ENGAGING CHINA

In recent years China has emerged as a vitally important political and economic power in the Asia Pacific. Sustained economic growth since the late 1970s combined with an increase in military capability and nationalism has forced the rest of the world to take notice.

The recent growth of Chinese power is reflected in many aspects of contemporary international politics. This book is concerned with the contemporary responses from various countries toward the rise of Chinese economic and strategic power. In particular, it explores the pressures that influence the choice of options and strategies those states can make in managing the uncertainties of a rising power. The authors provide both a theoretical background to the issues and individual chapters devoted to the policies of particular actors in the region including the United States, Japan, Singapore, Taiwan, Korea, Malaysia and Indonesia.

The combination of a theoretical approach, along with the use of case studies, will help to improve understanding of the complex nature of international relations surrounding China. *Engaging China* is written by some of the best scholars in this field, with upper level undergraduates or researchers in Asian Studies, International Relations or Political Science in mind.

The editors: Alastair Iain Johnston is John L. Loeb Associate Professor of the Social Sciences in the Government Department at Harvard University. **Robert S. Ross** is Professor of Political Science at Boston College and Research Associate at the John King Fairbank Center for East Asian Research, Harvard University.

The contributors: Randall L. Schweller, Victor D. Cha, Steven M. Goldstein, Michael Leifer, Yuen Foong Khong, Amitav Acharya, Michael Jonathan Green, Margaret M. Pearson, Paul Evans.

D0162320

POLITICS IN ASIA SERIES
Edited by Michael Leifer
London School of Economics

ENGAGING CHINA

The Management of an Emerging Power

*Edited by Alastair Iain Johnston
and Robert S. Ross*

London and New York

First published 1999 by Routledge
11 New Fetter Lane, London EC4P 4EE

Simultaneously published in the USA and Canada
by Routledge
29 West 35th Street, New York, NY 10001

Routledge is an imprint of the Taylor & Francis Group

© 1999 Selection and editorial matter Alastair Iain Johnston and Robert S. Ross;
individual chapters, the contributors

Typeset in Baskerville by Keystroke, Jacaranda Lodge, Wolverhampton
Printed and bound in Great Britain by T.J. International Ltd, Padstow, Cornwall

All rights reserved. No part of this book may be reprinted or reproduced or
utilized in any form or by any electronic, mechanical, or other means, now
known or hereafter invented, including photocopying and recording, or in
any information storage or retrieval system, without permission in writing
from the publishers.

British Library Cataloguing in Publication Data
A catalogue record for this book is available from the British Library

Library of Congress Cataloging in Publication Data
Engaging China: the management of an emerging power / edited by
Alastair Iain Johnston and Robert S. Ross.
p.   cm. – (Politics in Asia series)
Includes bibliographical references.
1. China – Relations – Foreign countries. I. Johnston, Alastair
I. II. Ross, Robert S., 1954– . III. Series.
DS779.27.E56   1999
327'.095'09045–dc21   99–17495

ISBN 0–415–20840–8 (hbk)
ISBN 0–415–20841–6 (pbk)

CONTENTS

v

ILLUSTRATIONS

Figures

Tables

CONTRIBUTORS

Amitav Acharya is Associate Professor of Political Science at York University, Toronto. He has been a Fellow of the Institute of Southeast Asian Studies and taught international relations at the National University of Singapore, Sydney University and Nanyang Technological University's Institute of Defence and Strategic Studies. He is a specialist on Southeast Asian affairs and Asia Pacific regional security. He is the author of *A New Regional Order in Southeast Asia: ASEAN in the Post Cold War Era* (IISS, 1993) and is completing a book on regional order in Southeast Asia.

Victor D. Cha is an assistant professor in the Department of Government and School of Foreign Service at Georgetown University. He is the author of *Alignment Despite Antagonism: The United States–Korea–Japan Security Triangle* (Stanford University Press, 1999). He has published articles and reviews on international relations and East Asia in survival journals including *Asian Survey*, *Political Science Quarterly*, *Journal of Asian Studies*, *Korean Studies*, *Security Dialogue*, *Korea and International Politics* and *Asian Perspective*. Professor Cha is a former Fulbright scholar, Olin National Security Fellow at Harvard University and CISAC postdoctoral fellow at Stanford University. He has also consulted for the US Department of Defense. For 1998 to 1999 he is a National Fellow, Hoover Institution, Stanford University and a Senior Fulbright Scholar.

Paul Evans has taught international relations at York University, Toronto since 1981, and between 1991 and 1996 he directed the University of Toronto–York University Joint Centre for Asia Pacific Studies. For the 1997–98 and 1998–99 academic years he has been a visiting scholar at the Asia Center at Harvard University. From July 1999 he will be taking a professorship in the Faculty of Graduate Studies at the University of British Columbia in Vancouver. His recent writings have focused on track-two security processes and multilateral institution building in Asia Pacific. His most recent publication is, with David Capie and Akiko Fukushima, *Speaking Asia Pacific Security: A Lexicon of Terms with Chinese and Japanese Translations and a Note on the Japanese Translation* (Joint Centre for Asia Pacific Studies, 1998).

Yuen Foong Khong is Deputy Director and Associate Professor at the Institute of Defence and Strategic Studies, Nanyang Technological University, Singapore. He has taught at Harvard and Oxford Universities and is Vice-President of the International Studies Association (1999 to 2000). He is the author of *Analogies of War: Korea, Munich, Dien Bien Phu, and the Vietnam Decisions of 1965* (Princeton University Press, 1992), and is completing a book on the sources of security cooperation in Southeast Asia.

Steven M. Goldstein is Sophia Smith Professor of Government at Smith College in Northampton, Massachusetts. He has written on a wide range of subjects including the evolution of Chinese Communism; Sino–Soviet relations; Sino–American relations and contemporary Chinese domestic politics. His current research focus is politics in Taiwan and cross-strait relations.

Michael Jonathan Green is Olin Fellow for Asian Security at the Council on Foreign Relations. He is also acting director of the Edwin O. Reischauer Center for East Asian Studies (SAIS) of the Johns Hopkins University and a consultant to the Office of the Secretary of Defense. He is the author of *Arming Japan: Defense Production, Alliance Politics and the Postwar Search for Autonomy* (Columbia University Press, 1995); co-author of *The US–Japan Security Alliance in the Twenty-first Century* (Council on Foreign Relations, 1997); and a forthcoming co-edited volume, *The US–Japan Alliance: Past, Present and Future* (Council on Foreign Relations, 1999).

Alastair Iain Johnston is a John L. Loeb Associate Professor of the Social Sciences in the Government Department at Harvard University. He is the author of *Cultural Realism: Strategic Culture and Grand Strategy in Chinese History* (Princeton University Press, 1995). He is currently working on a book on socialization in international institutions.

Michael Leifer is Director of the Asia Research Centre at the London School of Economics and Political Science where he was previously Professor of International Relations and also Pro-Director between 1991 and 1995. He is currently Secretary and co-Chair of the European chapter of the Council for Security Cooperation in the Asia Pacific (CSCAP). He is the author of *Dictionary of the Modern Politics of South-East Asia* (Routledge, 1996), and his earlier publications include *Indonesia's Foreign Policy* (Allen and Unwin, 1983).

Margaret M. Pearson is Associate Professor of Government and Politics at the University of Maryland, College Park. She is author of *China's New Business Elite: The Political Results of Economic Reform* (University of California Press, 1997), and *Joint Ventures in the People's Republic of China* (Princeton Press, 1991). Her current research interests include the incorporation of China into the global trade regime and the impact of this process on Chinese trade policy and behavior.

Robert S. Ross is Professor of Political Science, Boston College and Associate, John King Fairbank Center for East Asian Research, Harvard University. His most recent books are *Great Wall and Empty Fortress: China's Search for Security* (co-authored, W.W. Norton, 1997), and *Negotiating Cooperation: US–China Relations, 1969–1989* (Stanford University Press, 1995).

Randall L. Schweller is associate professor in the Department of Political Science at the Ohio State University. He is the author of *Deadly Imbalances: Tripolarity and Hitler's Strategy of World Conquest* (Columbia University Press, 1998). He has also published articles in journals such as *World Politics, International Studies Quarterly, American Journal of Political Science, International Security*, and *Security Studies*. In 1993 he received a John M. Olin Post-Doctoral Fellowship in National Security at the Center for International Affairs, Harvard University.

PREFACE

One of the most prominent elements of post-Cold War international relations is the increasing importance of China to both economic and strategic outcomes at the global and regional levels, and relatedly to individual states' long-term considerations of their national interests. China's importance reflects two related factors. The first is the sustained expansion of the Chinese economy since 1979 and the implications for Chinese long-term economic and strategic power. The second is that China's growing strategic and economic presence is most felt in East Asia, which many observers believe will become the economic and strategic focus of major powers in the twenty-first century.

The recent growth of Chinese power is reflected in many aspects of contemporary international politics. China's economic influence has affected the course of the 1997 Asian monetary crisis. Its light-industrial exports affect employment conditions in many advanced industrial economies and in many export-led economies. Its growing industrial base raises fears of greater transboundary pollution and the consumption patterns in its population raises concern for global food and energy shortages. Its weapons and military technology exports influence global non-proliferation regimes and impact regional balances of power, including in the Middle East. Its modernizing military capability contributes to security fears among its neighbors in East Asia. There is hardly a global agenda which does not reflect the development of China's growing economic and strategic capabilities.

While China's immediate impact on regional and global outcomes is obvious, what exacerbates preoccupation around the world with contemporary Chinese foreign policy is the recognition in some quarters that should China's development continue at its current pace and should it realize its full economic and strategic potential, the PRC may aspire to and perhaps realize regional-wide primacy in East Asia and develop global influence rivaling that of the United States. China's potential in this regard strongly colors assessments of present Chinese behavior and the formulation of short-term bilateral and multilateral policies toward China on a wide range of issues. It is responsible for discussions of the "China threat" and for controversies over China policy in countries around the world.

The relationship between China's post-Cold War economic and strategic importance and its long-term great power potential are reflected in the widespread international uncertainty over how current policies toward China should reflect long-term national and multilateral responses to the rise of Chinese power. In the United States, the debate is between vague and often internally contradictory visions of "engagement" and something more hardline, less accommodating, and often referred to as "containment". But to a considerable degree, regardless of the terminology, similar debates are taking place among policy makers and academic communities throughout East Asia, Southern Asia, Central Asia, Europe, North America and elsewhere around the world.

Post-Cold War debates over the "China threat" and over the appropriate policy response reflect a dilemma faced by leaders throughout history – how to respond to a rising power in a manner consistent with both their countries' short-term parochial national interests and their instrumental and/or normative interest in global order, particularly the absence of great power war. Throughout history, the emergence of great powers has been a turbulent process and diplomats and policy makers have long grappled, usually unsuccessfully, with developing constructive policy responses. The political science and history literature amply demonstrates the relationship between the rise of new powers and major war, and the diplomacy aimed at managing great power conflict.

Contemporary international uncertainty over the rise of Chinese power is the latest manifestation of this political process. For some, the prospect of China's emergence as a global power suggests the likelihood of significant international instability. Decision makers' responses to this possibility have, as in the past, varied, but the dominant policy option for most states is something called "engagement". But engagement is only the most recent term attached to a long tradition of trying to peacefully accommodate a rising power. Before British Prime Minister Neville Chamberlain's visit to Munich in 1936, the preferred term was "appeasement", but the term is now in such disrepute that contemporary leaders are compelled to deny that engagement is appeasement, despite the identical policy options and objectives.

Successful engagement of the rising power is the preferred policy outcome. In contrast to containment and the associated great power tension and risk of war, successful engagement enables pre-existing great powers to preserve their vital interests without incurring either extensive short-term costs of heightened tension or the future costs of international instability and hegemonic war. Nonetheless, successful engagement is, at best, rare, because decision makers in the past have chosen containment, wisely or not, or because they have pursued engagement strategies toward "unappeasable" powers, or because they have adopted flawed engagement strategies.

This volume is an effort to consider contemporary responses from various actors toward the rise of Chinese power. To this end, it examines the extent to which engagement has been the preferred policy choice and why, and what are the components of these engagement strategies. It seeks to understand how the decision to engage a rising power reflects not only the intrinsic difficulty of pursuing competing values with a single policy, but also reflects the unique strategic and economic relationships a country has with China. In so doing, the contributors to this volume want to broaden understanding of the pressures that affect the choice of options and strategies that states make in managing the uncertainties of a rising power.

The volume begins with a discussion of the intellectual and historical traditions of engagement of rising power. The objective is to place the volume's subsequent analyses of contemporary engagement of China within a historical and analytical context. Engagement is not a new concept. By developing our analyses within the intellectual and diplomatic perspectives of the past, we hope to build on existing scholarly work and diplomatic practice to enhance understand of a recurring diplomatic problem. In particular we hope to place engagement in the heretofore standard pantheon of strategies that states have adopted to deal with rising power: balancing, bandwagoning, hiding and capitulating.

The volume then addresses engagement from two relatively unique perspectives. First, it broadens the focus of engagement from the traditional perspective of great power relations to include the experiences of a wide range of countries. The volume concedes that great powers play a primary role in determining international strategic adjustment to a rising power. It includes chapters on the role and character of engagement in Japanese and US policy toward China. Nonetheless, the contributors recognize that smaller powers also face the policy imperative of adjusting current policy in preparation for the long-term implications of an emerging power for their respective security interests and for regional order. They recognize that an understanding of how local powers engage an emerging power can be instructive of the broad implications of an emerging power for a wide range of actors and of the full complexity of engagement, including the many policy options and the different factors that can influence policy choice. This focus on actors that vary in terms of geostrategic and geoeconomic importance to China, in types of political systems, and in types of historical relationships with China, allows for useful cross-national comparisons of the nature and effectiveness of different bilateral engagement strategies.

The local actors included in this volume are South Korea, Taiwan, Indonesia, Malaysia, and Singapore. South Korea is one of the local powers which has close cooperative ties with the PRC. Beijing and Seoul share many strategic perspectives and enjoy close and expanding economic ties. At the other extreme is Taiwan, which competes with mainland China for diplomatic recognition and faces the prospect of Chinese military coercion. In between South Korea and Taiwan are Indonesia, Malaysia, and Singapore. Possessing greater diplomatic flexibility *vis-à-vis* China, they are more likely to develop a multifaceted policy in which the polar opposites of engagement and containment coexist, reflecting both their distinctive positions in regional politics and their long-term strategic objectives toward China. The combination of great and local power perspectives on engagement provides an opportunity to develop a comprehensive under-standing of strategic responses to an emerging power.

The volume's second unique approach to engagement is its consideration of multilateral engagement of China. The development of multilateral strategic and economic institutions has accelerated since the end of the Cold War. Old institutions are gaining wider scope and new institutions are developing in order to address emerging issues. International rule-making institutions and multilateral diplomacy are assuming greater importance in creating and maintaining post-Cold War regional and global orders. Successful management of a rising power thus requires multilateral engagement strategies and comprehensive engagement requires developing long-range adjustment of multilateral institutions to the implications of the rise of Chinese power.

Chapters in this volume address multilateral engagement of China in security and economic issues from both regional and global perspectives. They not only consider how China's counterparts' bilateral policies manage PRC member-ship in multilateral institutions, but specific chapters also evaluate how well the international community is engaging China, so that Beijing is becoming an active member of various collaborative rule-making and confidence-building institutions. These chapters also assess the extent to which PRC membership in multilateral institutions is promoting Chinese "entanglement" in these institu-tions, creating new Chinese interests in international stability, and socializing China into developing consensus approaches to resolving international conflict.

The volume's comprehensive approach to studying engagement means that the contributors have vastly different research agendas. To encourage a common dialogue among the contributors and to facilitate the generation of a common understanding of engagement with cross-national applications, the contributors have worked within a common definition of engagement. For the purpose of this volume, engagement is defined as follows:

> The use of non-coercive methods to ameliorate the non-status-quo elements of a rising major power's behavior. The goal is to ensure that this growing power is used in ways that are consistent with peaceful change in regional and global order.

In this approach, amelioration of the rising power's behavior does not include efforts to hinder the accretion of relative power. This is better understood as "containment". We have neither defined nor limited the methods of amelioration, preferring that individual authors characterize the methods used by the respective countries and/or multilateral institutions. "Non-coercive methods" include such strategies as accommodation of legitimate interests, transformation of preferences, and entanglement in bilateral and multilateral institutional constraints.

The contributors clearly differentiate engagement from containment. In contrast to containment, engagement seeks neither to limit, constrain, or delay increases in the target country's power nor prevent the development of influence commensurate with its greater power. Rather, it seeks to "socialize" the rising power by encouraging its satisfaction with the evolving global or regional order. Our definition of engagement specifically excludes coercive policies.

We understand that this definition of engagement may fail to fully capture the complexities of specific national policies. Nonetheless, we hope that by working within a common framework, the contributors will help to develop a common understanding of the management of a rising power and generate conclusions, concepts and hypotheses facilitating further comparative and historical research.

The contributors met on two occasions to discuss the project and their work. At the first meeting, they presented and discussed their research plans and their tentative conclusions. They also developed a common understanding of the project, including the definition of engagement. The second meeting was attended by both the contributors and other specialists on both international politics and foreign policy. At this meeting the contributors presented their papers and received comments and suggestions from the other conference participants. On the basis of the conference discussions, the contributors revised their papers and completed the final versions of the chapters. From beginning to end, it has been a collaborative process.

The discussants in the second meeting were:

Robert Art	Wang Yizhou
Allen S. Whiting	Thomas J. Christensen
Ezra Vogel	Steven Vogel
Joseph Fewsmith	Richard Samuels

We thank them for their thoughtful and rigorous contributions to the conversation around the table. Also, this project would not have been possible without the generous contribution of Halpern Associates and the gracious assistance of the staff of the John King Fairbank Center at Harvard University.

The Editors

1

MANAGING THE RISE OF GREAT POWERS

History and theory

Randall L. Schweller

The history of world politics is commonly told as a story of the rise and decline of different countries and regions. At times, the tempo of these shifts in fortune resembles a carousel spinning at dizzying speed. This motion was evident among the Greek city-states during the time of Herodotus, who observed that "the cities that were formerly great, have most of them become insignificant; and such as are at present powerful, were weak in olden time."[1] It also describes the period between the congress of Westphalia in 1648 and the conclusion of the Napoleonic wars in 1815, when Spain, the Netherlands, and Sweden fell from the top tier of powers (Poland was wiped off the map!), and France, Britain, Prussia, Austria, and Russia emerged as great powers.

No such wheel of fortune existed during the nineteenth century, which saw Britain, Prussia/Germany, France, Russia, and Austria hold on to their exclusive status as great powers. By the century's end, however, America, Japan, and Italy were all knocking at the great power door. Since 1945, no new power has been able to vault into the great power category, though one fell from the ranks.

Whether structural transformation is dramatic or barely perceptible, turbulent or smooth, the important point is that the pecking order of states continually changes. As Paul Kennedy puts it, the "relative strengths of the leading nations in world affairs never remain constant, principally because of the uneven rate of growth among different societies and of the technological and organizational breakthroughs which bring a greater advantage to one society than to another."[2] Recognizing that this is so, this chapter addresses the question: How has the international system adjusted to the rise of new powers? More specifically, how successful have the established great powers been in managing and peacefully assimilating rising, *dissatisfied* challengers into the existing international order?

Great power transitions are never easy, but it is better when they happen slowly, surely and, in any event, not in an atmosphere of general crisis. A cursory glance at the historical record reveals that the nature and success of the

1

established powers' responses to rising powers has varied not only from one historical epoch to another but on a case-by-case basis within the same era. As is true for most explanations of history, this variance is a function of both situational factors (e.g. the structural characteristics of the international system) and dispositional ones. With regard to the latter causes, the key questions are: How dissatisfied, if at all, is the rising power with the existing order and its place within that order? What is the extent and nature of its revisionist demands? How are its demands and intentions perceived by the established powers? Can the rising power acquire the requisite strength (either through internal or external means) to change the system by force of arms? How, if at all, will the desired changes affect the interests of the other great powers?

The chapter begins by addressing the questions of why and when rising powers are dangerous. The next section lays out the various policies available to the established powers in response to a rising power. This is followed by a typology of rising powers according to their goals and risk propensity. In the final section, the nature of the rising power (discussed in the prior section) is linked to the choice and success of the established powers' policy responses.

The dangers of rising powers

The question of how to manage a rising power presupposes that such a situation is dangerous and therefore requires a strategy or plan of action on the part of the established powers. This raises several questions: Why are rising powers dangerous? What are the causal links between national growth – which typically accounts for the rising power's gain in relative strength – and international conflict and possibly war? When and why does an additional member of the great power club cause systemic instability?

Why rising powers are dangerous: the temptation to expand

According to Classical Realism, a nation's interests are shaped in the first place by its power (measured in terms of material resources and political influence). Specifically, as Martin Wight puts it: "It is the nature of powers to expand. The energies of their members radiate culturally, economically and politically, and unless there are strong obstacles these tendencies will be summed up in territorial growth."[3] In this view, states expand when they can; that is, when they perceive relative increases in state power[4] and when changes in the relative costs and benefits of expansion make it profitable for them to do so.[5] Thus Gilpin writes: "a state will attempt to change the international system only if it has some relative advantage over other states, that is, if the balance of power in the system is to its advantage."[6]

Acknowledging that political and military power must have an economic base, realists view economic prosperity as a preliminary to expansion and war; a full war

2

chest and the ability to replenish it are essential prerequisites to support the costs of military build-ups, arms races, and massive and prolonged armed violence. Accordingly, realists predict that, as states grow wealthier and more powerful, they not only seek greater world-wide political influence (control over territory, the behavior of other states, and the world economy)[7] commensurate with their new capabilities; they are also more capable of expanding their interests and, if necessary, of waging large-scale, hegemonic wars to revise drastically or overthrow entirely the established order. Simply put, the stronger and richer a state becomes, the more influence it wants and the more willing and able it will be to fight to further its interests.

The expansion of powers is a product not only of internal pressure but also of threats and opportunities in the external environment. The weakness of surrounding states, for instance, engenders both types of external compulsion. The powerful nation that finds itself bordering on a power vacuum feels compelled for reasons of appetite and temptation to fill the void with its own power.[8] The danger of not expanding into the power vacuum is that other powerful states will not be equally restrained from doing so. Bandwagoning dynamics also dictate a policy of expansion. Because "a buffer state that lacks internal strength and stability will gravitate, irrespective of its own wishes, away from a declining power towards an expanding power,"[9] it is doubly dangerous for a great power to appear weak and irresolute – in this case, by resisting the temptation to expand when the opportunity presents itself. Finally, because weakness implies political instability, the great power has to fill the power vacuum in order to prevent the threat of the region's instability spilling across its own borders; that is, to innoculate itself against the contagious effects of war (interstate, civil, and ethnic) and revolutionary ideas.[10]

The need to expand: national growth and colliding interests

In their study of the long-term causes of World War I, Nazli Choucri and Robert North developed the theory of lateral pressure to explain the dynamics of national growth and international competition and war.[11] The basic argument is that growth in a nation's population density and advanced technology generates demands for larger amounts and a wider range of resources, which often cannot be met by the state's domestic resource endowments. This domestic deficiency, in turn, generates *lateral pressure*, which refers to the tendency among rising powers to expand their external activities, whether for raw materials, markets, living space, religious converts, military or naval bases, or simply adventure.[12] When several states adopt expansionist policies, their external interests and commitments are increasingly likely to collide with each other. These clashes of interests increase the likelihood of war.

This theory is based on a positive feedback process, whereby rapid growth requires external expansion to sustain itself. Thus virtually every modern, industrialized country, they claim, has manifested strong, extensive lateral pressure in some form.[13] Whether motivated by exploration, commerce, investment, or conquest, lateral pressure establishes extraterritorial national interests among the great powers. Depending on type, extent, and intensity, lateral pressure generally leads to major power conflict when the foreign activities and interests of two or more major powers collide. Choucri and North's analysis of great power policies during the years between 1870 and 1914 revealed that:

> expansionist activities are most likely to be associated with relatively high-capability countries, and to be closely linked with growth in population and advances in technology. Also, growth tends to be associated with intense competition among countries for resources and markets, military power, political influence, and prestige.[14]

A related problem is raised by the security dilemma: "many of the means by which a state tries to increase its security decrease the security of others."[15] The rise of new great powers, particularly when they have or seek to acquire empires and/or other less formal far-flung interests and commitments, will likely engender security dilemmas and/or intensify existing ones. As Jervis puts it: "Any state that has interests throughout the world cannot avoid possessing the power to menace others."[16] Thus, when the US emerged as a world power after the Spanish–American war, it found that its new Pacific possessions could not be protected without threatening the security of Japan's home islands and insular colonies. Despairing over the US acquisition of the Philippines and the security dilemma it created with Japan, Theodore Roosevelt prophetically observed in 1907:

> The Philippines form our heel of Achilles. They are all that makes the present situation with Japan dangerous. . . . To keep the islands without treating them generously and at the same time without adequately fortifying them and without building up a navy second only to that of Great Britain, would be disastrous in the extreme. Yet there is danger of just this being done.[17]

For its part, Japan's quest for East Asian hegemony also could not be achieved without seriously compromising the security of the United States. Thus in vain President Wilson objected to the Council of Four's decision on May 7, 1919 to mandate to Japan the German islands in the Pacific north of the equator. A. Whitney Griswold paraphrases Wilson's concerns:

> The Japanese mandate, [Wilson] confided to one of his closest advisers, lay athwart the path from Hawaii to the Philippines. The mandated islands were nearer Hawaii than was the California coast. They could easily be fortified; in fact he could conceive of no use for them except as

naval bases. . . . The entire mandate . . . would, in the hands of a naval rival, menace the security of the Philippines.[18]

Colliding interests leading to war, however, do not always involve security. For example, following Elizabethan England's surprising defeat of Spain's "Invincible Armada," the Stuart Navy found itself confronting the rise of a new, more formidable maritime and commercial rival, the Dutch Republic, which had been thriving (ironically, with Elizabeth's aid) despite more than thirty years of continuous struggle to resist Spanish subjugation. The ensuing Anglo–Dutch rivalry and series of wars that ended in 1688 were fueled entirely by motives of prestige, power, and profit:

> This basic cause of a long-lasting rivalry over trade and primacy at sea set the style of the Anglo–Dutch wars: more than any others fought by the British in the past four centuries, they were trade wars. Invasion was not really planned or attempted by either side (except in 1673), and if a threat to territorial security had been the main criterion for assessing potential foes, then both countries would have regarded France as a more likely danger. It was, instead, a quarrel about who should rule the waves and reap the commercial benefits of that privilege.[19]

The Anglo–Dutch rivalry was a classic case of two rising powers with expanding and overlapping non-security interests headed for an inevitable showdown. Because their national identity as trading powers depended, they believed, on maritime supremacy, because their coasts and respective naval forces were separated only by the Narrow Seas, and because their commercial and colonial interests brought them into collision in almost every part of the world, the English and Dutch were locked into a "rivalry which was unavoidable, inexorable, a rivalry which could eventually have only one of two issues, either the voluntary submission of one of the rivals to the other, or a trial of strength by ordeal of battle."[20] The town, so to speak, simply wasn't big enough for both of them.

The significance of the arguments summarized above is that they imply that a rising power need not be an aggressor to cause instability in the system. Because there is no Leviathon in world politics to enforce agreements made between, or to keep the peace among, nation-states, international conflict is inevitable. In this regard the above arguments stress that, even among states seeking only to survive, conflict arises because of the constant condition of scarcity in terms of raw materials, markets, social goods (prestige, leadership), and security. National growth, by generating new resource demands in excess of the state's domestic endowments, exacerbates competition for scarce resources, regardless of the rising power's intentions. Equally significant, under conditions of global economic expansion, states must run faster simply to stay in place; fearing losses in relative power and prestige in the system, great powers will feel pressure to expand merely to keep up with the Jones's (e.g. the scramble for African colonies in the 1880s).

For all these reasons, interstate interactions in the periphery will intensify, making it more likely that interests will collide.

System structure: when are rising powers dangerous?

[handwritten: QUESTION — POLIALITY. POLAR SYSTEMS.]

The central questions of whether the emergence of a new great power will be destabilizing and what is the likelihood that the established powers can and will peacefully incorporate the rising power into the existing order are partly functions of the structure of the international system. All other things being equal, the rise of a sixth (or seventh or eighth) great power will have less impact on system stability and will be easier for the established powers to manage than will the rise of a second or third great power. In international relations parlance, the former situation represents a change *within* the structure of the system; that is, the addition of a sixth great power does not change the basic structural condition of multi-polarity (a system composed of four or more great powers) that existed prior to the emergence of the rising power.

In contrast, the latter two hypotheticals are changes *of* system structure: the emergence of a second great power transforms a unipolar system into a bipolar one; the rise of a third great power transforms a bipolar system into a tripolar one. This is important because the system dynamics (or characteristic behaviors) of unipolar, bipolar, tripolar, and multipolar structures differ significantly from each other. This is, after all, the theoretical justification for using the concept of "polarity" to categorize systems and for maintaining four separate categories of polarity. If, for example, tripolar systems behaved just like multi-polar ones, there would be no theoretical reason to distinguish the two types of structures.

While scholars agree that these various structures behave differently, a consensus has yet to emerge about the precise nature of that behavior. Waltzian neorealists, for example, claim that bipolarity is more stable (less prone to system-wide war) than is multipolarity; many scholars within the "quantitative empirical" school, however, make precisely the opposite claim.[21] More basic, there is no consensus over how to define, operationalize, and measure the concept of polarity.[22] Little wonder that the current system has been variously described as unipolar, tripolar, multipolar, uni-multipolar, and multi-multipolar. Unfortunately, any attempt to settle these prolonged scholarly disputes is well beyond the scope of this chapter.

What can be said with some confidence is that multipolarity is more conducive to the emergence of new great powers than are systems with fewer numbers of poles. This is because the power capability requirements for polar status in a multipolar system are less demanding than in tri-, bi-, and unipolar systems. Simply put, as the number of poles in the system increases, each pole's share of the total capabilities within the great power subset correspondingly decreases. Hence, emerging powers will find it easier to vault into the great power ranks under multipolarity than under any other type of system.

6

The question of whether multipolarity is more conducive to the successful management of rising powers than are other types of systems can be answered in several contradictory ways. On the positive side, potential blocking coalitions of various combinations of poles will be most plentiful under multipolarity. It is most unlikely, therefore, that a rising, revolutionary power will be able to gain the necessary strength to overthrow the existing order before a blocking coalition forms to counterbalance it. Further, because there are many established powers in a multipolar system, it is most likely that the interests of the rising power will coincide with those of one or more of the established powers. This suggests that the process of co-opting and socializing rising powers into the balance of power will be easiest under multipolarity. In contrast, when the advent of a rising power transforms the system from bipolarity to tripolarity, the danger of ganging up in an overpowering "two against one" coalition is always present. In other words, under tripolarity, even amity between two poles causes instability.[23]

On the down side, the logic of collective action implies that the temptation to ride free on the balancing efforts of others will increase with the number of poles in the system. The danger is that, by passing the "balancing" buck, the established powers allow the rising, dissatisfied state to substantially increase its relative strength through piecemeal aggression.[24] In addition, sheer numbers alone suggest that revolutionary powers are more likely to emerge under multipolarity than other types of systems.

State responses to rising powers

The historically most significant consequence of the rise of new great powers is international political change. As Gilpin points out, "a precondition for political change lies in a disjuncture between the existing social system and the redistribution of power toward those actors who would benefit most from a change in the system."[25] Of particular relevance here is that the rise of new powers, by altering the configuration of relative power in the system, inevitably presents the established powers with both threats and opportunities: some stand to benefit by its emergence, others fear that they will be disadvantaged.

How states are affected by the emergence of a new power differs not only in kind but also in degree: neighboring states and world powers with substantial interests in the region of the rising power will be affected more than distant powers with minor or no interests in the area of its growth. These two factors largely account for the variety of state responses to rising powers, e.g. balancing, bandwagoning, preventive war, engagement, appeasement, economic and political sanctions, accommodation, containment, and "roll back", to name a few. Some of these strategies involve alliances, others do not; some use alliances for capability-aggregation purposes, others use them as tools of management; some seek security from the rising power, others aim to profit by it.

For the purposes of analysis, these various state responses may be grouped into six basic policy options: (1) preventive war, (2) balancing, (3) bandwagoning,

(4) binding, (5) engagement, and (6) distancing/buckpassing. Which option is chosen depends on the established power's goal; that is, whether it seeks to eliminate the rising power, contain it, profit by it, bind it, convert it, or ignore it.

Preventive war

As articulated by Alfred Vagts: "The problem of preventive war is, simply put, the problem of whether a war considered inevitable in the long run is to be fought now, rather than later when the advantages may lie with the opposite camp."[26] Note the three basic requirements for preventive war contained in Vagts's definition: (1) war is viewed as inevitable, (2) the threat is a long-term one, and (3) it is better to fight now than later. Preventive wars are unique in that they are "wars of anticipation," and therefore their justification, if any is given, can rest only upon the inherently unprovable assumptions of human foresight.

In practice, states have waged preventive wars for either offensive or defensive reasons: to take advantage of a closing window of opportunity or to prevent the opening of a window of vulnerability.[27] Moreover, statesmen may rationally choose preventive war with little or no hope of victory if the expected costs of peace are thought to be even higher than those of war; for example, Japan's decision to opt for war against the US in 1941.[28]

Theorists disagree, however, on the causal links between power shifts and war. Robert Gilpin sees preventive action as "the most attractive response" for a declining dominant power confronting a rising power: "When the choice ahead has appeared to be to decline or to fight, statesmen have most generally fought." Similarly, Jack Levy writes: "Statesmen have often convinced themselves that war will reverse or retard the rising military power of the adversary . . . and history provides few examples of states' nonviolent acceptance of their national decline."[29] Conversely, A. F. K. Organski and Jacek Kugler appear to rule out preventive action altogether, arguing that recent history shows that rising dissatisfied challengers have initiated wars against leading nations "long before they equaled them in power."[30]

While there have been occasional instances of established powers waging preventive wars against rising threats (e.g. Sparta's initiation of the Peloponessian wars; the Athenian war against Philip *circa* 349 BC; Caesar's war against the Helvetii in 58 BC; the Florentine–Venetian war against Visconti's Milan in 1424),[31] the historical record strongly supports the proposition that it is not declining hegemons but risk-acceptant leaders of rising dissatisfied challengers – Philip II, Louis XIV, Frederick the Great, Napoleon I, the Kaiser, and Hitler – who, in their failed bids for hegemony, have been the great makers of preventive war. Indeed, even the most fledgling of rising powers, countries that were no match for any of the true great powers of their day, have waged preventive wars against far stronger established powers. Consider Drake's 1587 preventive attack upon Cadiz and the resounding defeat inflicted upon the Spanish Armada in the following year, when England was little more than an aspiring great power;[32] or

Charles II's preventive war against the Dutch in 1664; or Japan's preventive wars against Russia (1904–5) and the United States (1941) when it was far weaker in terms of its overall power capabilities than either of its opponents.

In contrast, there is not a single "clear-cut" case in the modern era of a hegemonic power initiating war to prevent the rise of a serious challenger.[33] One explanation for this surprising finding is that, as I have argued elsewhere, liberal democracies, for normative and institutional reasons, do not wage preventive wars.[34] Thus the two most recent hegemons, Britain in the eighteenth and nineteenth centuries and the United States in the twentieth century, did not exercise this option or even seriously contemplate it.

Another explanation is that leaders of dominant status quo powers are accustomed to actors who seek only to modify the existing system, not to overthrow it; consequently, they are slow to recognize the threat posed by revolutionary powers.[35] "Lulled by a period of stability which had seemed permanent," Kissinger notes, the:

> defenders of the status quo . . . tend to begin by treating the revolutionary powers as if its protestations were merely tactical; as if it really accepted the existing legitimacy but overstated its case for bargaining purposes; as if it were motivated by specific grievances to be assuaged by limited concessions. Those who warn against the danger in time are considered alarmists.[36]

For both these reasons, preventive wars have rarely been waged to close windows of vulnerability; far more often than not, they are wars of aggression to take advantage of windows of opportunity.

Balancing / containment

Balancing means opposing the stronger or more threatening side in a conflict.[37] Balancing may be accomplished in two ways: (1) internal balancing: individual attempts by the threatened states to mobilize their national resources to match those of the enemy; or (2) external balancing: the establishment of formal or informal alliances directed against the rising state or coalition. If they have the capacity to do so, threatened states would be well advised to engage in both types of balancing behavior to counteract the threat. This is because states that attempt to avoid the costs of internal balancing but want the security benefits that an alliance offers will appear as unattractive allies to potential partners.

Several conditions are required for the balance of power to work. First and most basic, there must be a sufficient number of powerful states that wish to survive as autonomous actors, and whose combined strength at least equals that of the strongest state in the system. Second, defender states must be vigilant and sensitive to changes in the distribution of capabilities, such as their ally growing weaker or their enemy growing stronger. Third, states must possess some mobility

9

of action, that is, they must be able to respond quickly and decisively to changes in the balance of power. Fourth, external balancing often relies on the ability to project military power; therefore, status quo states must not adopt strictly defensive military postures. Fifth, states that are essential to the balance must accept war as a legitimate tool of statecraft, even if they consider it to be a last resort. Finally, ideology, religious affiliation, and prior territorial disputes must not rule out alignments needed to maintain the balance; that is, balancing is most likely to be effective when there are no alliance handicaps.[38]

Related to the two traditional forms of balancing (harnessing internal resources along with those of allies) is the strategy of containment, which seeks not to defeat the rising power but to prevent its further expansion. It is a strategy designed to maintain the balance, not to restore it. John Gaddis makes the useful distinction between two styles of containment: symmetrical and asymmetrical response.[39] Symmetrical response means countering the enemy's provocation at the location, time, and in the manner of its original occurrence (for example, the way in which the US fought the Korean and Vietnam wars, and the strategy behind NSC 68 and Flexible Response). Asymmetrical response entails reacting to aggression at times, in places, and by means of one's own choosing; that is, instead of responding in kind, the defender shifts the location and nature of its reaction "onto terrain better suited to the application of [its] strengths against adversary weaknesses."[40] US Cold-War strategies of this type included Kennan's original containment strategy, the doctrine of "massive retaliation" and the "New Look" of 1953, the Nixon Doctrine, and Kissinger's use of linkage.

Bandwagoning[41]

The term "bandwagoning" as a description of international alliance behavior first appeared in Quincy Wright's *A Study of War* and later in Kenneth Waltz's *Theory of International Politics*.[42] Both Wright and Waltz employ the concept of bandwagoning to serve as the opposite of balancing (which Wright calls "the underdog policy"): bandwagoning refers to joining the stronger coalition, balancing means allying with the weaker side.[43] Unlike Waltz, Wright believed that, under certain circumstances, great powers may engage in bandwagoning to preserve the balance of power. This occurs when "the stronger in a given war is a relatively weak state whose strengthening is necessary to hold a more powerful neighbor in check."[44]

Curiously, and in stark contrast with the predictions of balance of power theory, the strongest and most revolutionary of the rising powers have been precisely the ones that have historically attracted the greatest number of bandwagoners. Consider the responses of the great powers to Revolutionary France and Hitlerite Germany. At various times between 1795 and 1814, Prussia, Russia, Spain, and Austria all bandwagoned with Imperial France; similarly, Italy, Japan, Russia in 1939, and some say France in 1940, bandwagoned with Nazi Germany. Only Britain and the United States can claim that they did not bandwagon with either

10

Revolutionary France or Nazi Germany. The United States, however, was not a great power during the Napoleonic wars, and it only actively balanced against the Nazi threat after Hitler declared war against it.

There is a good explanation for this seemingly illogical behavior: powerful revolutionary states are best positioned in the international system to use positive sanctions to lure others to their cause. Unlike defenders of the status quo, revolutionary states will not hestitate to offer other dissatisfied nations substantial gains in territory and prestige as a reward for helping them to create a new order. In other words, like delegates at party conventions, states are often motivated to join the stronger side for reasons of profit, that is, to secure a share of the rewards of victory.[45] To induce bandwagoning behavior, revolutionary powers have historically used the spoils of their early victories or the promise of future gains to bribe hitherto neutrals and enemies to align with them; or, in the latters' case, to pledge neutrality.[46] In this way, the rising power builds up the strength of its own coalition, while at the same time it weakens the military power and political solidarity of the opposing status quo side.

During the period 1667 to 1679, for example, Louis XIV's France achieved hegemony over Europe largely by promising rewards to attract bandwagoners. In the War of Devolution (1667 to 1968), the Austrian emperor, Leopold I, bandwagoned with France to partition Spain. By the secret Franco–Austrian treaty of 1668, the French Bourbons were to inherit Spanish Navarre, the Southern Netherlands, Franche-Comté, Naples and Sicily, and the Philippines in exchange for which Louis ceded his rights to the Spanish Crown.[47] In preparation for the Dutch War (1672 to 1679), Louis used rewards to gain the support of virtually all the powers that had previously opposed him. In June 1670, Charles II of England signed the treaty of Dover, which included plans for a joint Anglo–French attack against the Dutch in 1672. In exchange, Louis agreed to provide England with subsidies of £225,000 a year and territorial gains around the Scheldt estuary. In April 1672, Sweden, too, abandoned what was left of the Triple Alliance and jumped on the French bandwagon against the Dutch. Between 1670 and 1672, Louis offered the payment of French subsidies to gain alliances with many of the former members of the defunct League of the Rhine, including the Rhenish archbishop-electors, Saxony, the Palatinate, Bavaria, the Archbishop-Elector of Cologne, and the Bishop of Münster; and, while he did not ally with France, Leopold I signed a neutrality agreement in November 1671.[48] The peace of Nymegen which ended the Dutch War in 1679 proved that Louis could take on all his enemies and still dictate the peace. Declared the Great Elector: "France has already become the arbiter of Europe . . . henceforth no prince will find security or profit except with the friendship and alliance of the King of France."[49]

Like his predecessor, Napoleon Bonaparte used territorial rewards and spectacular military victories to attract bandwagoners. For example, in creating the Confederation of the Rhine (1806) as a counterweight to Prussia and Austria, Napoleon strengthened Bavaria, Baden, Hesse-Darmstadt, and Württemberg at the expense of the tiny German states. Tempted by the promise of aggrandizement, these middle-sized German states voluntarily climbed aboard Napoleon's bandwagon.[50]

Similarly, Tsar Alexander I bandwagoned with the French Empire in 1807, when Napoleon used his decisive victory over the Tsar's army at Friedland to propose the Vistula as the new frontier of Russia. Napoleon also offered Russia control over European Turkey and Finland, and he encouraged further Russian conquests in Asia. In exchange, the Tsar was asked to join the Continental System against England, use his influence to compel Denmark and Sweden to follow suit, and send the Russian Navy to aid France in the capture of Gibraltar.[51] As the historian, R. B. Mowat, put it: "Thus a prospect was held out to the defeated autocrat not merely of keeping what he possessed, but actually of gaining more territory: a strange sequel to the *débâcle* of Russia at Friedland!"[52]

Not surprisingly, Alexander welcomed the alliance with France, which "put the Continent of Europe at the disposal of the two Powers of France and Russia, with, however, the balance distinctly in favour of France."[53] During the Franco–Austrian war of 1809, Alexander proved his loyalty to Napoleon by "fail[ing] to avail himself of the opportunity to 'hold the balance' between the antagonists, with the result that France once more defeated Austria, added more territory to her already bulging empire, and threw the European system still further out of balance."[54]

In contrast with this wise treatment of Russia, Napoleon's peace terms to Austria and Prussia were "so rigorous that the treaties invariably were little more than truces under which the defeated powers thirsted for revenge and constantly sought a favorable opportunity to resume their contest of arms."[55] In the end, the victorious Allied coalition, whose forces doubled those of France by February 1814, would never have come together in the first place, much less held together, had Napoleon not foolishly attacked his own allies and neutrals – most fatefully, Russia. By repeatedly thwarting the bandwagoning strategies of Spain, Austria, Prussia, and Russia, Napoleon finally succeeded where the British had failed in creating a coalition with the strength and resolve to defeat Imperial France.[56]

Like Napoleon, Hitler blocked the formation of a powerful counter-coalition by encouraging dissatisfied states – Italy, the Soviet Union, Japan, Hungary, and Bulgaria – to feed on the pickings of the Nazi lion's kill.[57] Thus, Hitler promised (though he never delivered) Mussolini spoils in the Mediterranean and North Africa; he gave away half of Poland and Eastern Europe to the Soviets; and he simply handed over to Japan the French and Dutch colonies in Indo-China and the East Indies that Germany had won in the battle of the West.[58] In this way, the Reich became master of Europe by 1941. But just as Napoleon had gratuitously destroyed the source of his own success by attacking his allies, Hitler likewise brought Germany to ruin by declaring war against his Soviet ally and the United States, "two World powers who asked only to be left alone."[59] In so doing, the Führer forced into creation the only coalition powerful enough to prevent a German victory in Europe.

Binding

As the historian Paul Schroeder has pointed out, sometimes the function of alliances is not capability aggregation but rather restraint or control over the actions of the partners themselves in the alliance. In such cases, states forgo a counter-alliance against a threatening state, which they fear may provoke greater conflict and perhaps war, and instead ally with the rival for the purpose of managing the threat by means of a pact of restraint (*pacta de contrahendo*).[60]

The state seeking to "bind" the rival hopes that, by allying with the source of threat, it will be able to exert some measure of control over its policy. An alliance accomplishes this by increasing both the state's influence over its ally and the number of opportunities it gets to voice its concerns. Along these lines, Joseph Grieco posits a "voice opportunities" thesis, according to which "weaker but still influential partners will seek to ensure that the rules [of a collaborative arrangement] so constructed . . . provide sufficient opportunities for them to voice their concerns and interests and thereby prevent or at least ameliorate their domination by stronger partners."[61]

The goal of management was one of the motivations behind Britain's decision to ally with the rising power of Japan in 1902: "In Britain's eyes, one of the objects of the alliance was to act as a restraint upon a wilful Japan whose strength was acknowledged but whose self-control was thought to be doubtful."[62] To the dismay of the British, the alliance had precisely the opposite effect: it emboldened Japan to initiate war against Russia in 1904.[63] The British should not have been surprised by this, however. Logically, if the rising, dissatisfied power is inherently reckless or aggressive, aligning with it will doubtless encourage it to excessive boldness in disputes with other powers; it is unlikely to restrain it from undesired actions or to make it more cautious in disputes and crises with neighboring powers.[64]

When available, multilateral alliances and arrangements, such as collective security systems, are often used as a complement to or in lieu of bilateral "binding" strategies.[65] There are several objectives in adopting a multilateral binding policy. First, by incorporating the rising power in existing institutional arrangements, giving it a "place at the table" so to speak, the established powers seek to satisfy the prestige demands of the rising power. Second, through its membership in global institutions, the rising state is afforded a greater opportunity to voice its concerns and to build, in conjunction with the other great powers, a new international order that better reflects its enhanced power and interests. The established powers hope that this cooperative approach to international change based on consensus will foster a renewed sense of legitimacy in the international order among all the great powers, including the rising power. Finally, the established powers use multilateral arrangements for the purpose of entangling the rising power in a web of policies that makes exercise of its power too costly. This assumes that the gains derived by the rising power from membership in the existing institutions are substantial, and that "belonging confers additional benefits from which outsiders can be excluded."[66]

13

Engagement

The policy of engagement refers to the use of non-coercive means to ameliorate the non-status quo elements of a rising major power's behavior. The goal is to ensure that this growing power is used in ways that are consistent with peaceful change in regional and global order.

The most common form of engagement is the policy of appeasement, which attempts to settle international quarrels "by admitting and satisfying grievances through rational negotiation and compromise, thereby avoiding the resort to an armed conflict which would be expensive, bloody, and possibly very dangerous."[67] Typically, this process requires adjustments in territory and "spheres of influence" and the reallocation of global responsibilities and other sources of prestige commensurate with the growth in power of the rising state.

Engagement is more than appeasement, however. It encompasses any attempt to socialize the dissatisfied power into acceptance of the established order. In practice, engagement may be distinguished from other policies not so much by its goals but by its means: it relies on the promise of rewards rather than the threat of punishment to influence the target's behavior.

The primary objective of an engagement policy is to minimize conflict and avoid war without compromising the integrity of the existing international order. In essence, the established powers seek to restore system equilibrium by adjusting the international hierarchy of prestige and the division of territory in accordance with the new global balance of power, while at the same time maintaining the formal institutional arrangements and informal rules of the system, that is, its governance structures.[68] The policy succeeds if such concessions convert the revolutionary state into a status quo power with a stake in the stability of the system.

Engagement also serves three other important goals. First, it enables the status quo powers to gain a clearer picture of the real (as opposed to declared) intentions and ambitions of the rising, dissatisfied power. Only by "engaging" Hitler's legitimate, pan-German aspirations could Britain and France discover whether Germany truly sought limited revision, as Hitler had repeatedly stated, or Continental hegemony and ultimately world conquest. Second, it is a useful policy for buying time to rearm and gain allies in case the rising power cannot be satisfied and war becomes necessary. Third, it can be used to break up dangerous combinations or to prevent them from occurring in the first place. For these purposes, engagement may be seen as an alternative to the formation of a counter-balancing alliance that risks uniting the dissatisfied powers into a rival coalition. The British government, viewing tight alliances as a primary cause of World War I, applied this insight in 1935, when it attempted to keep Italy out of the German orbit by appeasing Mussolini at the expense of Ethiopia and Spain. Indeed, Chamberlain's engagement policy toward Germany sought to accomplish all of the various goals associated with engagement, namely to satisfy Germany without recourse to war and without destroying the existing order; to uncover Hitler's true intentions; to buy time for rearmament; and to prevent the formation of a German–Italian alliance.

Engagement, when successful, is the most efficient and sensible solution to the rise of a dissatisfied power. It is a very tricky and sometimes dangerous policy to implement, however. For the policy to succeed, the rising power must have only limited revisionist aims and there can be no irreconcilable conflicts of vital interests among the powers.[69] As Martin Wight points out:

> It is no good a satisfied power (let us say, Philip II's Spain) telling a dissatisfied power (let us say, Elizabethan England) that its legitimate interests can be fully secured within the existing arrangement of power, for there will be no possibility of agreement between what Spain calls "legitimate" and what England calls "vital".[70]

Moreover, engagement is most likely to succeed when the established powers are strong enough to mix concessions with credible threats, to use sticks as well as carrots, in their attempts to satisfy the rising power. Otherwise, concessions will signal weakness that emboldens the aggressor to demand more. For this reason, engagement should not be viewed as an alternative to balancing but rather as a complement to it – one that seeks a peaceful end to the rivalry and the balancing costs that accompany it. In Churchill's words:

> Appeasement in itself may be good or bad according to the circum-stances. Appeasement from weakness and fear is alike futile and fatal. Appeasement from strength is magnanimous and noble, and might be the surest and perhaps the only path to world peace.[71]

Another problem in carrying out an engagement strategy is that the two sides' expectations often diverge in accordance with their discrepant motivations for negotiation: the status quo power desires changes in the revisionist power's behavior, while the latter desires changes in the status quo order. Consequently, to the status quo power, engagement involves the use of rewards and threats to influence the revisionist state such that it behaves more in accordance with the rules of the established order. The dissatisfied power, in contrast, sees engagement as a tool for peaceful change of the existing order.

Finally, it must be remembered that the problem of managing peaceful change is not all on the side of the rising dissatisfied power. For the process to work, the status quo powers must exhibit empathy, fairness, and a genuine concern not to offend the prestige and national honor of the rising power. Above all, this means not judging the rising power's behavior according to principles that they them-selves are unwilling to live by. The estrangement of Japan and America after 1909, for instance, had less to do with a clash of vital interests than a clash of principles.

From Japan's perspective, America's insistence on the Open Door and Equal Opportunity policy in China contradicted its own Monroe Doctrine. If the US believed that it was entitled to exercise a monopoly right to interfere in the internal affairs of the other republics of Central and South America, why should not Japan be allowed a Monroe Doctrine for the Far East? Was not Korea to Japan's security what the Low Countries have been to Britain's defense since the time of Marlborough?[72] Thus, when the Shanghai incident of 1932 confirmed the basic cleavage between the Western nations and Japan over the issue of special rights and interests in China, the Japanese, exasperated at Anglo–American hypocrisy, pointed out that they merely sought to "advance with a policy of Asia for the Asiatics – an Asiatic Monroe Doctrine." In an address to the Council of Foreign Relations, for instance, Viscount Kikujiro Ishii reminded the audience that Japan's foreign policy was "activated by the same principle incorporated in the Monroe Doctrine."[73]

Buckpassing / distancing

Buckpassing occurs when a state attempts to ride free on the balancing efforts of others. In a buckpassing situation, effective balancing against the attacker will benefit all potential targets of aggression whether or not they have been involved in the defeat or substantial weakening of that aggressor. It is therefore to each state's advantage not to incur the costs of balancing (i.e. the dilemma of the "free-rider") by redirecting the threat elsewhere and remaining on the sidelines. In other words, the buckpasser assumes that it can safely "bystand" while the defending state or coalition absorbs the initial blow of the attacker and in the process critically weakens or destroys it.

For this reason, buckpassing has been associated correctly with the perception of defense advantage and wars of attrition.[74] If the buckpassing state believed otherwise (namely that the attacker would quickly overrun the defenders), it would not be in its interest to remain on the sidelines, since it would then be confronted by a newly triumphant and thus stronger rising power with fewer or no allies.

Related to buckpassing is the policy of distancing or hiding. Confronted by the threat of a rising, dissatisfied power, states have often attempted to hide rather than to meet the challenge by aligning with other threatened states, especially when their combined strength is insufficient to deter or defeat the aggressor(s). In such cases, less directly threatened states distance themselves from more immediately threatened states by refusing to coordinate their diplomatic and military strategies with the latter.[75] Distancing is frequently combined with the more positive strategy of trying to engage the enemy.

The logic behind distancing is that joining the weaker side not only fails to make the state safer, it is also dangerous: the alliance may provoke the enemy and/or embolden its ally. In either case, the state is more likely to be dragged into a war it cannot win. Associating with the weaker alliance also increases the likelihood that the state will be seen as a potential target, while at the same time it risks diverting precious resources needed for home defense to the defense of its allies.

Geography plays a significant role in determining which states among the status quo powers will exhibit distancing behavior and which will be desperately trying, despite the odds, to forge a coalition. The surplus security afforded by geostrategic insularity, which is unavailable to land powers, makes insular states (e.g. Britain, the US) the most likely candidates for a distancing strategy. For example, in response to the rise of Nazi Germany, Britain's foreign and military policy was designed to distance itself from the French. Obviously, a state that is contiguous to the rising aggressor, such as France during the interwar period, cannot hope to gain security by distancing itself from other status quo states.

Mixed strategies

The literature has incorrectly treated many of these strategies as if they are mutually exclusive. It is assumed, for instance, that a state can either balance, bandwagon, or buckpass but it cannot simultaneously do all three. It is easily shown, however, that all three behaviors and their respective goals can be achieved in one strategic move.

Consider, for instance, Stalin's response to the rising power of Nazi Germany. The Nazi–Soviet Nonaggression Pact from the Soviet's perspective was bandwagoning because the Soviets joined the strongest and most threatening side to avoid a German attack and to gain essentially unearned spoils in Central Europe. It was buckpassing because the German attack was redirected westward, where, Stalin believed, the two sides would bleed each other white to the advantage of the Soviet Union. The pact was therefore a clear example of "free-riding": by facilitating war among the Western capitalist states, the Soviet Union would gain the benefits of a greatly diminished German and world capitalist threat without incurring the costs of fighting. Finally, it was also balancing because, by delaying a German attack, the Soviets were both buying time to bolster their depleted military forces and gaining additional territory and resources to defend themselves against Germany if and when it returned east.

The reason why these strategies can be implemented simultaneously is that, as Waltz has pointed out, balancing can be accomplished by both internal and external means. A threatened state, therefore, can bandwagon by joining the stronger or more dangerous side in order to redirect the threat elsewhere (pass the balancing buck to others) and/or gain time, space, and resources in preparation for war (internal balancing purposes).

With regard to managing a rising, dissatisfied power, there are few, if any, historical cases of "successful" engagement that were not part of a larger policy of balancing a more dangerous threat. For example, Britain's successful engagement of Japan between 1900 and 1907 was motivated primarily by the two powers' common desire to balance the growing Russian threat to their East Asian interests. Once the Russian threat disappeared (when Japan smashed their fleet in 1905), Anglo–Japanese relations grew more distant, and Britain annulled the alliance soon after World War I. Likewise, Britain successfully engaged the rising

American power because the French, Russian, and German threats were far more dangerous. Unable to defend itself against all of its potential enemies, Britain used diplomatic means to reduce the number of its potential enemies, and the US was a major beneficiary.

The interests of rising, dissatisfied powers

In addition to state power and system structure, the interests of states have been a traditional concern of international relations theory. Power tells us how much influence a state can be expected to have over others; interests tell us how and for what purposes that influence will be used. Wilsonian liberals divided the world into good (democratic) and bad (non-democratic) states; traditional realists distinguished between revisionist and status quo powers.[76] Unlike Wilsonian liberals, however, traditional realists viewed this international struggle not in Manichean terms (as a morality play between the forces of light and dark, good and evil) but rather as a natural power struggle between the established, satisfied powers and the rising, dissatisfied ones – often the victors and vanquished in the last major power war.

In the eyes of traditional realists, the concept of power politics applied equally to both "haves" and "have nots," sated and hungry states. It is the centrality of this belief that most clearly separates traditional realism from Wilsonian liberalism. As E. H. Carr put it:

> It is profoundly misleading to represent the struggle between satisfied and dissatisfied Powers as a struggle between morality on one side and power on the other. It is a clash in which, whatever the moral issue, power politics are equally predominant on both sides.[77]

At issue in the enduring conflict between satisfied and dissatisfied states is the legitimacy of the institutional arrangements or governance structures that define the established international order. Here, "legitimacy" does not imply justice. In Kissinger's words:

> [legitimacy] means no more than an international agreement about the nature of workable arrangements and about the permissible aims and methods of foreign policy. It implies the acceptance of the framework of the international order by all major powers, at least to the extent that no state is so dissatisfied that, like Germany after the Treaty of Versailles, it expresses its dissatisfaction in a revolutionary foreign policy. A legitimate order does not make conflicts impossible, but it limits their scope.[78]

In a legitimate order, even the most dissatisfied states desire only changes within the system, not a change of system; and adjustments of the status quo are acceptable as long as they are made within the framework of existing institutional arrangements and not at their expense.

It is worth noting that not all rising powers are dissatisfied with the status-quo order or their prestige and position within that order. Further, rising powers do not necessarily threaten other states. As Stephen Walt has pointed out, threat does not inhere in power alone.[79] Thus, nineteeth-century Britain controlled three-quarters of the world and yet remained in "splendid isolation"; similarly, America's rise to great power status did not provoke a counter-coalition. Geographic proximity plays an important role here: strong insular powers are inherently less threatening than continental ones; and contiguous land expansion into untapped hinterlands is far less threatening than similar expansion within the core. Thus Russia and America, sometimes called flank states, expanded to continental size without greatly disturbing the old world powers.

Revolutionary and other dissatisfied, rising powers

Rising, dissatisfied powers may be distinguished along two dimensions: the extent and nature of their revisionist aims and their risk propensity.

The nature and extent of revisionist aims

There are basically two types of revisionist states: limited-aims revisionists and unlimited-aims revisionists or revolutionary powers. In Kissinger's view, "the distinguishing feature of a revolutionary power is not that it feels threatened – such feeling is inherent in the nature of international relations based on sovereign states – *but that nothing can reassure it.*"[80] The goal of revolutionary states is not "the adjustment of differences within a given system which will be at issue, but the system itself;"[81] it is a quest for global dominion and ideological supremacy.

While all revolutionary states are dissatisfied, not all dissatisfied powers are revolutionary ones. The key question is whether the rising power views the protection and promotion of its essential values as dependent on fundamental changes in the existing international order; or whether it is merely dissatisfied with its prestige and position within that order. If the former, then it is a revolutionary state that cannot be satisfied without destroying the status quo order. If the latter, then it is a dissatisfied state but not a revolutionary one. Consequently, its demands can be satisfied while at the same time preserving and perhaps strengthening the established order. These limited-aims revisionist states are typically regional powers that seek either compensatory territorial adjustments, recognition as an equal among the great powers, and/or changes in the rules and decision-making procedures within existing regimes.

The key to the success of a strategy designed to cope with a rising, dissatisfied power is accurately distinguishing limited-aims revisionist states, which merely seek changes within the existing order, from revolutionary powers, which aim to overthrow the system. Engagement, for example, is an appropriate strategy with regard to limited-aims revisionist states. Satisfaction of their grievances through reasonable concessions in the face of legitimate demands not only can be accomplished within the existing order but, by converting these disgruntled states into defenders of the new general settlement, it strengthens the legitimacy and stability of the system and promises to preserve the peace. Attempts to appease revolutionary states, by contrast, are not only misguided but dangerous: they weaken the appeaser's relative power position and simply whet the voracious appetite of the unlimited-aims adversary; it "errs in transferring a policy of compromise from a political environment favourable to the preservation of the status quo, where it belongs, to an environment exposed to imperialistic attack, where it does not belong."[82]

In Edmund Burke's eyes, for instance, the war against Revolutionary France was not a clash of interests but of ideologies, and so he saw no chance of reconciliation. Unlike the prior war against the American colonies, which Burke condemned, the present war was:

> not with an ordinary community, which is hostile or friendly as passion
> or as interest may veer about: not with a State which makes war through
> wantonness, and abandons it through lassitude. We are at war with a
> system, which, by its essence, is inimical to all other Governments, and
> which makes peace or war, as peace and war may best contribute to their
> subversion. It is with an armed doctrine that we are at war.[83]

In 1940, Hore-Belisha took the Burkean view that Naziism and British values could not coexist: "We did not enter the fight merely to reconstitute Czechoslovakia. Nor do we fight merely to reconstitute a Polish State. Our aims are not defined by geographical frontiers. We are concerned with the frontiers of the human spirit. This is no war about a map."[84]

John Lewis Gaddis similarly views the Cold War as one between a status quo and a revolutionary power:

> Throughout the history of the Cold War, the United States has, on the
> whole, been reconciled to living with the world as it is; the Soviet Union
> . . . has seen its security as dependent on changing it. In this sense . . . the
> United States has been the *status quo* power and the Soviet Union has
> been the revolutionary power – a fact that should not be overlooked in
> assessing responsibility for the Cold War.[85]

The crux of the problem is that, without the benefit of hindsight, it is a very tricky business to infer intentions from behavior. State actions are rarely unambiguous at the time. Consider, for instance, the seemingly clear-cut case of Hitlerite Germany. To Chamberlain and the appeasers, Hitler's actions, prior to the German seizure of Prague in 1939, were consistent with a "normal" German statesman; like his predecessors, Hitler merely desired to free Germany from the "shackles of Versailles" for reasons of security not aggrandizement. They therefore endorsed Hitler's role of the injured instead of contesting it. Of this view, Lothian wrote to Eden in 1936: "I believe that if we assist Germany to escape from encirclement to a position of balance in Europe, there is a good chance of the twenty-five years peace of which Hitler spoke."[86] Similarly, Neville Henderson asserted in the Spring of 1939: "The Corridor and Danzig were a real German national grievance, and some equitable settlement had to be found if there was ever to be genuine peace."[87]

To Churchill and those who advocated a hard-line policy toward Germany, Hitler's actions prior to 1939 were unambiguously consistent with a revolutionary state with unlimited revisionist aims. Anti-appeasers pointed out that, unlike traditional German nationalists, such as Stresemann and Brünig, who would have been more than satisfied with the frontiers of 1914, Hitler made it clear that his territorial ambitions far exceeded even a restoration of the enormous gains Germany made by the Treaty of Brest-Litovsk.[88] In the eyes of anti-appeasers, Hitler's many grievances were a mere cover for his program of greedy expansion. Thus, Lord Robert Cecil argued:

> I do not think that the present grievances of the Germans are genuine so far as Hitler and his entourage are concerned. They are merely being used in order to justify his armaments policy, and if we were successful in taking away one or more of his grievances, he would only produce others, and at the same time use our concessions as a proof of how well his policy was succeeding.[89]

In retrospect, we know that Churchill's assessment of Hitler's intentions was more accurate than Chamberlain's. This does not prove, however, that Chamberlain's image of Hitler was the product of misperception, irrationality, or plain naïvité. Given the evidence available to them at the time (prior to Germany's seizure of the rest of Czechoslovakia), both British leaders could reasonably conclude as they did: Hitler's actions were generally consistent with both a limited-aims revisionist and a revolutionary state. That one of these two interpretations would ultimately prove correct does not mean that the other interpretation was the result of cognitive biases or any other type of information-processing problem. Thus, even in this seemingly clear-cut case, the process of inferring motivation from behavior is problematic and riddled with ambiguity.

Risk propensity

"Risk propensity" refers to the probability of success that a particular decision maker requires before embarking on a course of action.[90] For example, in deciding whether to increase the nation's power through war or war-threatening conflict, leaders of revisionist states must make decisions under conditions of uncertainty, that is, the extent to which the probability of success of a course of action is unknown. The sources of uncertainty of particular concern to a revisionist leader contemplating war would include: (1) its own country's military strength relative to that of the target of the attack; (2) the balance of resolve, that is, how much it values what is at stake compared with the value the opponent attaches to what is at stake; (3) will other states get involved and, if so, who will align with whom; and (4) the relative capabilities of potential alliance partners.

Let us assume that a revisionist leader attaches a probability of p to its chances of winning a war it wants to initiate. Because the probability of any event occurring can range from zero to one, its estimated probability of losing the war is $1 - p$. Let us further assume that, if the revisionist state wins, it believes that it will increase its power (or utility) by some increment x; if it loses, it believes it will be less powerful than it was prior to the war by an increment of y. The subjective expected utility of the war option, then, is the leader's estimation of the utilities of the possible outcomes times their probabilities, or $(p)x + (1 - p)y$.

In terms of risk propensity, it is useful to distinguish between two types of actors: those that are risk-acceptant and those that are risk-averse. Risk-acceptant actors are gamblers, while risk-averse actors are cautious under conditions of uncertainty. A risk-averse revisionist actor, for example, would be opportunistic in its attempts to improve its power position. "Risk-acceptant leaders, because they attach some added utility to the act of taking a gamble, are less constrained in making war decisions than are risk-averse actors."[91]

Figure 1.1 categorizes various rising, dissatisfied states according to the two dimensions articulated above.

Risk-averse, limited-aims revisionist powers are opportunistic expanders that generally seek regional dominance. By contrast, risk-acceptant, limited-aims revisionist powers tend to have more ambitious aims than do their risk-averse counterparts; and, related to this, they often advance prestige demands as well

RISK PROPENSITY

NATURE OF REVISIONIST AIMS	Risk-averse	Risk-acceptant
Limited	Fascist Italy Japan, 1894–1930 Brezhnev's USSR France, 1871–1914	Bismarckian Germany Wilhelmine Germany Japan, 1931–45 Khrushchev's USSR 2nd Empire France
Revolutionary	Stalinist Russia Maoist China	Louis XIV's France Napoleonic France Hitlerite Germany Philip II's Spain

Figure 1.1 Typology of rising, dissatisfied powers

as territorial ones. Moreover, risk-acceptant, limited-aims revisionists are typically more dissatisfied with the status quo order than are their risk-averse counterparts; and they tend to place less value on their current possessions than do the latter. Risk-acceptant, revolutionary powers are the most virulent expanders. These are the states that have periodically emerged to mount a serious challenge to the very existence of the modern state system. In contrast, risk-averse, revolutionary powers – while they, too, desire a new order – are unwilling to risk system-wide war to overthrow the system. Instead, they seek revolutionary change as a long-run, almost utopian, goal. Consequently, they are opportunistic and incremental in their attempts to revise the status quo.

Policy responses to rising, dissatisfied powers

Foreign policy debates over how to respond to a potential threat generally revolve around differing perceptions of the adversary's intentions. Along these lines, Robert Jervis distinguishes between deterrence and spiral models – two generic types of belief systems that posit contradictory views of the other state's intentions, how conflict arises, and how peace can be had and preserved.[92]

The crux of the deterrence model is that great danger arises when "an aggressor believes that the status quo powers are weak in capability or resolve."[93] Evidence of weakness and irresolve by the defenders of the status quo emboldens aggressors to advance their revisionist aims, which will cease only when the expansionist state or coalition is confronted by firm resistance. The deterrence model of conflict applies, therefore, when the defender of the status quo faces a formidable, expansionist adversary – such as a revolutionary power. Under these circumstances, deterrence theory prescribes competitive policies: active balancing and, if feasible, preventive war.

The spiral model, by contrast, views conflict as a result of enduring structural factors: international anarchy and the security dilemma. Because states exist in an anarchic, self-help realm, wars are always possible and superior military power is the final arbiter of interstate disputes. Moreover, operating under anarchy and an ever-present security dilemma, states often misperceive the arming of others for security reasons as hostile and provocative. If both sides operate under this misperception, a dangerous and unnecessary action–reaction process will ensue. In the absence of deliberate efforts to reverse this process, conflict will eventually spiral out of control. The important point, one that distinguishes this model from the deterrence view, is that conflict in the spiral model is merely apparent not real; there is no underlying conflict of interest, only a vicious cycle of distrust and exaggerated fears of the other side's aggressive intentions. Thus, in contrast to the deterrence model, the spiral model prescribes cooperative policies to reassure the other side of one's benign intentions. Specifically, a spiral model view would dictate a strategy of Graduated and Reciprocal Initiatives in Tension-reduction (GRIT), which uses unilateral, costly concessions to gain the other side's trust.[94]

The problem with Jervis' "two-model" scheme is that it excludes situations in which there are real conflicts of interests between two states but their interests are not irreconcilable; that is, their relationship, while adversarial, is not a pure zero-sum conflict. To cover this historically common situation, I propose the engagement model as a third alternative between the deterrence and spiral models. Here, the established power is confronted by a limited-aims revisionist power. The former's primary goal is to end the rivalry with the rising, dissatisfied power. For this, the appropriate strategy is neither purely cooperative nor purely competitive but instead a mixture of both carrots and sticks. Specifically, the established power attempts to satisfy the rising power's limited revisionist aims and to modify its behavior through economic and political rewards as well as the threat of force.

Figure 1.2 lists the policies that are most appropriate for the established powers to adopt in response to the various types of rising, dissatisfied powers. Because I am concerned about the policies of directly threatened established great powers, I have omitted bandwagoning for profit, distancing, and buckpassing as prudent responses – though these may indeed be wise policy responses for weak states, unthreatened remote states, and/or other revisionist powers.

Conclusions

This brief historical and theoretical survey suggests certain conclusions. First, the pace and context within which power shifts occur affects how declining and rising powers react to each other and to changes in the ladder of power. Sudden and dramatic power shifts within small-N systems (regional or global) tend to produce instability and war. Conversely, gradual and incremental changes in the relative distribution of power, especially in the context of large-N (multipolar) systems, can often be managed successfully; that is, peacefully and without destroying the basic framework of the established order.

	RISK PROPENSITY	
	Risk-averse	Risk-acceptant
NATURE OF REVISIONIST AIMS — Limited	1. Engagement 2. Binding 3. Mixed strategy	1. Containment/ balancing 2. Engagement through strength
Revolutionary	1. Containment/ balancing	1. Preventive war

Figure 1.2 Politics in response to rising, dissatisfied powers

24

Second, the nature of the rising power – whether it is risk-acceptant or risk-averse, a revolutionary or limited-aims revisionist power – should determine which policies the established powers adopt and whether or not such policies will be successful. The existence of a risk-acceptant revolutionary power rules out any chance of managing the situation peacefully. In these situations, preservation of the status-quo order and, indeed, the state system itself requires the established powers to band together against the revolutionary power, which seeks to over-throw, not alter, the essential framework of the international order. If the rising power does not have revolutionary goals, however, then engagement becomes an option; though it may be an unnecessary one (e.g. if the rising power views the status quo as legitimate or can expand its territory and influence without disrupting the vital interests of the established powers).

Third, accurate recognition of the rising power's true nature on the part of the established states is a crucial step in the process of system management. Unfortunately, because the international environment is one of constant uncertainty and ambiguity regarding the intentions of others, this basic task, which may seem so simple in hindsight, is often botched with disastrous consequences in real time.

Great danger arises when, for instance, a rising revolutionary power, particu-larly a risk-acceptant one, is misidentified as a limited-aims revisionist state. Policies of accommodation and engagement, which are appropriate responses to a limited-aims revisionist state, will simply further a revolutionary power's ability to make relative gains. Though less dangerous, the opposite mistake in recognition (namely viewing a limited-aims revisionist power as a revolu-tionary one) will also lead to unnecessary conflict and possibly war as a result of spiral-model dynamics. Further, this type of recognition error can become a self-fulfilling prophesy: by treating a limited-aims revisionist as if it were a revolutionary state, the defenders of the status quo unwittingly induce such a conversion.

There is no magic formula for managing a rising challenger and maintaining international peace and stability. The characteristics of the external environment in which a rising power emerges are beyond anyone's control. Even if the status quo defenders are fortunate enough to operate within an international structure conducive to successful management, they must still search for the right policy devices to keep the peace, maintain the integrity of the system, and ultimately convert the revisionist state into a status quo one. Moreover, the success of any effort to manage a power transition is largely a function of factors that are internal to the rising and declining powers themselves. The problem here is that domestic sources of foreign policy, like international structural factors, also tend to be beyond the control of outside powers.

With regard to these internal–external linkages of foreign policy, China's current growth in power is troubling for three reasons. First, both history and scholarship show that countries undergoing economic transitions tend to pursue assertive and expansionist foreign policies.[95] Second, China is not only in the midst of transforming its entire political and economic system, it is also ruled by a regime trying to maintain its own legitimacy. Third, while "analysts can reasonably estimate China's economic and military power a decade or more hence," it is far more difficult to predict "China's internal political and social cohesion, and how Beijing will wield its new strength."[96] Taking these factors into account, David Shambaugh concludes: "The insular and defensive character of Chinese politics and nationalism suggests that China will be reluctant and difficult to engage and to integrate in the existing international order."[97]

In the end, the best that can be hoped for is that the established powers will properly identify the challenger's long-term goals and will avoid over-reacting or under-reacting to the developing situation. The least that can be expected is that the policies adopted to deal with a rising power do no harm.

Notes

1 Quoted in Mancur Olson, *The Rise and Decline of Nations: Economic Growth, Stagflation, and Social Rigidities* (New Haven and London: Yale University Press, 1982), p. 1.
2 Paul Kennedy, *The Rise and Fall of the Great Powers: Economic Change and Military Conflict from 1500 to 2000* (New York: Random House, 1987), pp. xv–xvi.
3 Martin Wight, *Power Politics*, edited by Hedley Bull and Carsten Holbraad (Leicester: Leicester University Press, 1978), p. 144.
4 Fareed R. Zakaria makes an important and often overlooked distinction between national and state power: "Power, for the statesman, must be 'usable' and hence involves not the nation's power but instead the national government's power or 'state power.' The latter can be defined as the central government's ability to extract resources from society and the ease with which central decision-makers can implement their preferences." Fareed R. Zakaria, *From Wealth to Power: The Unusual Origins of America's World Role* (Princeton, NJ: Princeton University Press, 1998), p. 7.
5 See Robert Gilpin, *War and Change in World Politics* (Cambridge: Cambridge University Press, 1981).
6 Ibid., p. 54.
7 Ibid., pp. 23–4.
8 Arnold Wolfers, *Discord and Collaboration: Essays on International Politics* (Baltimore, MD: The Johns Hopkins University Press, 1962), pp. 14–15. Wolfers uses a race-track analogy to explain this type of external compulsion.
9 Wight, *Power Politics*, p. 163.
10 This motivation often leads to "deathwatch" wars. See Geoffrey Blainey, *The Causes of War*, 3rd edn (New York: The Free Press, 1988), Chapter 5.
11 Nazli Choucri and Robert C. North, *Nations In Conflict: National Growth and International Violence* (San Francisco, CA: W. H. Freeman, 1975).
12 Ibid., pp. 16–19.
13 Ibid., p. 17. Categorizing states according to population density and per capita indicators, Choucri and North designate the strongest core powers as *alpha* profiles: "Countries with populations, technologies, and resource accesses that are large and advancing commensurately – technological advancement maintaining a substantial lead over population growth – are typically high-lateral pressure states, the most powerful and influential in the international system." Nazli Choucri, Robert C. North, and Susumu Yamakage, *The Challenge of Japan Before WWII and After: A Study of National Growth and Expansion* (London: Routledge, 1992), p. 14.

14 Choucri and North, *Nations in Conflict*, p. 28.

15 Robert Jervis, "Cooperation Under the Security Dilemma," *World Politics*, Vol. 30, No. 2 (January 1978), p. 169.

16 Robert Jervis, *Perception and Misperception in International Politics* (Princeton, NJ: Princeton University Press, 1976), p. 64; also see Jervis, "Cooperation Under the Security Dilemma," pp. 183–5.

17 Quoted in Charles E. Neu, *An Uncertain Friendship: Theodore Roosevelt and Japan, 1906–1909* (Cambridge, MA: Harvard University Press, 1967), p. 142.

18 A. Whitney Griswold, *The Far Eastern Policy of the United States* (New York: Harcourt, Brace & Co., 1938), pp. 246, 265.

19 Paul M. Kennedy, *The Rise and Fall of British Naval Mastery* (London: The Ashfield Press, 1976), pp. 48–50.

20 George Edmundson, *Anglo-Dutch Rivalry During the First Half of the Seventeenth Century* (Oxford: Clarendon Press, 1911), p. 5.

21 For the argument that bipolarity is more stable than multipolarity, see Kenneth Waltz, "The Stability of a Bipolar World," *Daedalus*, Vol. 93, No. 3 (Summer 1964), pp. 881–909; and Kenneth Waltz, *Theory of International Politics* (New York: McGraw-Hill, 1979). For the opposite argument, see Karl W. Deutsch and J. David Singer, "Multipolar Power Systems and International Stability," *World Politics*, Vol. 16, No. 3 (April 1964), pp. 390–406. Other key works on the general stability implications of multi- and bipolarity include Thomas J. Christensen and Jack Snyder, "Chain Gangs and Passed Bucks: Predicting Alliance Patterns in Multipolarity," *International Organization*, Vol. 44, No. 2 (Spring 1990), pp. 137–168; and Richard N. Rosecrance, "Bipolarity, Multipolarity, and the Future," *Journal of Conflict Resolution*, Vol. 10, No. 3 (September 1966), pp. 314–27.

22 See J. L. Nogee, "Polarity: An Ambiguous Concept," *Orbis*, Vol. 18 (1975), pp. 1193–224.

23 See Arthur Lee Burns, "From Balance to Deterrence: A Theoretical Analysis," *World Politics*, Vol. 9, No. 4 (July 1957), pp. 494–9; Theodore Caplow, *Two Against One: Coalitions in Triads* (Upper Saddle River, NJ: Prentice Hall, 1968); and Randall L. Schweller, "Tripolarity and the Second World War," *International Studies Quarterly*, Vol. 37, No. 1 (March 1993), pp. 73–103.

24 For buckpassing, see Christensen and Snyder, "Chain Gangs and Passed Bucks."

25 Robert Gilpin, *War and Change in World Politics* (Cambridge: Cambridge University Press, 1981), p. 9.

26 Alfred Vagts, *Defense and Diplomacy: The Soldier and the Conduct of Foreign Relations* (New York: King's Crown Press, 1956), p. 263.

27 See Richard Ned Lebow, "Windows of Opportunity: Do States Jump Through Them?," *International Security*, Vol. 9, No. 1 (Summer 1984), pp. 147–86.

28 The logic of expected-utility theory posits that states go to war simply when they expect to do better than by remaining at peace. See Bruce Bueno de Mesquita, "The War Trap Revisited," *American Political Science Review*, Vol. 79, No. 1 (March 1985), pp. 157–76; Bueno de Mesquita, "The Contribution of Expected Utility Theory to the Study of International Conflict," in Robert I. Rotberg and Theodore K. Rabb, eds, *The Origin and Prevention of Major Wars* (Cambridge: Cambridge University Press, 1989), pp. 53–76. Using the logic of expected-utility theory, Sagan argues that the Japanese decision for war against the US was, contrary to conventional wisdom, rational. See Scott D. Sagan, "The Origins of the Pacific War," in ibid., pp. 323–44.

29 Gilpin, *War and Change*, p. 191; Jack S. Levy, "Declining Power and the Preventive Motivation for War," *World Politics*, Vol. 40 (October 1987), p. 97.

30 A. F. K. Organski and Jacek Kugler, *The War Ledger* (Chicago: University of Chicago Press, 1980), pp. 13–63; A. F. K. Organski, *World Politics*, 2nd edn (New York: Knopf,

1968), p. 371. For other examples of power-transition theories, see George Modelski, "The Long Cycle of Global Politics and the Nation-State," *Comparative Studies in Society and History*, Vol. 20 (April 1978), pp. 214–38; Charles F. Doran and Wes Parsons, "War and the Cycle of Relative Power," *American Political Science Review*, Vol. 74 (December 1980), pp. 945–65; and Joshua S. Goldstein, *Long Cycles: Prosperity and War in the Modern Age* (New Haven and London: Yale University Press, 1988), Chapter 12. Goldstein argues that periods of sustained growth in world production lead to Great Power wars initiated by challengers, who "try to 'catch up' with the leading economic and military power." Ibid., p. 277.

31 See Vagts, *Defense and Diplomacy*, pp. 265ff.

32 Kennedy, *The Rise and Fall of British Naval Mastery*, pp. 28–9.

33 Britain, for instance, had plenty of chances to wage a preventive war against the United States, particularly during its Civil War, but wisely chose not to do so; likewise, it remained in "splendid isolation" while Bismarck's wars established the near-hegemonic German state in Europe; and it aided Japan's rise to naval supremacy in the Pacific.

34 Randall L. Schweller, "Domestic Structure and Preventive War: Are Democracies More Pacific?" *World Politics*, Vol. 44, No. 2 (January 1992), pp. 235–69.

35 See Jervis, *Perception and Misperception*, p. 271.

36 Henry A. Kissinger, *A World Restored: Castlereagh, Metternich, and the Problem of Peace, 1812–22* (Boston, MA: Houghton Mifflin, 1957), pp. 2–3.

37 See Stephen M. Walt, *The Origins of Alliances* (Ithaca, NY: Cornell University Press, 1987).

38 These conditions are derived from Edward Vose Gulick, *Europe's Classical Balance of Power: A Case History of the Theory and Practice of One of the Great Concepts of European Statecraft* (New York: W.W. Norton, 1967), Chapter 3; and John J. Mearsheimer, "The False Promise of International Institutions," *International Security*, Vol. 19, No. 3 (Winter 1994/95), pp. 5–49.

39 See John Lewis Gaddis, *Strategies of Containment: A Critical Appraisal of Postwar American National Security Policy* (Oxford: Oxford University Press, 1982).

40 Gaddis, "Containment: Its Past and Future," *International Security*, Vol. 5, No. 4 (Spring 1981), p. 80.

41 The following discussion borrows heavily from Randall L. Schweller, "Bandwagoning For Profit: Bringing the Revisionist State Back In," *International Security*, Vol. 19, No. 1 (Summer 1994), pp. 72–107.

42 Quincy Wright, *A Study of War*, abridged by Louise Leonard Wright (Chicago: University of Chicago, [1942], 1964), p. 136. Waltz incorrectly credits the term to Stephen Van Evera. Waltz, *Theory of International Politics*, p. 126. Actually, Arnold Wolfers mentioned the term "bandwagoning" to mean the opposite of balancing long before Waltz, but only in a passing reference. See Wolfers, "The Balance of Power in Theory and Practice," in Wolfers, *Discord and Collaboration*, p. 124.

43 Wright, *A Study of War*, p. 136; Waltz, *Theory of International Politics*, p. 126.

44 Wright, *A Study of War*, p. 136.

45 "Delegates wish to be on bandwagons because support of the nominee at the convention will be a basic criterion for the later distribution of Presidential favors and patronage." Gerald Pomper, *Nominating the President: The Politics of Convention Choice* (Evanston, Ill.: Northwestern University Press, 1963), p. 144.

46 In contrast with this positive strategy, threats and reliance on naked force to coerce states to align with the rising power often backfire. Seeking revenge, the unwilling alliance partner becomes a treacherous ally that will turn against its more powerful master at the first possible oportunity.

47 David Kaiser, *Politics and War: European Conflict from Philip II to Hitler* (Cambridge, MA:

Harvard University Press, 1990), pp. 149 and 172. Derek McKay and H. M. Scott, *The Rise of the Great Powers, 1648–1815* (London and New York: Longman, 1983), pp. 14–23.

48 McKay and Scott, *The Rise of the Great Powers*, pp. 23–35.

49 Quoted in ibid., p. 36. For a detailed account of Louis' preparations for the Dutch War, see Paul G. Sonnino, *Louis XIV and the Origins of the Dutch War* (New York: Cambridge University Press, 1988).

50 David G. Chandler, *The Campaigns of Napoleon* (New York: Macmillan, 1966), pp. 449–50; Mowat, *The Diplomacy of Napoleon*, (New York: Russell & Russell, 1971), Chapter 16. In Article 1 of the Franco-Bavarian treaty of alliance (August 24, 1805), Napoleon pledged "to seize all occasions which present themselves to augment the power and splendour of the House of Bavaria," in return for the support of 20,000 Bavarian troops. Ibid., p. 152. Likewise, greed not security, Mowat claims, animated Baden's decision to bandwagon with France: "The Elector of Baden, in the preamble of the treaty, gives the curious reason for making it, that 'the renewal of hostilities threatened the independence of the States of the German Empire'; therefore he joined with that Empire's enemy. The real reason is that the Elector of Baden, through the support of France in 1802–3, had gained greatly in territory." Ibid., p. 154.

51 Chandler, *The Campaigns of Napoleon*, p. 588; Mowat, *The Diplomacy of Napoleon*, Chapter 18; Georges Lefebvre, *Napoleon: From 18 Brumaire to Tilsit, 1799–1807*, translated by Henry F. Stockhold (New York: Columbia University Press, 1969), pp. 272–5.

52 Mowat, *The Diplomacy of Napoleon*, p. 176.

53 Ibid., pp. 177, 182.

54 Gulick, *Europe's Classical Balance of Power* (see n. 38).

55 Steven Ross, *European Diplomatic History, 1789–1815* (Garden City, NY: Doubleday, 1969), p. 381. The defeated Austrian state, for instance, was shorn of most of its possessions in Italy, Illyria, and Germany.

56 For more on this point, see Paul W. Schroeder, "Napoleon's Foreign Policy: A Criminal Enterprise," *Journal of Military History*, Vol. 54, No. 2 (April 1990), pp. 147–62; and Schroeder, "The Collapse of the Second Coalition," *Journal of Modern History*, Vol. 59 (1987), pp. 244–90. Holland, Italy and the maritime states of Scandinavia, Denmark, and Portugal were similarly coerced into bandwagoning with the French Empire.

57 For example, Mussolini and Hitler successfully played on Hungary's and Bulgaria's revisionist aspirations to lure these states into the Axis camp. As part of the Munich agreement of September 30, 1938, a German–Italian court of arbitration pressured the Czech government to grant a broad strip of southern Slovakia and Ruthenia to Hungary. Then, when the Germans carved up the rest of Czechoslovakia in March 1939, Hitler, in a deliberate attempt to gain further favor with the Hungarian government, ceded the remainder of Ruthenia (Carpatho-Ukraine) to Hungary. In exchange for these territorial rewards, Hungary pledged its unshakeable support for the Nazi cause and its "foreign policy was brought into line with that of the Reich. On February 24, 1939, Hungary joined the Anti-Comintern Pact, on April 11 it left the League of Nations." Norman Rich, *Hitler's War Aims: Ideology, the Nazi State, and the Course of Expansion* (London and New York: W. W. Norton, 1973), p. 184.

58 See Hosoya Chihiro, "The Tripartite Pact, 1939–1940," in James William Morley, ed., *Deterrent Diplomacy: Japan, Germany, and the USSR, 1935–1940* (New York: Columbia University Press, 1976), p. 206.

59 Alan J. P. Taylor, *The Origins of the Second World War* (New York: Atheneum, 1961), p. 278.

60 Paul W. Schroeder, "Alliances, 1815–1945: Weapons of Power and Tools of

Management," in Klaus Knorr, ed., *Historical Dimensions of National Security Problems* (Lawrence: University Press of Kansas, 1976), pp. 227–62.

61 Joseph M. Grieco, "The Maastricht Treaty, Economic and Monetary Union and the Neo-Realist Research Programme," *Review of International Studies*, Vol. 21, No. 1 (January 1995), p. 34 (emphasis omitted).

62 Ian Nish, *The Anglo-Japanese Alliance: The Diplomacy of Two Island Empires, 1894–1907*, 2nd edn (London and Dover, NH: The Athlone Press, 1985), pp. 239–40.

63 George Monger, *The End of Isolation* (London: Nelson, 1963), pp. 419–20.

64 See Glenn H. Snyder, "The Security Dilemma in Alliance Politics," *World Politics*, Vol. 36, No. 4 (July 1984), p. 467.

65 The following discussion is borrowed from Alastair Iain Johnston and Robert S. Ross, "Engaging China: Managing a Rising Power," Project Proposal, Fairbank Center for East Asian Research, Harvard University, July 1996, pp. 5–6.

66 Lance E. Davis and Douglass C. North, *Institutional Change and American Economic Growth* (Cambridge: Cambridge University Press, 1971), p. 31.

67 Paul Kennedy, "The Tradition of Appeasement in British Foreign Policy, 1865–1939," in Paul Kennedy, *Strategy and Diplomacy, 1870–1945* (London: George Allen & Unwin, 1983), p. 16 (emphasis omitted).

68 For the effects of differential growth in power on changes in the governance structures of the international system, see Gilpin, *War and Change*, Chapter 1.

69 Johnston and Ross, "Engaging China," p. 5.

70 Wight, *Power Politics*, p. 95.

71 Quoted in Martin Gilbert, *The Roots of Appeasement* (New York: The New American Library, 1966), p. ix.

72 See Malcolm D. Kennedy, *The Estrangement of Great Britain and Japan, 1917–35* (Berkeley and Los Angeles: 1969), Chapter 4.

73 Both quotes are found in James B. Crowley, *Japan's Quest For Autonomy: National Security and Foreign Policy, 1930–1938* (Princeton, NJ: Princeton University Press, 1966), p. 188.

74 See Christensen and Snyder, "Chain Gangs and Passed Bucks."

75 See Schweller, "Tripolarity and the Second World War" (see n. 23), pp. 84, 87–92. Schroeder calls this "hiding"; Arquilla introduces the term "bystanding," defined as a state's propensity to avoid conflicts for reasons of self-preservation. See Paul Schroeder, "Historical Reality vs. Neo-realist Theory," *International Security*, Vol. 19, No. 1 (Summer 1994), pp. 108–48; and John Arquilla, "Balances Without Balancing," paper presented at the annual meeting of the American Political Science Association, Chicago, Illinois, September 1992.

76 See Hans J. Morgenthau, *Politics Among Nations: The Struggle for Power and Peace* (New York: Alfred A. Knopf, 1948), esp. Chapters 2, 3, 9, 10, and p. 156; Frederick L. Schuman, *International Politics: The Destiny of the Western State System*, 4th edn (New York: McGraw-Hill, 1948), pp. 377–80; Edward Hallett Carr, *The Twenty Years' Crisis: 1919–1939: An Introduction to the Study of International Relations* (New York: Harper & Row, 1946); Henry A. Kissinger, *A World Restored*; Johannes Mattern, *Geopolitics: Doctrine of National Self-Sufficiency and Empire* (Baltimore, MD: Johns Hopkins University Press, 1942); Arnold Wolfers, "The Balance of Power in Theory and Practice," in Wolfers, *Discord and Collaboration*, pp. 125–6; and Raymond Aron, *Peace and War: A Theory of International Relations*, translated by Richard Howard and Annette Baker Fox (Garden City, NY: Doubleday), esp. Chapter 3.

77 Carr, *The Twenty Years' Crisis*, p. 105. Similarly, Raymond Aron maintains: "Idealistic diplomacy slips too often into fanaticism; it divides states into good and evil, into peace-loving and bellicose. It envisions a permanent peace by the punishment of the latter and the triumph of the former. The idealist, believing he has broken with power politics, exaggerates its crimes. . . . States, engaged in incessant competition[,] . . .

are not divided, once and for all, into good and evil. It is rare that all the wrongs are committed by one side, that one camp is faultless." Aron, *Peace and War*, p. 584.

78 Kissinger, *A World Restored*, p. 1.

79 Walt, *The Origins of Alliances*.

80 Kissinger, *A World Restored* (New York: Grosset and Dunlap, 1964), p. 2 (emphasis in original).

81 Ibid.

82 Hans J. Morgenthau, *Politics Among Nations: The Struggle for Power and Peace* (New York: Knopf, 1967), p. 61. Similarly, Kissinger writes: "'Appeasement', where it is not a device to gain time, is the result of an inability to come to grips with a policy of unlimited objectives." Kissinger, *A World Restored*, p. 3. For the best conceptual treatments of appeasement, see William R. Rock, *British Appeasement in the 1930s* (New York: W. W. Norton, 1977), esp. Chapters 2 and 3; George A. Lanyi, "The Problem of Appeasement," *World Politics*, Vol. 15, No. 2 (January 1963), pp. 216–319; John H. Herz, "The Relevancy and Irrelevancy of Appeasement," *Social Research*, Vol. 31, No. 3 (1964), pp. 296–320; and J. L. Richardson, "New Perspectives on Appeasement: Some Implications for International Relations," *World Politics*, Vol. 40, No. 3 (April 1988), pp. 289–316.

83 Edmund Burke, Letters on a Regicide Peace (1796), in *Works*, Vol. 8 (London, 1815), p. 98.

84 Hore-Belisha, October 21, 1940, as quoted in Martin Gilbert and Richard Gott, *The Appeasers* (London: Weidenfeld & Nicolson, 1963), p. 327.

85 John Lewis Gaddis, "Containment: Its Past and Future," *International Security*, Vol. 5, No. 4 (Spring 1981), p. 79.

86 Quoted in Gilbert and Gott, *The Appeasers*, p. 42.

87 Quoted in Lewis B. Namier, *Diplomatic Prelude, 1938–39* (London: Macmillan, 1948) p. 219.

88 See Hugh R. Trevor-Roper, "A. J. P. Taylor, Hitler, and the War," in W. Roger Louis, ed., *The Origins of the Second World War: A. J. P. Taylor and His Critics* (New York: John Wiley & Sons, 1972), p. 52.

89 Quoted in Gilbert, *The Roots of Appeasement*, pp. 166–7.

90 The following discussion is drawn from Bruce Bueno de Mesquita, *The War Trap* (New Haven, CT, and London: Yale University Press, 1981), pp. 33–6.

91 Ibid., p. 35.

92 Robert Jervis, *Perception and Misperception in International Politics* (Princeton, NJ: Princeton University Press, 1976), Chapter 3.

93 Ibid., p. 58.

94 For GRIT, see Charles E. Osgood, *An Alternative to War or Surrender* (Urbana: University of Illinois Press, 1962).

95 For studies linking economic growth with foreign policy extroversion, see Charles Doran, *Systems in Crisis: New Imperatives of High Politics at Century's End* (Cambridge: Cambridge University Press, 1991); Joshua S. Goldstein, *Long Cycles: Prosperity and War in the Modern Age* (New Haven, CT: Yale University Press, 1988), and Brian M. Pollins and Randall L. Schweller, "Linking the Levels: The Long Wave and Mood Swings in U.S. Foreign Policy, 1790–1993," *American Journal of Political Science* Vol. 43, No. 2 (April 1999), pp. 431–64.

96 David Shambaugh, "Containment or Engagement of China? Calculating Beijing's Responses," *International Security*, Vol. 21, No. 2 (Fall 1996), p. 180.

97 Ibid., p. 209.

2

ENGAGING CHINA

The view from Korea

Victor D. Cha

Introduction

A snapshot of relations between China and the Republic of Korea (ROK) before and after 1990 presents two dramatically different pictures. For most of the postwar era, relations between these two powers were virtually non-existent. Two adversaries employed policies of containment, non-dialogue, and non-recognition against one another. The experience of the Korean War and the Cold War made for enemy images of the South as a forward base for US imperialist aggression, and images of China as a menacing patron of the North Korean threat. This dim picture starkly contrasts with the one after 1990. Rapidly expanding trade relations led to the establishment of trade offices in 1991. Non-dialogue of the past gave way to fully normalized and amiable relations in 1992. Beijing supported Seoul on a number of significant political and security issues against the wishes of its longtime ally in Pyongyang. Among other things, Beijing now fully accepts the ROK as a legitimate government on the peninsula. It has opposed the North's suspected drive for nuclear weapons, it has supported Seoul's United Nations membership, and it has opposed North Korea's desire to accommodate Taiwanese nuclear waste.

How does one explain this growth of cooperation between China and South Korea? To what extent has this been the result of successful engagement on the part of the ROK to "manage" China? To what extent has it been the result of factors beyond Seoul's diplomatic efforts? This chapter argues that the ROK case represents a somewhat successful example of Chinese engagement. Initiatives by Seoul from the late 1980s in the political, economic, and cultural arenas, and at unilateral, bilateral, and multilateral levels played a major part in eliciting unprecedented cooperation from Beijing. However, ROK engagement strategies alone were not a sufficient condition for this cooperation. A prior and necessary condition was a change in the strategic context surrounding China and the Korean peninsula that both raised the benefits of cooperation and the costs of non-cooperation. In this sense, engagement reinforced and built upon cooperative impulses enabled by Realist causes.

The argument proceeds in four stages. The first surveys the variations in ROK perceptions of China from the Korean War to diplomatic normalization in 1992. The second section looks at ROK engagement strategies. Although at present there is no explicit statement of an engagement "theory" in Seoul regarding policy to China, there are certain causal assumptions, goals, and means that become apparent. The third section analyzes the standards by which the ROK assesses the success of its engagement policy. Here, the dominant "measuring stick" of Chinese cooperation is with reference to North Korea. Finally, as noted above, the ROK–China case presents a case of successful engagement, but one in which cooperation can also be explained by basic Realist causes. As a result, the concluding section attempts to distinguish between Realist strategic cooperation and engagement-produced cooperation. I show how the "quality" of cooperation in the latter case is substantively different from the former as well as more longlasting, and present propositions about how one might test this in future China–ROK interaction.

Overview: from revolutionary threat to diplomatic opportunity

Perhaps more so than any other power in Asia, South Korean perceptions of China have experienced the most change over time. These perceptions have run the gamut from a China viewed as an unlimited-aims revisionist/revolutionary power, to a limited-aims dissatisfied power, to a power seen as basically content with the status quo. The first of these terms corresponds to a state that perceives its needs as fulfilled only through fundamental overthrow of the status quo.[1] A key agent of these perceptions was the strategic environment in which the relationship operated. For the ROK, the Cold War caused Chinese power to be seen in nothing other than adversarial and containment terms. First as part of the communist monolith and then later as patron of revolutionary regimes in Asia, China was one of the primary threats to ROK state survival. The Chinese People's Volunteers intervention in October 1950 obstructed the realization of Syngman Rhee's *Pukchin tongil* vision.[2] The July 1961 Friendship treaty, the "automatic intervention" clause, and the portrayal of Beijing–Pyongyang relations as close as "lips and teeth," cemented in South Korean minds the unity and longevity of the North Korean–Chinese threat.[3] Perceptions were equally hostile on the Chinese side. For Beijing, the ROK was the "fascist" axis of the iron triangle of American imperialism and Japanese militarism. South Korea's normalization with Japan in 1965, its engagement in the Indo–China conflict, and its support of the Nixon–Sato joint communique's Korean and Taiwan clauses fueled the view of Seoul as a forward base for US-sponsored Chinese containment.[4] Moreover, the breakup of the Sino–Soviet monolith from the early 1960s only reinforced Beijing's hostility towards Seoul. Allegiance with North Korea became important not only for Cold War reasons but also for strategic ones *vis à vis* the new Soviet threat.[5] As a result, Chinese rhetoric against the ROK was at times even harsher than that against Taiwan.[6] For a quarter century after the Korean war, therefore, the ROK viewed China as a revisionist, aggressive power manageable only through containment.

It was during the 1980s that these adversarial perceptions experienced gradual change. The vision of China became one of a limited-aims, "dissatisfied" power. In general terms, this refers to a state discontented with its relative position in the power and prestige hierarchy, but amenable to changes effected within (not of) the existing order.[7] While the two sides still viewed one another as threatening in military terms, they also increasingly saw each other as economic opportunities. One of the primary causes for this was domestic changes in China. The abandonment of Mao's model of economic development and the institution of Deng's modernization programs caused China to become more receptive to trade with the South. This was largely indirect trade through third countries, but by 1985, total trade with the ROK surpassed that of North Korea.[8] Thus, the willingness to separate politics from economics enabled an incremental change in perceptions (Tables 2.1 and 2.2).

The ROK's view of China as a status quo power, ripe for economic *and* diplomatic intercourse, came to fruition in the 1990s.[9] The establishment of trade offices between the Korea Trade Promotion Association (KOTRA) and the Chinese Chamber of Commerce in 1990 marked the start of government-

Table 2.1 China–South Korea trade: 1979–1996 ($1 million)

Year	China exports	China imports	Total
1979	15	4	19
1980	73	115	188
1981	75	205	280
1982	91	48	139
1983	69	51	120
1984	205	229	434
1985	478	683	1161
1986	621	699	1289
1987	866	813	1679
1988	1387	1700	3087
1989	1705	1438	3143
1990	2268	1553	3821
1991	3441	2371	5812
1992	3725	4493	8218
1993	3927	5151	9078
1994	5460	6200	11660
1995	7400	9140	16540
1996 (Jan–June)	4070	5280	9350

Source: Compiled from Chae-jin Lee, *China and Korea: Dynamic Relations* (Stanford, CA: Hoover Press 1996), 146; and Hieyeon Keum, "Normalization and After: Prospects for the Sino–South Korean Relations [sic]," *Korea and World Affairs* 20.4 (winter 1996), 579.

Table 2.2 China–North Korea trade: 1970–1995 ($1 million)

Year	China exports	China imports	Total
1970	61	54	115
1975	284	198	482
1980	374	303	677
1981	300	231	531
1982	281	304	585
1983	273	254	527
1984	226	272	498
1985	231	257	488
1986	233	277	510
1987	277	236	513
1988	345	234	579
1989	377	185	562
1990	358	125	483
1991	525	86	611
1992	541	155	696
1993	600	290	890
1994	425	199	624
1995	486	64	550

Source: Compiled from Chae-jin Lee, *China and Korea: Dynamic Relations* (Stanford, CA: Hoover Press 1996), 140; and Hieyeon Keum, "Normalization and After: Prospects for the Sino–South Korean Relations [sic]," *Korea and World Affairs* 20.4 (Winter 1996), 580.

sanctioned economic relations and the shift from indirect trade to open and direct transactions. Bilateral agreements followed that granted reciprocal most-favored-nation status (December 1991) and reciprocal protection of investments (May 1992).[10] In 1990, the Soviet Union opened the path to diplomatic normalization by abruptly recognizing the ROK despite North Korean protests. China was less blunt in its move to a two-Korea policy, eventually establishing formal diplomatic relations in August 1992.[11] Sino–Soviet reconciliation was a significant factor in Chinese calculations to normalize with Seoul. The Deng–Gorbachev summit of 1989 and the end of Sino–Soviet competition reduced in Chinese minds the strategic consequences of "losing" North Korea to Moscow. This made the opening with South Korea more feasible.

In sum, South Korea's view of China has evolved from revisionist power to status quo power. The primary criterion by which Seoul judges Chinese intentions is the priority which Beijing places on "unification" versus "peace maintenance" as the preferred security equation for the peninsula. Emphasis on "unification" essentially reflects on China as a revolutionary power, that defines peninsular security in terms of strong support for North Korean objectives to undercut the South through force and subversion. These views pervaded in Seoul during China's one-Korea policy of the Cold War. Although indirect trade in the 1980s improved ROK views of China as an economic opportunity, in the political-military realm, Chinese intentions were still perceived as revisionist.[12] It was only with Beijing's formal adoption of a two-Korea policy in the 1990s that perceptions of it as a status quo power emerged in Seoul. Recognition of the South as a legitimate government on the peninsula effectively represented a shift from "unification" to "peace maintenance" as Beijing's preferred security outcome for Korea. While this still meant support of the North Korean ally, it also meant a preference for a nonviolent settlement of disputes, and the discouragement of provocative acts by the North that might upset the delicate peace on the peninsula.

South Korean engagement: assumptions, goals, means, and measures

Changes in the strategic context of China–ROK relations (i.e. the end of the Cold War and Sino–Soviet *rapprochement*) played an important part in altering ROK perceptions of China as a revolutionary or status quo power. However, it would be incorrect to assume that cooperative relations between the two powers simply emerged from these structural causes.[13] Outcomes were as much a product of successful strategies of engagement employed by Seoul. At present, there is no systematic explication of the assumptions, goals, and means behind ROK policies to engage China.[14]

Assumptions of engaging China

Engagement is a process of strategic interaction. It is the use of non-coercive diplomatic tools and initiatives to elicit cooperative behavior from the target state and to develop norms of diffuse reciprocity.[15] Engagement generally aims to ameliorate the dissatisfied or revisionist inclinations of the problem state in a manner that is consistent with peaceful change in the existing order.[16] Unlike containment, this can be done through: (1) accommodation of the target state's interests (regardless of normative considerations); (2) an "enmeshing" of the state in international institutions upon which its well-being becomes based; or (3) the growth of a variety of transnational linkages that transform the preferences of the state.[17] In the end, the engagement's target is "socialized" to cooperate rather than "forced" through coercion, threats, or an undercutting of its power base.[18]

Several causal assumptions that are somewhat consistent with the generic definition above underlie ROK views of engagement. The first is that economic linkages, investment, and trade ties can raise the benefits of cooperation and the costs of non-cooperation to China (roughly approximating the "enmeshing" means of engagement above). The ROK sees certain political advantages to be gained from its status as a newly industrializing country proximate to China. With seventeen-fold increases in GNP (1961 to 1978) and export growth rates annually averaging 42 percent, the ROK's economic success provides potential lessons for Beijing's own modernization programs. The Asian financial crisis has certainly undermined this success; for Beijing's purposes, however, the crisis modifies but does not negate the basic lessons to be learned from South Korea's experience. In particular, the combination of tight political controls, government intervention in the economy, exploitation of labor, and utilization of foreign capital and technology practised in Seoul throughout the 1980s presents China with a model of authoritarian politics and "managed capitalism" worth interacting with.[19] In addition, the composition of trade between the ROK and China suits Beijing. Chinese exports of primary products (e.g. raw cotton, vegetables, soybean, maize, coal) and imports of manufactured goods (e.g. household electronics, televisions, refrigerators, cement, plastics) fit well with South Korea's own trade needs.[20] The attractiveness of the ROK as a trade partner is also enhanced by its potential as a source of investment and technology. This does not connote a naive South Korean belief in economics as the solution to interstate conflict, but a view that economics can lay the groundwork and open the door to incremental coopera-tion. Moreover, the accumulation of these ties can have cooperative spillover effects in other aspects of relations.[21] A key condition here is to avoid expressly linking politics and economics with Beijing given the nature of Chinese ties with the North. Instead, the proliferation of economic ties will gradually produce cooperative behavior in other arenas.

A second causal assumption behind ROK engagement is that cooperation can be achieved by adjusting one's own policies to accommodate the interests of the dissatisfied target state (i.e. means #1 above). In this sense, the strategy accords the opponent's needs and interests (regardless of normative considerations) a degree of legitimacy by offering a place at the decision-making table. This is evident in the extent to which the ROK seeks to include China in any proposals for establishing a new status quo on the peninsula (the US-ROK four-party proposal being the most recent example). It is also evident in ROK efforts to include China in various multilateral bodies in the region.[22] An additional assumption in this regard for the ROK is that the causal link between accommodation and cooperation is tenuous if the initiating party is weak. In other words, a prerequisite for successful accommodation of China is an improvement in the ROK's own position in the system. It is therefore incumbent upon Seoul that it become strong and rich enough for China to see worthwhile benefits from interacting with it.

The former two points follow in general line with what might be seen as "realist" (i.e. accommodation of a rising power) and "institutionalist" (i.e. enmeshing a rising power in interdependent institutions) techniques of engagement. Two additional sets of causal assumptions are more specific to the ROK case. Both of these relate to ways of overcoming Cold War legacies as a prerequisite to attempting institutional ties or accommodation to elicit Chinese cooperation. In other words, there are certain actions that need to be taken to make the target state believe that the initiator is "serious" about engagement. One of these is greater independence in policies. Actions contrary to past precedent or contrary to the policies of one's allies raise the credibility of initiatives to the target state. For example, ROK credibility towards China was infinitely enhanced by Seoul's flexibility on Taiwan. In spite of a history of Cold War ties dating back to

Syngman Rhee and Chiang Kai-shek, and the fact that the ROK remained the only power in the region that still maintained diplomatic relations with Taipei by the 1980s, Seoul expressed its willingness, in one stroke, to trade in this time-honored relationship for ties with Beijing. For instance, from the early 1980s, as indirect trade mounted between the two countries, both the Chun Doo-hwan and Roh Tae-woo regimes deliberately bypassed Taipei in state visits around Asia. In the 1992 normalization treaty, the ROK accepted the one-China policy (i.e. acknowledging Beijing as the only legal government in China and that Taiwan was a part of China); moreover, it immediately severed relations with Taiwan and demanded that Taipei officials promptly vacate the $1.7 billion embassy complex.[23] The attempt to gain credibility was also reflected in Seoul's bucking of international trends and refraining from overt condemnation of Beijing's actions in Tiananmen in 1989. Unlike the US, Japan, and European governments who all imposed some form of sanctions, the Roh regime neither officially condemned Chinese actions nor took punitive measures. On the contrary, Seoul promoted tourism to China which had been badly hurt by events in Tiananmen and provided technical support for Beijing's staging of the Asian Games the following year.[24]

Another causal assumption in this vein is that a general increase in communication flow enhances the target state's views of the initiator as credible. When relations between two countries have been marked by virtual silence for decades, raising the general level of "noise" and promoting "thickness" in good-will exchanges in diverse arenas is important. For the ROK, this is also intimately related to history. For Seoul, an appeal to historical affinity provides the basis for cultivating a common "we-ness" with Beijing. However, it also requires a degree of functional "amnesia." While tributary relations with China dated back to the tenth century (fully institutionalized during the Yi dynasty (1392–1910)), the most recent memory of interaction is war and China's prevention of unification. As a result, accentuating the former and fudging the latter was a necessary cost borne by Seoul. This was vividly illustrated at the time of normalization in 1992. While the basic relations treaty was couched in language celebrating the restoration of historical ties and common Confucian traditions between the two countries, only passing reference was made to an "unnatural and abnormal" past. As ROK negotiators of the treaty recounted, there was strong sentiment in Seoul for some form of Chinese acknowledgment of past aggression in Korea. However, when negotiators raised the issue of the Korean War, the Chinese emphatically stated there was no "issue" to discuss, and that an apology for the past was out of the question. The treaty clause making an ambiguous reference to the past was the only acceptable solution for the Chinese.[25]

Goals of engagement

The purpose of ROK engagement strategies is to reach a state of reasonably high mutual expectations of reciprocity. The ROK seeks more than using engagement as a means to "buy time" with Beijing (as might be the case with Taiwan), or to acquire more information that might later be used for non-engagement purposes (as might be advocated by some in the US). Instead, it seeks to cultivate Chinese cooperation through a combination of altering Beijing's payoffs in dealing with the ROK, and tying Chinese interests to the status quo on the peninsula. Transforming Chinese preferences through constituency-building is a desirable but much longer term goal on the part of Seoul.[26]

The ROK also seeks to enhance the "quality" of cooperation elicited from China. Cooperative behavior that is costless or based on specific reciprocal exchanges is less "durable" in that it is motivated by concerns pertinent only to that discrete moment of exchange. This sort of cooperation does not have longer term contagion or reinforcing effects on the general state of relations. At the less ambitious end of the spectrum, Seoul seeks through economic interaction to improve the quality of cooperation by altering the overall payoffs to China (i.e. non-cooperation becomes more costly than in the past). At the more ambitious end of the spectrum, it seeks to cause China to see cooperation in an "enlightened" sense. This is where cooperation is valued not for its immediate benefits, but for future benefits and transparency. And at the most ambitious end, the ROK seeks Chinese cooperation that is less functionally motivated and more normative; i.e. China cooperates because it is "good" regardless of the immediate situation.[27]

A third purpose of ROK engagement is related less to China and more to the ROK's own self-image. As a divided country that was ravaged by war and a pawn of Cold War balance of power politics, Korea suffered from a pariah complex. It was not a "normal" state and not a fully accepted member of the international community.[28] Its identity in the region was as a security "problem," and its fate was determined by others. In this context, the ability to successfully engage a former adversary like China held significance. It affirmed ROK developmental successes as an economy that others wanted to model and benefit from. If China took the ROK seriously, this affirmed Seoul's own view that its position in the system changed. It was now a "player" in the region and a proactive shaper, rather than passive subject, of its external environment. As a power that sought to bring China into multilateral organizations, the ROK fulfilled its own desires to be seen as a leader of regional tension reduction and dialogue rather than as a source of this tension. Before domestic audiences, engagement also provided benefits. It show-cased the government's foreign policy successes and offered evidence of genuine attempts to engage North Korea through alternative channels (discussed below). Thus another goal of engagement is prestige and self-validation. Although the tangible benefits from this are difficult to quantify, they generally translate to legitimacy, inclusion, and influence. The ROK gets a place at the table of regional security issues where its views are accorded weight and its presence is considered indispensable.[29]

Means of engagement

There are several means by which the ROK pursues engagement; some are general in nature while others are more specific to the China–ROK case. All of these reflect the causal assumptions and overall goals behind South Korean conceptions of engagement.

First, engagement as an overall strategy has been pursued through *Nordpolitik* or "northern diplomacy." Initiated by the Roh Tae-woo government in 1988 and inspired by the West German *Ostpolitik*,[30] the policy called for the improvement of South Korea's relations with socialist powers according to principles of equality, respect, and mutual prosperity.[31] *Nordpolitik* was a radical departure from the ROK's past hard-line Cold War policies as it was explicitly non-ideological in nature, and focused on mutual economic prosperity as a means of expanding diplomatic horizons with former adversaries. East European countries were certainly included in this initiative, but the clear targets were the Soviet Union and China. As two analysts noted, "[under northern diplomacy] Russia and China are no longer considered actual or potential enemies but partners in economic cooperation and regional security."[32] In subsequent statements, the ROK specifically cited China as the priority of *Nordpolitik*.[33]

Segyehwa or "globalization" represents another means by which Seoul implements engagement initiatives. *Segyehwa* generally aspires to an ROK in the twenty-first century that is "globalized" across a variety of areas including economic liberalization, social welfare, corruption-free government, and the environment.[34] In foreign policy, *Segyehwa* advocates a leading role for the ROK in international organizations and the continued expansion of the ROK's multi-directional diplomacy. As means of implementing engagement, both *Nordpolitik* and *Segyehwa* legitimize Seoul's initiatives to China by placing them in the context of a non-ideological overarching foreign policy vision. In addition, both policies are expressions of Korean self-validation about their rising position in the international system.

The ROK utilizes multilateral channels such as APEC, ASEAN PMC, and Northeast Asia dialogue through which to exchange views with China on issues.[35] Track two diplomacy sponsored by ministry-related research institutes (in particular, the Foreign Ministry's Institute for Foreign Affairs and National Security) offer additional fora for cultivating shared agendas and confidence-building. A relatively recent effort at increasing security transparency at the bilateral level has been high-level military exchanges. The two governments established defense attaché offices in December 1993 and at the initiative of the Koreans have augmented this with the first ever visit by a delegation from the People's Liberation Army in December 1996.[36] In contrast with some other powers in the region (e.g. Japan, Indonesia), South Korea has relatively few inhibitions in pursuing such security dialogue. While other powers face the mixed incentive of incorporating China into security dialogues yet at the same time seeing it as a major threat in the region, the ROK views China in more status quo terms than most because of Beijing's shift to a two-Korea policy.

The thick web of economic ties continues to be a mainstay of engagement between the two countries. China has become the ROK's third largest trade partner and the ROK has become China's fourth largest trade partner (see Table 2.1). Over twenty bilateral agreements relating to science and technology, trade, telecommunications, taxation, and industrial cooperation have been signed. Economic ties through direct investment have also become a prominent component of relations. China ranks as one of the top two investment targets of the ROK and the first in the number of projects. By 1994, more than 50 percent of all overseas investment loans approved by the Bank of Korea were for projects in China (in 1990 this was only 7.4 percent).[37] The most recent complement to these ties has been the initiation of ROK Official Development Assistance (ODA) to China (Tables 2.3 and 2.4).

Begun in 1994, the total amount of ODA is still somewhat modest, but it represents another step in the deepening of ties.[38] From Seoul's perspective, this combination of incorporating China into regional economic and political bodies, opening bilateral security dialogue, and expanding investment and aid flows constituted key means by which to pursue engagement goals with China.

As noted above, establishing credibility and goodwill is an important prerequisite for ROK engagement of China. Seoul sought to achieve this through

Table 2.3 South Korean investment in China: 1989–1996 ($1 million)

Year	No. of cases	Amount
1989	7	6.36
1990	23	15.97
1991	69	42.46
1992	171	141.16
1993	376	262.63
1994	836	630.96
1995	725	814.31
1996 (Jan–June)	366	405.00

Source: From Hieyeon Keum, "Normalization and After: Prospects for the Sino–South Korean Relations [sic]," *Korea and World Affairs* 20.4 (winter 1996), 581.

Table 2.4 ROK ODA and grant aid to China: 1994–1996 ($1 million)

Type	1994	1995	1996
Economic development Cooperation fund	43	74	68
Grant aid	2.2	3.2	3.7

Source: From Hieyeon Keum, "Normalization and After: Prospects for the Sino–South Korean Relations [sic]," *Korea and World Affairs* 20.4 (winter 1996), 581.

Table 2.5 China–ROK civilian exchanges: 1985–1995 (1000 people)

Year	Chinese visiting ROK	South Koreans visiting China
1985	0.1	0.3
1986	0.7	0.5
1987	0.2	0.8
1988	3.0	5.8
1989	5.4	13.6
1990	25.2	31.9
1991	44.2	43.2
1992	45.0	43.0
1993	40.0	112.0
1994	63.0	235.0
1995	80.1	400.7

Source: Compiled from Chae-jin Lee, *China and Korea: Dynamic Relations* (Stanford, CA: Hoover Press 1996), 166; and Hieyeon Keum, "Normalization and After: Prospects for the Sino–South Korean Relations [sic]," *Korea and World Affairs* 20.4 (winter 1996), 578.

a heavy flow of government-elite contacts.[39] In addition, it established direct civil air routes and removed controls on civilian travel to China (April 1994) to boost tourism and people-to-people exchanges (Table 2.5). These are quite standard means of promoting contacts and goodwill among governments. However, there are two additional means that might be more specific to the ROK case. The first is capitalizing on unforeseen events. An often-cited watershed in China–ROK relations was a succession of diplomatic incidents in the 1980s that compelled the two governments to break their Cold War silence. In May 1983, hijackers took over a Chinese civilian airliner and forced it to land in South Korea. In March 1985, a mutinied Chinese naval vessel drifted into ROK territorial waters and was recovered by ROK authorities.[40] In each case, unforeseen events suddenly brought the two governments into direct contact over the return of crewmen, craft, and vessel.[41] The successful handling of these negotiations was an unexpected windfall in political goodwill. Despite the absence of diplomatic relations, the two governments addressed each other in their formal capacities. Joint memoranda expressed the hope of maintaining the spirit of cooperation exhibited in the handling of these incidents. In the aftermath of these events, both governments relaxed their restrictions regarding casual contacts between diplomats in third countries.

A second method of engagement is sports diplomacy. Participation in athletic competitions hosted by each country provided a useful means by which to express goodwill and an interest in expanding on the economic cooperation of the 1980s. China sent the largest (and most successful) delegation of athletes to the 1986 Asian Games in South Korea, despite Pyongyang's protests. One outgrowth of this was a change in Chinese public attitudes and images of South Korea. Chinese coverage of the Asian Games highlighted the beauty of Seoul, and praised South Korea's ability to combine modernity with Confucian traditions.[42]

These contrasted with the predominantly negative North Korean-based images of degradation and poverty in the South. China's decision to participate in the 1988 Seoul Olympics (again, despite Pyongyang's protests) was another major vehicle for expanded contacts. Preparations for the Games required direct contact between the two governments regarding the details of participation. As Young Whan Kihl noted, "all of [these contacts] bore significance in a situation where hardly a word had ever been exchanged previously on an official level."[43] These sports channels also became a convenient means of exercising reciprocity. ROK officials were also extremely pleased by China's participation in 1988, since it made the Seoul Games the most successful and well-attended since 1976. As a result, the ROK went to extreme lengths to support the 1990 Asian Games in Beijing. This was a significant event for China as it sought to establish a degree of normalcy in its outward appearance after events in Tiananmen. Seoul attended the Games with enthusiasm, provided $15 million in advertising revenue, and made other substantial donations in kind to facilitate a successful staging of the event.[44]

Measuring the success of engagement

If the goal of engagement is to elicit more cooperative Chinese behavior, how does the ROK "measure" this? Over what issues does Seoul assess the success of its strategy? The most significant measure for the ROK (not only regarding China but virtually all its bilateral relationships in the region) is policy toward North Korea. For the Koreans, national security is defined in terms of unification, which in turn is defined almost wholly in terms of containment, exclusion, and isolation of the rival regime in the North. A zero-sum mentality prevails in which any losses by the North are equated with gains to the South and vice versa.[45] In this context, there exists a range of outcomes across which the ROK measures the success of engagement with China (Table 2.6).

At the most unsuccessful end of the spectrum (A) are engagement strategies that fail to move Beijing from its traditional alliance ties with the North. China would continue to provide full economic and political support for Pyongyang's objective of inciting revolution in the South. The minimally successful outcome (B) would

Table 2.6 Possible engagement outcomes

1-Korea policy: support of NK	"1.5" Korea policy: formal support of NK, *de facto* recognition of SK	2-K policy: equidistance between NK & SK	2-K policy: discourage NK aggression	1-K policy: support SK
failure (A)	*minimally successful (B)*	*more successful (C)*	*very successful (D)*	*most successful (E)*

be where China *de facto* acknowledges the South but still maintains strong ties with the North. The more successful outcome (C) would be where China sheds a one-Korea policy and formally recognizes the South as a legitimate government, but maintains relations with both Koreas at arm's length. Beijing's priority in this instance would be to maintain peace on the peninsula but strictly as a neutral balancer with no inclinations toward either side. Policies to increase goodwill and enhance transparency would have little effect on Beijing's policies. A very productive engagement outcome (D) would also see China adopt a formal two-Korea policy. However, the focus of Beijing's concern would be on the North as the primary threat to peace on the peninsula. In other words, in this outcome, Beijing might be opposed to containment and isolation of the North by regional powers (as this might result in a desperate backlash), but it would also explicitly oppose and criticize any North Korean acts of aggression. Confidence-building and the accumulation of goodwill between Seoul and Beijing would increase transparency and give rise to tacit collaboration to avoid a destabilization of the peninsula. On the surface, the marginally and moderately successful outcomes (C and D) appear indistinguishable; however, the primary difference is that in the latter case, Seoul would not feel threatened by Chinese affirmations of solidarity with the North. Finally, at the far end of the spectrum, engagement would be most successful (E) if China moved wholly to a one-Korea policy recognizing the South and containing the North.[46]

ROK engagement policies appear to be relatively successful when measured on this scale. Outcomes generally fall into the middle range (i.e. B to D). One obvious illustration is Beijing's decision to establish trade offices with Seoul in October 1990 and formal diplomatic relations in August 1992. In both cases, Beijing was initially reluctant because of ties with Pyongyang. China–ROK bilateral trade dropped between 1982 and 1983 (see Table 2.1) precisely because of Chinese deference to North Korean complaints. In spite of this, the ROK persistently took the initiative in pursuing China. It played up economic opportunities as well as goodwill gained from Seoul's support of the Beijing Games.[47] When the Chinese finally agreed to trade offices, they downplayed the event, stressing instead the doctrine of "politics separate from economics," and their continued honoring of alliance commitments to North Korea. However, from the South's perspective, this was a watershed turn in Chinese behavior to a *de facto* two-Korea policy.[48] Similar circumstances surrounded normalization in August 1992. The Chinese were initially reluctant to move beyond a *de facto* two-Korea policy; however, Seoul's persistent entreaties – in combination with its efforts to bring Beijing into APEC, a string of economic agreements emerging from the establishment of trade relations (i.e. MFN, investment protection, civ-air routes), and an expressed willingness to drop relations with Taiwan – were successful in eliciting Beijing's formal shift to a *de jure* two-Korea policy. For Seoul, engagement was successful not so much because of new economic markets, but because it effectively isolated the North by befriending its two primary patrons (following Soviet normalization in 1990).

Another measure of moderately successful engagement was Chinese behavior during the 1994 North Korean nuclear crisis.[49] Beijing sided with the US and the ROK on many aspects of this dispute. It opposed North Korea's reneging on the NPT treaty and counseled them to return to their commitments. It clearly stated that it saw the North Korean nuclear program (in conjunction with its ballistic missile program) as destabilizing for the region, and advocated, with its new diplomatic partner in Seoul, a non-nuclear peninsula. It also expressed support for the Agreed Framework.[50] At the same time however, Beijing strongly opposed any acts of coercion against the North. It persistently pressed for dialog and negotiation as the only acceptable means of settling the dispute. In particular, it vocalized strong opposition to any moves by the US and UN Security Council to contemplate sanctions against the North. This emasculated the sanctions option, either through the threat of a Chinese veto or through non-compliance with an implementation of such measures. China's actions in the course of this dispute reflected the shift from one-sided policies in support of the North to ones that were more equidistant between the two Koreas – a moderately successful outcome for ROK engagement.

From the ROK perspective, two outcomes at the very successful end of the spectrum were Chinese behavior on UN admission of the two Koreas in 1991 and its response to North Korean attempts to disrupt the Armistice agreement. In the former case, prior to 1991, Beijing had a long-established policy opposing dual membership for the two Koreas in the world body. In 1987, Beijing explicitly backed Pyongyang and opposed Seoul in criticizing this formula. However, by late 1990, concurrent with the establishment of trade offices with the ROK, Beijing's enthusiasm for this policy diminished.[51] During Li Peng's visit to Pyongyang in April to May 1991, the Chinese premier informed North Korean officials that it could not veto an ROK application for membership, and urged the North to apply as well. Li reasoned that dual membership would be an interim measure that did not inhibit unification in the future (i.e. the German case), and that membership would afford the North international recognition and improved relations with the world. Immediately after Li's visit, the North made its dramatic reversal in policy and sought UN membership. Both Beijing and Seoul welcomed this decision.[52]

In the latter case, a key North Korean objective in the post-Cold War has been to seek direct dialogue with the US on a peace treaty for the peninsula to the exclusion of South Korea.[53] This is part of a broader North Korean strategy designed to create a division of interests between South Korea and its allies with regard to security issues on the peninsula. One manifestation of this "wedge strategy" was Pyongyang's boycott of the Military Armistice Commission (MAC) at Panmunjom after the chief representative position was transferred to the ROK in 1991. Another was a series of North Korean armistice violations in 1994 and 1996 aimed at drawing the US into a direct security dialogue.[54] In contrast to past precedent, China strongly opposed these North Korean actions. It maintained that despite Pyongyang's boycotts, the armistice agreement remained valid until a new peace structure was constructed. Beijing refrained from any statements of support for North Korean provocative actions, and declared that no party had the right to unilaterally invalidate the 1953 agreement. Moreover, it firmly maintained that the negotiation of a future peace treaty must include South Korea. As one analyst's articulation of the Chinese position stated, the key prerequisite to a peace treaty is the development of tension-reduction and confidence-building measures; in this vein, "[a]ny solution that attempts to leave the South Koreans out of a security dialogue does not address the current realities."[55]

From Seoul's perspective, Chinese behavior in both cases was a successful product of engagement strategies. Beijing's support of UN dual admission was a marked shift from past policies. In addition, Beijing's policy toward the armistice violations reflected a clear disapproval of North Korean wedge strategies *vis-à-vis* the ROK. This not only represented China's new *de jure* two-Korea policy, but also a tacit understanding that the primary threat to peace on the peninsula stemmed from North Korean intransigence. China was careful not to signal anything resembling an abandonment of its North Korean ally or policies that exacerbated or played on the North's isolation. Nevertheless, from the ROK perspective, engagement strategies had successfully created a situation where these PRC statements of allegiance to the North were no longer seen as threatening.

Engagement or harmony?

The previous section has provided an empathetic analysis of the assumptions, means, and goals of ROK engagement strategies toward China. On the whole, these strategies appear from Seoul's perspective to have been quite effective at eliciting cooperative behavior. However, questions still remain about the future success of ROK–China engagement. These largely emerge when one looks at the structural conditions surrounding the initiation of these strategies. There are two related problems in this regard. The first is overdetermination. The primary indicator of the success of ROK engagement strategies is Chinese cooperation; however, this cooperation could also be seen as a causal product of basic Realist factors. The second problem relates to the "quality" of cooperation. For engagement to be considered "successful," the cooperation that emerges from the target state must be more than simply "costless."

In essence, the first problem is whether Chinese cooperation results from ROK engagement or simply from the emergence of parallel interests in mutually beneficial outcomes. The primary causal factors in the latter regard are the end of the Cold War and Sino–Soviet reconciliation. China and the ROK were tied into alliance networks on opposite sides of the East–West divide in Asia. In addition, China's relations with North Korea operated within the context of the Sino–Soviet conflict. As a result, the absence of interaction between Seoul and Beijing was in many ways structurally determined. It was only with the lifting of these structural constraints from 1989 that paths to cooperation were laid open. The end of the Cold War removed the overarching security and ideological impediments to realizing mutual economic gains. Perhaps most important, the end of the Sino–Soviet confrontation (and Moscow's move first to normalize with Seoul) removed China's need to avoid policies that alienated the North and pushed it into the Soviet orbit. The domestic push for economic modernization in China added another positive force for exploring dialogue with Seoul. Seen in this light, the establishment of ROK–China trade offices, normalization, and other instances of cooperation may be less a function of the ROK's engagement efforts, and more due to mutually beneficial outcomes created by a new strategic context and domestic-political imperatives.[56]

This relates to the second problem with regard to the "quality" of cooperation. Engagement aims to establish norms of diffuse reciprocity with the target state. The more diffuse the notions of reciprocity that underlie behavior, the more robust and long-term cooperation is likely to be. As noted earlier, ROK engagement strategies ideally seek to elicit cooperation from China that is durable and enlightened – in other words, behavior that does not stem merely from specific reciprocal exchanges or a general altering of payoff structures in the direction of cooperation. Successful engagement causes China to cooperate even when it may not be immediately expedient to do so (i.e. to cooperate for longer term benefits or as a result of spillover effects), or in the most ideal case, because cooperation is seen in and of itself as a good thing. Thus, the causal significance and success of engagement strategies become inextricably intertwined with the quality of cooperation. If the improvement in China–ROK relations stems from changing geostrategic factors, then cooperation is not durable and enlightened but costless and temporary – in which case the causal significance and success of engagement is less persuasive. For example, China's decision to establish trade offices and formal diplomatic relations in the early 1990s may be less a result of engagement and more because the costs of doing so were negligible. The end of Sino–Soviet competition for North Korea's allegiance reduced dramatically the consequences of seeking ties with Seoul. In addition, the precedent for "defecting" on Pyongyang had already been set by Moscow. In short, cooperation happened less because of engagement, and more because it was, in this instance, "cheap."[57]

Similarly, if there exist alternative explanations for Chinese cooperation with the ROK, engagement as the causal variable is again suspect. For example, Seoul–Beijing allegiance in castigating Japan for an irresponsible accounting of past history could be seen as a cooperation produced by engagement.[58] However, it could also be the result of a harmony of interests. In other words, given the common history of victimization by Imperial Japan, similar outcomes would have resulted regardless of engagement. Similarly, Chinese and South Korean opposition to Taiwan–North Korea arrangements on the storage of nuclear waste might be cited as additional evidence of engagement-based bilateral cooperation.[59] However, this cooperation, too, is relatively costless, and given the convergence of interests, a likely outcome regardless of engagement.

The key point is that a distinction is necessary between the causal effects of Realist factors and those of engagement strategies. Each is a necessary but not sufficient condition for cooperation. Engagement initiatives are not effective in the China–ROK case if the strategic context is not permitting.[60] On the other hand, favorable changes in the strategic context do not guarantee cooperation but only provide the potential for it. The end of the Cold War and Sino–Soviet split were the permissive conditions to China–ROK *rapprochement* (and made cooperation somewhat costless), but the process of engagement – increasing interaction, promoting transparency, and accumulating goodwill – facilitated the outcome. Engagement therefore reinforces and builds on the positive impulses created by changes in the strategic environment.

Conclusion: propositions for the future

In spite of engagement's facilitating role in the promotion of cooperation in the China–ROK case, it is still admittedly difficult to clearly separate this from basic Realist causes. This is because: (1) the strategic environment figured so heavily in conflict in the China–ROK relationship; and (2) cooperative changes in the environment and cooperative strategies for engagement occurred at virtually the same time. This final section attempts to draw out some propositions to help further isolate the effects (and success) of engagement strategies.

One way of approaching this problem is to focus on the expectations of the parties. Structural changes may be a necessary condition for cooperation, but they do not automatically change the expectations which states have about each other's actions. Thus, if engagement succeeds, it should have an effect on the baseline of expectations which states have with regard to what constitutes cooperative and non-cooperative behavior.[61] In other words, what might have been interpreted as non-cooperative behavior before engagement might be seen differently with engagement. A potential example of this in the China–ROK case was interaction over Hwang Jang-yop in spring 1997.[62] The defection of this prominent North Korean ideologue placed Beijing in a difficult position between its new partner in Seoul and its old ally in Pyongyang. The precedent in such cases was for China to return all defectors to the North. Given Hwang's prominence, Seoul wanted his immediate release to the ROK. Beijing's initial statements intimated that resolution of the case would take an extremely long time.

In an engagement-scarce environment, ROK officials might have interpreted China's statements as a delaying tactic, ultimately resulting in a back door deal with Pyongyang for Hwang's return; however, this was not the case. ROK statements during the incident were marked by a conspicuous absence of disapproval or pressure on China, and counseled patience in awaiting the Chinese decision. Similarly, in an engagement-scarce environment, Beijing might have found this an easily resolvable case, simply returning Hwang to face punishment in the North. However, engagement effectively changed Chinese perceptions of such an action. What was standard operating procedure prior to engagement was now seen as a very significant signal of non-cooperation with Seoul. In this sense, engagement matters because it changes the baseline of expectations of what constitutes cooperation and defection. For Seoul, what might have been seen as Chinese non-cooperation before was now seen benignly. For Beijing, what might have been standard operating procedure in the past was now seen in a wholly different light.

A final way of isolating the effects of engagement is to pinpoint issues over which there might arise conflicts of interest between China and the ROK. One of the problems of distinguishing between the causal effect of Realist factors and engagement strategies in China–ROK cooperation is because many of the situations are positive-sum. Thus if Seoul and Beijing successfully manage situations in which mutually beneficial outcomes are more difficult to achieve, engagement might be the cause.

Such conflictual situations might emerge as a result of Korean unification. For example, North Korea's absorption by the South may raise new strategic realities between a united Korea and China. The absence of the North Korean buffer would give rise to a situation in which two powers, of different regime types, share a contiguous border. Koreans would have to contend with an immensely powerful China whose intentions are not transparent, and most likely would do so without the same security guarantees from the US enjoyed in pre-unification days.[63] China would have to contend with a competing political system directly on its southern flank that might be a proxy for US or Japanese containment – historically a situation that China has dreaded.[64] If engagement strategies work, Seoul and Beijing should be able to manage this situation which otherwise would be ripe for misperception, distrust, and insecurity spirals.

Engagement strategies might also make a difference in the way Korea and China manage future economic competition. Although the composition of China–ROK trade is complementary (primary products for manufactured goods, making cooperation relatively costless), China's growth may change its trade needs and raise competition with Korea. In particular, a combination of high growth and fixed resource endowments may make China a net importer of food products and raw materials and a net exporter of labor-intensive manufactured goods. Given China's comparative advantage over Korea in labor costs, this could lead to fierce competition with Korean (sunset) industries for international markets.[65] Competition could also grow more fierce as Korea faces OECD pressures to liberalize and become vulnerable to a flood of Chinese imports. If engagement matters, it would affect the domestic debate in both countries on protectionism, and curtail spillover effects from trade friction.

Finally, another potential conflict between a united Korea and China centers on the issue of nationalism. A united Korean resurgence of nationalism might raise concerns in Beijing about its ethnic Korean minority population largely in Jilin province. Numbering two million, this constitutes the largest concentration of overseas Koreans in the world. Beijing's sensitivities to Korean appeals to this group have already been expressed on a number of occasions.[66] The ability of the two governments to avoid friction and build transparency over this issue may turn on the effects of engagement. In the end, the true test of ROK engagement strategies may be yet to come.

Acknowledgment

I thank Iain Johnston, Robert Ross, Allen Whiting, and Robert Lieber for comments.

Notes

1 See Randall Schweller, "Managing the Rise of Great Powers: History and Theory," Chapter 1, this volume.
2 "March north" or *songgong tongil* (unification through victory) were two slogans explicating the ROK vision that unification could only be achieved through military victory. Rhee vehemently despised the Chinese for obstructing the realization of this vision both in terms of the 1950 intervention and later in the armistice. Rhee instituted mass anti-China campaigns after 1953 with songs like "smash the Chinese barbarians." For the best works on the Chinese calculus for entering the Korean war, see Allen Whiting, *China Crosses the Yalu: The Decision to Enter the Korean War* (Stanford, CA: Stanford University Press, 1960); Sergei Goncharov, John Lewis, and Xue Litai, *Uncertain Partners: Stalin, Mao and the Korean War* (Stanford, CA: Stanford University Press, 1993); and Thomas Christensen, "Threats, Assurances, and the Last Chance for Peace: The Lessons of Mao's Korean War Telegrams," *International Security* (Summer 1992), 122–154.
3 The China–North Korea Treaty of Friendship, Cooperation, and Mutual Assistance was viewed as more permanent than the alliance signed between North Korea and the Soviet Union. This stemmed not only from rhetoric about how the Chinese–North Koreans had been "sealed in the blood" of the Korean war, but also from the legalities of the agreement. While the Soviet treaty could be abrogated unilaterally after ten years with advance notice, the Chinese treaty could only be abrogated with mutual agreement of the parties (see Chae-jin Lee, *China and Korea: Dynamic Relations* (Stanford, CA: Hoover Press, 1996), 60).
4 A statement by Liu Shaogi (PRC Chairman) in September 1963 was representative of China's attitudes:

> South Korea under the occupation of US imperialism is a hell on earth. The south Korean people living under intolerable conditions have time and again courageously launched a just struggle against US imperialism and for national salvation. The US puppet Syngman Rhee has been overthrown by the south Korean people. Another US puppet Park Chung Hee will be overthrown too by the south Korean people sooner or later. The scheme of US imperialism to perpetuate the division of Korea is doomed to failure.
> (Cited in Lee, *China and Korea*, 61)

For a discussion of the Cold War contexts of Japan–Korea normalization, ROK involvement in the Vietnam War, and the 1969 Nixon–Sato joint communique, see Victor Cha, *Alignment Despite Antagonism: The United States–Korea–Japan Security Triangle* (Stanford, CA: Stanford University Press, 1998), Chapter 3.
5 Aside from the ideological benefits of North Korean alignment against the Soviets,

China's concerns centered on the threat of Soviet access to warm water ports in North Korean areas like Najin and Nampo. In combination with Soviet access to Cam Ranh Bay, this could threaten China's northeastern region and the Bohai Sea. China's difficult relations with Vietnam, Cuba, Mongolia, and Albania only increased the strategic value of the North to China.

6 For these reasons, China–ROK relations were also uninfluenced by the proliferation of *détente* between 1972 and 1974. While there was a reduction in tension and normalization of relations among all the major powers (including increased dialogue between Japan and the Soviet Union and between North and South Korea), the China–ROK dyad remained conspicuously devoid of improvement. In addition to the Cold War and the Sino–Soviet split, another factor that inhibited Chinese dialogue with the ROK was the contradiction this would pose to Beijing's own situation regarding Taiwan. Recognition of the South would constitute a "two-Korea" policy completely at odds with Beijing's vehement insistence on a "one-China" policy. As discussed below, changes in geostrategic conditions and ROK engagement strategies made this less of an obstacle.

7 Schweller, "Managing the Rise of Great Powers," Chapter 1, this volume.

8 Much of the trade was transacted through third-party intermediaries or ROK trading firms in Hong Kong. ROK markings were removed from most goods prior to entry in the Chinese market and bills of lading were doctored to disguise the port of origin (Lee, *Korea and China*, 144).

9 The ROK view of China as a status quo power does not deny that China harbors certain irredentist and prestige-hierarchy grievances, but outside of this, finds China basically a supporter of the existing order.

10 For details of these events, see Hong Yung Lee, "China and the Two Koreas," in Young Whan Kihl, ed., *Korea and the World* (Boulder, CO: Westview Press, 1994); David Dollar, "South Korea–China Trade Relations: Problems and Prospects," *Asian Survey* 29.12 (December 1989); and Qin Yong Chun, "China–ROK Relations in a New Period," *Korean Journal of International Studies* 25.2 (1994).

11 For the joint communiqué, see "Source Material," *Korea and World Affairs* 16.3 (fall 1992), 544–545; see also Ilpyong Kim, "The Normalization of Chinese–South Korean Diplomatic Relations," *Korea and World Affairs* 16.3 (fall 1992), 483–492.

12 During the 1980s, Beijing maintained harsh Cold War rhetoric against the South; however, it also expressed a clear desire to avoid becoming entrapped in another war on the peninsula. For example, on several occasions, the Chinese made statements to the US and Japan that North Korea did not have the capabilities to attack the South and that China would not support such an act (see Lee, *China and Korea*, 79). Nevertheless, ROK perceptions of the threat from China remained salient as long as China maintained the one-Korea policy.

13 In fact, from a Realist perspective, one could also argue that post-Cold War changes in the strategic environment might give rise to greater friction between Beijing and Seoul, as the ROK is now seen as part of the American unipolar threat to China. The point is not that this view is right, but that Realism is indeterminate in its predictions, therefore begging the question of what other factors might have been at play in promoting the two countries' cooperation.

14 *Nordpolitik* or "Northern Diplomacy" is discussed below as a policy manifestation of ROK engagement thinking, but there is to my knowledge no systematic exposition of causal assumptions behind these policies toward China.

15 For a more detailed and slightly different definition, see Johnston and Ross, Preface, and Schweller, "Managing the Rise of Great Powers," Chapter 1, this volume.

16 The extent to which the goal of peaceful change is attainable greatly depends on the nature of the target state (i.e. less likely when the target is revolutionary with

unlimited aims; more likely when the target's aims are limited). See Schweller, "Managing the Rise of Great Powers," Chapter 1, this volume.

17 Johnston and Ross, Preface, and Schweller, "Managing the Rise of Great Powers," Chapter 1, this volume.

18 In a related vein, see George Shambaugh, "Threatening Friends and Enticing Enemies in an Uncertain World," in Gerald Schneider and Patricia Weitsman, eds., *Enforcing Cooperation: "Risky" States and the Intergovernmental Management of Conflict* (New York: Macmillan, 1996), 234–261, on the "socializing" effects of international organization memberships on "risky" states.

19 Lee, *China and Korea*, 144; see also William Overholt, "China After Deng," *Foreign Affairs* (May/June 1996); and Hieyeon Keum, "Normalization and After: Prospects for the Sino–South Korean Relations [*sic*]," *Korea and World Affairs* 20.4 (Winter 1996), 577–578. In the late 1980s the Chinese Academy of Social Sciences established a group to systematically study ROK development successes (Dong Sung Kim, "China's Policy Toward North Korea and Cooperation Between South Korea and China," *Korean Journal of International Studies* 24.1 (1994), 36.)

20 Dollar, "South Korea–China Trade Relations," 1167–1168. Potential problems in terms of trade complementarity are discussed below. Geographic proximity adds to the economic fit. Iron, copper, coal, and petroleum deposits in the Liadong and Shandong peninsulas and Bohai Sea areas are easily transported to Korea across the Yellow Sea.

21 One of the ways in which this assumption was validated in ROK minds was the establishment of trade liaison offices in 1990. Although trade up until this time was indirect, the volume of transactions became so great that it was difficult to continue without some formal agreements. For Koreans, these agreements in turn formed the basis and set the precedent for steps toward normalization. The growth of trade ties in the 1980s was also seen in Seoul as a major reason why China chose to participate in various sporting events in the ROK (i.e. 1986 Asiad, 1988 Olympiad), which was also an important spur to normalization.

22 The primary example here is the ROK's efforts to facilitate China's participation in the 1991 APEC meeting in Seoul despite the presence of Hong Kong and Taiwan.

23 Parris Chang, "Beijing's Policy Toward Korea and PRC–ROK Normalization of Relations," in Richard Mansbach and Manwoo Lee, eds., *The Changing Order in Northeast Asia* (Boulder, CO: Westview Press, 1994), 159, n. 6.

24 Lee, "China and the Two Koreas," 103; and Lee, *China and Korea*, 151.

25 Former Director, Treaties Division, ROK Ministry of Foreign Affairs, personal interview, Stanford, CA, September 1994; and Lee, *China and Korea*, 126.

26 One of the means by which the ROK has been increasing transnational ties has been through improved educational and cultural exchanges. A rash of Korea-related institutes and programs have emerged on Chinese university campuses, chiefly funded by large Korean corporations. The government and education ministry have also actively encouraged students who seek to study abroad to make China their destination.

27 As discussed below, this distinction in types of cooperation is useful in helping to differentiate between the causal effects of Realist factors and engagement strategies in explaining Chinese–South Korean cooperation.

28 For instance, until September 1991, Koreans have always viewed their exclusion from membership in the United Nations as a reflection of this pariah status.

29 An additional goal might be ROK engagement of China out of concerns about threats from Japan. This sort of engagement, however, would be slightly different in that the focus of the policy would be more "against" Tokyo than a desire to seek a workable accommodation with Beijing, in which case we may no longer be solely in the realm

of engagement, but more in that of pure balance of power. On the confluence of strategies like balancing, binding, and engagement, see Schweller, "Managing the Rise of Great Powers," Chapter 1, this volume.

30 An earlier version of *Nordpolitik* was attempted by Park Chung Hee in 1973, but, for reasons stated below, the initiative was not successful.

31 "Dialogue for Peace," Address at the 43rd Session of the General Assembly of the United Nations, October 18, 1988, reproduced in *Korea: A Nation Transformed, Selected Speeches of Roh Tae Woo* (Oxford: Pergamon Press, 1990), 8.

32 Chung-in Moon and Seok-soo Lee, "The Post-Cold War Security Agenda of Korea," *Pacific Review* 8.1 (1995), 101.

33 Lee, *China and Korea*, 112–113. In 1989, the ROK normalized relations with Hungary, Poland, and Yugoslavia. The following year, relations were established with Czechoslovakia, Bulgaria, Romania, Algeria, Congo, Mongolia, South Yemen, and Vietnam. The ROK exchanged trade offices with the Soviet Union in April 1989 and consular offices in March 1990. A series of high-level visits laid the groundwork for the Roh–Gorbachev meeting in San Francisco in June 1990, after which diplomatic relations were established in September (see Young Whan Kihl, "Foreign Relations: Diplomatic Activism and Policy Dilemmas," in Don Clark, ed., *Korea Briefing 1991* (New York: Asia Society, 1991), 58–61).

34 See In Duk Kang, "South Korea's Strategy toward North Korea in Connection with its Segyehwa Drive," *East Asian Review* 7.1 (Spring 1995), 55–70; Young-kwan Yoon, "Globalization: Toward a New Nationalism in Korea," *Korea Focus* 3.1 (January to February 1995), 13–28; and Victor Cha, "Globalization, Security, and the Alliance," in Samuel Kim, ed., *Globalization and South Korea* (forthcoming).

35 For example, it was at the October 1991 APEC meetings in Seoul that Foreign Ministers Qian Qichen and Lee Sang-ock discussed an expansion of relations beyond trade ties. Lee's follow-up meetings with Qian at the ESCAP (Economic and Social Council for Asia and the Pacific) meetings in Beijing in April 1992 overshadowed a simultaneous visit by President Yang Shangkun to Pyongyang for Kim Il Sung's eightieth birthday celebrations (Lee, *China and Korea*, 122–124).

36 A four-member delegation led by Major General Luo Bin met with Defense Minister Kim Dong Jin and Army Chief-of-Staff Do Il-kyu (*Joongang Ilbo*, December 4, 13, 1996).

37 The major areas of ROK investment are in the northern and northeastern regions (Tianjin, Beijing, Wehai, Qingdao in the Bohai Sea area). Average monthly wages in China are a fraction (approximately 10 percent) of those in the ROK. The pioneers of the Chinese market were the small and medium-sized ROK businesses in the 1980s, but these were followed by large-scale chaebol investment. Projects by Hyundai, Daewoo, and Samsung include pianos, semiconductors, computers, automobiles, and small passenger aircraft.

38 A major agreement in 1994 linked ODA to ROK–China industrial cooperation in automobiles, telecommunications, small aircraft, high-definition television, and nuclear energy (see Keum, "Normalization and After," 581).

39 Official visits have included individuals such as Jiang Zemin, Li Peng, Yang Shangkun, Qiao Shi, Qian Qichen, Roh Tae-woo, Kim Young Sam, Lee Hong-koo, Han Sung-joo, and Lee Sang-ock.

40 For the specifics of these events, see Chae-jin Lee, "South Korea in 1983: Crisis Management and Political Legitimacy," *Asian Survey* (January 1984); Chang, "Beijing's Policy Toward Korea," 160; and Lee, *China and Korea*, 106–112.

41 In both cases, crew and vessels were returned to Chinese possession, and in the latter case, Beijing also apologized for violating ROK waters in pursuit of the mutinied craft (Lee, *China and Korea*, 109–110).

42 Ibid., 145–146.

43 Kihl, "Foreign Relations: Diplomatic Activism and Policy Dilemmas," 59.

44 Seoul expressed its enthusiasm for the Games by sending a personal relative of Chun as the ROK delegation head as well as a number of government officials to hold high-level, low-profile discussions on trade offices. The ROK also donated over 400 vehicles for the transportation of athletes and officials as well (Kihl, "Foreign Relations: Diplomatic Activism and Policy Dilemmas," 67–68).

45 For a discussion of how zero-sum mentalities are changing under Kim Dae Jung and a comparison of Chinese engagement and the "sunshine" policy, see Victor Cha "Engaging China: Seoul-Beijing Detente," *Survival* Spring 1999, 73–98.

46 I realize that this last point is controversial. Some would argue that the spectrum should end at the penultimate point. Outcome E could easily produce the "hard-landing" unification scenario dreaded by the South. Nevertheless, I include this outcome because if one accepts that zero-sum mentalities pervade Korean interaction, then the logical extreme definition of "victory" is complete Chinese defection from the North Korean camp.

47 It was directly after the September 1990 Asiad in Beijing that KOTRA and the Chinese Chamber of Commerce representatives reached agreement on trade offices. During the Games as well, members of the ROK delegation carried out low-key talks on the issue (Kihl, "Foreign Relations: Diplomatic Activism and Policy Dilemmas," 67–68).

48 Lee, *China and Korea*, 90–91 and 150.

49 Although US intelligence was aware of the North's clandestine drive to develop atomic weapons since the early 1970s, it was not until 1989 that it began expressing concerns that the regime might be capable of producing a bomb. What followed from 1992 were two years of tense on-again, off-again negotiations between North Korea, the UN, and the US in which the North resisted International Atomic Energy Agency (IAEA) inspections, reneged on the Non-Proliferation Treaty (NPT), and defied US and UN threats to impose economic sanctions. Events came to a head in April 1994, when Pyongyang removed 8000 spent nuclear fuel rods from its five-megawatt reactor in Yongbyon and refused to segregate rods which held evidence of its plutonium reprocessing history. The US began consultations with Seoul and Tokyo to pursue sanctions, and plans were laid for the movement of minesweepers and amphibious vessels from Hawaii to the region. In what was most likely the final effort at negotiation, Jimmy Carter went to Pyongyang and brought back proposals for a freeze on the North's nuclear activities in exchange for a new round of US–North Korea talks and a summit between the two Koreas. A period of uncertainty followed after the death of Kim Il-sung in July 1994; however, US–North Korean talks resumed between Assistant Secretary Robert Gallucci and Vice-Minister Kang Sok-ju, ultimately leading to the October 1994 Agreed Framework. For analyses, see Leon Sigal, *Disarming Strangers* (Princeton: Princeton Univ. Press, 1998) and Senate Committee on Foreign Relations, *Implications of the US–North Korea Nuclear Agreement: Hearings Before the Subcommittee on East Asian and Pacific Affairs*, December 1, 1994, 103rd Congress, 2nd session (Washington: GPO, 1995).

50 Ji Guoxing, "Chinese Policy for Peace and Stability in the Korean Peninsula and Northeast Asia," in *Peace Regime-Building on the Korean Peninsula and the Roles of the Regional Powers* (Seoul: MOFA, Institute for Foreign Affairs and National Security, 1996), 126–127.

51 Quansheng Zhao, "China and the Two Koreas," paper presented at the SMU-Dallas Forum on Asian Affairs, Dallas TX, March 20–21, 1997, 15.

52 Zhao, "China and the Two Koreas," 15; Lee, *China and Korea*, 121; and Chang, "Beijing's Policy Toward Korea," 165–166.

53 The justification from the North's perspective is that any future peace structure for the peninsula must be negotiated by the original signatories to the 1953 Armistice, and South Korea (due to Syngman Rhee's opposition to a cessation of hostilities) was not party to this agreement (see Selig Harrison, "Promoting a Soft Landing in Korea," *Foreign Policy* 106 (spring 1997), 57–76).

54 In particular, the North refused to discuss through the MAC its downing of an errant US Army helicopter flight into the DMZ in Winter 1994, and instead demanded direct negotiations with the US on the return of the one surviving crewman (see *Joongang Ilbo*, December 27, 1994; and *Hangyôre Sinmun*, December 28, 1994 in *FBIS-EAS* 94–249, December 28, 1994). In 1995, the North instigated several armistice violations (i.e. moving forces into the Joint Security Area and conducting military exercises in restricted zones), and again refused to discuss these through regular MAC channels in an attempt at brinkmanship to force US authorities into a direct dialogue.

55 Ji, "Chinese Policy for Peace and Stability in the Korean Peninsula and Northeast Asia," 127; see also Zhou, "Chinese Position and Perspective on Peace Regime-Building on the Korean Peninsula," 66–67.

56 With regard to these last two points, there are two counter-arguments worth mentioning. First, there is no doubt that China's modernization programs of the 1980s were an important factor in developing cooperation between Beijing and Seoul; at the same time, however, one would be hard-pressed to explain variations in Chinese cooperative behavior along the A–E dimensions laid out in Figure 2.1 based on this single variable. Engagement strategies are useful in explaining these variations. Second, there is not necessarily a linear causal relationship between the new strategic context created by the end of the Cold War and China–Korea cooperation. Instead, this new context could also be the cause of Sino–Korean competition stemming from Chinese fears of American–Korean threats directed against them. Engagement acts by the ROK played a role here in that they caused the two actors to interpret the new strategic context as a cooperative opportunity rather than a conflictual one (thanks to Iain Johnston on this point). For more on the effect of engagement strategies on actor expectations and interpretations of behavior, see the section below.

57 The distinction here might be between "easy" engagement in which the circumstances faced by the target state are very conducive to cooperation with little engagement effort made by the initiator; and "hard" engagement in which the engagement strategies, more than the circumstances faced by the target, are responsible for ameliorating the target state.

58 For example, the November 1995 Kim Young Sam-Jiang Zemin summit conference produced a joint statement castigating Japan for insensitive remarks about past aggressions in Asia (see "Kim, Jiang Criticize Japanese Attitude on Past Wrongdoings," *Korea Herald*, November 15, 1995).

59 In spring 1997, Taipei negotiated an agreement to compensate Pyongyang for the interim storage of 200,000 barrels of low-level radioactive waste in North Korea.

60 Events during the 1970s validate this proposition. In 1973, the Park Chung Hee regime did attempt an engagement strategy of sorts in the "June Declaration," calling for the diversification of Korea's foreign relations and the opening to all nations regardless of ideology. This was in conjunction with the ROK's dropping of the Hallstein doctrine in which it refused relations with any country that recognized North Korea (see *Taehan min'guk woegyo yônp'yo: 1973 bu juyo munhôn* [Diplomatic Documents Annual of the Republic of Korea], Seoul: Ministry of Foreign Affairs, 1973). However, this initiative failed to produce discernible changes in Chinese behavior because the Sino–Soviet split and Chinese competition for North Korean allegiance made the costs of responding too high.

61 This section benefitted from discussions with George Shambaugh and Joe Lepgold.

62 For the details of this case, see Kevin Sullivan, "Defector Warns 2d Korean War 'Dangerously Close'" *Washington Post* April 21, 1997; and Kim Yong-ho, "Hwang Jang-yop's Defection: Its Impact on North Korea," *Korea Focus* 5.2 (March–April 1997), 37–49.

63 For this argument, see Cha, *Alignment Despite Antagonism*, Chapter 7.

64 As one analyst speculated:

> From a longer-term perspective, China is apprehensive about potential threats to its interests from a reunified Korea . . . the Chinese are uncertain about the role that a united Korea might play in the region and worried that Japan could eventually dominate the peninsula and undermine China's growing influence in Korea. Militarily, the prospect of a reunified Korea with at least a potential if not an actual nuclear capability is also a cause for Chinese concern. In addition, some Chinese foresee the possibility that a reunified Korea would seek to reclaim Chinese territory bordering Korea that both North and South view as the birthplace of the Korean nation.
> (Bonnie Glaser, "China's Security Perceptions: Interests and Ambitions," *Asian Survey* 33.3 (March 1993), 261–262)

65 Dollar, "South Korea–China Trade Relations," 1167–1176.

66 For example, in the course of normalization negotiations, the Chinese rejected ROK requests for a consulate in the area, and have discouraged ROK state visits to the area. Beijing was also the only party that lodged protests over ROK articulations of an "international community" of Koreans, and criticized Korean tour groups that referred to parts of China as original Korean territory (ROK foreign ministry official, personal interview, Stanford, CA, September 1994). On Beijing's complaints about the tour groups, see Steve Glain, "After 1300 Years, White Collar Armies Target Manchuria," *Wall Street Journal*, October 9, 1995, A1; see also "Beijing Asks Seoul to Curb Activities of Korean Civilian Body in Manchuria," *Korea Herald*, October 11, 1995, 3.

3

TERMS OF ENGAGEMENT

Taiwan's mainland policy

Steven M. Goldstein

On the face of it, Taiwan has gone a long way toward "engaging" the People's Republic of China (PRC). Until their suspension in 1995, cross-strait negotiations had become routine and institutionalized. Economic relations, both trade and investment, have flourished – although they have been somewhat one-sided, with Taiwan enjoying a huge trade surplus and investment going to the mainland. Second-track diplomacy has also grown. Since 1989 when Taiwan's reporters covered the Tiananmen demonstrations, there has been a steady stream of cross-strait people-to-people exchanges which have come to include an extraordinarily wide variety of groups, ranging from scientists to students to local government officials.

Yet, as the editors of this book note in their preface, engagement is not simply contact – no matter how diverse or active it may be. It is substance that counts; and particularly the manner in which the engaging state, in this case Taiwan, addresses those elements of the PRC's foreign policy orientation which are directed toward changing the status quo. In this respect Taiwan has a distinctive problem. The essence of its existence and, in an age of growing democratization on the island, the basis of the government's legitimacy is precisely the status quo which the PRC argues must be changed if there is to be any accommodation between the mainland and the island. These terms of engagement have produced a relationship with Beijing quite different from that of Taiwan's Asian neighbors.

Continuing the struggle: 1949–1988

Introduction

In 1949, the Communist Party, then in effective control of the mainland, declared the founding of the People's Republic of China which included the "province" of Taiwan. By December, the pathetic remnants of the Kuomintang (KMT) government of the Republic of China (ROC) had settled on Taiwan, the nearby Pescadores islands, and offshore island groups. It was assumed that the confrontation between the two governments – one in Beijing, the other in Taipei – both claiming to rule China would not last long. Communist forces were massing to invade Taiwan. President Harry S. Truman and Secretary of State Dean Acheson were ready to write off the island and deal with the Communists on the mainland.[1] However, when North Korea invaded South Korea in June 1950, everything changed.

Concurrent with the decision to defend South Korea, the Truman administration dispatched the Seventh Fleet to neutralize the Taiwan Strait. By August a small amount of US foreign aid had been approved for the KMT. When Chinese troops entered the Korean conflict in October 1950 and engaged American troops, the commitment to Taiwan was sealed. Fate – and American policy – had given the Kuomintang a second chance, thus frustrating the consummation of a Communist victory. For nearly five decades since, the KMT has ruled Taiwan.

In the sections which follow we examine the island's mainland policies during the presidencies of Chiang Kai-shek (1949–1975) and his son, Chiang Ching-kuo (1978–1988). The purpose of this discussion is to highlight a central element that is often overlooked in discussions of Taiwan's later relations with the mainland – the profound impact which the island's political evolution had on the trajectory of cross-strait relations in the 1990s.

Chiang Kai-shek 1949–1975

Chiang Kai-shek continued to act as if Chinese history stopped in the late 1940s when Nanking confronted Yan'an. The KMT claimed to be preparing for a "fourth military campaign" or a "second northern march" that would finally defeat the Communists.[2] The ROC government, with its temporary capital in Taipei, denied that it was an "exile government." Rather, it was governing a nation of which large parts were occupied by "rebels."

Neither mere defense of the island nor "containment" of the mainland was Chiang's goal. Rather, the *raison d'être* of his government was to return to the mainland. Although policy would change slightly toward the end of his life, the assumption throughout was that the cross-strait conflict was "a pure internal matter" to be resolved by military means – either in the form of an invasion from Taiwan or as part of an Asian confrontation with global communism.[3] The political slogans of the 1950s, 1960s, and 1970s were thus "*fangong dalu*" ("counter-attack the mainland") and "*guangfu dalu*" ("recover the mainland").[4] These were the only forms of "engagement" that interested Chiang Kai-shek.

This posture, of course, prevented any interaction with the mainland. Trade was impossible and even overseas Chinese were exhorted to look elsewhere for investment opportunities.[5] Negotiations on any subject with the Communist enemy were off-limits – "the loyal and traitorous cannot coexist" (*Hanzei bu liangwei*), Chiang insisted. There was, very simply, nothing to talk about. To settle for anything less than the surrender of the mainland was "to recognize the rule of traitors."[6]

The assumption that the civil war was continuing and that the next stage would be an inevitable military confrontation decisively shaped the manner in which the ruling KMT viewed both Taiwan and its people. The temporary nature of the regime on Taiwan was stressed throughout much of Chiang Kai-shek's life: policies were directed toward recovery of the mainland, not continued residence on the island. The KMT would never settle into the security of the island, nor would it develop Taiwan for any purpose other than that of a base for invasion. To do otherwise would be to admit defeat.[7]

This refusal to be resigned to a permanent existence on Taiwan, within the context of an ongoing "hot war" with the mainland, was integrally linked to the KMT's right to rule the island. The pledge to return was needed to maintain the morale of Chiang's key mainlander supporters – especially the army.[8] More important, it was also essential for the maintenance of the KMT's authoritarian rule on Taiwan through a unique set of political institutions which were structured both to sustain a mood of military alert and to preserve their continuity with earlier Kuomintang governance on the mainland.[9]

The Constitution of 1947 which mandated a Legislative Yuan, an indirectly elected president, and an Executive Yuan headed by a premier, remained in effect. The exiled representatives, chosen to represent mainland provinces, kept their seats even after the move to Taiwan. Similarly, the president continued to be selected by an electoral body (the National Assembly) whose members were all chosen years earlier on the mainland. The government, after all, represented all of China – not simply Taiwan. However, because it also represented a government seeking to suppress a domestic rebellion, two statutes, one granting Chiang extraordinary powers and the other continuing martial law that had originated during the anti-Communist conflict on the mainland, were extended to Taiwan.

Domestic political demands and policy toward the mainland were thus inextricably bound together. If the Civil War were to be unilaterally declared over, or were it to be resolved by negotiations, the logical basis for the party's authoritarian rule over Taiwan, as merely one province in a single country divided by civil war, would end. Political institutions could no longer be legitimized by elections held on the mainland and political rights on Taiwan could no longer be curtailed by the needs of civil war.

Until the end of the 1960s, this intransigent KMT posture was also sustained by the international environment – specifically, the policies of the mainland and the United States. The PRC's position held out little prospect for meaningful talks. It was, rather, the uncompromising mirror image of that articulated by the Generalissimo and the KMT. Beijing maintained that it represented the legitimate government of China; that the Cairo and Potsdam meetings had ceded Taiwan to China; that the ROC was a rump government on Chinese territory; and, most importantly, that the "Taiwan question" was an internal issue that would be settled between the two parties to the Civil War. In the years before 1955, the emphasis was on "armed liberation." Thereafter, there was some mention of "peaceful liberation," a third united front with the KMT, and the possibility of talks between the two parties.[10]

By 1958, Beijing was placing most of the blame for its failure to achieve closure in the Civil War on American military aid and diplomatic support for Taiwan. Condemning these as unwarranted intervention in internal affairs, the PRC was careful to note that while it was willing to discuss with Washington the tensions in the strait area, there would be no discussions of the purely domestic question of the status of Taiwan.[11]

There was considerable justification for Chinese charges regarding American intervention. There is no question that intervention by the United States had the effect of both denying the CCP its ultimate victory and perpetuating the blatant fiction that the KMT had not been defeated. It was American support, driven by Washington's perception of the demands of the Cold War, that allowed the ROC to maintain an international presence (particularly at the UN) that was larger than life.

Still, as time went on, the patience of the United States was tried even as the rhetoric of mainland recovery wore thin on Taiwan. By the late 1960s it was becoming clear that Washington's Asian policies were moving beyond the Cold War posturing that had sustained the ROC. Despite bitter warnings from Taipei about the dangers of negotiating with the Communists, the Nixon administration did just that with both the PRC and the Democratic Republic of Vietnam.[12]

On Taiwan, token yearly pledges to retake the mainland increasingly lacked credibility. In a particularly candid moment the ROC ambassador to the United States admitted to a State Department official in 1958 that these pledges had become "quite an ordeal" for Chiang Kai-shek.[13] There is also evidence that harsh realities were prompting subtle changes in Taiwan's mainland policy. Although the rhetoric of recovery and the claim to be the only legitimate "China" continued, emphasis was placed on using peaceful or "political" means to achieve these goals.[14] Specifically, Taiwan aimed to become a "model province" that would encourage the people on the mainland to seek unification on its terms.[15] This posture also provided the rationale for more attention to development of the island and to an expansion of the political rights of the local population.[16] In addition, although it fiercely held to its position that only the ROC represented all of China, Taipei had to adjust to the reality that it was no longer a member of the UN and that expanded international recognition of Beijing was becoming a fact of life. It was in the last years of Chiang Kai-shek's life that the roots of "substantive diplomacy" were developed, whereby diverse contacts (economic, social, and even political) were established with foreign states in the absence of formal, diplomatic relations.

These were, however, secondary themes. Until the day he died, Chiang and the party/government he led continued the themes of the Civil War: political legitimacy; recovery of the mainland; and refusal to have any dealings (economic links, negotiations, etc.) with the PRC. The policies of these years were antithetical to engagement diplomacy.

Chiang Ching-kuo, 1978–1988

During the presidency of Chiang Ching-kuo, the son of the Generalissimo, Taiwan remained intransigent in its public statements. The ROC held to its claim of being the only legal government of China; referred to Taiwan as a "national bastion"; continued to speak in terms of another stage in the Civil War; and, in a bitter reaction to President Jimmy Carter's announcement of the normalization of relations with the PRC in 1978, Chiang outlined what came to be known as the "three nos" policy – no contact, no compromise, and no negotiations with the mainland.[17]

Yet, as the 1980s wore on, Taiwan's international environment and domestic politics underwent significant changes which conditioned important shifts away from past practices. On the mainland, Deng Xiaoping initiated a reform that would not only beguile the entire world, but also present tempting economic opportunities. Taiwan's continued rejection of the mainland began to receive a less sympathetic audience abroad. This was particularly the case in the United States which, under the Carter administration, sought an economic and strategic relationship with the mainland.

Additional complications for Taipei resulted from a less hostile policy emanating from the mainland. The essentials of Beijing's policy remained the same: Taiwan was considered to be a local government within a single China ruled from Beijing; foreign interference in a domestic issue would not be tolerated; and the PRC's right to use force was reserved. However, in a series of statements from 1979 to 1984, the PRC leadership elaborated a place for a more autonomous Taiwan using the "one country, two systems" (*yiguo liangzhi*) concept which was later to be applied to Hong Kong.[18] Given the subsequent credibility accorded the Sino–British agreement on Hong Kong and the growing expectations created by the Chinese domestic reforms, Taipei's anti-Communist rhetoric was becoming a weak suit internationally.

Within Taiwan, the context of mainland policy was also changing. International isolation (even humiliation), an aging government, and increasing corruption were damaging the already frayed legitimacy of the KMT. In the years after his father's death, Chiang Ching-kuo, who finally became president in 1978, showed signs that he was sensitive to these trends and set about to transform the political system. Most prominently, the lifting of the martial law decree in July 1987 led to the removal of the military from direct governance and put an end to many restrictions on public assembly and speech. It also legalized Taiwan's first true opposition party, the Democratic Progressive Party (DPP), which traced its roots to the pro-independence opposition of the late 1970s.

Within the KMT, Chiang Ching-kuo sought greater inner-party democracy and the inclusion of more native Taiwanese. He moved with greater caution, however, in reforming formal government organizations. Despite expanded "supplementary elections," Chiang was never able to confront the aging and politically meaningless delegates who continued to govern Taiwan in the name of a bogus central government.

Yet the reforms were significant enough to have an impact on the making – and substance – of mainland policy. The admittedly tentative steps toward democracy resulted in a situation whereby Chiang, unlike his father, had to be responsive to opinions both inside and outside of the ruling party. In particular, he had to be attentive not only to the yearnings of the old-line KMT mainlanders, but also to the rising demands of the business community and the political challenge presented by the independence-oriented DPP. In short, Chiang had to formulate policy toward the mainland within a more complex and demanding domestic political environment. As a result, the actual policies implemented under the intransigent "three nos" strategy changed significantly.

Chiang legitimized these changes by maintaining continuity with elements of his father's policies. Promoting the "Taiwan experience" became the watchword of his mainland policy. Arguing that the experience would be attractive only if the island became more developed and democratic, Chiang presented his reforms on Taiwan as neither an admission of KMT defeat in the Civil War nor of its failure to govern the island. Rather, they were to be a means to the end of unification – still called "recovery" – on the KMT's own terms.[19] The implication of this act was to break with the past and begin a separation between KMT legitimacy on Taiwan and the party's continued, ideological commitment to unification. In addition, by combining an emphasis on democracy and economic growth on the island with the contention that any movement toward unification required "a lessening of the gap between the two sides and a maturation of conditions,"[20] Chiang implied that the onus was on the PRC to become more like Taiwan before closer ties would be considered.

However, promoting the "Taiwan model" was used by Chiang to do more than incrementally reorient his father's policies. It became the justification for the two most radical changes of his rule with regard to the mainland: the decision to allow visits to the PRC and to turn a blind eye to indirect cross-strait trade. Using the humanitarian excuse that aging KMT servicemen were entitled to return to their former homes to visit relatives and the political rationale that such travel would promote the "Taiwan experience," trips to the mainland for limited categories of ROC citizens were permitted beginning in 1987.[21]

Relaxing the ban on travel and at about the same time, permitting the export of capital led to the beginnings of Taiwan investment on the mainland and to cross-strait trade that would grow to more than US$2.5 billion by 1988.[22] Remarkably, statements by government officials on Taiwan did little to discourage these economic contacts. In fact, they were implicitly condoned. For example, Vincent Siew (Hsiao Wan-chang, currently Taiwan's prime minister, but at the time director-general of the Board of Foreign Trade) acknowledged that government policy stipulated "no direct trade with mainland China, no direct contact with Communist Chinese representatives, *and no interference with transshipment trade.*"[23]

Finally, again building on an earlier policy, Chiang Ching-kuo considerably expanded the practice of "substantive diplomacy." Through the creation of trade offices abroad and unofficial representations in Taipei by major trading partners, economic ties were strengthened. Work normally done by diplomatic offices – most importantly the issuance of visas – was carried out by organizations ranging from airlines to specially created quasi-diplomatic bodies. At the end of 1985, the minister of foreign affairs announced that "substantive trade and economic relations" were being maintained with 140 countries and there were trade representatives in 57 countries.[24]

Of equal significance, during Chiang Ching-kuo's presidency, Taiwan changed a long-standing policy against coexisting with the mainland in international organizations. In December 1985, the Executive Yuan announced that "the government will not dodge or shy away from private organizations in which Communist China is a member."[25] More concretely, this meant that Taiwan rejoined the Olympic Games in 1984 under the title "Chinese, Taipei"; remained in the Asian Development Bank despite a name change to "Taipei, Taiwan"; and rejoined the Asian Table Tennis Association under the name "Chinese, Taipei."[26]

These shifts in mainland policy, which reflected Chiang Ching-kuo's creative use of his father's policies, were without question evidence of the manner in which the beginnings of democratic reform on Taiwan were coming to influence mainland policy. Chiang's initiatives were, in the first instance, responsive to the concerns of the KMT mainlanders who still dominated the party. This was obvious in the decision to allow some travel to the mainland; the linkage of political and economic change on the mainland with future unification; and the continued adherence to the "three nos."

However, Chiang was seeking to please other constituencies as well. The "hands-off" policy toward cross-strait trade was a response to pressures from a business community which was increasingly coming to view the mainland as an important economic opportunity. Moreover, since the majority of the small business people flocking to the mainland were native Taiwanese, it is also likely that these initiatives were an attempt both to promote KMT ties with them as well as to blunt DPP influence and independence sentiment. Finally, the growing "substantive diplomacy" addressed the sense of global isolation which was under-mining KMT support and giving credence to DPP demands for independence.[27]

Chiang Ching-kuo died on January 13, 1988. The decade since has seen two dramatic developments that are rooted in his policies: the democratization of the island's politics, and the development of an economic relationship with the mainland. As others have noted, the simple fact that he – a mainlander and a member of the Chiang family – presided over these political and mainland policy reforms provided legitimization for the more dramatic changes initiated in these two areas by his Taiwan-born successor, Lee Teng-hui.

Mainland Policy, 1988 to 1999: from struggle to engagement?

During the past decade Taiwan has followed a very different mainland policy from that of the past. The government has promoted frequent organizational contacts, made proposals for the resolution of earlier conflicts, and facilitated expanded trade and investment on the mainland. Still, looks can be deceiving. Much of the civil war mentality persists and has even been reinforced by these contacts as well as by the dramatic democratization of Taiwan's politics.

The schizoid quality of the island's mainland policies must be described before any attempt can be made to relate Taiwan's policy to the concept of engagement. In other words, before we can judge the *nature* of Taiwan's mainland policy, we must understand its *substance*. The discussion which follows addresses the latter by examining the dimensions of the policy.[28]

Economics

The early development of economic relations across the strait was largely spontaneous. It was driven by the needs of the business community with little ongoing political supervision. This remains much the same today. Yet trade represents more than the initial dimension in which significant cross-strait contacts developed. It is also the most important and fully articulated. Indeed, many maintain that growing trade contacts hold out the promise of providing the basis for a more general expansion of cross-strait relations.

The passive, turn-a-blind-eye policy of Chiang Ching-kuo toward indirect trade with the mainland could not have come at a better time for some members of Taiwan's business community. Rising domestic costs, an appreciation in the value of the NT$, threats of protectionism in the West, and the growing environmental and labor movements on the island all combined to make coastal China, with its shared culture, low-wage labor, and lax legal regulations an attractive site.

The numbers are certainly dramatic. In 1986 cumulative contracted investment (usually through Hong Kong) stood at eighty projects valued at US$100 million. By 1993 this had grown to almost 11,000 projects valued at nearly US$10 billion and in early 1999, it was estimated that investment on the mainland by Taiwan companies had grown to more than US$30 billion.[29] More significantly, in May 1997 the Ministry of Economic Affairs in Taipei announced that 72.71 percent of "Taiwan's manufacturing companies making investments abroad" were active in the PRC, with the United States a distant second at nearly 13 percent.[30] Approximately 40 percent of the island's total foreign investment was PRC-bound. Taiwan's investments have had a strong impact on the mainland's economy as well. In 1995 the island's investment created 3.89 million jobs (2.2 percent of total employment in the PRC); produced US$33.57 billion in goods (3.1 percent of the mainland's industrial output); and accounted for US$21.45 billion in exports (14.4 percent of the PRC's exports).[31]

The changes in the size, nature, and location of Taiwan's investments are as significant as their dramatic growth. As noted above, initial investments were small, export-oriented, labor-intensive, and located along the southern coast. Although this remains the dominant pattern, there is evidence of change. By 1999, more Taiwanese investment was moving to Shanghai and Beijing as well as to the hinterland. Similarly, the type of products manufactured has been upgraded. Athletic shoes and clothing have been joined by electrical and computer components, while the number of upstream firms has also increased. Finally, Taiwanese companies, particularly in the beverage and food industries, are now producing increasingly for the mainland market.[32]

The growth of cross-strait trade has paralleled this growth in investments. In 1988, the year Chiang Ching-kuo died, two-way trade stood at US$2.7 billion, rising to US$15 billion in 1993. In 1998 it reached US$22.5 billion – or roughly 10 percent of Taiwan's total foreign trade. Moreover, since the beginning of cross-strait trade, Taiwan has enjoyed a favorable balance, which grew from US$1.7 billion in 1988 to US$14.3 billion in 1998.[33] The correlation with investment is obvious. Although firms on the mainland are increasingly sourcing components locally, Taiwan's exports to the PRC are overwhelmingly machinery, parts, and materials to support export-oriented firms on the mainland whose production goes to areas other than Taiwan. The PRC's exports to the island have been semi-finished goods destined for re-export and agricultural products.[34]

The fact that nearly three-quarters of Taiwan firms investing abroad are operating on the mainland suggests that investors from the island are no less immune to the PRC's lure than those from other countries. Although the strong growth documented above has been paralleled by a more general growth in foreign investment from Taiwan, the proximity of the mainland, the linguistic, cultural, and even family ties, as well as the complementary nature of its economy have made the PRC a natural target for an increasingly outward-looking Taiwan business community. Moreover, although individual firms on the mainland suffered during the Asian economic crisis of 1997 to 1998, the importance of the mainland as a whole remained, given the growing trade deficits with most other Asian countries.[35]

In sum, the trade ties that have developed since the late 1980s have been governed more by the needs of business than by the calculations of government. This is not to say that the government has continued the hands-off policy of Chiang Ching-kuo. By 1990 to 1991, the spontaneous growth of cross-strait economic links had become a matter of concern in Taiwan. President Lee Teng-hui's government came under attack as pro-unification forces became concerned about the lack of clarity on this issue; the independence-oriented DPP was warning of the dangers of too much contact with the mainland; and the business community was uneasy about investing without a clearly defined policy. In response to the *faits accompli* created by the spontaneous growth of PRC-oriented business, the government was compelled to begin creating programmatic and institutional bases upon which to manage mainland relations. This would not be the last time that government followed business in the making of mainland policy.

One strategy was to attempt to regulate mainland trade and investment. In 1988 officials began to monitor trade with the mainland and to draft ministerial guidelines regarding permissible imports and exports. In 1991 procedures were announced for the regulation of cross-strait investment and for the establishment of a warning system that would alert authorities when dangerous levels had been reached. There were also threats of punishment for those companies that failed to obey these guidelines.[36]

More significantly, steps were taken to place economic ties within a wider programmatic and institutional context for managing an increasingly complex relationship with the mainland. The first of these was the drafting, in February 1991, of the "Guidelines for National Unification" by the National Unification Council (NUC) under the president's office. These remain the foundation for Taiwan's mainland policy today.

Stating that the unification of China was "the common wish of the Chinese people at home and abroad," the guidelines laid out the conditions as well as a vague timetable for reaching that goal. The two central guidelines stipulate that any unification must "respect the rights and interests of the people in the Taiwan area" and unification must result in a "democratic, free, and equitably prosperous China." The timetable posited three stages to the unification process. The short-term (present phase) involved people-to-people exchanges; the end of hostility (including an end to the mainland's opposition to Taiwan's global role); the implementation of "democracy and rule of law" in the PRC; and the development of "mutual trust and cooperation." Upon realization of these goals, relations would then enter a second, intermediate stage characterized by "direct postal, transport, and commercial links"; official contacts; and mutual assistance in "taking part in international organizations and activities." The final phase envisioned government-to-government negotiations on the subject of unification.[37]

Along with these guidelines, two important bureaucracies were established at the beginning of 1991 to manage relations with the mainland. The first was the Straits Exchange Foundation (SEF) which was charged with making contacts to solve technical issues. Consistent with the requirement that all contacts be "unofficial" at the first stage, this body was to be a private foundation. It has remained the principal negotiator with mainland representatives throughout the 1990s.

However, its private status is only a useful fiction. The SEF is, in fact, a semi-official body. Government officials sit on its board; it receives government funding; and it is under the close supervision of a second bureaucracy, the Mainland Affairs Council (MAC), a cabinet-level body charged with coordinating mainland policy. The idea was that the NUC would draw up general guidelines; the MAC would translate these into policies to guide economic ties, cultural exchanges, and "non-official" contacts; and the SEF would be the "white glove" organization that would manage these contacts and meet with mainland counterparts.[38] Specifically, as trade and investment were the principal manifestations of "people-to-people" contacts, it was expected that the SEF would represent Taiwan's business interests in dealings with the mainland.

These initiatives did not, however, provide tools to give the government any real control over the economic dimension of its mainland policy. In the first place, the premises and principles of these bureaucracies reflected a basic ambivalence toward the question of trade that was symptomatic of government policy. On the one hand, there was a recognition that such ties were essential to the economy of the island. In addition, they might become, in the long run, a confidence-building tool in relations with the mainland and, in the more immediate future, a means by which to satisfy increasing mainland demands for movement in cross-strait relations. Moreover, promoting trade with the mainland would also serve the KMT's domestic political needs by securing support from the increasingly important business community. Finally, and especially until 1993, the promise of future unification and the sanctioning of current "people-to-people" economic ties were intended to reassure Lee Teng-hui's opponents among the elderly Kuomintang mainlanders that he was sincerely committed to the policy of unification.

On the other hand, there was a clear awareness of the economic and political dangers of growing links. Economic dependence would surely increase mainland leverage. Moreover, Beijing's announced policy of *"yi jingji cu zhengzhi . . . yi min bi guan"* ("promoting political amalgamation through economic integration . . . pressuring the government with popular demands") suggested an eagerness to use an over-committed business community to influence the island's politics.[39] As one military intelligence official put it, the mainland's strategy aimed "at carrying out a united front campaign against Taiwan through economic and trade activities."[40] Finally, even as unificationist sentiment had to be mollified by the promotion of ties, independence sentiment had to be mollified by the insistence that trade remain at an unofficial level. Thus the "three nos" policy remained.

This governmental ambivalence was compounded by the impact which the uncertainties of Taiwan's democratization had on the policies and institutions intended to manage policy. For example, the MAC and the SEF initially came to represent different factions of the KMT and were often bitterly divided; the government bureaucracies clashed, driven by different definitions of their missions (the trade offices seeking to expand ties, and the more political or security bureaucracies seeking to restrain them); and business groups used the dispersal of power throughout the government (primarily in the bureaucracies, but also in the Legislative Yuan) to increase their influence.[41]

In subsequent years, ambivalence and ineffective institutions continued to hamper government efforts to exercise effective control over the spontaneous economic boom that began in the last years of Chiang Ching-kuo's presidency. Until recently, there were few signs that the government was prepared to move commercial relations out of the category of unofficial relations. Moreover, the government continues efforts to dampen growing economic ties. Pointed comments have been made to the business community regarding the importance of considering the national interest over their own commercial needs. As late as the spring of 1997, more strict regulations on permissible investments in the PRC were promulgated – and seemingly enforced.[42] On the less coercive level, programs have been launched to encourage business people to "go South" to other parts of Asia and informal pressure has been exercised through the KMT as well as via the extensive ministerial links that tie the business to government. Finally, since 1997 President Lee Teng-hui has consistently warned of the dangers of "rash" investment and has called for "avoiding haste and demonstrating restraint."[43]

Yet, as the figures cited in the introductory portions of this section suggest, none of these measures have been effective in controlling the flow of investment from Taiwan to the mainland. Institutions remain weak and the government is ambivalent. Moreover, the business community still has considerable political clout in Taiwan. Both its essential role in promoting the nation's prosperity and its contributions to political coffers assure that its views get a careful – and sympathetic – hearing. More importantly, the major thrust of government-sponsored initiatives for future economic policy favors – indeed might even require – closer economic ties with the mainland. For example, the recent liberalization of the economy has provided the business community with the means (most importantly through foreign subsidiaries) to evade controls, while the island's much sought-after WTO membership will make it even more difficult to control mainland trade.

More important is the fact that a central element in the government's economic strategy for future development is the development of a "Regional Operations Center" that will transform Taiwan into a communications hub, a financial center, a source for high technology, and the site of regional headquarters for international corporations doing business in the region. Stable economic relations with the mainland are essential to the success of this strategy because, without links with the potential economic giant of Asia, the plan for a regional hub is a non-starter. Mainland economic ties are thus not simply part of the problem, they are also part of the solution to Taiwan's future economic development.

In short, despite the post-1995 deterioration in Taiwan's relations with the mainland, the government has continued to be supportive of the economic relationship. Even as it has promulgated new regulations, renewed calls for a reorientation of overseas investment, and cautioned against excessive dependence on the mainland, the government has also widened the boundaries of permissible trade and investment, calling for greater protection of Taiwanese investment on the mainland, assisting in the sending of commercial delegations to the mainland, and remaining receptive to business initiatives. A most dramatic response came in spring 1997 when the government began to permit foreign-registered ships from the mainland and Taiwan to move goods directly between the mainland to a bonded "offshore" warehouse in Kaohsiung. Rationalizations that this was not "direct trade" because goods never really passed Taiwan customs could not obscure the fact that a major breach had occurred in the "three nos" policy – a breach that some observers feel will likely stimulate even greater cross-strait investment.[44] In much the same vein, the government carefully responded to the transfer of sovereignty in Hong Kong. Despite the post-1995 break-off of negotiations with the mainland, solutions were found to ensure the continued use of the former colony as an entrepôt.[45]

The business response to this ambivalent government policy is to seek to evade its regulatory aspects even as it uses its permissive aspects. Although one should be careful not to overestimate the extent to which business has flaunted government restrictions, it is also true that economic relations continue to respond more to their own logic than to the state of cross-strait political relations. To be sure, these relations suffered in the immediate aftermath of Tiananmen (1989); after the "Qiandao Incident" in spring 1994 when a group of Taiwan tourists were murdered on the mainland; during the election tensions of 1995 to 1996; and as a result of doubts regarding the safety on the mainland of business people from Taiwan during mid-1998. But they have consistently bounced back.

Although, at times, government warnings have achieved temporary slow-downs and occasionally pressure has been effective in delaying large investments, significant control of business has been a frustrating matter for the authorities.[46] Moreover, the business community has pressured for greater access to the economic opportunities on the mainland. Such pressure has taken the form of demands for the expansion of categories of permissible trade and investment; threats of making large-scale investments through foreign subsidiaries; or dramatic public demands for major policy changes, such as those made by shipping magnate Chang Yung-fa in 1997, or by the highly successful chairman of the Formosa Plastics Group, Y.C. Wang, a year later.[47]

On the mainland, growing economic links with Taiwan have not escaped the leadership's attention. Since 1988, when the "Rules for Encouraging Taiwan Investment" were approved by the State Council, central and local authorities have taken a number of steps to facilitate Taiwan's investment in, and trade with, the mainland. These have included expanded investment opportunities as well as special investment districts and regulations to be applied to cross-strait trade.[48] Finally, after the retrocession of Hong Kong, the mainland seemed intent on assuring that Taiwan's trade with, and through, the former colony would be maintained.

Institutionally, in December 1991 Beijing established a counterpart organization to the SEF, the Association for Relations Across the Straits (ARATS). Although ostensibly "a mass organization in the form of a corporate body," ARATS was chaired by an influential former mayor of Shanghai, a former foreign ministry official served as secretary-general, and it operated under close party/state supervision.[49] It was this organization which, until 1995, was the sole mainland body negotiating directly with Taiwan on issues relating to economic links. However, as we shall see below, ARAT's dealings with the SEF have been stormy and, ironically, have suggested that the leadership in Beijing, like that in Taiwan, has ambivalent feelings regarding the role of economic ties in cross-strait relations.

The reasons for such ambivalence are not difficult to divine. On the one hand, as the earlier statistics suggest, the capital, technology, and export connections which the Taiwan business community brings with it to the mainland have made important contributions to the post-Mao economic reform – particularly in south China. Second, the mainland has been quite open in expressing its intention to use economic ties not only to create constituencies in Taiwan to press for change in other – particularly political – aspects of the relationship, but also as an opening wedge to raise political questions in "technical talks" on trade and other matters.[50] It is thus not surprising that even after the confrontation of 1995 to 1996 the mainland continued to promote cross-strait trade, despite the virtual absence of any other contacts.

Yet Beijing also has its suspicions about trade. The PRC leaders have, it seems, come to the conclusion that Taiwan uses trade as a means to satisfy mainland demands for greater contact and to give the illusion of substance to what is, in the mainland leadership's view, empty talk about unification. Beijing sees Taiwan using trade and investment as a means to achieve economic gain while maintaining the island's political status quo and avoiding mainland demands for political talks. In short, the mainland has sought spillover to other areas in its relations with Taiwan, while Taipei has rigorously resisted.

Politics

By 1991, the institutional and programmatic bases for what might have become a cross-strait dialogue on political as well as economic questions were in place. Yet it was clear at the outset that each side viewed the purpose of contact through "unofficial" organizations differently. In 1998, after seven years of lurching from crisis to crisis, these bases are in an uncertain state.

From the first meetings between Taiwan and the mainland in 1991 to 1992, difficult questions which reflected the asymmetrical goals of each side intruded into the discussions. Taiwan sought to avoid any discussion of politics while expanding the number of topics (mostly related to trade and investment) that it placed under the rubric of "technical issues." The mainland seemed intent on expanding discussions relating to issues considered to be political by Taipei (such as direct shipping). More basically, the two sides remained divided over the meaning of "one China." While the mainland meant it to relegate Taiwan to subordinate status within a China ruled from Beijing, Taipei insisted on recognition of its own sovereignty and equality *vis-à-vis* the mainland.[51]

In early 1993 there were signs of some movement to break this stalemate. Cheyne Chiu, a close associate of Lee Teng-hui, was appointed the new secretary-general of the SEF.[52] Chiu soon conveyed the impression that dramatic changes were afoot. He informed the press that the president would focus on "cross-strait and international relations" for the next three years; that "future exchanges . . . should go beyond current discussions on technical details"; and that efforts should be made to "tear down the Berlin Wall between Taiwan and the mainland."[53]

Speculation grew regarding an impending shift in policy toward the mainland. It is not surprising that the suggestion of such a shift immediately encountered resistance in the new and complex world of Taiwan's domestic and bureaucratic politics. Business groups pressed for a wide-ranging discourse. The opposition DPP depicted the talks as a sell-out of Taiwan by the KMT and thus they sought to embarrass the KMT in the Legislative Yuan. President Lee, seeing the direction of the political winds, moved to limit the scope of the talks. Even before the SEF delegation left for Singapore in April 1993 to attend the highest-level cross-strait meeting since 1949 (between the chairmen of the SEF and the ARATS), it was clear that Taiwan's domestic political pressures had severely narrowed its mandate.[54]

In the end, despite an earlier agreement to put the contentious "one China" question aside, the Singapore talks accomplished very little. Purely technical documents were signed, addressing such matters as registered mail, notary publics, and future regularly scheduled meetings of representatives from both organizations. The scheduling of regularized contacts was, of course, significant. Institutionalization is essential for engagement in its strictest sense. Of equal significance, however, was the fact that the discussions highlighted the continued asymmetry in the goals of the two sides, thus rendering more difficult any future progress within that institutional framework.

The SEF's request that investment guarantees for investors on the mainland be discussed was met with the response from the ARATS representative that this could only be negotiated when direct contacts had been established – an item considered by Taiwan to belong to a future stage of relations. Attempts by the mainland to discuss trade issues within the context of "reunification" – an indirect introduction of the "one China" question – were immediately rejected by the very constrained SEF delegation which characterized this issue as political and outside the scope of the talks. In short, even as Taiwan, seeking to mollify business interests and opposition sentiment, attempted to use the negotiations to serve narrow economic purposes and to avoid overt political issues, the mainland insisted that progress on economic matters be contingent upon the discussion of difficult political questions.

After the talks, the political dimension of Taiwan's relations with the mainland began to show signs of deterioration. In early 1993, the government was talking openly about the need to pursue a more aggressive policy regarding entry into international organizations and to expand the "pragmatic diplomacy," or "flexible diplomacy" (*wushi waijiao*) which had developed early in Lee's administration. This was a continuation – but also an extension – of the earlier policy of "substantive diplomacy." It was also a very political policy intended to assuage independence sentiments and to complement the more active mainland policy which was advocated by pro-unification forces as well as the business community.

Taipei aggressively sought to expand the scope and visibility of its foreign policy to include entry into international organizations (most prominently the United

Nations); expansion into new areas (most notably the former Soviet bloc); attempts to gain the recognition of countries already maintaining diplomatic ties with the PRC; and efforts to promote greater official and unofficial travel abroad by government figures, including the president himself.[55] Beijing's response was sharp. In the summer of 1993, the PRC came out with a strongly worded "White Paper" which reiterated its definition of one China; condemned Lee Teng-hui's "pragmatic diplomacy"; and reserved the right to use force in settling the issue of reunification.[56]

In early 1994, cross-strait political relations hit a post-1988 low with the "Qiandao Incident." This led to expressions of outrage and a temporary slow-down of Taiwanese investment.[57] During the summer, the MAC issued Taiwan's own "White Paper" on cross-strait relations. In it, the government gave up claims to represent all of China and called on the mainland to abandon the idea that Taiwan was a "subordinate" province of China. It argued that "two separate areas of a divided China" existed with different, but equal, governments which "should co-exist as two legal entities in the international arena."[58]

The response from Beijing was predictable – and bitter. This policy pronounce-ment was evidence of one more step toward independence, thus demonstrating that President Lee and the KMT were disingenuous in their statements regarding reunification. What they really sought, it was argued, was the continuation of the status quo of separation from the mainland while continuing to benefit economically from relations across the strait. Pragmatic diplomacy had to cease. Ironically, the PRC was demanding that Taipei dismantle the very foreign policy amalgam that, by catering to the demands of both those seeking unification and those seeking greater autonomy for Taiwan, made cross-strait political engagement acceptable on the island.[59]

Yet this did not become immediately apparent. By early 1995, momentum in the political dimension of engagement seemed to have been regained. In Taiwan, former minister of economic affairs, Vincent Siew, became the new head of the MAC. Siew had long argued for closer economic ties with the mainland and announced, upon his appointment, that he would consider ways to facilitate shipping ties.[60] In January, Jiang Zemin unveiled an Eight-Point Proposal which, while making no dramatic departures from previous mainland statements, suggested the possibility of broader negotiations – and even of a visit by a "leader of the Taiwan authorities . . . in the appropriate status" to the mainland.[61] Authorities in Taiwan characterized the statement as "constructive" and Premier Lien Chan suggested that relations with the mainland were entering an "era of consultations." In April, President Lee Teng-hui gave Taiwan's reply to Jiang's proposals which also restated old positions but remained open to negotiations.[62]

A second meeting of the chairmen of the SEF and MAC was scheduled for July. In May a Taiwanese delegation left for Beijing to make the final arrangements. There were reports that Taiwan "officials" might attend the forthcoming talks and that the scope of the meetings would be much wider than those in Singapore. Taiwan's representative stated that a "policy-oriented dialogue" might well begin, based on the proposals made by Jiang and Lee.[63] In the spring of 1995 cross-strait relations seemed on the verge of moving beyond narrow technical issues.

It was at this juncture that President Lee Teng-hui visited Cornell to attend a class reunion (he had received a doctorate in agricultural economics in 1968) and to deliver a major lecture. The trip incensed the leadership in Beijing, suddenly reversing the improving trend in Taiwan–mainland political relations. For Lee Teng-hui, who was to face his first electoral challenge within less than a year, the invitation to attend the reunion, as well as the support that he received in certain US Congressional quarters, offered an opportunity to validate his "pragmatic diplomacy" and to elevate his position as the leader of a new Taiwan. For the PRC, the trip struck two sensitive chords. It confirmed suspicions that Lee's diplomacy was really aimed at Taiwan's independence by fostering wider "official" relations and it again raised the specter of American meddling in the Taiwan question.[64]

Beijing postponed the second round of Taiwan–mainland talks and direct cross-strait dialogue virtually ceased. It was replaced by angry and defiant rhetoric as relations seemed increasingly to be driven by domestic politics. From the PRC, there were rumors that Jiang Zemin, who had invested considerable political capital in the Eight Points, had been embarrassed by the Cornell visit, thus increasing the influence of those in Beijing – particularly the military – who were dissatisfied with the slow progress toward reunification.[65] In Taiwan, Lee Teng-hui built on his diplomatic *coup* to bolster his political image as a president who could both stand up to the mainland and give Taiwan the international stature it deserved. The pre-election environment was not a time for him either to be conciliatory toward the mainland or to limit pragmatic diplomacy. When, in response, Beijing used military exercises (see the discussion in the next section) to express its indignation in the aftermath of Lee's Cornell visit and prior to the March 1996 presidential elections, developments in the political dimension of cross-strait relations came to a halt.

For the next two years, this stalemate virtually froze "semi-official" cross-strait contacts. The mainland press dismissed Lee's statements of commitment to unification as rhetorical cover for independence. Moreover, constitutional change downgrading the status of the provincial government on Taiwan and discussions regarding provisions for national referenda were both seen as moves toward independence.[66] With regard to Taiwan's international position, Beijing demanded that attempts to join the United Nations end; that visits by Taiwan leaders to countries with which the PRC had relations cease; and that the US stop intervening in cross-strait relations.

Most important, despite suggestions in early 1998 of some flexibility in the mainland's position, there was little movement away from Beijing's insistence that Taiwan's place in "one China" be based on the principle (recently applied to Hong Kong) of "one country, two systems" – which assumed Beijing's political dominance and Taiwan's subordination.[67] Beijing was not willing to set aside the definition of "one China" as it had in 1993. In the face of Taiwan's charges that acceptance of it was a precondition for talks, the PRC bluntly replied that this was not the case – "one China" was a reality.[68]

In addition, the PRC met the challenge of pragmatic diplomacy more aggressively than before. The summit meetings between presidents Jiang Zemin and Bill Clinton in the fall of 1997 and summer of 1998 were used as occasions to express continued opposition to American support of Taiwan. Moreover, Beijing exercised its veto power (its first such use of this power) in the UN Security Council to block the dispatch of peacekeeping forces to Guatemala until that nation dropped its support of Taiwan's bid to enter the UN; opposed attempts by Taiwan to join international organizations; began unofficial diplomacy with countries recognizing Taiwan; and criticized countries that allowed visits of officials from the island (such objections, for example, led to Vice-President Lien Chan's aborted trips to Spain in October 1997, and Lebanon in February 1998).[69] Finally, as the Asian economic crisis unfolded, Beijing was sharply critical of what it perceived as attempts by Taipei to use its relative economic stability to increase its influence in the area.[70]

Yet during these years, Taiwan gave little ground in the face of mainland objections. It continued to refer to itself as the "Republic of China on Taiwan" (an appellation condemned by the mainland); to declare itself as an "equal," "sovereign," and "independent" political entity; and to insist on a one China formula based simply on history and culture which in no way diminished its claim of being the equal, not the subordinate, of the PRC. Rather than easing up on its pragmatic diplomacy, Taipei publicly stated that it would continue this practice, even arguing that, from its perspective, such diplomacy was more important than relations with the mainland. Relations with countries with which it maintained official relations were carefully cultivated by visits and promises of aid; unofficial trade relations were expanded; and high-ranking officials from Taiwan continued to travel abroad.[71]

In short, until mid-1998 Taiwan's relations with the mainland seemed locked in a vicious circle which froze any semblance of political engagement. The demands of international economic integration and Taiwan's domestic politics (of which more in the conclusion to this chapter) required that the government continue to insist on the sovereignty and independence of the "Republic of China on Taiwan" and to present unification as a matter to be settled in the more distant future. This, in turn, provoked increasingly strident responses from the leaders of the PRC, who became even more insistent on *their* definition of "one China" and Taiwan's subordinate place within it. The underlying programmatic bases for cross-strait relations on both sides of the strait seemed more likely to promote collision rather than contact.

In addition, the institutional foundations for engagement had seriously eroded. Formal contact between the unofficial SEF and the ARATS ended in 1995. In the three years that followed, Taiwan continued to use the SEF for mainland dealings by including it in discussions over hijacker repatriation, visits to the mainland by other organizations, and in talks regarding trade with post-1997 Hong Kong. It also sought to restart direct talks between the SEF and the ARATS on the assumption that they would take up where they left off with the procedures and agenda items (of a largely technical nature) that had been agreed upon at the first talks. Although Taipei was willing to discuss political matters, it was clear that it preferred a continued focus on technical questions of trade and investment.[72]

Beijing, however, considered the institutions and practices initiated in the early 1990s to be of little value. It was not enough merely to address technical questions; rather, the talks had to deal with political matters. It seemed that the PRC was intentionally insulting Taiwan's SEF. At the same time, Beijing worked to broaden its influence in Taiwan by cultivating contacts outside of the SEF. Besides business figures, delegations from the island including legislators, party officials, local officials, and more unification-oriented political figures were all welcomed in Beijing.[73]

In the summer of 1998, just when it appeared that what would be considered "engagement" in the political realm had reached a dead-end, a visit to the mainland by the chairman of the SEF, C.F. Koo, was finally arranged for October 1998. Koo met with his PRC counterpart, Wang Daohan, the Chairman of ARATS, and with the President of the PRC, Jiang Zemin, in his capacity as chairman of the Communist Party. The principle accomplishment of the visit was an agreement to maintain cross-straits contacts and to arrange for a return visit by Wang to Taiwan. However, as of the spring of 1999 both the visit (now postponed until the fall of 1999) and the nature of the topics to be discussed remained mired in renewed mutual recriminations. The divisive legacy of the earlier engagement will not be easily dispelled.

Security

Since the KMT fled to Taiwan, there has not been any significant cross-strait dialogue on reducing military tensions.[74] Rather, whatever reductions that have occurred have been the result of unilateral statements or actions.

During the 1950s there were ongoing hostilities in the strait, with mainland military probes and infiltration efforts by Taiwan. By the 1960s, tensions were considerably reduced and, with the normalization of relations between Beijing and Washington in 1979, the PRC began to emphasize the use of political means for reunification. On Taiwan, under the leadership of Chiang Ching-kuo, official statements emphasized that the role of the military was to defend the island rather than to recover the mainland. More significantly, the major legal bases for continued civil war with the mainland (martial law and the Temporary Provisions) were repealed in the course of democratization on Taiwan.

Still, militant rhetoric across the strait has not ceased. In Taipei, the emphasis is on a defensive posture, but there have been no concessions on the commitment to a vigorous defense of Taiwan and the offshore islands. The government continues its program of military modernization as well as its aggressive efforts to obtain military hardware from abroad – especially from the United States. The mainland, for its part, still reserves the right to use military force to achieve reunification.[75]

However, it was only with the military exercises of 1995 and 1996 that this rhetoric seemed to be approaching reality.[76] In the wake of President Lee's visit to the United States and the presidential elections in 1996, the PRC used military exercises and/or missile firings into the Taiwan Strait to express its anger over Lee Teng-hui's policies and perceived American support. The threat of military confrontation was most intense during the elections when missiles landed between twenty-two and thirty-two miles from the Taiwan coast and extensive naval, air, and amphibious exercises took place in the strait area.[77]

In certain respects, Taiwan's strategic position improved after this confrontation. To be sure, there was evidence that some of the island's strongest supporters in the United States were taken aback by the strength of the mainland reaction and seemed ready to moderate their position as well as that of Taiwan. Moreover, Washington made it clear in private that its response to a future clash in the Taiwan Strait would be quite different if Beijing were to be provoked by the island's movement toward independence.[78]

Still, Washington's deployment of two aircraft-carrier battle groups during the crisis was the strongest indication since the expiration of the Mutual Defense Treaty in 1979 that the United States might defend Taiwan against an un-provoked attack.[79] Furthermore, expressions of support for the American position by Asian leaders and the guidelines for the US–Japan alliance of September 1997, which called for cooperation to meet "situations in areas surrounding Japan," provided a boost. Although Taiwan was not mentioned specifically, there were strong suggestions – fed by comments from the Japanese side – that it could very well be included in such cooperation in the event of conflict with the mainland.[80]

The confrontation of March 1996 also had an impact on Taiwan's policies. The exercises provided a dose of reality for those on the island who approached the rhetoric and reality of autonomy with little concern for Beijing's sensibilities. Specifically, many in the independence-oriented DPP began to reconsider their position. The mainland had sent a clear message. Thereafter it was unrealistic to think that the DPP could continue to garner support on the island by stressing a policy that appeared perilous.[81]

In response, the DPP gradually began to moderate its stand. It joined the KMT-dominated National Unification Council and expressed its willingness to negotiate with the mainland.[82] Most dramatically, at the December 1996 National Development Conference at which the DPP and the KMT came to a number of agreements on necessary constitutional amendments, some consensus was also reached regarding mainland policy. It included a rejection of the mainland's stance of "one country, two systems"; a declaration that the Republic of China was a "sovereign state that must promote foreign relations"; and a pledge to seek actively "accession to international organizations."[83] In the subsequent 18 months, the

DPP, particularly during the leadership of Hsu Hsin-liang, not only sent representatives to the mainland, but advocated even greater contact.[84] Ironically, then, even as the military confrontation of March 1996 served to moderate independence demands on Taiwan, it anchored the basis for pragmatic foreign policy more firmly in the island's domestic policy. In short, while one might say that a positive result of the events of March 1996 was to define more clearly the American position and to sober political forces in both Taipei and Washington.

A military solution to the cross-strait crisis weighs heavily on the minds of the people of Taiwan. For more than a decade Taipei has focused considerable energies and resources on defense. It has developed its own hardware, ranging from the Indigenous Defense Fighter (IDF) plane to the Tiangong ("sky bow") surface-to-air missile to the Xiongfeng ("male bee") ship-to-ship missile. It has also actively sought assistance, primarily from the United States, which, pursuant to the Taiwan Relations Act, has continued wide-ranging arms sales to Taiwan as well as the leasing of naval equipment. These sales have featured such important hardware as the Patriot anti-missile system and the F-16 fighter which, along with the French Mirage 2000, began arriving in Taiwan in April/May 1997.[85] Moreover, even as relations between Washington and Beijing warmed in 1998, Taipei received important upgrades for advanced American fighter planes as well as enhancements of its naval capabilities.[86]

These weapons upgrades have, of course, been matched by similar efforts by the PRC, which has sought to increase its own military clout through domestic development and the acquisition of arms from abroad – primarily from the former Soviet Union. However, by early 1999 concern was focused on the PRC's development of ballistic and cruise missiles and their deployment in the coastal province of Fujian. A Pentagon study suggested that by 2005, the PRC might be able to target Taiwan with 650 missiles.

More ominously, the report suggested that by that time the mainland might possibly have "the capability to attack Taiwan with air and missile strikes which would degrade key military facilities and damage the island's economic infrastructure" and a sufficiently strong navy to "blockade the island's principal maritime ports." With this military edge, Beijing would have a wide range of options available to intimidate – or to inflict serious damage on – Taiwan.[87] Moreover, as March 1996 demonstrated, for an island dependent on foreign trade even the threat of the use of force is extremely dangerous. Not only would it disrupt foreign trade, it would also undermine foreign business confidence and discourage further investment in Taiwan.

In response to these developments, Taiwan has increased the pace of its indigenous arms development and production, with particular emphasis on those areas related to defense technology. It has also sought more advanced weapons from the United States, ranging from early warning radar to Aegis class cruisers capable of serving as platforms for missile defense. However, the most controversial issue has been the inclusion of Taiwan in a proposed theater missile defense (TMD) system for Asia.

This American project, still in the planning stage, has as its stated purpose the defense of US forward deployed troops in Asia. However, once in place, it could be used to defend other areas in the region. Taiwan has expressed an interest in being included in such a defense and some in the Congress have lent their support, pointing to missile development on the mainland. Such inclusion is, of course, anathema to the PRC. They see it as interference in domestic affairs; a renewal of Taiwan's defense relationship with the United States; and, by providing protection from mainland threats, an additional factor promoting independence sentiment on the island.

By mid-1999 the TMD issue had further complicated cross-strait relations as well as US–PRC relations. It had also created the conditions for an escalation of the Taiwan–PRC arms race. There is presently little prospect that this race will be controlled. Besides proposals from Taiwan for a cross-strait peace treaty (not likely to be accepted by the PRC because it smacks of inter-state relations), vague statements from Beijing regarding its willingness to permit Taiwan to maintain its own armed forces (viewed as a spurious offer in Taipei), and some talk of confidence building measures such as a "hotline" between militaries, no real progress has been made on addressing security issues.

Conclusion

A study of Taiwan's relations with the mainland from 1949 to 1999 yields somewhat contradictory conclusions. It provides both a useful corrective to the tendency to view the democratization of the late 1980s and early 1990s as marking a decisive turning point in the island's development even as it reaffirms the significance of that revolution.

It is a fundamental argument of this chapter that Taiwan's present policies toward the mainland did not develop de novo during the presidency of Lee Teng-hui, but incrementally and organically from earlier policies. In this respect, three aspects of these policies are particularly important. The first relates to the impact which history has had on the tone of the relationship. The legacy of the civil war remains a powerful influence on the perceptions of both sides. This is particularly true in the case of the mainland, where inflexibility on the issue of Taiwan is integrally tied to questions of regime legitimacy. Even in Taiwan, where the issue of unification has become far more politically complex, historic ties with Republican China – even in defeat – remain the single most important element substantiating the government's demand that, internationally and in talks with the PRC, it must be treated as an independent, sovereign, and equal political entity.

Second, the past has given form to specific aspects of Taiwan's current mainland policies. The policy of pragmatic diplomacy grew out of the substantive diplomacy which, as early as the Chiang Kai-shek era, was used as a means to break out of the isolation which had resulted from the increasing global recognition of the PRC. In addition, economic relations, which represent the most developed dimension of cross-strait relations at present, also had their origins in this earlier period. As suggested above, not only did Chiang Ching-kuo sanction such trade, but his hands-off policy was a major factor in creating the spontaneity that his successor has been as yet unable to bring under control.[89]

A final area of continuity, but also of fundamental change, has been the enduring linkage between mainland policy and domestic politics on Taiwan. In the period before democratization, the connection between regime legitimacy on Taiwan and the right to rule the mainland was a major obstacle to dealing with the PRC. Ironically, although KMT's dominance on the island would have facilitated talks with the mainland on an equal, party-to-party basis, for the Nationalists to have done so would have called into question their right to rule in Taiwan. Anti-Communist intransigence was required if the KMT's authoritarian rule was to be maintained on Taiwan.

Domestic politics remain at the core of the island's mainland policy. However, democratization has changed the fundamental nature of this linkage. The basis for regime legitimacy has changed from the KMT's claim to rule the mainland to its responsiveness to the views of the island's electorate, which seems to favor a centerist status quo position of neither independence nor unification . Since 1996 both ends of the political spectrum have shifted toward a similar centerist position, with the pro-unification New Party and the independence-oriented DPP focusing their criticism more on the *practice* of KMT mainland policy than on its *substance*. The effect of these shifts has been to embed the commitment to the concept of the island's sovereignty and independence even more deeply into domestic politics. In short, as in the 1950s, dealings with the mainland are still constrained by domestic politics, but for very different reasons.

The continued importance of this linkage, and the direct contradiction of the mainland position on "one China" that results from it, have been the most important factors shaping the peculiar nature of Taiwan's engagement of the PRC. In the definition offered by the editors of this volume, "engagement" has three qualities: it is non-coercive; it seeks to "ameliorate the non-status quo elements of a rising major power's behavior"; and its goal "is to ensure that this growing power is used in ways that are consistent with peaceful change in the regional and global order."

Taiwan's mainland policy, especially in the past decade, has been consistent with the letter of certain elements in this conception of engagement, but less so with its spirit. Indeed, Taiwan's mainland policy is best characterized as "pseudo-engagement." In this variant, the purpose is to buy time and security on the assumptions that mutual goals are basically irreconcilable, but that talk and some contact is better than conflict. In other words, by pursuing a policy of "pseudo-engagement," Taiwan has hoped to lower tensions, avoid crisis situations, and stave off further demands from the PRC. Moreover, such engagement has also served the KMT's domestic political needs by solidifying its centerist position on relations with the mainland.

However, the focus of Taiwan's engagement policy is on the *process* of diplomacy rather than its *substance*. While this is a non-coercive strategy, it does not really ameliorate the non-status quo elements of Beijing's position since it merely seeks to evade or, at least, to ease the pressure on Taiwan from the mainland's demands without satisfying them. Moreover, over time this policy has served to frustrate rather than accommodate a central – perhaps *the* central–demand of the PRC: discussion and eventual acceptance of the "one China" principle on PRC terms. The result has been sporadic crises that do little to advance peaceful change.

Of course, one might argue that such "pseudo-engagement" is merely a preliminary stage in an evolution toward a more comprehensive engagement which, rather than stalling the mainland or keeping it at arm's length, actually "engages" Beijing by seeking resolution of real questions. This is precisely what Taipei offers the mainland when it speaks in the National Unification Guidelines of a three-stage process of unification. This framework envisions a progressive spillover process whereby progress on one set of issues leads to the addressing of more complicated questions. In particular, the guidelines speak of a progression from "people-to-people" contacts (primarily trade and investment) to official contacts on a broad range of issues. In the short run, the guidelines seem to offer the promise that progress in the areas of trade and investment will be enough to sustain the relationship as it builds confidence for future development.

However, this has not been the case. Burgeoning economic relations have not provided the basis for Taiwan's engagement of the mainland in the manner in which the term is used in this volume; rather, they have rendered that engagement more problematic. The principal reasons for this conflict are to be found in the linkage between mainland policy and domestic politics discussed above. In the first place, any attempt to seek spillover from economic relations into other areas is hampered by the fact that the government in Taipei has very little control over this most active area of cross-strait relations. The origins of business ties with the mainland and their evolution during the decade of democratization have resulted in diminished governmental control of a potential policy instrument, thus contributing to the intensification of official ambivalence regarding the uses of economic relations. In essence, such relations are seen by the government as a two-edged sword that could easily be turned against Taiwan as dependence on the mainland and the influence of the mainland-oriented business community grows. This, in part, accounts for past insistence on limiting the scope of economic negotiations so as to exclude any discussion of political questions – a stance consistent with a strategy of buying time, but which hardly meets the demands of the business community.

Second, and more importantly, the likelihood of any evolution from "pseudo-engagement" is diminished by the terms which Taiwan itself has set for such movement. The demand that the mainland treat the island as an equal, sovereign, and independent entity before relations can be strengthened is in direct conflict with a fundamental mainland demand that negotiations must be predicated on the "one country, two systems" principle which presupposes Beijing as the central government and Taiwan as a subordinate unit. The basic issue remains the final resolution of the civil war of nearly fifty years ago, an issue upon which neither side has much room to compromise.

During the early 1990s the PRC was willing to have contacts with Taiwan within the context of pseudo-engagement. It sought not only the benefits of trade, but also the promise of policy spillover through growing leverage on the business community. After 1995, however, this willingness eroded as the mainland became increasingly aware that Taipei's policy was not an open-ended one which sought final resolution of the basic issue of sovereignty. Rather, it was intended to divert the mainland from its goal, enhance the global status of Taiwan, and secure economic as well as political benefits from mainland links. Beijing's insistence after 1996 that acceptance of its definition of "one China" be the virtual precondition for cross-strait negotiations was intended to put an end to this policy of "pseudo-engagement."

Instead, however, it froze negotiations as neither side could yield without compromising a fundamental tenet of its self-definition and a major prop of its domestic political legitimacy.

In September 1998, events moved both sides to re-examine the post-1996 deadlock. In Taiwan, the business community, joined by foreign commercial representatives, warned of the deleterious effects of continued cross-strait tensions.[88] Moreover, the impact of the PRC's international efforts to blunt Taiwan's pragmatic diplomacy lessened the credibility of this policy. Finally, the conditional nature of American support, as well as concerns growing out of the warming of Beijing's relations with the United States during 1997–1998, prodded Taipei.

For the PRC leadership, and particularly President Jiang Zemin, the resolution of cross-strait relations came to the fore following the return of Hong Kong. Moreover, given the focus on domestic economic reform, the improving atmosphere of Sino–American relations (as well as the symbolism of President Clinton's statement on Taiwan during his June–July 1998 trip to the PRC), and the increasing domestic and foreign pressure on Taipei, Beijing concluded that it was time to explore the possibilities of a second round of engagement.

It was the confluence of these factors that most likely lay behind Beijing's decision to invite C.F. Koo for an October 1998 visit. Yet, as noted above, the results of the trip were meager. There was no resolution of the fundamental issues that divide the two sides and regularized, institutionalized contacts were not re-established. This should not be surprising. Cross-strait relations could not begin where they left off in 1995. Over the years, both sides have not only sharpened their mutually contradictory positions on the nature of "one China," they have also embedded these positions more deeply into their domestic politics and international posture.

We thus end with an irony. The circumstances and results of Taiwan's post-1987 engagement of the mainland have intensified rather than ameliorated the tensions of the past. They have created a tenuous foundation for the process of resolving the PRC's most pressing demand for a change in the regional status quo. Rather than contributing to a future solution, the era of "pseudo-engagement" may be seen in retrospect to have added more weight to the burden of history which will continue to complicate any resolution of the cross-strait conflict.

Acknowledgments

The author thanks the Chiang Ching-kuo Foundation for International Scholarly Exchange. Thanks also to Hu Wanli for research assistance and to Nancy Hearst for her editorial assistance.

Notes

1 This is well covered in Nancy Bernkopf Tucker, *Patterns in the Dust: Chinese–American Relations and the Recognition Controversy, 1949–1950* (New York: Columbia University Press, 1983) and recently in Thomas J Christensen, *Useful Adversaries: Grand Strategy, Domestic Mobilization, and Sino–American Conflict, 1947–1958* (Princeton: Princeton University Press, 1996).

2 *Free China Weekly* (hereafter *FCW*) , January 7, 1963 and October 10, 1965.

3 Hungdah Chiu, ed, *China and the Question of Taiwan: Documents and Analysis* (New York: Praeger Publishers, 1973), p. 339; and *Foreign Relations of the United States 1955–1957*, vol. 2: *China* (Washington, DC: Government Printing Office, 1986), pp. 347 and 511.

4 Zhang Zhanhe, *Liang'an guanxi bianqian shi* (A changing history of the relations between the two shores) (Taipei: Shangzhou wenhua faxing, 1995), p 193.

5 *FCW*, April 13, 1969 and October 25, 1970.

6 Chiu, *China and the Question of Taiwan*, p. 261; Wang Mingyi, *Bu queding de haixia* (Uncertain strait) (Taipei: Shibao wenhua chuban qiye youxian gongsi, 1993), p.41; and *FCW*, February 23, 1975.

7 Nancy Bernkopf Tucker, *Taiwan, Hong Kong and the United States, 1945–1992* (New York: Twayne Publishers, 1994), p 54. See also Gary Klintworth, *New Taiwan, New China: Taiwan's Changing Role in the Asia-Pacific Region* (New York: St Martin's Press, 1995), pp. 81–90.

8 See, e.g. *Foreign Relations of the United States 1955–1957*, vol 2: *China*, pp. 323, 353, and 482.

9 The discussion of political structure which follows is based on Hung-mao Tien, *The Great Transition: Political and Social Change in the Republic of China* (Stanford, CA: Hoover Institution Press, 1989), Chapters 1,4, and 5; Yun-han Chu, *Crafting Democracy in Taiwan* (Taipei: Institute for National Policy Research, 1992), Chapter 2; Shao-chuan Leng and Cheng-yi Lin, "Political Change on Taiwan: Transition to Democracy?," *The China Quarterly*, No. 136, December 1993, pp. 805–839; and Jaushieh Joseph Wu, *Taiwan's Democratization: Forces Behind the New Momentum* (Hong Kong: Oxford University Press, 1995), Chapter 2.

10 Zhang, *Liang'an guanxi bianqian shi*, pp125–129.

11 Gordon Chang, *Friends and Enemies: The United States, China, and the Soviet Union, 1948–1972* (Stanford, CA: Stanford University Press, 1990) and Chiu, *China and the Question of Taiwan*, pp. 288–290.

12 *FCW*, June 20, 1971, January 28, 1973, and October 18, 1973.

13 *Foreign Relations of the United States 1958–1960*, Vol 19: *China* (Washington, DC: Government Printing Office, 1996), p. 467.

14 *FCW*, January 28, 1973
15 Ibid., October 14, 1973.
16 Ibid., November 18, 1973.
17 Tun-jen Cheng, Chi Huang, and Samuel SG. Wu, eds., *Inherited Rivalry: Conflict Across the Taiwan Straits* (Boulder, CO: Lynne Rienner Publishers, 1995), p. 236. The only possible exception to this policy occurred in early 1986 when the national airline of the ROC held talks in Hong Kong with their mainland counterparts to negotiate the return of one of their cargo planes. This was dismissed by Chiang Ching-kuo as an "isolated case." *FCW*, October 20, 1986.
18 Zhang, *Liang'an guanxi bianqian shi*, Chapter 7.
19 *Free China Journal* (hereafter *FCJ*), January 6, 1986 and February 9, 1987.
20 Ibid., June 20, 1982, August 5, 1984 and February 9, 1987. For an early statement by Lee Teng-hui along these lines, see ibid., March 17, 1986.
21 On the decision-making process that lay behind this decision, see Wang, *Bu queding de haixia*, pp 81–98.
22 *FCJ*, June 15, 1989.
23 Ibid., September 21, 1987; emphasis added. Earlier, in 1986, Chiang Ching-kuo had told an American reporter: "it is beyond our control to prevent indirect trade through a third country." Ibid., October 20, 1986.
24 For a general discussion of the roots of this diplomacy, see Ralph Clough, *Island China* (Cambridge, MA: Harvard University Press, 1978), pp 153–158. The figures come from *FCW*, December 30, 1985.
25 Ibid., December 14, 1985.
26 *Republic of China Yearbook, 1994* (Taipei: Government Information Office, 1993), p. 437; *FCJ*, March 17, 1986 and April 7, 1986. See also Wang, *Bu queding de haixia*, pp. 136–146.
27 Ralph Clough, *Reaching Across the Taiwan Strait: People to People Diplomacy* (Boulder, CO: Westview Press, 1993), pp. 23–24.
28 The three dimensions discussed below are similar to the categories used by Chong-Pin Lin in his "Beijing and Taipei: Interactions in the Post-Tiananmen Period," *China Quarterly*, No 136 (December 1993), pp. 770–804.
29 *FCJ*, April 19, 1991; Chi Schive, *Taiwan's Economic Role in East Asia* (Washington, DC: Center for Strategic and International Studies, 1995), pp. 26–27, 72–73, and 86; China News Agency (henceforth CNA), May 6, 1997; and *Wall Street Journal*, March 5, 1999.
30 CNA, May 12, 1997.
31 Ibid., May 6, 1997.
32 CNA, May 14, 1997 and *Wall Street Journal*, February 2, 1998.
33 Schive, *Taiwan's Economic Role in East Asia*, p 86, and *Dow Jones Newswires*, February 27, 1998.
34 Schive, *Taiwan's Economic Role in East Asia*, p 86.
35 CNA, March 7, 1998 and September 18, 1998.
36 *FCJ*, May 10, 1991.
37 See Wu, *Taiwan's Democratization*, pp 147–48; "Introduction to the Republic of China's Organization for the Handling of Mainland Affairs" (Taipei: Mainland Affairs Council, nd) and *FBIS-CHI*, September 14, 1990, p. 65.
    The guidelines can be found in John F. Copper, *Words Across the Taiwan Strait* (Latham, MD: University Press of America, Inc., 1995), pp. 125–127.
38 See Wang, *Bu queding de haixia*, pp 178–210, *Caituan faren haixia jiaoliu jijinhui bashinian niangao* (1991 Report of the Strait Exchange Foundation) (Taipei: Haijihui chuban, 1992), Chapters 1 and 2, and Clough, *Reaching Across the Taiwan Strait*, pp. 131–135, on the background to the founding of these organizations and their relationship to one another.

39 Yu-shan Wu, "Economic Reform, Cross-Strait Relations and the Issue of Policy Linkage," in Cheng *et.al.*, *Inherited Rivalry*, p. 128. See also *FCJ*, April 17, 1992.

40 *FBIS-CHI*, July 26, 1997.

41 In his book *The Taiwan–China Connection: Democracy and Development Across the Taiwan Straits* (Boulder, CO: Westview Press, 1996), Tse-Kang Leng presents an excellent discussion of these activities, arguing that democratization has made it impossible for the government to control cross-strait economic relations. See especially Chapters 4, 5, and 6.

  I discuss some of these questions in Steven M. Goldstein, "The Cross-Strait Talks of 1993 – The Rest of the Story: Domestic Politics and Taiwan's Mainland Policy," *Journal of Contemporary China*, Vol. 6, No. 15, 1997, pp.259–285.

42 *FBIS-CHI*, April 2, 3, and 19, 1997 *FCJ*, March 21, 1997.

43 *FBIS-CHI*, May 20, 1997.

44 CNA, April 20 and 22, 1997. For a good general discussion of this system, see Stephane Corcoff, "Direct Cross-Strait Links Linger Beyond the Horizon," *FCJ*, April 11, 1997, p. 7.

45 *FCJ*, March 7, 1997 and May 30, 1997; *South China Morning Post*, April 24, 1997.

46 See, e.g. *FCJ*, February 28, 1997.

47 For Chang Yung-fa's statements, see *South China Morning Post*, October 16, 1997. For Y.C. Wang, see *China News*, August 22, 1998.

48 For some examples, see *FBIS-CHI*, August 28, 1997, and September 15, 1997, October 10 and 12, 1997,

49 Zhang, *Liang'an guanxi bianqian shi*, pp 353–55; Clough, *Reaching Across the Taiwan Strait*, pp. 129–31; and Hsin-hsing Wu, *Bridging the Strait: Taiwan, China, and the Prospects for Reunification* (Hong Kong: Oxford University Press, 1994), Chapter 3.

50 On the building of a business constituency, see Chu Yun-han, "The ABC of Cross-Strait Policy," *Free China Review*, May 1997, pp 44–45. A typical mainland commentary to this effect can be found in *FBIS-CHI*, September 16, 1997.

51 Examples of efforts to raise politically sensitive topics are the November 1992 Hong Kong talks and the April 1993 Koo-Wang talks in Singapore. Wang, *Bu queding de haixia*, pp. 245–253 and Chapter 6.

52 *China News*, March 11, 1993, and *Shijie ribao*, January 21, 1993.

53 *China Post*, March 1 and 12, 1993, and *FBIS-CHI*, March 8, 1993, p 79.

54 The discussion which follows draws from Goldstein, "The Cross-Strait Talks of 1993 – The Rest of the Story".

55 Zhang Huiying, *Chaoqi waijiao guan: Li Denghui he tade wushi waijiao* (Beyond the foreign ministry: Lee Teng-hui and his pragmatic diplomacy) (Taipei: Shibao wenhua chuban qiye youxian gongsi, 1996), and Clough, *Reaching Across the Taiwan Strait*, Chapter 6.

56 *FBIS-CHI*, September 9, 1993.

57 Ibid., April 2 and 17, 1994 and May 10, 1994.

58 The quotations are from Jean-Pierre Cabestan, "Taiwan's Mainland Policy: Normalization, Yes: Reunification, Later," *China Quarterly*, No 148 (December 1996), pp. 1260–1283.

59 *FBIS-CHI*, December 16, 1994.

60 For Siew's earlier statements see e.g. ibid., January 5, 1994. For reactions to his appointment see ibid., January 9, 1995 and January 17, 1995.

61 A summary can be found in *FCJ*, February, 10, 1995.

62 Ibid., April 14, 1995.

63 Ibid., February 24, 1995 and May 19, 1995. On the Eight-Point Proposal and Lee's response, see also the discussion in John W. Garver, *Face Off: China, the United States and Taiwan's Democratization* (Seattle, WA: University of Washington Press, 1997), pp. 41–46.

64 *FBIS-CHI*, October 7 and 17, 1995, September 6, 1995, and January 23, 1996. For

a sample of mainland comments at the time, see David Shambaugh, "Taiwan's Security: Maintaining Deterrence Amid Political Accountability," *China Quarterly*, No. 148 (December 1996), p. 1286.

65 For a general discussion of domestic divisions in China over the Taiwan question, see Garver, *Face Off*, Chapter 10.

66 CNA, July 19, 1997; *FBIS-CHI* September 9 and 25, 1997; and *Far Eastern Economic Review*, July 24, 1997.

67 For suggestions of flexibility, see *South China Morning Post*, January 2, 1998, and *FBIS-CHI*, January 5, 1998. For the insistence on the "one country, two systems" principle, see *FBIS-CHI*, February 4, 1998 and *South China Morning Post*, May 15, 1998.

68 *CNA*, January 22, 1998.

69 The Guatemala issue is noted in my *Taiwan Faces the Twenty-First Century: Continuing the Miracle* (New York: Foreign Policy Association, 1997), p 70. See *FBIS-CHI*, September 27, 1997 and October 2, 1997, as well as *South China Morning Post*, October 17, 1997 and February 27, 1998.

70 *Dow Jones Newswires*, March 5, 1998.

71 *FBIS-CHI*, April 30, 1996, July 11, 1996, January 11, 1997, and April 14, 1997. See also *Far Eastern Economic Review*, May 8, 1997 and July 17, 1997.

72 See, e.g. Premier Vincent Siew's remarks to the Legislative Yuan, CNA, March 13, 1998.

73 Ibid., July 9, 1997, August 2, 1997, August 21 and 26, 1997; Cabestan, "Taiwan's Mainland Policy: Normalization, Yes: Reunification, Later," pp 1271–1272; and CNA May 6, 1998.

74 This section draws heavily from Lin, "Beijing and Taipei: Interactions in the Post-Tiananmen Period".

75 Copper, *Words Across the Taiwan Strait*, p.85.

76 The next two paragraphs draw from Garver, *Face Off*, Chapters 4–9.

77 For a sample of interpretations of these events, see "Forum," *China Journal*, No 36 (July 1996), pp. 87–134.

78 *Far Eastern Economic Review*, March 26, 1998, p 28.

79 Indeed, during his April 1997 visit to Taiwan, House Speaker Newt Gingrich flatly stated that the United States would defend Taiwan *Far Eastern Economic Review*, April 10, 1997.

80 See e.g. *FBIS-CHI*, September 25, 1997. For a discussion of this issue, see Dennis Van Vranken Hickey, "The Revised US–Japan Security Guidelines: Implications for Beijing and Taipei," *Issues and Studies*, Vol. 34, No. 4 (April 1998), pp. 72–89.

81 See *FCJ*, September 26, 1997.

82 *FBIS-CHI*, August 3, 1997 and September 19, 1997.

83 *FCJ*, January 4 and March 21, 1997.

84 See, e.g. *FBIS-CHI*, January 5, 1998.

85 Richard A Bitzinger and Bates Gill, *Gearing Up for High-Tech Warfare: Chinese and Taiwanese Defense Modernization and Implications for Military Confrontation Across the Taiwan Strait* (Washington, DC: Center for Strategic and Budgetary Assessments, 1996) and Shambaugh, "Taiwan's Security: Maintaining Deterrence Amid Political Accountability", pp. 1284–1318.

86 *Washington Post*, January 28, 1998 and *South China Morning Post*, June 3, 1998.

87 United States Department of Defense, "Report to Congress Pursuant to FY99 Appropriation Bill," MS. p. 25.

88 For a discussion of these scenarios, see Shambaugh, "Taiwan's Security: Maintaining Deterrence Amid Political Accountability", and *Far Eastern Economic Review*, May 28, 1998, pp 31–33.

89 This is a central thesis of Leng, *The Taiwan–China Connection*. The author argues

that democratization has been the major factor in the lack of control. Certainly democratization has complicated control, but the origins of this issue pre-date democratization. See also Cheng-Tian Kuo, "The Political Economy of Taiwan's Investment in China," in Cheng *et. al.*, *Inherited Rivalry*, pp. 153–69.

90 I refer here to the criticisms of the American Chamber of Commerce in Taiwan. CNA, September 27, 1997. On impatience in the business community, see *Far Eastern Economic Review*, October 9, 1997.

4

INDONESIA'S ENCOUNTERS WITH CHINA AND THE DILEMMAS OF ENGAGEMENT

Michael Leifer

The concept of engagement is both ambiguous and alien as a criterion for assessing Indonesia's changing relationship with China. It is replete with alternative meanings in the English language and, more to the point, does not have an equivalent in Indonesia's vernacular lexicon of foreign policy. In Jakarta, the concept of engagement with reference to China has entered into the discourse of international relations because it has been employed by the government in the United States to describe its policy towards the People's Republic. Indonesia's policy towards China fits within America's parameters only up to a point, however. It differs from them in one very important respect. The underlying objective is to try to influence the external conduct of China and not the way in which the People's Republic orders its domestic politics.

Indonesia's policy towards China has also been driven in part by very different considerations to those of its two closest regional neighbours and partners, Malaysia and Singapore, which are also the subject of consideration in this volume. Indonesia's position is distinguished, above all, by an incipient geo-political rivalry with China which does not obtain in the cases of Malaysia and Singapore. That rivalry has its roots in Indonesia's foreign policy elite's sense of standing and entitlement within Southeast Asia based on an extensive geographic scale, a strategic location, a large population as well as on a national revolutionary tradition. It has been based also on an economic promise which has been set back dramatically from the second half of 1997. That prerogative stance has been combined, in some contradiction, with a sense of national vulnerability arising from the fissiparous physical and social condition of the archipelagic state which has been the source of a shared concern with its close regional neighbours about the hegemonic potential and intent of a rising China. That concern has its source also in Indonesia's experience of past encounters with China which has generated an adverse perspective of the People's Republic and which has informed the practice of engagement.

Indonesia's version of engaging China has been distinguished in the main by participation in multilateral dialogues with a view to encouraging the government in Beijing of the advantages of regional cooperation and good citizenship. It has also been supplemented by a limited measure of balance of power practice. Indonesia's political reopening to China after a break in direct diplomatic ties of some twenty-three years has never been envisaged as sufficient in itself to cope with the rising power and influence of the People's Republic. The break and restoration of diplomatic ties occurred during the long tenure of President Suharto which came to an end in May 1998. His resignation from office against a background of economic adversity and political turmoil, and his succession by his Vice-President, Dr B. J. Habibie, has not made any appreciable difference in national outlook and policy towards China.

An adverse perspective

The Republic of Indonesia is exceptional within Southeast Asia in its experience of dealing with the People's Republic of China. Diplomatic ties were established first in July 1950 quite soon after Indonesia had assumed sovereignty from the Dutch in December 1949. A close and radical political alignment developed between the two states for a limited period during the mid-1960s. That alignment was expressed in a shared revisionist view of the international system. In the main, however, the bilateral relationship has been problematic and even turbulent. Indeed, between October 1967 and August 1990, diplomatic ties were held continuously in a suspended state. Suspension had occurred at Indonesia's initiative in the wake of China being charged with complicity in an abortive *coup* in Jakarta in October 1965 in support of an attempt to seize power by Indonesia's Communist Party. For well over two decades, Indonesia's policy towards China was distinguished by a calculated practice of disengagement.

Among the decisive factors underlying that lengthy period of disengagement was a judgement by President Suharto that Jakarta had no need of diplomatic ties or for that matter of any equivalent to "engagement" with Beijing, although several years before suspension was brought to an end direct economic ties were re-established. In considering Indonesia's policy towards China with reference to the concept of engagement, it is important to understand that the relationship has been a matter reserved for presidential prerogative, with all important initiatives taken by or with the sanction of the State Secretariat, in effect his private office, and not by the Department of Foreign Affairs. Indeed, the actual announcement of an impending restoration was made unexpectedly, and to great surprise, not in Jakarta but in Tokyo, where President Suharto had gone in February 1989 to attend the funeral of Japan's Emperor Hirohito. It was during that visit that he met privately with China's Foreign Minister, Qian Qichen, in a positive response to a request for a restoration of relations from the government of the People's Republic which had been communicated to Indonesia's Permanent Representative to the United Nations in New York.

President Suharto's dismissive view of the need to deal at close hand with China had been sustained through the mid-1970s even after three of Indonesia's regional partners within the Association of South-East Asian Nations (ASEAN) had entered into diplomatic relations with Beijing and also after the United States and Japan had followed suit by the end of the decade. He saw no need to accommodate to Beijing in the wake of the success of revolutionary Communism in Indo–China or in the wake of Sino–American *rapprochement*. Diplomatic relations were only restored when domestic circumstances in Indonesia permitted and when their continued absence was judged to be of economic disadvantage and also an impediment to the Republic's diplomatic ambitions in seeking to promote a resolution of the Cambodian conflict and in assuming the chair of the Non-Aligned Movement. Restoration occurred in August 1990 concurrently with the Cold War coming to an end. It was only after then that the term "engagement," with China in mind, began to enter generally into the discourse of international relations.

Whether that elliptical and confusing term of Western provenance, which has been used to differentiate American policy, above all, from that of an earlier doctrine of containment, translates readily to Indonesian ideas and experience is debatable. But irrespective of any semantic perplexity and also the lack of a systematic statement of engagement and its terms, there has been a conspicuous political opening towards China on Indonesia's part for quite pragmatic reasons which have corresponded partly to those which have driven policy in Washington.

Indonesia's significant change of approach towards the People's Republic has not, however, erased a heavy historical legacy of encounters with China and Chinese which predisposes the country's political establishment towards a deep suspicion and apprehension of Beijing. Engagement, so-called, is an ambivalent stance on Indonesia's part, reflecting those national fears. Indeed, in February 1989, news of the impending restoration of diplomatic relations was received in Jakarta with very mixed feelings, especially within the Armed Forces which have long occupied a dominant position within the foreign policy elite. The author of a recent study of Indonesia's Armed Forces has pointed out that from its corporate perspective "China continues to be seen as the greatest potential direct threat to Indonesian sovereignty."[1] To that extent, while it has since come to be accepted in Jakarta that it would be incongruous for a state of Indonesia's regional standing and aspirations not to have diplomatic relations with a rising China, there is a shared corresponding view that in supping with China, as with the devil, it is best to use a long spoon. And although China is viewed as being too preoccupied with domestic economic reforms and their social consequences to trouble Indonesia's security in the short term, the prospect of its success in that endeavour being translated into modern military power for the pursuit of irredentist goals in Southeast Asia is a matter of deep and abiding concern. The most recent statement of Indonesia's defence policy has pointed out that China's continuing growth will make it, at some time, "the pre-eminent country in the region, both economically and militarily." It noted also China's extensive claims in the South China Sea and the prospect of "military conflict with other claimant countries."[2]

Indonesia's concern with China's irredentist agenda touches the innate physical vulnerability of the distended archipelago with its fissiparous political potential. Jakarta's strategic outlook is expressed in a long-standing *Wawasan Nusantara* or "Archipelagic Doctrine" which binds together the extensive combination of land and water in more than symbolic form.[3] The Republic enjoys archipelagic status under the terms of the United Nations Convention on the Law of the Sea which came into force in November 1994. Under that Convention, Indonesia is permitted to draw maritime baselines linking the outermost points of its outermost islands. In consequence, sovereign jurisdiction now extends over some three million square miles of land and sea beyond which there is an entitlement to an extensive Exclusive Economic Zone. The prerogative role in politics of the Army and the prime focus of security from independence on countering domestic challenges have led to a neglect of the country's naval capability until recently. Its ability to effectively monitor, let alone protect, Indonesia's extensive maritime domain is limited. Nonetheless, as pointed out in an earlier defence policy document: "The Doctrine serves as a guide to the entire nation in building up, maintaining and consolidating the whole national territory as one political, economic, socio-cultural, defence and security entity."[4]

It is well understood in Jakarta that should China ever be able to extend its jurisdiction so as to realize in full its irredentist agenda in the South China Sea, a revolutionary geopolitical fusion of Northeast and Southeast Asia would occur. Such a worst-case fusion would make the People's Republic as much of a Southeast Asian state as Indonesia, with the prospect of its being in a position to contend for command of the maritime heart of the region. Although China is no longer regarded in Jakarta as a revolutionary state, it is viewed as a territorially revisionist one which cannot be trusted to respect the regional status quo and which might well, in time, employ its rising power to advance its irredentist ends.

One consequence of that judgement has been to cause a significant modification in Indonesia's regional security practice which has long been based on the notion of "comprehensive security" and not on that of the balance of power.[5] That modification has been expressed in an unprecedented security agreement with Australia concluded in December 1995. Engaging China through both direct and multilateral dialogue underpinned by the nexus of economic cooperation is accepted as a necessary practical measure suitable for a post-Cold War Asia-Pacific but without either deep confidence in the process or trust in China's ultimate intentions. Indonesia's approach to engagement is replete, therefore, with an ambivalence of outlook. Ambivalence arises also from the concern that Indonesia, which looks to China for economic opportunity, might be weakened by the competitive economic strength of the rising power which was an impression made on President Suharto as a result of his first visit to the People's Republic in November 1990. A complementary concern adding to ambivalence has arisen over the extent to which Indonesia's economically powerful Chinese community has invested heavily in China at the expense of local capital needs.

Indonesia's experience

China has long occupied the position of prime potential adversary in the strategic perspective of those responsible for the security policy of Indonesia. Indeed, a historical apprehension of an imperialist China pre-dates the advent of the post-colonial Republic going back in particular to the invasion of Java in the late thirteenth century during Kublai Khan's reign as well as to the celebrated expedition of Admiral Cheng Ho in the early fifteenth century. Such historical episodes have been interpreted to confirm a perception of China as an expansionist power. An abiding, and at times violently expressed, resentment of the economic role of ethnic Chinese domiciled in Indonesia as well as a suspicion of their loyalties also pre-dates the post-colonial Republic. Their privileged economic position during Dutch dominion and their perceived political ambivalence during the period of national revolution gave rise to a national stereotype. It was the ethnic-Chinese community as a subversive conduit which bulked largest in perception with the success of the Communist revolution in China rather than a fear of the export of Communism as such.[6]

An Indonesian view of a menacing China has arisen in the main, however, from national experience since the acquisition of sovereignty. The immediate post-independence governments of Indonesia were not well disposed to Communist countries but diplomatic relations were entered into with the People's Republic of China in order to register the credibility of an "independent and active" foreign policy distinguished by not taking sides in the Cold War. To that end, for example, Indonesia's representative abstained from voting on the United Nations General Assembly resolution branding China as an aggressor for its military intervention in Korea.

Indonesia was established as an independent state through armed and diplomatic struggle against a dogged Dutch colonial power between 1945 and 1949. In the process, its revolutionary government had crushed an armed challenge from a radical faction with which the local Communist Party had become aligned. In that context, it was deemed necessary to demonstrate that the embryonic Republic was not beholden to Western powers towards which its leaders looked for diplomatic intervention against the Dutch as well as for economic assistance. The seminal expression of an ideal "independent and active" foreign policy course for Indonesia was articulated by Vice-President Mohammad Hatta in a celebrated statement in September 1948, and has remained the national credo ever since.[7] The subsequent diplomatic opening to China took place in order to lend credence to Indonesia's declaratory policy. Moreover, Indonesia sustained a one China policy from the outset which was upheld through the period of suspension of diplomatic ties. The initial establishment of those ties involved a domestic political price, however, which served to mar relations between Jakarta and Beijing from early on.

The relationship with China was a problem for Indonesia from the outset. As indicated above, the Republic had inherited a settled ethnic-Chinese community (of around 3 percent of the population) which had long played an important economic role out of all proportion to their number.[8] The Chinese Embassy in Jakarta sought actively to attract the political and financial support of this community, in part to compete with the Nationalist government in Taiwan with which Indonesia's Chinese had enjoyed long-standing links. Such intervention was most unwelcome and served only to confirm national prejudices. The issue of the citizenship status and the loyalty of the ethnic Chinese in Indonesia, as well as China's renunciation of any political claims on them, was addressed by treaty in April 1955 when Premier Zhou Enlai visited Jakarta after the historic Bandung Conference.[9] That treaty proved to be inadequate in its application, however. Sino–Indonesian relations then deteriorated markedly during the late 1950s when the Armed Forces enforced a law prohibiting ethnic Chinese from engaging in retail trade in rural areas by expelling them in large numbers from the countryside. China reacted by despatching ships to Indonesia to facilitate their repatriation which was interpreted in Jakarta as an act of intimidation.[10]

The issue of the legal status of ethnic Chinese resident in Indonesia took decades to resolve and was not laid to rest until diplomatic relations had been restored. Even so, the issue of their alien identity and doubtful loyalties has continued to remain just below the surface of the relationship sustained by the continuing dominant role of ethnic Chinese in the economic life of the Republic. It reappeared, for example, in April 1994 in the wake of labour unrest and racial violence in Medan in north Sumatra which prompted an expression of concern by a Chinese Foreign Ministry spokesman which in turn provoked an angry response in Jakarta at an apparent reversion to a past meddling practice.[11] Significantly, there was a conspicuous absence of adverse comment from China during the recurrent incidents of racial violence in Indonesia during the second half of 1996 and into the first months of 1997 leading up to parliamentary elections in May that year as well as before and after presidential elections in March 1998. Indeed, China's newly appointed Foreign Minister, Tang Jiaxuan, while visiting Jakarta in April 1998, went out of his way to stress that anti-Chinese rioting was an internal matter for Indonesia's government to handle.[12] Such forbearance on China's part was not sustained in the wake of a revival of anti-Chinese violence in Indonesia concurrent with the political downfall of President Suharto the following month. A number of official expressions of concern about attacks on "Chinese-Indonesians" emanated from Beijing, including one from Vice-Premier Qian Qichen made conspicuously at a National Day reception held by the State Council's Office of Overseas Chinese Affairs in late September 1998.[13] Notably, the Indonesian government failed to respond in the way in which it had in April 1994, probably because it had little stomach for international controversy which might have aggravated its dire economic circumstances. Nonetheless, the diplomatic reassertion by China on behalf of the interests of Indonesian citizens was deeply disturbing in Jakarta.

In the past, however, China's involvement in Indonesia's domestic affairs had been highly controversial through its conspicuous support, including funding, for the large indigenous Communist Party, especially after July 1959 when President Sukarno imposed his authoritarian political system of guided democracy. Although its inauguration enjoyed military support, the Armed Forces regarded the Communist Party, which claimed a membership of over three million, as an anti-national political rival. They resented the way in which President Sukarno employed the party as a balancing factor in order to sustain his own political centrality and its burgeoning political alignment with its Chinese counterpart. They became alarmed subsequently by China's offer of light weapons for a so-called "fifth force" of armed workers and peasants required ostensibly to defend the country against an alleged impending attack by Britain on behalf of Malaysia which was then the object of Indonesia's policy of "confrontation."

Despite the resistance of the Armed Forces, Sino–Indonesian relations blossomed towards the end of President Sukarno's regime. China provided enthusiastic support for Indonesia's challenge to the international legitimacy of Malaysia and also rallied to Indonesia's side when it was frustrated in an attempt to deny the Federation a non-permanent place on the United Nations Security Council. China was also openly sympathetic when Indonesia withdrew from the United Nations in January 1965. For example, later that month, Foreign Minister Dr Subandrio travelled to Beijing where he concluded an agreement on political principles with Premier Zhou Enlai in which a shared revisionist view was expounded of the international system. Premier Zhou endorsed President Sukarno's proposal for a conference of like-minded radical states represented as a possible alternative to the United Nations. In the following August, on the anniversary of Indonesia's proclamation of independence, President Sukarno enthused publicly over building "an anti-imperialist axis" between his government and that in Beijing together with others in Phnom Penh, Hanoi and Pyongyang.[14] This public enthusiasm was not shared by the Armed Forces and Muslim groups, in particular, who regarded the so-called axis as politically unhygienic.

This rhetorical "axis" proved to be short-lived. Within a few months, Sino–Indonesian relations were in tatters as a consequence of the political outcome of an abortive *coup* which occurred in the early hours of 1 October 1965. In the event, the Armed Forces led by General Suharto seized effective power in March 1996, having become an active party to the bloody destruction of Indonesia's Communist Party which was then declared illegal. The Republic then changed course in political economy and correspondingly in its foreign policy with China translated to the role of adversary. It was denounced for providing asylum and facilities to "Indonesia's counter-revolutionaries and subversive elements," which was the term applied to a delegation from Indonesia's Communist Party which had been visiting Beijing coincidentally with the *coup* attempt and which had been granted asylum there. Moreover, Chinese diplomatic personnel and property in Jakarta and in consulates outside the capital were made the object of inspired demonstrations and physical attack.

Subsequently, the ferment of China's Cultural Revolution, which found expression in an endorsement of a revolutionary line for the remnant of

Indonesia's Communist Party, led on to Indonesia's Department of Foreign Affairs succumbing to military pressure and withdrawing its depleted embassy staff from China's capital in October 1967. Foreign Minister Adam Malik deliberately employed the term "frozen" to describe the new state of relations between the two countries. The object was to obstruct any attempt to promote diplomatic relations with Taiwan as an alternative to Beijing as well as to hold out the prospect of normalization in the future. Trade was continued between the two countries but had to be conducted through third parties such as Hong Kong.

Although the full circumstances of the abortive *coup* of October 1965 have never been revealed, China's complicity is a central part of national conventional wisdom about the episode.[15] This conventional wisdom has been central to the claim to legitimacy and prerogative political role of the Armed Forces and of President Suharto's rule, albeit in his case modified over time. An early restoration of diplomatic relations with China would have undermined both corporate and personal credibility by raising doubts about the claim to have quashed an externally inspired threat to national security. In the event, restoration had to wait for more than two decades until President Suharto had managed to free himself of undue political dependence on the support of the Armed Forces and also until a change in the basis of his legitimacy had occurred from that of upholding order to one of material achievement in development.[16] Indonesia's government had also to pronounce itself satisfied that China no longer posed a threat to national security either through support for any remnant of its banned Communist Party or through any claim on the loyalty of the country's ethnic-Chinese community. Restoration was a matter of political pragmatism for Indonesia, however. It did not presage the revival of a past warmth. Indonesia's calculation was cold and based on national advantage. Restoration was only contemplated and concluded when President Suharto judged that its price was acceptable. It did not mean that the strategic perspective of the Republic had changed in any substantive way.

The perspective had been confirmed, for example, in the course of the Cambodian conflict early on during which China had launched a punitive military expedition into Vietnam. China's use of force in February 1979 alarmed Jakarta and also reinforced a foreign policy dilemma. Indonesia had been the prime founding member of ASEAN which had been set up in August 1967 in an attempt to serve the Republic's security interests through building confidence and trust among new-found regional partners. This multilateral structure had been conceived in part as a shield against Chinese political intrusions. The invasion of Cambodia by Vietnam in December 1978, however, had posed an unprecedented threat to Thailand, one of Indonesia's regional partners. For the sake of intra-ASEAN cohesion, Indonesia had been obliged to tolerate being drawn into a tacit alliance with China directed at weakening Vietnam's political resolve in Indo-China, despite shared geopolitical interests between Jakarta and Hanoi. That experience deeply troubled Indonesia's foreign policy establishment which resented the strategic priorities of the state being distorted to China's advantage.[17]

By the time diplomatic relations had been restored in 1990, China was well advanced along the road to economic modernization. Indeed, the opportunity for direct trade relations with China had been taken up from July 1985 in response to a fall in the world price of oil and the need to promote compensating non-oil exports. Trade offices were pointedly not established automatically in respective capitals. With a restoration of diplomatic relations, however, it seemed as if all outstanding issues between Indonesia and China had been resolved, but that proved not to be the case as the People's Republic began to engage in a maritime assertiveness to its south which served to point out an underlying sense of geopolitical rivalry.

Although not a claimant state, Indonesia shared a concern with its regional partners about China's irredentist agenda in the South China Sea as a pointer to its likely hegemonic intent. From 1990, its Foreign Ministry began to sponsor a series of workshops, formally at a "track-two" or unofficial level, on managing potential conflicts there. Chinese representatives began to participate in these workshops in 1991 after diplomatic relations had been restored. These workshops, based on the model of preventive diplomacy, became a frustrating experience for Indonesian officials involved, partly because of the seemingly obstructionist tactics of China's delegations over even limited functional cooperation, especially from the mid-1990s.[18] In addition, their proceedings became clouded by a growing concern about China's maritime claims extending to Indonesia's domain, so prejudicing the Republic's assumption of a neutral non-claimant status which was the basis on which its Department of Foreign Affairs had taken the initiative in mounting the workshops. It is worth noting the extent to which Indonesia has sought to conciliate China in an attempt to achieve progress in that venture. For example, at the Non-Aligned Summit which convened in Jakarta in September 1992, the final wording of a paragraph welcoming an ASEAN Declaration of the previous July on the South China Sea for inclusion in the Final Document on Political Issues was worked out in consultation with the Chinese delegation. That delegation was present with observer status only, and Indonesia's officials did not have any obligation to consult it but deemed it appropriate to do so in order to facilitate the workshop process.

Concern about China's irredentist intent had been registered during the late 1980s when Beijing took advantage of an unplanned naval clash with Vietnam to occupy a limited number of islands in the Spratly group. This concern was reinforced acutely with the revelation in February 1995 of China's seizure of Mischief Reef, an unoccupied atoll within the Spratly group in an area claimed by both Vietnam and the Philippines. As noted above, in July 1992, arising partly from deliberations at the Indonesian-sponsored workshops, the ASEAN states, meeting in Manila, had endorsed a Declaration on the South China Sea. The Declaration called for the employment of peaceful means only in settling contending claims to jurisdiction. It had been prompted by China's promulgation of a law on its territorial waters and contiguous areas in the preceding February which reaffirmed extensive claims to all the islands in the South China Sea and by implication to all of the interjacent waters.

China's Foreign Minister, Qian Qichen, who had been invited as a guest to the ASEAN foreign ministers' meeting at which the Declaration was issued, was highly equivocal in his response. China's subsequent use of naval forces to seize Mischief Reef confirmed the apparent unwillingness of the People's Republic to be bound by a regional code of conduct. Even more disturbing for Indonesia has been China's apparent claim to maritime jurisdiction within Indonesia's Exclusive Economic Zone arising from its sovereignty over the Natuna Islands which are situated to the south of the Spratly Islands. The Natunas constitute a chain of some three hundred small islands and atolls spread midway between the east coast of the Malay Peninsula and northern Borneo and comprise part of the Republic's territorial inheritance from Holland under an Anglo–Dutch Treaty of 1824. Considerable natural gas reserves are believed to lie below the sea-bed of those waters, and Indonesia's state oil company, Pertamina, entered into a joint venture for their exploration and exploitation with the American oil company Exxon in January 1995.

The matter was of sufficient concern for Indonesia's Foreign Ministry to send a diplomatic note to China via its Embassy in Jakarta in September 1994 seeking clarification, in particular, as to whether or not China intended to use its claim to the Spratly Islands as a basis for measuring the country's Exclusive Economic Zone and its continental shelf. There was a clear implication in the note that, if it were so, an overlap would arise with the waters of Indonesia's Exclusive Economic Zone extending from its jurisdiction over the Natunas. A failure to secure a satisfactory response prompted Foreign Minister Ali Alatas to visit Beijing in July 1995 specifically to seek clarification of the extent of China's maritime claims arising from its assertion of sovereignty over the Spratly Islands. Alatas pronounced himself satisfied with the clarifications received but without allaying the concerns of Indonesia's military establishment.

In response to a strong, albeit private, diplomatic reaction from ASEAN to the seizure of Mischief Reef, China made concessions of form and, in particular, expressed a willingness to recognize International Law, including the United Nations Convention on the Law of the Sea, as a basis for negotiating a settlement to the contentious issue of the Spratly Islands. However, when it came to ratifying the Convention in May 1996 and to defining its maritime baselines, China employed the terms of the archipelagic principle in the case of the more northerly Paracel Islands, disputed with Vietnam. Such a principle is generally held to be valid under the United Nations Law of the Sea Convention only with respect to mid-ocean archipelagos, of which Indonesia is one. Although China reserved its publication of baselines in the case of the Spratly Islands, such an alleged illegal use of the archipelago principle was received with deep apprehension in Jakarta and elsewhere within ASEAN as a deliberate attempt to establish a precedent for delimitation in the case of the more acutely contested Spratlys. China's likely intention to employ the archipelagic principle in the case of the Spratlys was indicated in a volume published in September 1996 by a retired PLA officer, whose writings on the South China Sea carry a stamp of authority.[19]

This act of delimitation for the Paracels prompted an official note of protest from Jakarta to Beijing in July 1996 for having acted contrary to International Law. It warned that should a similar line be drawn in the case of the Spratly Islands it would be considered "as possibly provocative to the ASEAN countries, including Indonesia." For Indonesia, in the light of that episode and despite a restoration of diplomatic relations with China, the People's Republic has not purged its reputation as an expansionist power. Indeed, its maritime assertiveness since that restoration has served to confirm the apprehension by the country's political and military establishments of the potential strategic threat posed by a rising China dissatisfied with the regional status quo. This maritime assertiveness has also been a factor in Indonesia's narrow interpretation of its obligation under the United Nations Law of the Sea Convention to declare sea lanes for unimpeded passage through its archipelagic waters. The prospect in the future of a Chinese blue-water fleet able to penetrate the Java Sea has been an underlying consideration in withholding assent to an east–west sea lane.

Indonesia's experiences of dealing with China before and after its extended diplomatic break have served to confirm a deep-seated apprehension of the malign intent of the People's Republic. And although China has become a minor benefactor in providing limited financial support with others in helping Indonesia to overcome an acute economic adversity and has avoided any strident interference in the country's internal affairs, the underlying outlook of its foreign policy elite has not changed. China continues to cast a looming shadow over Indonesia's domain.

Dilemmas of engagement

For Indonesia, the restoration of diplomatic relations with China in August 1990 may be construed as a form of engagement without explicit employment of that concept. Direct diplomatic contact was seen as a way of becoming better informed about the People's Republic, although the linguistic skills of Indonesia's embassy staff in Beijing have been limited. Indeed, within Indonesia, the teaching of Chinese language and the use of its characters remain tightly restricted. As indicated above, from the mid-1980s, the lack of direct diplomatic contact with Beijing was considered to be an impediment to Indonesia promoting a resolution of the Cambodian conflict and also to its assumption of the chair of the Non-Aligned Movement. It is doubtful, however, if much more was anticipated of the restored relationship by way of securing China's practical endorsement of Indonesia's vision of regional order. This vision had been articulated by ASEAN's foreign ministers in November 1971 in a collective commitment to make Southeast Asia a "Zone of Peace, Freedom and Neutrality" (ZOPFAN) which would be "free from any manner of interference by outside powers." This statement had been precipitated by the People's Republic's assumption of China's seat in the United Nations in October with Indonesia abstaining in the decisive vote. It was a declaratory way of announcing to external powers that the ASEAN states reserved the exclusive right to define the terms of their own regional order and was directed, among others, at China. Indeed, for Indonesia, ASEAN has always been regarded as a political shield of a kind against an assertive China.

Despite mixed feelings among ASEAN's governments about the utility and appropriateness of ZOPFAN, it has become part of the official security doctrine of Indonesia and its regional partners. Although China has been supportive of that doctrine in principle, it has not been willing to endorse all of ASEAN's expressions of its application. For example, China, together with the United States, raised practical objections to the terms of a Southeast Asian Nuclear Weapons-Free Zone (SEANWFZ) Treaty concluded by the ASEAN states in December 1995 which was represented as integral to the realization of ZOPFAN. Although China has encouraged ASEAN's role as a vehicle for promoting multipolarity in Asia-Pacific within which it is obliged to cope with troubling relationships with the United States and Japan, the Association has not made any headway in persuading Beijing to moderate its irredentist agenda. Moreover, within ASEAN there are differences of strategic perspective towards China with Thailand, for example, more concerned about Vietnam's intentions within Indo–China and willing to rely on China's regional countervailing power as a check to its possible ambitions. For this reason, in part, ASEAN has not been a robust vehicle of engagement to the extent of being able to effect a substantive change in China's conduct. For example, ASEAN did not take a collective stand on Vietnam's behalf in an oil-drilling dispute with China in March/April 1997 in contested waters between Danang and Hainan Island.[20]

Nonetheless, ASEAN has demonstrated some utility in its collective engagement with China to Indonesia's satisfaction. For example, ASEAN and China have begun a series of annual security dialogues at the level of senior officials. It was at the first of these dialogues held in Hangzhou in April 1995 that the ASEAN side made known its strong objections to China's seizure of Mischief Reef. The outcome was a political accommodation in form by China in the context of its acute tensions with the United States and Japan with an evident temporizing for a time over any further pressing of its maritime claims by show of force.[21] Such a response may be judged to have been a success of a kind, albeit determined by China's assessment of the disadvantages of driving ASEAN into a united front against its interests. For Indonesia, however, ASEAN has served in the main as a quasi-familial undertaking in cooperative security from which China is excluded as a non-regional state. Indonesia has also supported the progressive enlargement of ASEAN to include all other Southeast Asian states, including those which have been at odds with China and those over which China is seen to enjoy undue influence. To this end, Vietnam became a member in July 1995 and Myanmar and Laos joined in July 1997, with Cambodia's entry being postponed because of an intervening violent *coup* which was a source of acute political embarrassment. Despite its limitations as a diplomatic community, an enlarged ASEAN, speaking with one voice, has been regarded in Jakarta as likely to be a more effective instrument for managing relations with a China regarded with apprehension and some foreboding. Indonesia has also suggested expanding ASEAN cooperation "to include a security dimension," without pressing its regional partners on the matter.[22]

In its limited engagement of China, Indonesia is faced with a dilemma not experienced by other regional partners within ASEAN. Indonesia shares a mirror image with China in its view of its rightful place within its regional environment. In geopolitical terms, there is a sense in which they may both be described as "middle kingdoms," and therefore natural geopolitical rivals within an East Asia incorporating a fused Northeast and Southeast Asia, especially since the end of the Cold War. For its part, at least until its economic tribulations from late 1997, Indonesia has sought to occupy the role of prime manager of regional order within Southeast Asia; a call for a greater assertiveness to that end was endorsed by members of its foreign policy establishment at a seminar in 1988 to commemorate the fortieth anniversary of Mohammad Hatta's seminal statement.[23] Indonesia's initiative to restore diplomatic relations with China was one expression of that greater self-assertiveness in foreign policy, but it was taken in the light of changes in the regional balance or distribution of power seen to be working to the advantage of the People's Republic. To that extent, there was evident interest in cooperating with like-minded governments which argued for trying to incorporate China constructively within a post-Cold War regional order based on shared norms of interstate conduct. The problem for Indonesia has been how to reconcile such incorporation with its own long-standing sense of regional entitlement. Such a perspective rules out an intervening role for external powers, especially for a territorially dissatisfied and menacing China which is not regarded as a resident Southeast Asian state.

It was with this dilemma in mind that in May 1993 in Singapore, Indonesia joined in an unprecedented joint meeting of ASEAN's senior officials and their counterparts from dialogue partners among the industrialized states which participated in the Association's annual Post Ministerial Conference (ASEAN-PMC). At its fourth summit in January 1992, ASEAN's heads of government had decided to address regional security cooperation through "external dialogue." In May 1993, in Singapore, the senior officials recommended extending the ASEAN-PMC with security in mind to include, among other countries, China and Russia. Indonesia was among a number of governments represented which exhibited some nervousness about extending the multilateral dialogue beyond the familiar context of the Western-aligned grouping. In the event, Indonesia's representatives were persuaded of the merits of trying to encapsulate China within a structure of relations which would include the United States and Japan as well as ASEAN. At a special dinner meeting in Singapore the following July, Indonesia's Foreign Minister, Ali Alatas, together with seventeen counterparts, including China's Foreign Minister, Qian Qichen, agreed to inaugurate the ASEAN Regional Forum (ARF) as a multilateral security dialogue.[24]

By the time the ARF had convened for its first working session in Bangkok in July 1994, an institutional change had occurred within Asia Pacific Economic

Cooperation (APEC), a multilateral forum set up in 1989 to promote greater regional free trade and investment to which Indonesia and China were both parties. As a result of an initiative by President Clinton in mid-1993, annual meetings of its heads of government were convened after the regular meeting of its finance ministers. With this change in format, APEC acquired an enhanced significance and an informal security relevance given the opportunity for heads of government to address matters of mutual concern in private conversation. President Suharto did not have any qualms about participating. Indeed, he volunteered Bogor as the venue for the second APEC summit in 1994. APEC registered the dynamism of the time among the economies of Asia-Pacific and the incentive and likely constraining influence of interdependence for a country like China with pressing domestic economic priorities. APEC was therefore seen as an underpinning complementary structure to the ARF which was viewed as the security analogue of APEC. Indonesia went along with this cooperative approach to regional security which well fitted its declared philosophy of foreign policy, but with the ARF constituted geographically on a far more extensive basis than ASEAN.

Indonesia accepted the logic of employing the vehicle of multilateral security dialogue underpinned by institutionalized economic cooperation as a way of playing on China's sense of self-interest. In order to accelerate the momentum of economic development, the official view in Beijing has been that a stable regional environment is required. Indonesia has been encouraged by the extent to which the ARF is itself predicated on the security model and experience of ASEAN and to a degree by China's willing and sustained participation in inter-sessional dialogues on confidence-building, however limited their practical accomplishments. At issue for Indonesia, however, has been a concern that in engaging with China through the ARF, ASEAN may come to lose its distinct and distinctive identity and become subordinate to the wider Asia-Pacific multilateral enterprise which could then serve as the equivalent of a "Trojan horse" for the intervening attentions of external powers. In other words, the price of engaging China may be at the expense of Indonesia's exclusivist vision of regional order. That view has also been reinforced by the way in which, so far, China's participation within the ARF has not appeared to have affected the steely rectitude with which it has asserted its irredentist agenda in the South China Sea.

For Indonesia, what passes for engagement is both a process and a goal. The process has been expressed in the restoration of diplomatic relations and participation with China in multilateral enterprises within the Asia-Pacific. That process may be seen as an attempt to promote an entanglement on China's part because of the expectation that self-interest, both economic and security, will influence its conduct to Indonesia's advantage. Such an entanglement would seem directly related to the goal of engagement which has not been articulated explicitly but which may be inferred as an attempt to secure China's respect for norms of state conduct that have come to distinguish the collective culture of ASEAN and which serve the cause of a stable regional order. That said, Indonesia's government is not naive about the limitations of engagement through multilateral security dialogue within the ARF. Its salutary experience of frustration in the workshops on the South China Sea as well as concern over the incipient conflict of maritime interests with China have served to confirm an underlying apprehension which has not been assuaged by the experience of engagement. In addition, Indonesia has not come to terms with the prospect of China being able to play a leading role in Southeast Asian affairs through the vehicle of engagement.

Supplementing engagement

Indonesia cannot be described as an enthusiastic advocate of engagement with China. The decision by President Suharto to restore diplomatic relations did not express a full consensus on the part of the foreign policy elite with evident misgivings registered by the military establishment which constitutes its dominant part. Moreover, there was a grudging quality about the response of Indonesia's Department of Foreign Affairs to the advent of the ARF within which the Republic would have to cope with the diplomatic weight of the three major Asia-Pacific powers, including China. With those reservations in mind, it is important to take note of the measure of change in Indonesia's regional security policy, albeit without any declared change in principle.

Outright containment of China has never been considered a realistic proposition by Indonesia. Indeed, its defence establishment would be quite inadequate for such an ambitious undertaking. The Republic's security doctrine has been overwhelmingly inward-looking, with its navy geared primarily to coastal defence. It has been noted that, with the possible exception of the Philippines, "Indonesia still affords less attention to external security than probably any other state in Southeast Asia."[25] Moreover, it was pointed out in 1997 by the Department of Defence and Security that "in the medium-term instability will tend to be caused by internal rather than external factors."[26] That said, limited measures of collective external defence have been entered into by way of compensation for military weakness. For example, an initial irritation with Singapore for concluding a memorandum of understanding on military access with the United States in November 1990 gave way to a common outlook. The government in Jakarta speedily came to terms with the underlying intent of providing limited facilities to offset its significant loss in the Philippines as a way of helping to sustain America's military deployment in the region. Indonesia followed up with an offer of limited repair and port visit facilities at the headquarters of its Eastern Fleet in the port of Surabaya.[27] Whatever the view, in principle, of the undesirability of major external powers playing a role in Southeast Asian affairs, the United States was judged to be a necessary informal defence partner as the only countervailing force capable of balancing a rising China.

A more striking example of Indonesia's conversion to the merits of the balance of power has been registered in the security agreement concluded with Australia in December 1995, to the surprise of the Republic's Department of Foreign Affairs as well as to that of its ASEAN partners. The accord, which exhibits the spirit of an alliance, states *inter alia* that the two parties will consult "in the case of adverse challenges to either party or to their common security interests and, if appropriate, consider measures which might be taken either individually or jointly and in accordance with the processes of each party."[28] The terms of the treaty would seem to violate the traditional tenets of Indonesia's foreign policy as well as to be out of keeping with the spirit of multilateral security dialogue which both Indonesia and Australia had viewed as a prime vehicle for engagement. Moreover, the treaty had been concluded within only months of President Suharto vacating the chair of the Non-Aligned Movement; his tenure having been represented as one of the concluding triumphs of his long rule. In that respect, the treaty may be viewed as the most significant break in continuity in Indonesia's foreign policy since the late President Sukarno embarked on his ill-fated axis with China in the mid-1960s. It is important to note that, for Indonesia, the decision to conclude the treaty was made by President Suharto in great secrecy in much the same way as he had made the decision to restore diplomatic relations with China.

Indonesia's primary motivation for concluding the agreement with Australia was to institutionalize the changing dynamics of the bilateral relationship. However, China's new-found strategic latitude and rising power is believed to have played some part in Jakarta's change of course.[29] The security agreement with Australia does not have the potential for transforming Indonesia's defence capability with China's maritime assertiveness in mind but it serves to enhance it to a degree, as well as communicating an important political point to Beijing. In addition, the agreement has provided an additional linkage in defence ties with the United States with which direct defence cooperation and sales had become less reliable because of the interposing issue of East Timor. Such additional linkage was indicated in July 1996 when Australia stepped up its defence cooperation with the United States.

The bilateral security agreement between Indonesia and Australia did not in itself repudiate the ARF process. Indeed, in July 1996, Indonesia's capital served as the venue for its third working session. At issue, however, is the utility of the ARF and its related processes in an undeclared role of seeking to restrain regional assertiveness on China's part. By concluding an unprecedented security agreement with Australia, Indonesia's former president indicated his reservations about engagement through the vehicle of the ARF and conveyed a willingness to commit his government to complementary undertakings with national security in mind. Moreover, within days of concluding this accord in December 1995, President Suharto backed a proposal by Singapore's Prime Minister, Goh Chok Tong, at the meeting of ASEAN's heads of government in Bangkok that India should become a dialogue partner of the Association and also, by implication, a member of the ARF on the grounds that it would provide an element of balance to China.

A more conspicuous signal was communicated by Indonesia to China through unilateral action. Indonesia could not have failed to have noted, with some concern, China's use of military display in March 1996 in the Taiwan Strait with the object of exercising an intimidating influence on the island's presidential elections. Limited steps had already been taken for greater surveillance and protection of the Natunas and their waters by increasing air patrols from the main island of Greater Natuna and by augmenting its small garrison. In August 1997, Indonesia ordered twelve Russian Sukhoi SU-30K fighters which, according to its Air Force Planning Director Air Vice-Marshall Richard Haryono, would be deployed to assist in the maritime defence of the Natuna Islands.[30] In the previous September, Indonesia's armed forces had engaged in a conspicuous military display through combined military exercises in and around the Natuna Islands involving nearly 20,000 armed servicemen supported by fifty-four aircraft and twenty-seven naval vessels.

Irrespective of the efficacy of these operations, the largest of their kind ever staged in the Republic, it was an attempt to demonstrate Jakarta's resolve and willingness to use military force should its national resources be subject to challenge. At the time, one well-informed Indonesian commentator explained that the Republic's officials had "begun to reappraise this policy of engagement which they adopted from their neighbours" because of the growing evidence that China was "not going to be deterred" from pursuing its regional territorial ambitions. He went on to suggest that the Republic's "wariness does not mean it will deviate from a policy of constructively engaging China. But it reveals the country's growing assertiveness in shaping security arrangements in the Asia-Pacific region."[31] Moreover, it seemed more than coincidental that during the period in which the combined exercises were being conducted, Indonesia's Foreign Minister Ali Alatas was willing to receive his Taiwanese counterpart John Chang, albeit disclaiming any official status for the meeting.

This meeting provoked Chinese protest in the light of Beijing's sensitivity over President Lee Teng-hui's controversial presence in the United States the previous June and also his so-called "vacation" visit to Indonesia in February 1994. In August 1996, President Suharto had taken the unusual step of commenting publicly on the prospect of China becoming a threat to Asia, at least in economic terms, explaining that he was "concerned that it may dominate the global market with its economic power which is capable of producing low-priced goods."[32] Indeed, it had been President Suharto's astonishment at the pace and extent of China's economic development during his visit in November 1990 and his attendant concern about its regional implications, as well as recognition of the economic opportunities involved, that had influenced his government to support initiatives within ASEAN for a wider framework for regional security dialogue beyond the limited bounds of the Association.

It should be pointed out that the underlying reserve towards China on Indonesia's side has not obstructed the development of a working relationship of a kind. Reciprocal visits of senior political and military figures have taken place.

Coincidentally or not, Major-General Prabowo Subianto, then Commander of Indonesia's Special Forces and President Suharto's son-in-law, was present in Beijing concurrently with the onset of the combined military exercises in and around the Natuna Islands but without attracting hostile attention. Moreover, Foreign Minister Ali Alatas and State Secretary Moerdiono were invited to attend the ceremonies marking the reversion of sovereignty of Hong Kong to China at the end of June 1997. Trade has been a rising factor in the relationship with its two-way value put at around US$3.23 billion in 1995, with a small surplus in Indonesia's favour, compared with only US$232 million in 1984.[33] Despite presidential encouragement for increased trade relations, Indonesia's misgivings about China rise regularly above the surface, as they did when Foreign Minister Ali Alatas appeared before a Commission of Indonesia's Parliament in September 1996. He registered national concerns about its maritime assertiveness, while expressing hope that the People's Republic's participation within the ARF would have a moderating influence.[34] For its part, China has gone out of its way to strengthen the bilateral relationship. For example, US$200 million in export credit facilities has been extended, in addition to US$400 million in stand-by loans as part of an IMF rescue package. In addition to avoiding any impression of interfering in Indonesia's internal affairs over the predicament of its ethnic-Chinese community, forbearance has been shown at visits by senior figures from Taiwan where the matter at hand has been trade and investment. Such forbearance was displayed in January 1998 when Taiwan's Prime Minister Vincent Siew visited Jakarta.

The limits of engagement

Indonesia's post-Cold War relationship with China has been conducted on the basis of evident misgivings and within a context of national limitations. Irrespective of the Republic's long-standing sense of regional entitlement, it is not capable of embarking unilaterally on a policy towards China which would be able to keep the People's Republic at a distance and so assuage deep-seated anxieties about its mid- to long-term intentions. Indeed, President Suharto's decision to restore diplomatic relations reflected, in part, a pragmatic recognition of the political utility of direct communications with the government in Beijing as the Cold War was coming to an end. Beyond a diplomatic opening as a form of engagement, Indonesia was persuaded, albeit with some reluctance, of the complementary merits of encapsulating China within the framework of a multilateral regional security dialogue in an attempt to influence its external behaviour.

Indonesia had objected strongly nearly a quarter of a century before to Malaysia's proposal for the neutralization of Southeast Asia based on the guarantees of the major powers, including China. It had been argued in Jakarta that such a proposal would take the management of regional order out of the hands of its resident states and allocate virtual policing powers to those from outside. It was as an alternative to neutralization in the classical sense that in 1971 ASEAN's foreign ministers were persuaded to endorse the alternative ZOPFAN concept which was in keeping with Indonesia's regional vision.[35]

The ARF, to which Indonesia has been a party from the outset, has been based on ASEAN's model of regional security. However, its far more extensive geographic remit threatens the integrity of the ZOPFAN concept because it holds out the prospect of ASEAN's prerogative role becoming subordinate within the multilateral enterprise and with it the loss to Indonesia of a valued diplomatic centrality reflected symbolically in the location of ASEAN's Secretariat in Jakarta. Accordingly, the endorsement of the ARF has represented a pragmatic accommodation to the change in regional strategic circumstances attendant on the end of the Cold War, and especially the disturbing emergence of a new distribution of power to the apparent advantage of China. A compelling argument in favour of the ARF was not only that it would locate China within a multilateral structure of dialogue with the prospect of influencing its external conduct. It was maintained correspondingly that the collateral participation of the United States would encourage its continuing post-Cold War interest in the region as a factor in the regional balance. To that extent, Indonesia was disposed to acquiesce in the extension of cooperative security arrangements beyond the ambit of Southeast Asia because they would incorporate a balance of power factor with China in mind. Such acquiescence did not register a strong enthusiasm for engagement in the sense articulated in Washington.

Indonesia has sustained its long-standing declaratory commitment to an "independent and active foreign policy" which is fully compatible with its involvement in both the ASEAN and ARF versions of cooperative security. There has been a measure of revision in Jakarta's practice, however, in the form of limited collective defence measures complementary to the process of engagement, while unilaterally asserting a determination to protect national assets against Chinese predatory intent. The purchasing order for advanced Russian fighter aircraft in August 1997 should be viewed in that light. Naval access facilities granted to the United States and the security treaty with Australia are indications also of how Indonesia has sought to mix a measure of balance of power policy with that of engagement in managing its relations with China without being a party to any overt acts of containment.

China is not perceived as an imminent security threat in Jakarta, but it *is* viewed as casting a growing shadow which has begun to encroach on the periphery of Indonesia's archipelagic and strategic bounds. For the time being, engagement as a way of trying to encourage China in cooperative practice serves economic and, up to a point, security interests. Moreover, it is not deemed to be costly in political terms. For its part, China has responded positively up to a point. Stereotypes of China die hard in Jakarta, however, and the displays of regional good citizenship by government in Beijing have not served to dispel them. For Indonesia's foreign policy elite, engaging China is a stratagem undertaken without any deep-seated conviction in its merits and also without much enthusiasm for its outcome.

Acknowledgements

In writing this chapter I have benefited, in particular, from the helpful comments of Alan Dupont and Yuen Foong Khong.

Notes

1 Robert Lowry, *The Armed Forces of Indonesia* (Allen & Unwin, St Leonards, Australia, 1996), p.4. See also Tim Huxley, 'Indonesia's armed forces face up to new threats', *Jane's Intelligence Review*, January 1997.

2 See *The Policy of the State Defence and Security of the Republic of Indonesia 1997* (Department of Defence and Security, Jakarta, 1997), p.7.

3 For an account of the origins and assertion of that doctrine, see Michael Leifer, *Malacca, Singapore and Indonesia*, Vol.2, *International Straits of the World* (Sijthoff & Noordhoff, Alphen aan den Rijn, 1978).

4 See *The Policy of the State Defence and Security of the Republic of Indonesia* (Department of Defence and Security, Jakarta, 1995), p.12.

5 Ibid., p.14.

6 For a summary of Indonesian perceptions of China, see Franklin B. Weinstein, *Indonesia's Foreign Policy and the Dilemma of Dependence* (Cornell University Press, Ithaca, 1976), pp.88–95 and 118–25.

7 See Mohammad Hatta, *Mendajung Antara Dua Karang* (Rowing Between Two Rocks) (Djakarta, Department of Information, 1951). An English-language version of Hatta's views may be found in 'Indonesia's Foreign Policy', *Foreign Affairs*, April 1953.

8 For accounts of the ethnic-Chinese community within Indonesia as well as of the relationship between China and Indonesia up to the suspension of diplomatic relations in 1967, see Victor Purcell, *The Chinese in Southeast Asia* (Oxford University Press, London, 1965), Part vii, Leo Suryadinata, *China and the ASEAN States* (Singapore University Press, Singapore, 1985), and David Mozingo, *Chinese Policies Towards Indonesia* (Cornell University Press, Ithaca, 1976).

9 See Stephen Fitzgerald, *China and the Overseas Chinese. A Study of Peking's Changing Policy, 1949–1970* (Cambridge University Press, Cambridge, 1972).

10 A significant incident of Chinese intimidation over this episode is recounted by George McT. Kahin in 'Malaysia and Indonesia', *Pacific Affairs*, fall 1964.

11 For an account of the episode in April 1994, see Rizal Sukma, 'Recent Developments in Sino–Indonesian Relations: An Indonesian View', *Contemporary Southeast Asia*, Vol. 16, No. 1, June 1994, pp.40–3. The prominent role of ethnic Chinese in the economic life of President Suharto's Indonesia is addressed well in Adam Schwarz, *A Nation in Waiting* (Allen & Unwin, St Leonards, Australia, 1994), Chapter 5.

12 For an indication of the tone of the visit, see BBC, *Summary of World Broadcasts 15 April 1998* (FE/3201 B/4), and Michael Richardson, 'Japan's Lack of Leadership Pushes ASEAN Toward Cooperation With China', *International Herald Tribune*, 17 April 1998.

13 Xinhua News Agency, 29 September 1998, in *BBC Summary of World Broadcasts*, FE/3344 G/2.

14 See Sheldon Simon, *The Broken Triangle: Peking, Djakarta and the PKI* (The Johns Hopkins University Press, Baltimore, MD, 1969), and J.D. Armstrong, *Revolutionary Diplomacy. Chinese Foreign Policy and the United Front Doctrine* (University of California Press, Berkeley, 1977), Chapter 4.

15 For an authorized version of this episode see Nugroho Notosusanto, *The Coup Attempt of the 'September 30 Movement'* (P.T. Pembimbing Masa, Djakarta, 1968).

16 The most scholarly and comprehensive account of the issue and circumstances of

Indonesia's restoration of diplomatic relations with China may be found in Rizal Sukma, *Indonesia and China: The Politics of a Troubled Relationship* (Routledge, London and New York, 1999). See also Leo Suryadinata, *Indonesia's Foreign Policy Under Suharto* (Times Academic Press, Singapore, 1996), Chapter 7, and Michael Williams, 'Indonesia and China Make Up: Reflections on a Troubled Relationship', *Indonesia*, Special Edition, 1991.

17 For an assessment of the frustration evident in Jakarta during the course of the Cambodian conflict, see Michael Leifer, 'Indonesia in ASEAN – Fed up Being Led by the Nose', *Far Eastern Economic Review*, 3 October 1985.

18 For an account of the underlying approach to and experience of these workshops by their originator, see Hashim Djalal, *Indonesia and the Law of the Sea* (Centre for Strategic and International Studies, Jakarta, 1995), Chapters 32 and 33.

19 See Pan Shiying, *The Petropolitics of the Nansha Islands – China's Indisputable Legal Case* (Hong Kong Economic Information and Agency, Hong Kong, 1996), pp.163–4.

20 See Michael Richardson, 'China–Vietnam Dispute Revives Regional Fears', *International Herald Tribune*, 14 April 1997.

21 Note the revival of maritime assertiveness in the first half of 1997 with the establishment by China of hut-like structures on Scarborough Shoal to the north of the Spratly Islands and the passage of Chinese warships close to Philippines-occupied islands in the Spratly group. See *The Economist*, 24 May 1997.

22 See *The Policy of the State Defence and Security 1997*, p.4.

23 See Michael Leifer, *Indonesia's Foreign Policy* (George Allen & Unwin, London, 1983), p.xv and *passim*, and *The Jakarta Post*, 6 September 1988.

24 For an account of the origins and role of the ARF, see Michael Leifer, *The ASEAN Forum. Extending ASEAN's model of regional security*, Adelphi Paper No.302, International Institute for Strategic Studies, London, 1996.

25 See Alan Dupont, 'Indonesian Defence Strategy and Security: Time for a Rethink?', *Contemporary Southeast Asia*, Vol. 18, No. 3, December 1996. For an official public statement of Indonesia's defence doctrine, see *Policy of the State Defence and Security of the Republic of Indonesia, 1997*, and Robert Lowry, *The Armed Forces of Indonesia*. For an account of Indonesia's order of battle involving fewer than 300,000 military personnel (excluding police and reserves) out of a population of around 200 million with a responsibility for defending a distended archipelago with sovereign jurisdiction over an area of land and sea of almost ten million square kilometres, see *The Military Balance* (The International Institute for Strategic Studies, London, 1997/98), pp.179–81.

26 *Policy of the State Defence and Security of the Republic of Indonesia, 1997*, p.12.

27 For an Indonesian interpretation of this security burden-sharing exercise, see Jusuf Wanandi, 'ASEAN's China Engagement: Towards Deeper Engagement', *Survival*, autumn 1966, p.120.

28 The text of the treaty has been reprinted in Desmond Ball and Pauline Kerr, *Presumptive Engagement. Australia's Asia-Pacific Security Policy in the 1990s* (Allen & Unwin, St Leonards, Australia, 1996), Appendix 5. See also Rizal Sukma, 'Indonesia's Bebas-Aktif Foreign Policy and the "Security Agreement" with Australia', *Australian Journal of International Affairs*, Vol.51, No.2, 1997.

29 See the discussion in Bob Lowry, *Australia–Indonesia Security Cooperation: For Better or Worse*, Strategic and Defence Studies Centre, Working Paper No.299 (Australian National University, Canberra, August 1996), and also in Alan Dupont, 'The Australia–Indonesia Security Agreement', *Australian Quarterly*, Vol.68, No.2, 1996.

30 *The Australian*, 6 August 1997.

31 Rizal Sukma, 'Indonesia Toughens China Stance', *Far Eastern Economic Review*, 5 September 1996.

32 In a rare interview in Jakarta to the Japanese publication *Nihon Kezai Shimbun* reprinted by *Agence France Presse*, Jakarta, 14 August 1996.
33 See *Jakarta Post*, 10 September 1996.
34 See *Suara Pembaruan*, 12 September 1996.
35 See the discussion in Leifer, *Indonesia's Foreign Policy*, pp.147–54.

5

SINGAPORE

A time for economic and political engagement

Yuen Foong Khong

A defining feature of the next quarter century in international politics
will be the emergence of the Chinese juggernaut, the world's largest non-
status quo power. . . . With over 1.2 billion people, and an economy
growing at ten percent a year on a path to overtake the United States as
the world's largest economy, China comes into the international stage
with an identity, a history, and presumptions distinct from those of any
other state.[1]

China, according to the Commission on America's National Interest, is likely
to be a revisionist power with hegemonic ambitions in East Asia. A vital interest
of the United States is to prevent the emergence of such a hostile hegemon.

Singapore's Lee Kuan Yew may quarrel with the tone of the Commission's
prognosis, but he is unlikely to object to its substance. As the prime architect and
chief spokesperson of Singapore's China policy, Lee has described China's rise in
not dissimilar terms: "It's not possible to pretend that this is just another player.
This is the biggest player in the history of man." Consequently, "[t]he size of
China's displacement of the world balance is such that the world must find a new
balance in 30 to 40 years."[2] Indeed, Lee does the Commission one better by
providing a structural explanation for the source of US–China tensions:

China has the potential to become a super-power. America's interest is to
maintain the status quo, where it is the only super-power but in 30 years
China's growth could challenge this pre-eminence. So there will always
be some underlying tension in US–China relationships.[3]

The critical issue for Lee, Singapore, and arguably the world, is how to
"manage" China's growing power such that peace and stability, the prerequisites
of rapid economic growth, can be maintained in the Asia Pacific. One possible
answer is to focus on containment, as the United States and its allies did during the
Cold War. The aim of containment was to prevent the communist bloc – Russia,

China, and their allies – from expanding their influence and power, by military means if necessary. As students of the era know, although containment worked, it was a high cost and high risk strategy. It was also associated with nuclear brinkmanship, regional wars, military crises, high tensions, and political enmity. The two "hot wars" which were direct offshoots of containment and which involved the United States – Korea and Vietnam – were fought in East Asia. In part because of memories of these wars, there is a consensus among policy-makers in the Asia Pacific today that the time for containment has not yet arrived. Singaporean officials, like their United States counterparts, believe that embarking on the containment path now will be counter-productive: it is likely to lead to the very outcome to be averted; namely, a paranoid and militarily aggressive China.[4]

Singapore's preferred response is to engage China. This chapter suggests that Singapore has adopted a three-pronged approach to engaging China. The first and most important prong focuses on economic engagement, which consists of providing China with a set of economic incentives that allows it to prosper and develop a stake in the existing "rules of the game." A China doing well by these rules will have strong disincentives against upsetting or revising these rules through conflict and war. This understanding is manifested in a China policy which seeks to fully integrate China into the regional and world economy.[5]

Political engagement is the second prong of Singapore's policy. Political engagement is more than diplomacy as usual, in that China is viewed less as an adversary and more as an important, legitimate player in the Asia Pacific whose participation and cooperation in regional initiatives are to be welcomed. This has not always been Singapore's perspective; in fact, for much of the 1960s and 1970s, political disengagement would be a better characterization of Singapore's China policy. Since the early 1980s however, Singapore has had excellent informal relations with China. The then Prime Minister and current Senior Minister, Lee Kuan Yew, has been granted access to the Chinese leadership available to few other foreign leaders. Beyond bilateral engagement, Singapore has also been very active in engaging China as a member of ASEAN. China has been an invited "observer" to ASEAN's Post-Ministerial Conference (PMC) since 1992, ASEAN-China senior officials' meetings have become institutionalized, and, despite its initial reservations, China is playing its part in the ASEAN Regional Forum (ARF).

Both economic and political engagement aim to facilitate the creation of a China that takes the "rules of the [interstate] game" seriously, i.e. a China that adheres to contemporary norms of international behavior. Such a China will respect the territorial integrity and political sovereignty of other states and refrain from using military force to settle disputes. Diplomacy and negotiations will be its preferred mode of settling differences and it will not seek drastic changes in the very rules of the game. Singapore's interest in advocating and pursuing an engagement strategy is not to uphold the rules of the game in some abstract way. A China that subscribes to the rules and norms of contemporary international society is less likely to destabilize the Asia Pacific; investments can continue to flow in, commercial transactions can continue uninterrupted, and trading states like Singapore can continue to prosper. A China that flouts those rules is likely to force Japan to rearm and acquire nuclear weapons, thus delivering a double whammy to the security of Southeast Asia. Singapore will suffer the repercussions of an assertive China most: Singapore's neighbors and friends might begin to wonder whether Singapore – being 77 percent ethnic Chinese – will bandwagon with China and perhaps even do its bidding in Southeast Asia.[6] Although Singapore has made strenuous efforts to cast itself as a Southeast Asian state, its political and military security are more easily upheld if the region experiences a well-behaved China.

While engagement is the preferred mode to getting a well-behaved China, Singapore's leaders would be remiss to place all their hopes in the engagement basket. Hence the existence of a third prong or a fall-back position. Simultaneous with economic and political engagement, Singapore – like most in ASEAN – is also modernizing its armed forces and augmenting its military strength. Defense spending in constant US dollars has clearly shown an upward trend since 1987, even though it remains around 6 percent of GNP. Since Singapore's traditional security concerns have focused on its closest neighbors, and since the latter are also increasing their arms spending, one should be cautious about attributing Singapore's arms buildup to an emerging China. It would be more accurate to attribute Singapore's – and its neighbors – military spending to the strategic uncertainty pervading the Asia Pacific.[7] However strong Singapore's defense posture, it cannot act as a deterrent against China; its utility lies in acting in concert with other Southeast Asian states. Should economic and political engagement fail, Singapore, along with the rest of ASEAN, will most likely move in the direction of the US–Japan alliance.[8] In this worst-case scenario, a militarily capable Singapore, together with ASEAN, will at least be poised to augment the US–Japan deterrence posture in non-negligible ways.

These three facets of Singapore's engagement policy accord well with the notion of engagement adopted by this volume. China is recognized as a rising power, with possible non-status quo ambitions. Singapore has no wish, nor does it see it possible or wise, to block the growth of Chinese power. The goal is to ensure that China's growing power will be channeled in peaceful and productive directions, or, in this volume's terms, "used in ways that are consistent with peaceful change in the regional and global order." Singapore's preferred means of achieving this goal, as manifested in its economic and political approaches to China, are predominantly non-coercive.[9] They stress the provision of incentives to make it possible for China to prosper and feel secure, on the assumption that a prosperous and secure China will develop a vested interest in the existing rules of the game. A China that takes these rules seriously is more conducive to regional order than one that seeks their whole-scale revision.

What follows elaborates on the content of each of these components of Singapore's engagement strategy and the reasoning or logic behind them. The single best source for piecing together these components are the frequent public discourses on China by Senior Minister Lee Kuan Yew. As Singapore's Prime Minister from 1959 to 1990, Lee has been the chief formulator of the republic's foreign policy, especially that toward China. Despite having relinquished the prime ministership, Lee remains the prime architect and chief spokesperson of Singapore's China policy. Whether measured by length, frequency, or profundity, Lee's pronouncements on Singapore's China policy tower above those of his cabinet colleagues. Moreover, Lee's prestige as a strategic analyst both within Singapore and internationally adds to the seriousness with which his comments are taken. The pronouncements of Lee's cabinet colleagues, including Prime Minister Goh Chok Tong, will also be consulted, although they tend to be less systematic and detailed than Lee's. The interpretation of these discourses is helped considerably if the following caveats about their context are borne in mind.

Assured and confident though Singapore may be on "Asian values" and "Asian democracy," it has always demonstrated a certain humility about its place when it comes to great power relationships. Singapore's leaders understand that by itself, Singapore can do little to shape the security dynamics of the Asia Pacific. There might be some understatement here, since Singapore has consistently succeeded in punching above its weight, whether in helping draft the concept paper detailing the ARF's future trajectory, housing the APEC Secretariat, persuading ASEAN to reach out to Europe via an Asia-Europe Meeting (ASEM) and the Asia-Europe Foundation, or through Lee Kuan Yew's intellectually weighty and much sought-after counsel. Still, Singaporean officials are realistic about the limits of the island-state's influence. At the global level, it assumes and counts on a United States supporting, if not underwriting, a liberal economy, a system of military alliances, and a credible forward military presence in the Asia Pacific. In this context, Singapore sees itself – sometimes together with its ASEAN neighbors, sometimes against them – as playing a supporting role by welcoming American, Japanese, and European investments (and hence giving them an economic stake in the region); bringing together the major powers through the regional institutions; exhorting the Americans when their will is lagging, and providing naval facilities for their vessels when circumstances require it.[10]

What the above implies is that by itself, Singapore does not expect to have much influence over China. Is it a misnomer then to speak of its policy as one of engaging China? Not at all. Engagement is a process in which interested members of the international community can participate; nothing in our definition suggests that to qualify as an "engager," states like Singapore – or Malaysia or Indonesia – must be able to unilaterally move the "engagee" toward the goal of using its power responsibly.[11] In fact it is important to separate the process of engagement from the engager's ability to realize the goal (of engagement): if the latter were part of one's notion of engagement, even the United States may not qualify as an "engager."[12] Thus Singapore's inability to unilaterally change China does not prevent it from engaging China on multiple fronts: bilaterally and in concert with its ASEAN and Asian Pacific partners such as the United States and Japan.

A second point is that the pronouncements of Singaporean officials are often more than just an elaboration or explanation of Singapore's strategic perspective. They tend also to be "calculated perceptions";[13] that is, they are part of a self-conscious and explicit discourse aimed at influencing the relevant audiences. More than others in the region, Singapore's leaders – especially Lee – are aware that "voice" plays an important role in shaping the terms of any debate (in this case the vociferous debate about whether to engage or contain China) and they have not been shy about making their version heard. Thus even when Lee speaks to the People's Action Party's (PAP) constituency leaders, he seems to be addressing China, Taiwan, and the United States: how else is one to interpret a speech with nothing about local politics but in which every single one of its twenty paragraphs is devoted to the US–China–Taiwan issue?[14] This kind of speech-act does raise questions about the extent to which the speech is an adjunct to the act and how seriously we should take the narrative or analysis contained within it. This chapter does not pretend to have an answer to this question other than to note that the narratives examined here are not only intuitively plausible, but are also more elaborate and "fleshed out" than most policy makers' "theories" (such as the domino theory) with which we are familiar. It will be sufficient for the purposes of this chapter to treat Lee Kuan Yew and his colleagues' ruminations and narratives as conjectures, but conjectures that provide insight into Singapore's China policy.

Finally, the time frame for Singapore's ruminations about China is not now, or even five years down the line; it is twenty to thirty years hence. In analyzing Singaporean statements therefore, it is important to remember that they are referring to long-term developments, with the implication that there is time to act and that what one does between now and the distant future will affect the outcome. As the classic anticipatory state, its leaders have been trained to think in terms of possible scenarios for the future and how they might affect Singapore. They waste little time in glorifying past successes or fuming over present dilemmas: their energies are aimed at positioning Singapore to enable it to take advantage of future developments while avoiding dangerous currents.

The origins of Singapore's engagement discourse

Singapore's Lee Kuan Yew has believed in the importance and necessity of engaging China for at least thirty years. In his first meeting with Richard Nixon, in April 1967, the former Vice-President asked Lee what US policy toward China ought to be. Lee's answer then was that the line drawn by the United States "across the Taiwan Straits was a line drawn on water and need not be perpetual. There was much to be gained by engaging China." Two years later in the White House, Lee reiterated the same point – "there was something to be gained by engaging China because it was a key player in Asia" – to President Nixon and his National Security Adviser, Henry Kissinger.[15]

While Lee was free to counsel Nixon on the benefits of America's engaging China, Singapore's own room for maneuver was more restricted. In the 1960s China was still providing material and moral support to communist insurgents in virtually all the ASEAN states. Indonesia, Malaysia, and Singapore considered China to be a major threat to their national security. As a state with a pre-dominant Chinese population, Singapore found itself in an unusually delicate position: it was suspicious of China but it also had to worry about Malaysian and Indonesian suspicions – however unjustified – that it (Singapore) may be China's henchman in the region. Sensitivity to the latter explains why Singapore took the position that it would only establish diplomatic relations with China after Indonesia had done so.

Deng Xiaoping's visit to Singapore in 1978 was a turning point in Singapore–China relations. While Deng's strategic aim was to corral support for an anti-Vietnam coalition from the ASEAN states of Thailand, Malaysia, and Singapore, he was also keen to see for himself the economic payoffs associated with the more open market economies of ASEAN. By the time he left, Singaporean officials knew that Deng had seen China's economic future in Singapore. Singapore was Deng's preferred model because it showed that rapid economic growth was not inconsistent with tight central governmental control.

In the 1980s Singapore began to play advisory as well as investment roles in China's economic modernization. The architect of Singapore's successful economic strategy, Dr Goh Keng Swee, was appointed special adviser to two special economic zones. In 1986, ninety Singaporean companies had invested US$200 million in China; in 1992, Singaporean companies were involved in 700 projects, worth about US$1 billion, in China.[16] The Singapore government signed an agreement with China in 1993 to build an entire township, known as the Suzhou Industrial Park (SIP), where business will be done Singapore-style, i.e. with superior infrastructure, bureaucratic efficiency, probity, and general predictability. The Park had attracted about US$2 billion worth of investments by 1996, although the development of a rival park nearby has raised questions about SIP's future profitability. Although Singapore would be deeply disappointed if the SIP project falters, it is unlikely to alter Singapore's continued economic engagement of China. China's economic take-off in the 1980s elicited widespread praise from the international community. Lee Kuan Yew was among those who saw a link between such economic progress and peace:

> China is seeking growth through trade, not territorial aggrandisement. Its quest for a better life for its people is through peaceful cooperation in trade, investments and transfer of technology and know how, not the use of force for territorial conquests and the carving out of a sphere of influence or a trading bloc.

Comparing Deng's era with that of Mao, Lee proclaimed:

China's decision [to open up] is a most significant factor for peace, stability and growth in Asia. For nearly 30 years, from 1949 until Mao died in 1976, a poor but ideological fervent China was a ceaseless spoiler of other countries' economic plans as it undermined their stability. It was an exporter of revolution. It provided arms, ideology and radio support to guerrilla insurgencies in Southeast Asia. China has, for the present discontinued such support.[17]

Four years later, as the Cold War was winding down, Lee sought to spell out the consequences of America's withdrawal from the Philippines. He saw "medium powers" jockeying to be the "front runner" if the United States left. Lee's explanation for this will to power was based on his conception of human nature: "That's the way human beings have been. In tribes, in smaller nations and in modern big nations." Interestingly, the medium powers he identified as potential muscle flexers were India and Vietnam, not China.[18] The omission of China is quite comprehensible: China had been a helpful ally of ASEAN in putting pressure on Vietnam to withdraw from Cambodia, the Soviet Union was still a force to reckon with in Asia, the Taiwan issue was dormant, and Singapore was actively participating in China's economic liberalization. In fact, even in the early 1990s, it was Japan, and not China, that struck American and Singaporean observers as the possible new contender in Asia. In the United States, worries about economic decline went hand-in-hand with consternation about Japan as the new aggressive economic juggernaut playing by a different set of rules. In Singapore, Lee's response to Japan's participation in a United Nations peacekeeping force in Cambodia was the pithy, "It's like giving liquor chocolates to an alcoholic."

It was in 1992 or 1993 that China became the object of widespread consternation. Perhaps this was the lagged aftermath of the Tiananmen crackdown: there had been too many breathtaking and world-transforming events in the intervening years to notice China's rising power or contemplate its implications. Or perhaps for those in need of an (adversarial) "other" in order to define "themselves," the implosion of the Soviet Union and the bursting of the Japanese economic bubble left them with no plausible "other" other than China. More likely, that was the year in which the National People's Congress approved a maritime law reaffirming China's claim to virtually all of the South China Sea and "empowering" the People's Liberation Army to enforce those claims.

Memories of the less pleasant side of Chinese international behavior began to surface. China had used force to eject Vietnamese troops from Paracel Islands in the South China Sea in 1974 and 1988. Tiananmen and China's treatment of its dissidents indicated its disregard for democratic norms, which in turned reinforced worries about its willingness to abide by international norms. In February 1995, Chinese naval forces occupied Mischief Reef in the Spratly Islands, which was also claimed by the Philippines. The high point of Chinese belligerence was of course the launching of a series of "missile tests" off the coast of Taiwan between July 1995 and March 1996. The last batch of "tests" – just prior to the Taiwanese elections – caused the United States to dispatch two aircraft-carrier groups to Taiwan and some rather acrimonious exchanges between Chinese and US officials.

While Singapore had always taken a contrary view of the Tiananmen crackdown to that of the United States' or CNN's – in essence viewing the demonstrating students as impatient and arguing that they could have achieved their objectives with a longer term strategy – it too began to seriously contemplate the implications of China's growing power. China's growth became viewed as an opportunity *as well as* a challenge. Singapore's point of entry into this debate – as articulated by Senior Minister Lee – was that issues of human rights and democracy have "distracted attention away from the world's major challenge in the next century: to obtain China's cooperation in maintaining world peace, stability and prosperity, as it emerged as a great power in the next 20 to 30 years."[19] According to Lee,

> [p]eace and security will turn on whether China emerges as a xenophobic, chauvinistic force, bitter and hostile to the West because it tried to slow down or abort its development, or educated and involved in the ways of the world, more cosmopolitan, more internationlised and outward looking.[20]

It should be apparent from this passage that, for Lee, a xenophobic China is the likely outcome if the international community tries to restrict its growth. For a cosmopolitan China, the international community should educate and involve China in the ways of the world. It is now possible to examine the path by which such a form of engagement is to bring about an outward looking and responsible China.

Economic engagement and its incentives

Of the three prongs of Singapore's engagement policy, the economic prong is best developed, in theory and in practice. The basic idea is that a China engaged in profitable economic activities and international trade will continue to want more of a good thing. Hegemonic ambitions, irredentist tendencies, and memories of national humiliation (and the urge to right historical wrongs) will not disappear, but they are likely to be held in check by the greater glory and comfort of being rich. Over time, China will develop a stake in not just the rules of the international economic game (such as the WTO or APEC) but also the underlying political norms and practices that make commerce possible.[21] In Lee's own words:

> As China's development nears the point when it will have enough weight to elbow its way into the region, it will make a fateful decision – whether

to be a hegemon, using its economic and military weight to create a sphere of influence in the region for its economic and security needs, or to continue as a good international citizen abiding by international rules to achieve even better economic growth.

Meanwhile, the world should give China "every incentive to choose international cooperation over hegemony," for the former will absorb China's energies "constructively for another 50 to 100 years." Thus:

> China must have the economic opportunities to do this peacefully, without having to push its way to get resources like oil, and have access to markets for its goods and services. There are fair and equitable rules in multilateral organizations like WTO for a free exchange of goods and services, so that each country can stay within its borders and improve its people's well-being through trade, investments and other exchanges. . . .
>
> If such a route is not open to China, then I say the world must live with a pushy China. . . . All countries in Asia, medium and small, [will then] have this concern: will China seek to re-establish its traditional pattern of international relations of vassal states in a tributary relationship with the Middle Kingdom? Any signs of this will alarm all the countries in the region, and cause most, not all, countries to realign themselves closer to the US and Japan. . . . The United States should use the time available to encourage and help China to integrate itself into the world community, and to play a part in shaping the international order.[22]

This is a remarkably elaborate and revealing theory about the importance and dynamics of engaging China.[23] Several observations are in order. First, running through this theory of economic engagement is the conviction that the point of fateful decision is not yet here; it is in fact a generation – twenty to thirty years – away. The implication is that there is time to act, and how the international community chooses to treat China in the interregnum will have a direct bearing on the China that emerges. Second, economic incentives provide the master key to China's good naturedness; the imperative to be rich is able to suppress or deflect other possible desires such as the will to power.[24] It is pointless to speculate about China's internal politics because foreigners can do little more than set up a system of external incentives that rewards rather than frustrates coalitions favoring economic growth. In this sense Singapore's attitude is closer to that of Indonesia and Malaysia's than to the United States.[25] The political "thinness" of this model of engagement can be seen in the process by which China is supposed to be socialized into being a responsible member of the global community. Lee is counting on Chinese students who are educated in the advanced industrial democracies to return home and eventually take over when the present generation retires:

Every year there are more Chinese students, scientists and officials studying in America, Europe and Japan. The Chinese people will change in order to plug into the global community to maximise their growth and development. However, China will change in keeping with its own history and culture and at is own pace. . . . America's greatest long term influence on China comes from playing host to the thousands of students who come every year from China, some of the ablest of Chinese scholars and scientists. They will be the most powerful agents for change in China.[26]

The motor of change remains the "dynamics of economic development"; the agents, Chinese nationals with Wharton MBAs, or Stanford Ph.Ds keen on plugging China into the global economy and community. Implicit in this emphasis on students educated abroad may be the notion that they are the likely locus of China's "liberalizing coalitions," and economic engagement is likely to strengthen their position while weakening that of anti-liberalizing or "statist–nationalist" coalitions.[27] There are also echoes of Lee's and Singapore's past here. The generation that led Singapore to independence and sustained economic growth were all educated abroad and they learned their economics and politics from Cambridge and London. They may have sought political inspiration from Harold Laski, but they would find P.T. Bauer's economic teachings more helpful when it came to deciding whether and how to plug Singapore into the world economy. The second echo is Deng's 1978 visit to Singapore: if he was able to adopt the Singapore model for China after a short visit, it stands to reason that Chinese students who have lived and breathed neoclassical economics and liberal democracy while abroad are likely to adopt and implement some of these principles at home, especially when enough of them rise to positions of power within the next twenty years. Hence Lee's advice to the hosts of these Chinese students: invest in this younger generation of potential Chinese leaders.[28]

Not surprisingly, Singapore has matched Lee's words with deeds. As Chan Heng Chee puts it, "The PRC looks to Singapore as a potential source of capital, business enterprise, and technical and managerial skills." Singapore has provided all these in abundance because it sees China "as a vast potential market and a business partner."[29] Throughout the 1980s Singapore engaged China economically. In 1986, Dr Goh Keng Swee became economic adviser to China for developing the special economic zones of Zhuhai and Shenzhen. Bilateral agreements on investment protection, tourism, and double taxation were also signed.[30] Economic engagement and cooperation culminated in the 1993 China–Singapore agreement to build from scratch a township of twenty-seven square miles where things would be run the Singapore way. Thousands of Chinese nationals are also studying, working, or performing post-doctoral work in Singapore's tertiary institutions and research institutes. Within its limits, Singapore seems to be practicing what it is exhorting America, Europe, and Japan to do in terms of socializing China's next generation of leaders.

Beyond bilateral efforts, Singapore has also been keen to elicite Chinese participation in regional economic initiatives such as APEC and ASEM. Acting in concert with other ASEAN members, it has been possible to assuage Chinese fears about American domination of APEC. ASEM was a Singaporean idea – hatched in the aftermath of the Seattle APEC meeting as a means of reassuring Europe – implemented under the auspices of ASEAN; and China is enthusiastic about ASEM in part because it may be considered an economic counterweight to APEC. Singapore has been at the forefront in championing China's early admission into the WTO. In sum, Singapore is practicing, at both the bilateral and multilateral levels, the very kind of economic engagement it is counting on to make China into a responsible member of the international community.

Political engagement and its sensitivities

Until the establishment of Singapore–China diplomatic relations in 1990, official bilateral political engagement lagged behind economic engagement. Singapore had delayed formalizing diplomatic relations with China until all the other ASEAN states – Indonesia in particular – had done so. This was a policy born out of geopolitical necessity as well as deference to the ethnic sensitivities of Singapore's neighbors. Always conscious of the fact that it is "a Chinese island in a Malay sea," Singapore is anxious to dispel any impressions that it is an outpost of China.[31] Any hint that Singapore is doing China's bidding in Southeast Asia will seriously strain relations with Indonesia and Malaysia (which have historical suspicions about China) as well as endanger Singapore's national security. Hence there is a self-imposed limit on the extent to which Singapore can pursue political engagement on a bilateral basis. Perhaps this also explains why Lee Kuan Yew's notion of engagement is predominantly economic.

Singapore's sensitivity to the ethnic factor has not been limited to the timing of diplomatic relations with China or its diplomats' insistence on using English (with their Chinese interlocutors) and interpreters even when they are Mandarin speakers. In recent years, Singaporean leaders have also found it necessary to point out that the republic's extensive investments in China are based on the profit motive and not on ethnic solidarity. Home Affairs Minister Wong Kan Seng, for example, was anxious to dismiss perceptions of Singapore as a "third China" as "absurd" and "utter rubbish." Singapore's China policy, according to Wong, was "founded on the premise of economic opportunities, not ethnic affinity."[32]

There have also been domestic ramifications. In the 1997 general elections, the ruling PAP turned on an opposition candidate, lawyer Tang Liang Hong, with unusual vehemence. Concerned about Tang's ability to draw the crowds and worried about the possibility that he might play the racial card, the PAP went on the offensive. Tang was branded as a dangerous Chinese chauvinist who not only threatened inter-ethnic peace in Singapore but also regional stability. In the context of an emerging China, it was deemed dangerous for Singapore to identify ethnically and culturally with China, something that Tang might champion as a

Member of Parliament. The government's efforts to construct a Southeast Asian identity – necessary for Singapore's survival – would be undermined. Tang had to be prevented from winning a parliamentary seat and the PAP brought out its heavy hitters – Prime Minister Goh and Senior Minister Lee – to warn the electorate about Tang.[33] There is no need to get into the lawsuits launched by the PAP leaders against Tang and the resulting political spillovers that led to a major Malaysia–Singapore quarrel. The more pertinent point is that for Singapore, engaging China politically does not extend to cultural/emotional identification with China – in fact the two must be rigorously separated in part because Singapore's leaders take the multi-racial character of their society seriously, but also because, according to Singapore's Minister for Information and the Arts, George Yeo, "the long-term peace and stability in the Asia Pacific will partly depend on this clear distinction being made, not just by ethnic Chinese outside China but also by China itself."[34] A major tenet of Singapore's foreign policy is not to be China's agent in Southeast Asia.

Engaging China multilaterally via regional political institutions such as ASEAN, the PMC, ARF, APEC, and ASEM is also an important component of Singapore's policy. For much of the 1980s, ASEAN and China cooperated to put pressure on Vietnam and the State of Cambodia. China participated in the founding of the ARF and, although it harbored initial reservations about the enterprise, it has gradually warmed to the idea, especially after discovering that ASEAN was determined to run the Forum according to its own agenda and not that of the United States or Japan. After China's occupation of Mischief Reef in 1995, an ASEAN–China senior officials' meeting in Hangzhou proved useful because ASEAN remonstrated with China in unison. Somewhat taken aback by the display of ASEAN unity, China went to the Brunei ARF agreeing to discuss the South China Sea on a multilateral basis with ASEAN. At a another recent ASEAN–China senior officials meeting in Huangshan, China was keen to sign an accord on the Pacific settlement of disputes in the South China Sea. Initiatives like ASEM also give China an opportunity to band together with the rest of Asia – without the United States – to engage Europe. Coming at a time when China is anxious to show the United States that it can seek alternative economic and strategic partners, ASEM is likely to grow in importance in the years ahead.

China is therefore voluntarily enmeshed in a web of Asian Pacific institutions. Neither Lee Kuan Yew nor other Singaporean ministers have fleshed out the implications of these kinds of multilateral, constant, criss-crossing political interactions and engagement. But officials who have participated in such consultations and consensus-building sessions admit that they play important confidence-building roles and help jack up comfort levels essential in securing cooperative outcomes. Lee himself has alluded to the inadequacy of relying on "the old power politics of the world . . . to accommodate China's growing strength" and to the necessity of trying out new arrangements where "there will be many discussions between officials and ministers as they meet informally, and a consensus will develop."[35] Here, the politicians may be a step behind international relations theorists who argue that repeated interactions in such multilateral settings may actually transform states' definitions of self-interest in more cooperative directions.[36]

Nixon's (and Singapore's) fall-back position

Lee's understanding of economic man, together with his intimate familiarity with China, gives him confidence that engagement has a good chance of working. But, like most of his ASEAN neighbors, he refuses to be caught unprepared should it fail. Lee's view on the importance of having a fall-back position was made explicit in his remarks to a group of Nixonites on the occasion of his receiving the Architect of the New Century Award from the Nixon Center. Part of Lee's acceptance speech has already been cited earlier, and most of it was devoted to spelling out how important it was for the United States to engage China. Toward the end of his remarks, Lee summarized his position by invoking (the ghost of) Nixon: "President Nixon was a pragmatic strategist. He would engage, not contain, China, but he would also quietly, if I know him, set pieces into place for a fall back position should China not play in accordance with the rules as a good global citizen."[37]

In not so many words, Lee had also revealed Singapore's and arguably ASEAN's position. But what does setting "pieces into place" involve? Lee did elaborate:

> In such circumstances, where countries are forced to take sides, he [Nixon] would arrange to win over to America's side of the chess-board, Japan, Korea, Asean, Australia, New Zealand and the Russian Federation, for in 30 years, maybe less, Russia may again be on the march.[38]

On Singapore's side, preparing for this worst-case scenario involves modernizing its armed forces, increasing their technological sophistication, and maintaining constant vigilance. Should China prove unsocializable and should it show increasing signs of flexing its military muscles (as in repeated skirmishes in the South China Sea), Singapore, in unison with ASEAN, is likely to move closer to the US–Japan and Australia–New Zealand–United States alliance systems.[39] In this sense, arguments about how ASEAN states like Singapore and Malaysia are likely to bandwagon with a rich and mighty China on ethnic or civilizational grounds betray a lack of understanding of the security dynamics of the region.[40]

Engagement and its preliminary results

Has Singapore's three-pronged approach to engagement led to any of the anticipated results? Bearing in mind that Lee was talking about a twenty- to thirty-year process, it is probably too early to expect real results. Moreover, the question is unanswerable with respect to Singapore; however intense or significant Singapore's engagement of China may be, it will have only minor influence on China's international predilections. The better question may be: if one assumes that the international community has, by and large, engaged China since the mid-1980s, have there been any noticeable results so far?

The answer is mixed, as might be expected at such an early stage. On the minus side of the ledger are instances when China used force, such as the 1988 military clash with Vietnamese forces in the Paracel Islands, or tried military intimidation such as the test firing of missiles during the Taiwanese elections of March 1996. The occupation of Mischief Reef in 1995, the extensiveness of its claims in the South China Sea, and its unwillingness to negotiate with other claimants about the sovereignty of contested parts of the South China Sea suggest a haughty and opportunistic power capable of using force to achieve its aims.

On the plus side China has exhibited a willingness to join existing multilateral economic and security institutions such as APEC, WTO, ARF, and ASEM. Joining such institutions implies recognizing their legitimacy and a willingness to abide by their rules and understandings. An aspiring hegemon bent on revising the international order would be wiser to keep some distance from such institutions. Even seeking exemptions from the rules or exploiting their loopholes suggest acceptance of their general framework. In other words, the first step in engagement requires that the actor to be engaged is part of, and participates in, the relevant institutions. China seems to have met this requirement.

Bilateral diplomacy gives great powers more leverage over smaller powers; hence joining these multilateral institutions implies some willingness to trade that leverage for some other goals (such as cultivating a good reputation). Multilateral interaction might also allow one to be persuaded on certain issues. For example, China had initial reservations about joining the ARF for fear of being ganged up upon. On discovering that ASEAN was more interested in being a neutral arbiter than a henchman of "the West," China became less anxious. Michael Leifer has written about how Australian Foreign Minister Gareth Evans, through his "strident intervention," persuaded China to relent to intersessionary ARF meetings between government officials.[41] China also came to the second ARF meeting agreeing to discuss the South China Sea on a multilateral basis with ASEAN, something it had previously refused to do. In March 1997, China and the Philippines (of all parties!) co-chaired in Beijing an ARF intersessionary seminar on confidence-building measures.[42] Johnston and Evans have found preliminary evidence that China has become less reluctant to participate in regional institutions and regimes over time and that China's participation may have encouraged it to re-evaluate its national interests on some issues.[43]

Still, in recent years Lee has found it necessary to qualify or refine his rather economistic view of what it means to engage China. He has had to incorporate some political "nos" into his notion of engagement. According to Lee, issues like MFN, intellectual property, and WTO are negotiable issues for China; the "integrity" or "unity" of China, however, is not. Taiwan and Tibet are "neuralgic" areas over which China is willing to risk war. Lee came to this conclusion as a result of an August 1995 meeting with Chinese Premier Li Peng and President Jiang Zemin. Concerned about the state of US–Chinese relations and their impact on economics, he told the Chinese leaders that if Chinese–US relations "remained unstable and tensions across the Taiwan Straits high, Singapore's industrial park project in Suzhou would not take off." The response: "Jiang listened. Li listened. But they said nothing." Three days later, Vice-Premier Li Lanqing, the official in charge of the Suzhou project gave Lee a reply: "Taiwan must understand it cannot continue to go down this road (of leveraging the US against the mainland in pursuit of greater independence), but if it does, then we cannot rule out the use of force." For Lee, this "was not an off-the-cuff comment, but a considered response after three days of consultation at the top" and it meant that "China's unity cannot be subordinated to China's economic development"; "if necessary, Suzhou or other such development projects may have to wait a decade or more." Hence his advice to the United States and those serious about engaging China (such as Singapore): accept that both Tibet and Taiwan are part of China and stop challenging this reality.[44]

Conclusion

Singapore's leaders feel that they already know China and Chinese economic man well. The number one priority for China's leaders and people is economic modernization so that China will be a prosperous, industrialized country by 2020. Frustrate those economic hopes, and other less laudable tendencies – hyper-nationalism, militaristic irredentism – will creep to the fore.[45] Hence anything that Singapore, ASEAN, and the international community (i.e. the United States, Europe, and Japan) can do to facilitate China's economic modernization will be beneficial to the economic prosperity and political-military security of the Asia Pacific. China will concentrate on getting rich; it will develop a stake in the existing rules of the political-economic game; and it will be a satisfied great power.

This is a profoundly economic take on the process and consequences of engagement. Singapore's assumption is that when Deng Xiaoping unleashed the forces of capitalism in China twenty years ago and experimented with "socialism with Chinese characteristics," an irreversible process was set in motion. For Lee, China's growth was unstoppable because of its immense size and hugh potential; moreover, "there was nothing which Taiwan, Hong Kong and Singapore had done which China could not do."[46] Prime Minister Goh concurs: "I do not believe that China's growth can be stifled. The genie is already out of the bottle. . . . There is sufficient internal dynamism for China to grow robustly even without outside help."[47] Given these assumptions, facilitating rather than frustrating China's growth is the safer bet.

The assumption that a rich, strong China is likely to be responsible instead of vengeful also reflects Singapore and ASEAN's experience. Singapore's single-minded devotion to the economic well-being of its citizens has occupied the energies of its leaders since independence. Success has given it a vested interest and unusual influence in upholding the (existing) rules of international economic and political order, whether it is Tommy Koh chairing the UN's Law of the Sea conference, Lee Kuan Yew exhorting the United States Congress to keep America's markets open in the 1980s, Singapore fighting for the right to host the inaugural meeting of the WTO, or initiating ASEM to induce the European Union to take Asia seriously.

Equally relevant is ASEAN's experience with post-Sukarno Indonesia. Sukarno's preference for revolutionary nationalism and regional hegemony over economic development plunged the region into turmoil and military strife. Suharto reversed those priorities, emphasized economic modernization, and brought interstate relationships in the region to an even keel. A China similarly bent on economic development – and given the opportunity to do so – is likely to renounce hegemony; in time, it may even be as pro-active as Singapore in upholding the rules and norms that have underwritten its material progress.

Singapore's leaders will not deny that this emphasis on economic engagement serves Singapore's economic interests. Singaporean firms have invested close to US$1 billion in China. If the capital and technology-rich countries were to stop engaging China and opt for economic isolation or containment, it would make it all that much harder for Singapore to profit from its investments. Lee's theory of economic engagement also legitimizes Singapore's "go regional" strategy where its entrepreneurs are encouraged to invest in, and reap profits from, the opening and expansion of regional economies such as China, Vietnam, Laos, and Myanmar.

In recent years, however, the pure and optimistic version of economic engagement has had to be tempered by messier political variables. Taiwan and to a lesser extent Tibet have been introduced as "neuralgic" areas over which China may risk war even if they retard China's economic progress. This brings us to the second prong of Singapore's engagement strategy: political engagement. Lee's position on Taiwan and Tibet is unambiguous: they are part of China and those serious about engaging China politically should treat them as such. Lee's patience with Taiwanese President Lee Tenghui's "creeping independence" has clearly been exhausted. Referring to China's missile diplomacy during the Taiwanese elections, Lee opined that "The region has not reacted with alarm because regional countries understand what it is about." But Lee stopped short of saying China could do what it liked. His recent speeches also contain a warning to China:

> But actual use of force is another thing altogether. The countries of the region will not understand why China cannot be patient and resolve the matter peacefully, when using force will damage both China and Taiwan, and also hurt third parties, the countries of ASEAN and East Asia.[48]

Lee's penchant for talking straight to the Chinese in public and in private – and to be taken seriously – is a form of political engagement available to few others.[49] It is unclear if Singapore will have that clout after Lee passes from the scene. But, even with Lee around, Singapore has devoted enormous energies to engaging China via ASEAN, and ASEAN-related institutions such as the PMC, ARF, and ASEM. In the future, an increasing proportion of Singapore's engagement strategy is likely to be channeled through multilateral venues like the ARF and ASEM. The theory of how bilateral and multilateral political engagement might "tame" China is not well articulated, perhaps because they do not seem to be that different from normal diplomacy. Unlike some of its neighbors, Singapore has not pushed the idea of an Asian Pacific community and how such an identity might lead to common definitions of interests. Such transformative notions are probably at variance with the world views of those who lead Singapore, who prefer the language of interests and incentives. Which leads to the third prong of Singapore's engagement strategy: have a fall-back position because there is no guarantee that engagement will work. Letting China know that one is not disarming or repudiating the United States while one is actively engaging China will also give the latter extra incentive to take engagement seriously.

More than a decade ago, one of the editors of this volume had already anticipated "the future dilemma for Asia" as "adjustment to the rise of a new power [China]." Ross worried about the historical inability of nation-states to make that adjustment peacefully but went on to suggest: "If there is one lesson that can be gleaned from the European experience, it is not that accommodation is an inherently flawed policy but that accommodation from strength, rather than from weakness, is a surer way to socialize peacefully a new power into an existing order."[50] Ross will probably be relieved to learn that Singapore is committed to accommodation and to ensuring that the world gives accommodation a concerted try. Yet, taking a leaf from the Nixon book – which absorbed the lessons of the European experience (too uncritically, some would say) – Singapore is also putting into place the pieces of a fall-back position by quietly augmenting its military strength. Would one expect anything less of the classic anticipatory state?

Notes

1 The Commission on *America's National Interest*, America's National Interest (Cambridge, MA: 1996), p. 29.
2 *The Straits Times Weekly Edition* (STWE), May 22, 1993.
3 Lee Kuan Yew, "How the United States and Japan can help Integrate China into the World Community," Speech at the Create 21 Asahi Symposium, Osaka, Japan, November 19, 1996. Reprinted in *The Straits Times*, November 20, 1996.
4 *The Washington Post*, March 17, 1996, cited Lee as saying, "Containment will not succeed . . . you will have absolutely no influence on how China – and its attitudes will develop. It will be hostile and xenophobic to the West, and that's not good for us."
5 See Chapter 9, this volume, p. 207.
6 See Chapter 8, this volume, p. 176.
7 Yuen Foong Khong, "Southeast Asia and the United States: Managing

Preponderance and Its Decline," Paper prepared for delivery at the Stiftung Wissenschaft und Politik (SWP) Institute of Southeast Asian Studies Conference on Strategic Concepts and Strategic Cultures in East Asia and Europe, May 9–10, 1996, Ebenhausen, Germany.

8 Philippine President Fidel Ramos is on record as saying that continued Chinese encroachment on the South China Sea is likely to "accelerate deeper security cooperation among the Southeast Asian countries – and between them and the United States and Japan as well." Cited in Michael Richardson, "Asian States Ponder Defense Strategy: Regional Countrweight is Sought for China's Belligerence," *International Herald Tribune*, August 23, 1995.

9 The third prong, or fall-back position, of Singapore's policy – increasing military spending and favoring a continued US military presence – seems to possess a coercive dimension. But this dimension pales into significance when compared to the first two prongs of the policy which emphasize economic and political cooperation. Moreover, China is not the only reason for having a fall-back position; for historical and geographical reasons, other regional powers are equally compelling incentives for Singapore wanting a fall-back position. In other words, the target of any "coercive" strands in Singapore's policy is diffused. Finally, a fall-back position is precisely that: something which one activates in the worst-case scenario. In Singapore's case, the coercive dimension of its fall-back position will only be fully realized when it asks – probably in concert with other ASEAN states – to join the US–Japan alliance in order to counter a China using its power aggressively.

10 In the wake of the American withdrawal from the Philippines, Singapore was the first to offer the United States access to its facilities. A Memorandum of Understanding signed in 1990 provided for increased use of Singapore's air and naval facilities. Singapore's predilection for a strong American military presence has not always been welcomed by its neigbors Indonesia and Malaysia, which view the American presence as being targeted against them. However, in wake of China's rise, both Indonesia and Malaysia have become less critical of the American presence and have increased security cooperation with US forces. From Singapore's perspective this is fortunate, because the American presence serves a multitude of functions – balancing China, reassuring Japan, and deterring other potential aggressors – all of which are conducive to Singapore's national security.

11 Neither Singapore, Malaysia, nor Indonesia have any illusions about their independent influence on China. As the Chapters by Leifer and Acharya in this volume suggest, the three states show different degrees of enthusiasm in engaging China, with Indonesia being the most cautious, Malaysia in the middle, and Singapore relatively enthusiastic.

12 The importance of not defining the outcome into the process of engagement (or its obverse, containment) can be seen in the following: Even if Western Europe did not join the United States in containing the Soviet Union between 1945 and 1989, America's policy would still be one of containment; whether it would have accomplished its goal is another question. Similarly, whether or not Europe and Asia join the United States in engaging (or containing) China, America's policy may still be termed as engagement (or containment). However, without Europe and Asia, the United States is unlikely to achieve its goal(s).

13 *Financial Times* (London), May 5, 1997.

14 Lee Kuan Yew, speech at Reception for Constituency Leaders, Shangri-La Hotel, Singapore, March 3, 1996.

15 Lee Kuan Yew, "How the United States Should Engage Asia in the Post-Cold War Period," acceptance speech on receiving the Architect of the New Century Award, Nixon Center for Peace and Freedom, Washington, DC, November 11, 1996. Reprinted in *The Straits Times*, November 13, 1996.

16 Chan Heng Chee, "Singapore: Domestic Structure and Foreign Policy," in Robert Scalapino *et al.* (eds) *Regional Dynamics: Security, Political, and Economic Issues in the Asia-Pacific Region* (Jakarta: Center for Strategic and International Studies, 1990), p. 146; *The Economist*, August 21, 1993, p. 52.

17 *The Nation* (Bangkok), October 20, 1985.

18 *The Straits Times*, August 21, 1989.

19 Ibid., November 16, 1993.

20 Ibid., May 16, 1993.

21 See also Chapter 9, this volume.

22 Lee, "How the United States Should Engage Asia."

23 A strand of contemporary research seems to support Lee's argument. Dale Copeland has argued that under conditions of economic interdependence, states whose expectations of future trade are positive are unlikely to go to war. See his "Economic Interdependence and War: A Theory of Trade Expectations," *International Security*, spring 1996, pp. 5–41. For inexplicable reasons, Copeland codes China as having low expectations of (future) trade (pp. 39–40); Lee believes that China's expectations are high and positive and wants the world to help it realize them.

24 For a view that emphasizes the importance of learning instead of economic incentives, see Insight interview with former Foreign Minister Wong Kan Seng, *STWE*, June 24, 1995. In the interview, Wong, the current Home Minister, argued that "Singapore believes that helping China join entities such as the Asia-Pacific Economic Cooperation forum and the Asean Regional Forum will *enable it to learn the rules and conduct of multilateral relations* and integrate better. This is more conducive to regional peace and stability than isolating China" (emphasis added).

25 In Chapter 4, this volume, Leifer makes the critical point that unlike the United States, Indonesia's China policy aims to influence the external – not the internal – conduct of China. The United States is interested in influencing both.

26 Lee, "How the United States and Japan can help Integrate China."

27 I would like to thank Ezra Vogel for alerting me to the differing impact of engagement on different political coalitions within China. The terms "liberalizing" and "nationalist-statist" coalitions are borrowed from Ethel Solingen, "Economic Liberalization, Political Coalitions, and Emerging Regional Orders," in David Lake and Patrick Morgan (eds) *Regional Orders: Building Security in a New World* (University Park: Pennsylvania State University Press, 1997), pp. 71–79.

28 Ibid.

29 Chan, "Singapore: Domestic Structure and Foreign Policy," p. 145.

30 Ibid.

31 Acharya makes the same point in Chapter 6, this volume.

32 *STWE*, June 24, 1995.

33 Ibid., January 4, 1997.

34 Ibid., May 20, 1995.

35 *The Straits Times*, May 19, 1993.

36 Alexander Wendt, "Collective Identity Formation and the International State," *American Political Science Review* 88: 2, 1994, pp. 384–96. Iain Johnston has suggested that middle-level Chinese policy-makers who participate in the tracks I and II activities of ASEAN Regional Forum become more committed to multilateral initiatives. See his "The Myth of the ASEAN Way: Explaining the Evolution of the ASEAN Regional Forum," Paper prepared for Conference on Security Institutions, Center for International Affairs, Harvard University, March 16–18, 1997.

37 Lee, "How the United States Should Engage Asia."

38 Ibid.

39 Whether the United States will welcome such a move is an interesting question. If only

a couple of ASEAN states seek closer military ties with the US–Japan alliance system, the latter may well be ambivalent. If, however, the China threat is sufficiently serious to cause ASEAN as a whole to seek more formal military ties with the United States and Japan, it is unlikely that ASEAN will be rebuffed.

40 Cf. Samuel Huntington, *The Clash of Civilizations: The Remaking of World Order* (New York: Simon & Schuster, 1996), pp. 236–37.

41 Michael Leifer, *The ASEAN Regional Forum: Extending ASEAN's Model of Regional Security* (London: Oxford University Press, 1996). International Institute for Strategic Studies, Adelphi Paper No. 302.

42 Summary Report of the ARF Inter-Sessional Support Group on Confidence Building Measures, Beijing, China March 6–8, 1997.

43 See Chapter 10, this volume.

44 *STWE*, October 14, 1995.

45 For an earlier version of this thesis without specific reference to China, see Lee Kuan Yew's speech before a joint session of the United States Congress, October 1985. Excerpts from *The Nation* (Bangkok), 20 October 1985.

46 *The Straits Times*, May 19, 1993.

47 Goh Chok Tong, "Give China Time and Space," *Far Eastern Economic Review*, May 25, 1995, p. 30.

48 Lee, speech at Reception for Constituency Leaders.

49 In his letter of condolence to Chinese President Jiang Zemin on the occasion of the death of Deng Xiaoping, Lee praised Deng as "a small man but a giant among world leaders." More interesting for our purposes is Lee's account of his first meeting with Deng:

> I met him for the first time in November 1978, when he came to Singapore to mobilise support against Vietnam before the Vietnamese invaded Cambodia.
>
> In our discussions, he urged us to get ASEAN to unite with China and isolate the Soviet Union and its pawn, Vietnam, the Cuba of Southeast Asia.
>
> I told him that on the contrary, my ASEAN neighbours wanted Singapore to unite with them to isolate China, not the Soviet Union.
>
> This was because China supported local communist parties, led by ethnic Chinese out to overturn their governments, and China was appealing over radio to the overseas Chinese to return and help China in its "Four Modernisations."
>
> He listened intently. His face and body language registered consternation. He knew I had told him the truth.
>
> Instead of denouncing me, he abruptly asked: "What do you want me or China to do?" I took courage and replied to this grizzled old veteran of the Long March: "Stop these broadcasts appealing to Chinese kinship and patriotism. Stop helping the communists to overthrow these governments."
>
> (*STWE*, February 22, 1997)

Lee's propensity to speak to Chinese leaders this way is one reason why he has unusual access to them.

50 Robert Ross, "China's Strategic Role in Asia," *Proceedings of the Academy of Political Science*, 36:1, 1986, pp. 116–28.

6

CONTAINMENT, ENGAGEMENT, OR COUNTER-DOMINANCE?

Malaysia's response to the rise of China[1]

Amitav Acharya

Introduction

Coping with a rising China is a key concern for Malaysia's security policy in the post-Cold War era. Malaysian leaders view China's ascendancy with mixed feelings: as both a major economic opportunity and a potential threat to national security and regional stability. Historic suspicions of China, derived from its past support for communist insurgency in Malaysia and the perceived potential of Malaysia's substantial Chinese population to act as a fifth column, are perhaps less important today in colouring Malaysia's perception of China. But China's growing military power and its claim on the Spratly Islands, contested by Malaysia, Taiwan, the Philippines, Vietnam and Brunei, have created new fears of Chinese hegemony. Malaysian leaders want to avoid an openly adversarial relationship with China, generally preferring a policy of engagement to a posture of containment. China's actions in the Asian economic crisis have served to increase Beijing's positive political image in Malaysia. But Malaysia remains sufficiently worried about the potential of China becoming a threat to regional security so as to prepare for confronting Beijing militarily and politically.

Malaysia is a relatively small state with internal and external vulnerabilities characteristic of most developing countries. Post-colonial Malaysia has been chiefly preoccupied with internal threats, notwithstanding Indonesian President Sukarno's war against Malaysia in the mid-1960s (called *Konfrontasi*) and the Philippine claim to the Malaysian state of Sabah (which peaked in the late 1960s). Malaysian armed forces have until recently maintained a counter-insurgency orientation and were slow to develop self-reliance in meeting external threats. Its multi-ethnic population, especially the fragile balance between the Malays and Chinese, has been a key factor not just in domestic politics, but also in shaping its foreign policy and regional security posture. But Malaysia is also a relatively prosperous state with abundant natural resources, and it has been one of the most dynamic industrializing economies in the Asia Pacific region. Prosperity has helped to reduce ethnic strife and allowed Malaysia to devote attention and resources to external threats. Under Prime Minister Mahathir Mohammed, it has pursued an activist foreign policy both at regional and global levels. Mahathir has been an outspoken critic of Western political and cultural dominance, an ardent champion of Third World solidarity and an active participant in efforts to build regional multilateral institutions, such as the ASEAN Regional Forum and his very own brainchild, the East Asian Economic Caucus (EAEC).

In dealing with China, Malaysia clearly favours a strategy of engagement. As Abdullah Badawi, then Malaysia's Foreign Minister, put it in 1997, "The most important thing is engagement, not containment."[2] The usage of the term "engagement" by Malaysian officials to describe its policy towards China is a recent practice. It seems to have been adapted from the debates in the West and Asia Pacific security meetings on the implications of the rise of China, debates which Malaysian officials and security specialists have followed and actively participated in. But the meaning of the term is somewhat more narrow and specific in Malaysia than in the US, especially in terms of its objectives. As with Indonesia (see Michael Leifer, Chapter 4, this volume), Malaysia does not seek to influence the domestic politics of China, keeping the focus instead on China's external behaviour. A strategy of engagement, in the sense used by the editors of this volume (see their Preface), is a deliberate policy of socialization of a rising power using non-coercive methods. Its aim is not to prevent or block the growth of the latter's influence or status, but to ensure that any change in the regional and global order caused by its ascendancy is peaceful. An engagement policy is pursued through essentially non-coercive methods. It may involve the creation of institutional constraints on the rising power's geopolitical behaviour, accommodation of its legitimate interests, and the devising of other means to transform its policies that are deemed to be destabilizing. In contrast, containment is a strategy pursued through coercive means in order to constrain a rising power, including engendering its military defeat or internal collapse.

From a Malaysian perspective, a policy of engaging China means a conscious effort by its neighbours and the international community at large to develop a normative framework and a range of bilateral and multilateral linkages which will constrain Chinese unilateralism and encourage its role as a peaceful and responsible member of the regional and international system. Engagement is both a process and a goal. The goal is to ensure that Malaysia benefits from the economic opportunities offered by China's economic growth while discouraging a Chinese security posture that would pose a threat to Malaysia's security interests. Malaysia's policy toward China is designed to create a mutual accommodation of legitimate interests. A related objective is to maximize positive economic and functional interdependence, which China will find costly to break. Beyond this, Malaysia sees multilateral institutions such as the ASEAN's external dialogue mechanism and the ASEAN Regional Forum as an important instrument in socializing and eventually integrating China into a system of regional norms and order.

Yet Malaysian elites are not fully convinced that engagement, as defined above, will work. They recognize the difficulties in creating a workable regional mechanism for conflict prevention and resolution. As a result, Malaysian policy exemplifies the kind of ambivalence that marks the attitude of many other Asia Pacific nations toward Chinese power. While publicly speaking the language of engagement, Malaysia is also quietly but firmly reorienting its security posture that will enhance its ability to respond to Chinese provocation.

Malaysia's perception of China as a threat

At a declaratory level, Malaysian political elites downplay the potential of China as a threat to Malaysia's national security. In this respect, they share the approach of their counterparts in other ASEAN countries who are generally reluctant to speak publicly of a "China threat," notwithstanding their private misgivings about the rise of Chinese power. Malaysian Prime Minister, Mahathir Mohammed, argues that identifying China as a threat could become a self-fulfilling prophecy. As he put it: "Why should we fear China? If you identify a country as your future enemy, it becomes your present enemy – because then they will identify you as an enemy and there will be tension."[3]

Mahathir has even argued that the rise of China should not become a justification for an American containment posture. He once derided US naval presence in the East Asia region as "a waste of money as there was nothing to fear from either Japan or China."[4] Some Malaysian commentators have dissociated themselves from the so-called "China threat," blaming it on Western governments and analysts.

However, Malaysian defence and security planners and analysts are much more forthcoming than its political leaders in voicing concerns about the rising power of China. These concerns encompass three aspects. The first is the general uncertainty in the region's strategic climate. The chief of the Malaysian Navy points out that one of the most serious security concerns of Malaysia is the "uncertainties in the region's evolving security situation and military modernization programme by some Asian countries, and the issue of how the balance of power is going to evolve especially where there exist competition and rivalries between China, Japan, Russia and the US." The rise of China is a key and worrying factor in this climate of strategic uncertainty:

> China, Japan and the US are important players that would determine regional security developments in the Pacific Asia. The state of their inter-relationships obviously affects the stability of the region. Thus, it is important that the existing triangular relationship is maintained in a state of equilibrium. . . . However, as the years progress, there exist . . . uncertainty in the form of China's behaviour once she attained her great power status. Will she conform to international or regional rules or will she be a new military power which acts in whatever ways she sees fit?[5]

A related source of Malaysian concerns regarding China is the latter's military buildup, which for Malaysia assumes a greater significance in view of the post-Cold War decline of American and Russian military presence in the region. Comparing the three regional powers, India, Japan and China, the former Chief of Malaysia's Defence Forces, General Hashim Mohammed Ali argued that while India is constrained by domestic problems and Japan by constitutional constraints, China continued to increase its defence spending and military modernization and threatened the use of force to support its territorial claims in the South China Sea.[6] Malaysian defence planners have noted the shift in China's defence posture from a people's defence to an offensive power projection capability. Reviewing China's military buildup, two Malaysian officials concluded that the new Chinese military strategy "treats the ocean as strategic space and the navy an instrument for control of the ocean. . . . This strategy envisages the encounter and defeat of enemies in the ocean rather than at its doorstep." They pointed specifically to the PLA's emphasis on rapid reaction forces, creation of naval and air assets to "meet regional contingencies," extension of the "operational range" and the "sustained operational capability" of the Navy, provision of air cover for the fleet, training of highly mobile airborne troops and the acquisition of an "amphibious offensive capability" as indicated in the creation of a marine corps.[7]

The Chief of the Malaysian Army gave an even clearer hint of Malaysia's fears about China's military buildup:

> The country to watch today would be the People's Republic of China. Lately China has engaged in a large defence build-up. Besides the purchase of 26 × SU-27 [sic] Flanker, a proposed acquisition of an aircraft carrier and a planned procurement of the Russian made strategic backfire bomber, if materialize, China's military capabilities, especially in its power projection will be significantly higher. Despite recent friendly utterances, suggesting that China wants to see peace in the world and particularly in East Asia, it seems likely that the long-term aim is dominance, though not necessarily aggression. That surely must be the meaning of the proposed large fleet and this factor immediately focuses attention on the most sensitive territory in Southeast Asia – the group of Spratly Islands.[8]

Of particular concern to Malaysia is the growth of Chinese naval power. This may be especially unsettling since Malaysia historically has been a naval power itself (in contrast to its neighbour, Thailand) and therefore feels a greater sense of threat from a competing naval prowess. Moreover, to a larger extent than its ASEAN neighbours, Malaysia's security concerns have increasingly shifted from counter-insurgency to conventional warfare, with the sea assuming a major place in its strategic planning. As the chief of the Malaysian Navy put it, "the main challenge . . . to the Pacific Asia region will be maritime in nature."[9] In his view, regional countries are "becoming more aware and competitive over natural resources which lie on or under the sea-beds." Issues such as the law of the sea, maritime boundaries, conflicting claims to offshore territories, offshore resources, sea-borne (trade), transit rights and piracy "are growing in importance and have now become sources of conflicts."[10] Malaysia itself is involved in a number of maritime disputes; indeed, it is the only ASEAN member to have a maritime territorial dispute with all other members.

A third and more direct source of Malaysia's strategic perceptions regarding China relates to the Spratly Islands dispute. Four Southeast Asian countries are involved in the Spratlys dispute with China and Taiwan. While China, Taiwan and Vietnam claim the entire chain of islands on a historical basis, Malaysia (as well as the Philippines and Brunei) claims portions of the Spratlys on the basis of maritime rights under the Law of the Sea Convention. Between September and November 1983, Malaysia troops occupied three South China Sea atolls: Layang-Layang (Swallow Reef), Manatanani (Mariveles Reef) and Permatang Ubi (Ardasier Bank). Malaysia is developing the Layang-Layang island into a holiday resort and is building an airstrip on the island.

In the words of Malaysian Chief of Defence Force: "In the immediate term . . . the biggest problem to regional stability will be the settling of the claims to the Spratly and Paracel Islands and whether China will want to pursue its claims militarily."[11] In the wake of the Sino–Vietnamese naval clashes in the South China Sea in March 1988, the Spratly issue was raised from "secondary to very much top priority" in Malaysian defence planning.[12] The Director of Military Intelligence admitted that military planners pay "serious attention" to the protection of the Malaysian garrison on three atolls in the Spratly Islands, which had become Malaysia's "front line in the area."[13] The China factor, and the more general concern with maritime security undoubtedly plays a role, aside from increased buying power and prestige considerations, in Malaysia's ambitious military modernization drive. This includes the acquisition of the British *Hawk*, the Russian MiG-29 *Fulcrum*, and the US F-18 combat fighter aircraft, large surface platforms such as 2200-ton guided missile frigates, and a long-term programme to acquire a submarine capability (this was cancelled due to the economic crisis).[14]

China and Malaysia have explored the idea of joint development as a possible way of resolving the Spratlys dispute;[15] but Malaysian officials are sceptical of Chinese assurances in this regard, pointing to a mismatch between Chinese declaratory policy and its actual behaviour. In the words of the Chief of the Malaysian Navy:

> Everybody would like to believe in the wisdom, statesmanship and restraint of the PRC. In recent years, there have been no lack of instances of such admirable behaviour. But we are bound to ponder with alarm the Chinese pronouncements in 1992 on the subject of the Spratly Islands that it would not "budge an inch" over questions of sovereignty.[16]

The growth of Chinese power, especially the true extent of its power projection capabilities, remains a matter of debate among analysts and policy-makers, including those in Malaysia. Malaysian planners are aware of the challenges and constraints facing China's military in its efforts at modernization. Whether China will acquire a genuine blue-water navy and a power projection capability in the near term remains doubtful. It is unlikely that China will achieve military superiority in the areas adjacent to Malaysia. Yet Malaysian defence planners may regard the uncertainty about China's long-term intentions and capabilities as a useful rationale for acquiring modern weapons systems which would be difficult to justify in the context of a relatively tranquil immediate post-Cold War order.

Malaysia's domestic demographic and economic balance is important in shaping its perceptions of, and policy towards, China. Malaysia has a larger ethnic Chinese minority, measured in terms of percentage of total population, than any other Southeast Asian country. Malaysia's ethnic Chinese constitute about 29 per cent of its total population, compared to 15 per cent in Brunei, 5 per cent in Cambodia, 3.5 per cent in Indonesia, 20 per cent in Burma, 2.0 per cent in Philippines, and 10 per cent in Thailand. While the decline and end of the insurgency carried out by the Communist Party of Malay (consisting of a largely ethnic Chinese cadre and supported by Beijing) removed an important source of Sino–Malaysian friction, the economic dominance of the ethnic Chinese (as will be discussed later) remains an incipient source of domestic ethnic strife in Malaysia with possible consequences for its China policy. In this context, the fear of China continues (albeit in a low-key manner) to serve as a device for shoring up Malay unity and hence as a basis of regime legitimation in Malaysia. Moreover, the domestic ethnic mix may also explain why Malaysian leaders worry not just about a prosperous and powerful China which can pose a military threat, but also about a weak and unstable China which may upset its domestic ethnic balance by precipitating an influx of refugees into Malaysia. A comment by the then Foreign Minister Badawi is particularly suggestive:

> The talk of China as a threat presupposes it has a planned agenda. I don't think it has one. If China's economic reforms fail miserably, there will be no need for an agenda; the outflow of people will knock all of us down.[17]

Malaysia–China bilateral relations

Sino–Malaysian bilateral relations have been historically shaped by a combination of domestic and external factors, chief among them the state of Chinese-backed communist insurgency in Malaysia and the relationships between the major powers in the region. The latter was particularly important in spurring a positive turn in bilateral relations in the late 1960s, with the announcement of the British decision to withdraw from "east of Suez" and the Nixon adminis- tration's urging of Asian states to be more self-reliant on defence. The diminished prospect of receiving Western assistance to cope with its internal and external security challenges prompted a pragmatic decision by Malaysia to improve relations with China, even before the latter ceased aid to the CPM. Indeed, during negotiations leading to the establishment of diplomatic relations in 1974, Malaysia chose to live with Beijing's refusal to break ties with the CPM (which had already been defeated at home, with its remnants forced to retreat to the Thai–Malaysia border). But Kuala Lumpur was reassured by a clear affirmation of China's new position on the "overseas Chinese," i.e. Beijing would no longer regard those who have obtained citizenship in other countries as Chinese nationals.[18]

Although Malaysia continued to view China, rather than Vietnam, as the most serious long-term threat to regional stability during the decade-long Third Indo–China War (the Vietnamese occupation of Cambodia from 1978 to 1989), China's backing of ASEAN's position against Vietnam contributed to a better political climate for Sino–Malaysian bilateral relations. The surrender of the CPM to Malaysian authorities in 1989 and the cessation of its clandestine radio broadcasts from China contributed to another positive turn in Malaysia–China relations.

The early 1990s saw intensified bilateral political contacts and economic ties between China and Malaysia, highlighted by Chinese Premier Li Peng's visit to Malaysia in December 1990 as the head of a delegation that included Foreign Minister Qian Qichen and a number of other senior government figures.[19] Subsequent visits by the Chief of the People's Liberation Army (PLA) General Chi Haotian and Chairman Qiao Shi of the Standing Committee of China's National People's Congress in 1993 underscored the expanding scope of bilateral ties.[20] Initial efforts at cooperation in the highly sensitive defence sphere were indicated during the visit in August 1992 by the then Malaysian Defence Minister Najib Tun Razak to Beijing to meet with his Chinese counterpart, General Chi Haotian. The visit was reciprocated by the latter in May 1993 when the two sides discussed the situation in the South China Sea and bilateral military cooperation.[21] In November 1995, China and Malaysia agreed to expand bilateral military cooperation, including defence industrial cooperation and an officer exchange programme.[22] While the scope of defence cooperation remains extremely modest, the high-level visits have proved useful in confidence-building.

While political and strategic consideration were crucial in shaping bilateral ties in the previous decades when China was not a significant economic player, the lure of economic opportunities in China in the 1990s helped the two countries to shift the focus from contentious high politics issues and to cast the relationship on a broader, more positive footing. A visible symbol of China's new economic importance to Malaysia was Mahathir's visits (two during the 1993 to 1994 period) to China as the head of large Malaysian business delegations. Similar to visits by many Western leaders to China in recent years, Mahathir's June 1993 visit, for example, included a 290-strong Malaysian business delegation, and resulted in trade and investment deals worth approximately $600 million.[23] One cannot go too far in characterizing the growth in economic ties between Malaysia and China as part of an engagement strategy. Such ties are based primarily on calculation of economic opportunity, rather than being the result of a considered strategic approach. But economic interdependence has been viewed by Malaysian officials and academics as an important source of peace and stability in the Asia Pacific region. The importance of Malaysia's trade with China is highlighted by structural changes in the Malaysian economy that is becoming increasingly reliant on the export-oriented manufacturing sector. Manufacturing now accounts for about 80 per cent of the export earnings compared to 13 per cent for the agricultural sector.[24] Thus the large Chinese market is an obvious attraction for Malaysian exporters. Malaysia's trade (the total volume of exports and imports) with China registered a fourfold increase between 1985 and 1993 (see Table 6.1). In 1997 it was estimated to be US4.4 billion.[25] The balance of Sino–Malaysian trade is in China's favour, causing concern and some resentment in Kuala Lumpur. In this sense, while Liberal international theory expects interdependence to foster improved political ties, one should also be aware of the potential of interdependence to create new sources of friction.

Before the Asian economic crisis hit Malaysia and halted the overseas investment ventures of Malaysian companies, investments by the latter in China had almost tripled between 1993 (RM113 million) and 1997 (RM316 million).[26] These investments, while of doubtful value in terms of the economic benefits they might have brought to Malaysia, carried a domestic political significance, because of the involvement of Malaysia's ethnic Chinese entrepreneurs. The emergence of China as a major investment destination offered Malaysian Chinese entrepreneurs a new opportunity to escape the limitations imposed by the pro-*bumiputra* national economic framework. Despite periodic criticism from some opposition groups, this did not cause resentment among the Malay elite because non-Chinese Malaysians themselves were almost as interested and active in seeking economic opportunities in China. Malaysian leaders (some with close links with ethnic Chinese business concerns with interests in China) have presented economic linkages with China as a matter of national priority serving the national interest, not the narrow economic interests of a particular ethnic group. Mahathir has underscored this issue by including in his trade delegations to China a substantial number of ethnic Chinese businessmen.[27] "I don't see investing in China as a loyalty issue," stated Badawi, adding: "We used to question the loyalty (of overseas Chinese) but I don't think it is in the minds of (indigenous Malaysian) today . . . Chinese Malaysian are [*sic*] proud of being Malaysian. They will invest where they can make the most money."[28]

This relatively benign view could change if the economic downturn in Malaysia threatens its overall political stability, and renders domestic inter-ethnic relations more volatile. The economic downturn in Malaysia also has the potential to strain bilateral political ties, including a possible rekindling of Malaysia's fear of Chinese interference in its domestic affairs. The May 1998 anti-Chinese riots in Indonesia prompted China to issue a series of strong demands for the Indonesian

Table 6.1 Malaysian–Chinese trade: Malaysian exports and imports: 1985–1995

	1985	1986	1987	1988	1989	1990	1991	1992	1993	1994	1995
Exports	215.0	212.0	351.7	503.6	558.6	688.9	685.0	805.1	1,228.8	1,971.3	1,986.2
	(1.0%)	(1.2%)	(1.6%)	(2.0%)	(1.9%)	(2.1%)	(1.9%)	(1.9%)	(2.6%)		
Imports	335.2	366.7	471.4	585.0	707.2	624.4	859.7	1,016.8	1,118.6	1,390.0	1,737.2
	(2.0%)	(2.6%)	(2.9%)	(2.9%)	(2.7%)	(1.9%)	(2.2%)	(2.4%)	(2.4%)		

Sources: Figures derived from International Monetary Fund, *Direction of Trade Statistics Yearbook* (Washington, DC: International Monetary Fund, various years).

Notes:
Exports and imports are rendered in 1994 constant million US dollars.
Figures in brackets are percentages of total exports/imports.

government to act swiftly and bring the perpetrators to justice. Such statements by Beijing might have been seen as ominously assertive and unduly interventionist by its Southeast Asian neighbours, reviving memories of the past when "the welfare of 'overseas Chinese' was indeed employed [by Beijing] for political purposes when it had suited Chinese geo-strategic objectives," as an editorial in Singapore's *Straits Times* warned.[29] While it did not publicly react negatively to China's statements, the Malaysian government warned its own Chinese political parties not to criticize the Indonesian government for the anti-Chinese violence. Relatively less affected by the economic crisis, the prospects for Indonesia-like ethnic violence in Malaysia is more remote, but the Malaysian government remains sensitive to any contagion effect of the Indonesian situation on its own ethnic balance.

On the other hand, the Asian economic crisis has helped to improve China's image in the region, dampening, at least for the time being, the fear of China turning into an expansionist and politically uncooperative regional giant in the minds of Malaysian leaders. Reeling from the economic crisis, Malaysia has been appreciative of China's promise not to devalue its currency, which might have hurt Malaysia's exports and sparked another round of currency devaluations in the region. Acknowledging this point, the Malaysian Foreign Minister stated: "ASEAN is grateful to China for all its assurance not to devalue the renminbi despite pressures upon it to do so."[30] China's regional image has also benefited from its contribution of US$4 billion dollars to the IMF's operational budget to help Thailand and Indonesia weather the crisis and its provision of export credits and emergency medical assistance to Indonesia.[31] Like other ASEAN members, Malaysia has taken a positive view of China's actions and therefore the potential for China's act of "leadership," especially in the light of Japan's failure to deal with its own economic woes.

Malaysia–China relations: the regional and multilateral dimension

Dealing collectively with China through regional institutions and fora such as the ASEAN-Post Ministerial Conferences (ASEAN-PMC), the ASEAN–China security consultations, the Asia Pacific Economic Forum (APEC) and the ASEAN Regional Forum (ARF) runs parallel to Malaysia's bilateral dealings with China. In looking at this regional aspect, one must bear in mind that Malaysia's own perceptions of China are not always identical to those of other ASEAN members. The ASEAN members' attitudes toward China are shaped by conditions, both domestic and international, which differ from member to member. For example, differences in the domestic political context explain why anti-Chinese sentiments, a key determinant of foreign policy toward China, are much less pronounced in Malaysia than in Indonesia. The government's official redistributive approach, the New Economic Policy (NEP), helped to spread the benefits of economic growth in the 1970s and 1980s to the *bumiputras*, thereby dampening the potential for ethnic strife. Today, the ethnic Chinese in Malaysia are less economically dominant *vis-à-vis* the *bumiputras* than their counterparts in most other parts of Southeast Asia, particularly Indonesia.[32]

Apart from such domestic level differences, the regional context of Malaysia's China policy is affected by bilateral tensions among the ASEAN members. Many members of the Malay political elite in Malaysia see Singapore's move to establish close economic and political relations with China as evidence of what the Malaysian envoy to the UN has described as "the increasing Chineseness of the island republic".[33] This is an aggravating factor in the fragile relationship between Malaysia and Singapore. ASEAN has put up a collective front *vis-à-vis* China's territorial claims in the South China Sea, and secured Beijing's participation in multilateral ASEAN–China security consultations to reduce tensions in Sino–ASEAN ties. But Beijing's preference for separate bilateral dealings with the individual claimant states (in areas such as joint development of resources and negotiating codes of conduct in managing disputes) is a source of potential intra-ASEAN discord which would shape Malaysia's regional engagement policy toward China.

From a Realist perspective, the engagement of one's potential adversary by a relatively weaker actor or group of actors could be the result of a pragmatic recognition by the latter of the limits of its countervailing power. ASEAN does not have the option of pursuing a containment strategy on its own. Notwithstanding the substantial sums spent by ASEAN members in recent years on sophisticated weapons, the military power of individual ASEAN countries will not be adequate for a containment posture. A collective ASEAN military response, even an *ad hoc* one (which does not require ASEAN to form itself into a military alliance in advance), to China is an extremely remote possibility, because of well-known intra-ASEAN suspicions and conflicts. The individual national capabilities of Malaysia and Vietnam, but not the Philippines, may suffice for a denial strategy, one that inflicts severe costs on any Chinese attempt to dislodge their forces from the Spratly area. But even this may be a daunting challenge for Malaysia, given the limitations of manpower, logistics support, and the difficulties of maintaining and operating highly sophisticated weapon systems in an actual combat environment.

Thus the ASEAN states cannot meaningfully pursue a containment or countervailing strategy *vis-à-vis* China except in alliance with the US (as well as other Western powers including Australia). In this context, moves by several ASEAN states to establish closer defence relationships with the US, based on granting of access to military facilities and joint exercises, assumes significance. Malaysia and Singapore have also maintained their defence relationship with Australia, New Zealand, and Britain under the Five Power Defence Arrangements (although Malaysia did not participate in a FPDA exercise in 1998 due to its row with Singapore). Malaysia's defence ties with the US are less elaborate and less formal than those between the US and Singapore or the US and Thailand. Nonetheless, they are an important element of Malaysia's regional security posture. American access to Malaysian facilities include: (1) port calls to Malaysian ports since the early 1980s; (2) offer of ship repair facilities on a commercial basis; (3) occasional use by US forces of jungle warfare facilities in Malaysia; and (4) low-visibility exercises since the mid-1980s between the US navy and Malaysian naval and air forces, including naval passing exercises in the Straits of Malacca and South China Sea.[34] It is important to note that these ties pre-dated the end of the Cold War and may not be seen as a response to the rise of Chinese power.

However, Malaysia and other ASEAN members are also wary of relying on a military strategy that increases their dependence on the US security umbrella. The US credibility as a security guarantor remains problematic, partly but not entirely due to continuing doubts regarding the future of the US military presence in the region which have not been assuaged by frequent US assurances. Washington's action in deploying two aircraft-carrier battle groups in response to the crisis in the Taiwan Straits in 1996 might have brought some private relief to ASEAN strategists, but it has not brought about an appreciable increase in ASEAN's faith in the American deterrent. Mahathir himself has been a leading member of the doubter's camp. In his co-authored book entitled *The Asia That Can Say No*, Mahathir took a Gaullist swipe at the US, stating: "I don't think the U.S. military presence guarantees security in Asia" and "If we are invaded it is not certain that the U.S. would extend a helping hand. I think the U.S. would only help us when its own position is threatened."[35]

However, while Malaysia does not seek and cannot rely on a containment strategy led by the US, it certainly sees the US military presence as a necessary factor in ensuring a regional balance of power. As Malaysia's Director of Armed Forces Intelligence stated:

> America's presence is certainly needed, at least to balance other powers with contrasting ideology in this region. America's presence is also needed to ensure that shipping lanes are always safe and not disturbed by suspicious powers. The power balance is needed in this region to ensure that other powers that have far-reaching ambitions in Southeast Asia will not find it easy to act against countries in the region.[36]

Malaysia's outlook is similar to that of the other ASEAN members, who doubt that the US would be capable of mobilizing enough resources to pursue a credible containment strategy, but see the balance of power maintained by the US military presence as a critical element of regional stability.

But, from a Malaysian point of view, military power balancing alone cannot ensure regional stability. The latter also hinges on the framework of multilateral security dialogues and confidence-building that is being undertaken by ASEAN and the ARF. Malaysia has been strongly supportive of the development of multilateral security dialogues and security cooperation in the region. As early as 1989, Mahathir urged the two superpowers to adopt a set of confidence-building measures, including prior notification of joint naval exercises, joint measures to avoid incidents at sea and in the air and transparency through information exchanges, including a hot line between the military establishments of the superpowers and regular dialogues between their military personnel. Later, in 1992, the then Defence Minister, Najib Razak, suggested that ASEAN and its dialogue partners should encourage greater transparency in arms acquisitions and create a regional arms register, so that "suspicions among each other could be minimised, and managed."[37] Although the ARF was not a Malaysian initiative, these proposals formed an important part of the security debate in the Asia Pacific region which culminated in the establishment of the ARF in Bangkok.[38]

Since its inception, the ARF has outlined a three-step approach to regional security cooperation, consisting of confidence-building, preventive diplomacy, and conflict resolution (later changed to "elaboration of approaches to conflicts" as a concession to China which had warned against rapid institutionalization of the ARF).[39] The initial measures of confidence-building selected by the ARF include exchange of annual defence postures on a voluntary basis, increased dialogues on security issues on a bilateral, sub-regional and regional basis, forging of senior-level contacts and exchanges among military institutions and partici-pation of the ARF members in the UN Conventional Arms Register. These measures are rather modest in scope, and reflect the preference of the ASEAN states to develop the ARF in a manner and at a pace that is comfortable for China and the ASEAN states. Malaysia and other ASEAN members see the ARF as a "soft" institution which could promote dialogue and consultations on security issues, rather than develop elaborate mechanisms for conflict resolution in the manner of the Organization for Security and Cooperation in Europe (OSCE). In this respect, Malaysia's position is similar to that of China and differs from the position of the Western members of the ARF, such as the US and Australia, which favour a more "fast-track" approach to security cooperation. China's position on the ARF was stated by an editorial in the *People's Daily* in the following terms:

> new forms of security cooperation [in the Asia Pacific region] can only evolve in a gradual process . . . it must not affect the basic defence systems of any country. . . . Security through cooperation does not mean the collective intervention in disputes among countries or seeking the thorough settlement of all concrete security problems.[40]

But the views of Malaysia and China regarding the ARF's purpose and role differ in other respects. While the former views the ARF as a mechanism for responding to and managing the rise of China and its effects on the regional balance of power, the latter harbours suspicions that the ARF may be used by its neighbours such as the ASEAN states to gang up on China and oppose its strategic interests. Malaysia, like other ASEAN members, hopes that the socialization of China can be brought about by the process of consultations organized under the ARF framework as well as its more specific measures of transparency and confidence-building once they are developed beyond their present rudimentary stage. Acting through the ARF, Malaysia can convey to Beijing the high diplomatic costs of any use of force in the South China Sea, including the risk of regional political isolation which Beijing seems so keen to avoid. While the ARF may never develop into a fully fledged instrument of conflict resolution, the norms created within the framework of the ARF and other regional security fora, such as the ASEAN–China dialogues on regional security, may impose greater and more meaningful constraints on Chinese military options in the South China Sea. In this respect, the development of normative and institutional restraints on Chinese behaviour will constitute an alternative form of containment ("containment by other means," as some have called it).

Malaysian leaders argue that the ARF has already launched a process of socialization involving China and other countries of the Asia Pacific region; but Malaysia does not foresee the ARF producing a fundamental transformation of China's interests in the near to medium term. In the context of China's role in multilateral institutions, Johnston and Evans argue (Chapter 10, this volume) that "institutions merely obstruct non-cooperative behavior, but do not change the interests motivating this behavior." This is true of Malaysia's expectations concerning the ARF's potential impact on China. While Foreign Minister Badawi recently asserted that the policy of engaging China was "proving to be effective,"[41] he did not define what "effectiveness" meant except for vague references to China's willingness to become "a part of the ARF." Malaysian leaders are yet to be convinced that joining the ARF has produced on the part of China what Johnston and Evans call "fundamental changes in Chinese calculations of interest and strategy." The prospects for such transformation remain uncertain.

A somewhat different element of Malaysia's multilateral approach in Asia Pacific is its controversial proposal for an East Asian Economic Caucus (EAEC). The EAEC reflects Malaysia's misgivings about the Asia Pacific Economic Cooperation (APEC). Malaysia does not take kindly to the fact that APEC grew out of an Australian initiative, a country with which it has had a difficult and ambivalent relationship. Mahathir views the EAEC as East Asia's answer to the rise of protectionist trading blocs in North America and Europe, as represented in NAFTA and the EU. He has actively but unsuccessfully sought Japan's support for the idea (Tokyo's refusal is partly due to the strong US opposition to the idea). China's support is therefore crucial to Mahathir's efforts to realize the EAEC concept. In 1991, the then Chinese President Yang Shangkun described the EAEG (East Asia Economic Grouping, as the initiative was originally called) as an idea "of positive significance to the increasing of economic cooperation in East Asia." This was seen by the Malaysian media as an indication of China's backing,[42] although there are no firm indications that China is actually enthusiastic about the EAEC concept. Although Mahathir has attached greater priority to securing Japan's backing for the idea, Tokyo's persistent refusal to do so and China's growing economic clout led him to turn to China for support as well.

While the EAEC idea remains officially moribund, Malaysia has sought to push it through the back door by engineering an "informal" summit of the ASEAN leaders with their counterparts from Japan, South Korea and China in December 1997. China's consent to participate was crucial to this meeting, and Mahathir was "especially appreciative of the support expressed by China for ASEAN's proposal for the East Asian Nations to engage in purposeful exchange of views on matters affecting the peace, stability and economic growth of the region."[43]

To create a favourable climate for multilateralism, Malaysia wants the US to steer a middle course between withdrawal and unilateralism. American security policy, like that of Malaysia, should not be needlessly provocative to China, nor should it allow Beijing to miscalculate the diplomatic and, if necessary, military costs of its action which threatens regional stability. From a Malaysian perspective, the US should also avoid unilateralism in the sense of not pursuing a strategy that ignores ASEAN's views and interests. This means eschewing a containment policy *vis-à-vis* China. Indeed, to discourage a containment-oriented American posture is one of the key goals being pursued by ASEAN through the ARF. At the same time, the normative evolution of ARF, ASEAN hopes, will constrain China's military options, even if it falls short of its avowed goal of bringing about a complete socialization of China.

Thus ASEAN seeks to play a moderating role in the US–China rivalry. Malaysia, more than any other ASEAN state, wants neither Beijing nor Washington to dominate the region. Chinese dominance will threaten Malaysia's security, while Malaysia is apprehensive of American dominance because of Washington's tendency to be meddlesome over issues of political freedom and labour rights. Mahathir has warned that Washington's crusade on human rights (including its promotion of labour rights) constitutes a form of protectionism, aimed at undermining Asian competitiveness. It is interesting to note that while dismissing the China threat, Mahathir "foresees a lot of pressures" from a dominant US, suggesting that the rise of China is less of a security concern to Asia than the American tendency to "impose things on others," including an attempt to seek extra-territorial rights and heavy-handed promotion of values such as human rights and liberal democracy.[44] In this respect, Malaysia's attitude toward Japan deserves notice. Malaysia has been more tolerant of an expanded Japanese security role in the Asia Pacific region than China or some other ASEAN states. While this is explained by Malaysia's continuing hope that Japan may be persuaded to lead an East Asian Economic Caucus, it may also have to do with political and security concerns stemming from the potential role of Japan as a counterweight to the growing Chinese military and economic power and to US political and strategic dominance in the region.

Implications for the theory of containment and engagement

The implications of containment and engagement as ways of responding to the rise of great powers have not been fully explored in the international relations theory. Although containment is an old concept, the idea of engagement is relatively new. Moreover, we know little about the practice of containment in a multipolar international system, since the concept was developed in the context of the Cold War. Identifying the conditions under which states are likely to opt for either containment or engagement in the post-bipolar era constitutes a rich and interesting area of theoretical reflection and innovation.

Theorizing about containment and engagement becomes even more complicated when the actors making the choice are not great powers, but relatively weaker states with a limited degree of security self-reliance. Realist international theory provides some clue to understanding how weaker states may adjust to shifts in the balance of power caused by the ascendancy of a particular great power. Simply put, the weaker states have two alternatives: balancing and bandwagoning (see Randall Schweller, Chapter 1, this volume).[45] But balancing a stronger and rising power is a meaningful option for weaker actors (given the inherent limitations on how far they can balance by increasing their national strength) only if they can obtain and count on security guarantees from an existing status quo power whose strength approximates that of the rising power. If no such guarantee is available or is sufficiently credible, weaker actors may seriously consider bandwagoning with the rising power rather than pursue a futile and dangerous balancing strategy. On the other hand, choosing the balancing option by joining hands with the status quo power means increasing one's reliance on external security guarantees, which may not be appealing to independent-minded weaker powers that abhor client status.[46]

For Malaysia, choosing containment or a pure balancing strategy toward China would mean increasing its dependence on American (and to lesser extent Australian, Japanese, or even Indian) power. But such a strategy is politically unappealing, especially to Malaysia, which values its independent and non-aligned international posture. In the early 1970s, Malaysia proposed the idea of neutralization of Southeast Asia to be secured through great power guarantees of non-intervention. It has since emphasized the need for regional autonomy and security self-reliance under ASEAN's concept of Southeast Asia as a Zone of Peace, Freedom and Neutrality (ZOPFAN). If balancing China entails band-wagoning with the US beyond loose and informal security ties, Malaysia will not find it politically attractive.

On the other hand, Malaysia cannot bandwagon with China, no matter how loosely one defines the term bandwagoning. (Here, my assessment is similar to Khong's dismissal, Chapter 5, this volume, of a possible bandwagoning strategy for Singapore, in spite of its Chinese majority.) To be sure, Malaysia will find China to be a useful partner on a range of issues, such as human rights, especially in offsetting American pressure in this area. But Malaysia's domestic ethnic mix, and fears held by its leaders regarding China's long-term intentions, rule out the possibility of even a rudimentary China–Malaysia alliance. But if neither balancing China nor bandwagoning with China is a desirable option for Malaysia, what is the alternative? The idea of engagement may be a more desirable alternative because it lies somewhere between balancing and bandwagoning. But while containment and balancing require increased dependence on great power alliances, which Malaysia seeks to avoid, even a strategy of engagement requires a certain degree of equality in status and capabilities between the parties in order to be meaningful. Moreover, China may not be seriously interested in being "engaged" by Malaysia. "Engaging" a vastly superior rising power may not be a credible option for a weaker power because it does not mean much for the "power-prestige demands" (see Margaret Pearson, Chapter 9, this volume) and needs of the superior power. When the capacity of two sides to damage each other's interests is unequal, the weaker side's policy of engagement may be seen by the stronger side as a form of appeasement. In this context it is worth noting that some observers of ASEAN find the grouping to be simply too soft on China, reluctant to publicly confront Bejing over its controversial actions in the South China Sea (although there are indications that this may be changing). The danger is that engaging a vastly superior power may amount to a *de facto* appeasement posture, which will encourage the latter to miscalculate the political and military costs of territorial aggrandizement.

For these reasons, weak actors may perceive the logic of containment and engagement differently from the great powers. In the case of Malaysia, neither containment nor engagement is desirable in itself if it entails vastly increased dependence on external security guarantees. Even if the US develops a clearly defined strategy of containment, Malaysia is unlikely to accept the political costs of identifying completely with the US posture. As a developing country with considerable distrust of Western security guarantees and as a potential middle power itself, Malaysia will do its utmost to avoid being seen as an American client. Neither will Malaysia (nor most other Southeast Asian countries) opt for band-wagoning with China, even though Malaysian leaders have made common ground with China over issues such as human rights and accept China as a legitimate great power.

For Malaysia, therefore, the preferred way of dealing with the rise of China is to steer a middle course somewhere between containment and engagement. It implies a generally cooperative posture on the part of the weaker state (Malaysia) toward a rising power (China); but it is also backed up by a range of political, diplomatic (especially multilateral), and military instruments aimed at discouraging threatening policies and actions by the rising power. Moreover, such a posture requires that to the extent possible the weaker state does not take sides in the bilateral conflicts between the competing great powers (in this case the US and China) unless they seriously threaten the stability of the region as a whole (such as some scenarios of a Sino–US conflict involving Taiwan).[47] It also means not providing unconditional support to either side which may encourage their unilateral and extremist behaviour. Finally, this strategy places considerable emphasis on multilateralism. While liberal-institutionalist theory points to a range of ways in which international institutions may promote cooperation and peace, including information-sharing, development of norms and enhancing predictability, Malaysian interest in multilateralism assumes that it is only through their collective efforts that the ASEAN countries can make their voices heard and count in the club of great powers, no matter whether the latter are friendly or adversarial. Multilateralism is often used by weak powers to enhance their bargaining clout which they cannot achieve through unilateral action. The ARF gives Malaysia a chance to affect the preferences of both China and the US without accepting the dominance of either side.

Taken together, these various elements of Malaysian posture are best described as one of "counter-dominance" (See Table 6.2). Such a strategy incorporates a strong element of multilateral "engagement," in the sense that the term is defined by the editors of this volume; but it goes beyond the policy of engagement as defined from an American vantage point. The Malaysian policy is conditioned by an aversion to a region dominated by any great power, including the US. In other words, while Malaysia may favour an "engagement strategy," it does not wish to be identified with an *American* engagement strategy. Engagement must be pursued through a multilateral framework in which the weaker actors play a major norm- and agenda-setting role. This strategy may be elaborated in terms of four principal aspects.

1 No single power should dominate in the region

This may be described as a key element of regional security framework of ASEAN as a whole, but Malaysia, one of the more neutrality-minded members of ASEAN (especially when compared to Singapore and Thailand) has been a key promoter of this idea. As Mahathir puts it, the security of the ASEAN region requires that "nobody should dominate anybody else."[48] In other words, Malaysia will seek to ensure that countering Chinese military dominance does not require acceptance of American political dominance.

Table 6.2 Balancing, bandwagoning, and counter-dominance

The options of an autonomy-seeking weaker state such as Malaysia in dealing with a rising power (China) are presented as part of a continuum beginning with A (outright containment) and ending with E (joining the camp). Malaysia's preferred approach at present appears to be C. It is important to note that B, C, and D are not mutually exclusive. Depending on changing circumstances, C may draw upon some elements of B (balance without containment) and even, at times, D (siding with the rising power on certain issues without appeasement or bandwagoning).

(A) participate in the containment strategy of a competing Great Power with firm alliance ties to the latter – (B) balance the rising power through increased national strength and loose military ties with other Great Powers but stop short of outright and aggressive containment – (C) develop a counter-dominance posture that avoids firm alliances with, and maintains relative neutrality between, the rival Great Powers, while promoting bilateral and multilateral norms and linkages to constrain the strategic options of the rising power – (D) side with the rising power on certain key economic, political and security issues, but stop short of outright bandwagoning (including alliance-building) with the rising power – (E) bandwagon (join the camp) with the rising power.

2 There should be no great power concert

A logical corollary to the first principle, this also constitutes a key goal of Malaysia's and ASEAN's regional security posture. A concert implies a cooperative relationship among the great powers in which the latter assume the primary responsibility for the maintenance of order in a given regional/ international system. A concert system acknowledges the hierarchical distribution of power and the special status, privileges and responsibilities of the great powers in the management of international order.[49] Such a system may marginalize the interests and role of weaker actors in shaping international order. The vision of an Asia Pacific concert of powers comprising the US, China and Japan (and to a lesser extent Russia and India) has been firmly rejected by the ASEAN states. ASEAN's preferred vehicle for regional order is the ARF, a multilateral institution in which ASEAN itself hopes to remain in the "driver's seat."

3 The primacy of national and regional autonomy

To a greater extent than most of its ASEAN neighbours, Malaysia is wary of an unequal alliance relationship. It was an outspoken critic of Cold War clientelism, even though it received significant military support from the West (Britain, Australia and New Zealand) in combating communist insurgency, and it has opposed the idea of a New World Order as a mask for renewed American and Western unilateralism and dominance in the post-Cold War era. But the concept of autonomy need not mean the total exclusion of outside powers. Rather, its goal is to ensure that the role of outside powers is not coercive and serves the interests of the regional actors. Thus while Malaysia acknowledges the legitimate interest and role of outside powers in regional stability, this involvement is acceptable only to the extent that it conforms to prevailing regional norms and promotes the security interests of the regional actors.

4 National and collective military power is a necessary but not sufficient basis for counter-dominance

Military power needs to be supplemented by multilateral norms and institutions. Malaysia, like most other East Asian nations, is undertaking a major programme for defence modernization aimed at acquiring a modern fighting force. Malaysian armed forces may realistically aim for a limited capacity for denial, i.e. preventing China from occupying territory and exploiting resources in areas claimed by Malaysia. But they are unlikely to match China's growing power projection capabilities. A strategy of countering Chinese regional primacy must involve other elements, especially multilateralism. Multilateralism is not an idealistic quest for regional governance, but a practical response to regional order in view of Malaysia's limited military power. By pursuing multilateralism, Malaysia hopes to raise the diplomatic and political costs of Chinese militarism.

Conclusion

Malaysia is willing to live with rising Chinese power as long as it does not become preponderant. In view of its distrust of both the US and China, Malaysia is unlikely to bandwagon with either power except in the extreme case of outright Chinese aggression. Given the fluidity of the regional strategic environment and the uncertainties about China's future security posture, Malaysia and other Asian countries will keep their options for dealing with China relatively open.

A counter-dominance strategy may be seen as the preferred approach of weak actors without the will or the way to pursue balancing. For Malaysia, the appeal of pursuing a fully fledged engagement policy is tempered by uncertainty as to whether it will work, as well as the close association of the term with American policy toward China (which Malaysia will seek to distance itself from, at least for political reasons). A balancing strategy, on the other hand, involves accepting a dominant role for external powers. Faced with these difficult choices, weaker actors are likely to adopt as much of a middle ground (including relative political neutrality) between rival great powers as possible while working multilaterally to regulate the behaviour of the latter. International norms and institutions and multilateralism play a key role in a counter-dominance strategy pursued by weak powers, for which a key goal of collective action is to avoid being a pawn in the hands of great powers as they compete for power and influence.

Acknowledgement

1 My thanks to Ezra Vogel, discussant of the paper at the Harvard workshop during 30–31 May 1997, Mak Joon Num of the Maritime Institute of Malaysia for advice and assistance during research for this paper, and Hari Singh of the National University of Singapore for helpful and detailed critique of an earlier draft of the chapter

Notes

2 "Engaging China: The View from Kuala Lumpur," *Asiaweek*, 1 August 1998 (http://ftdasia.ft.com/info-api/sh, p.1).

3 "I Am Still Here," Interview with Mahathir Mohammad, *Asiaweek*, 9 May 1997, p. 34.

4 Cited in J.N. Mak, "The ASEAN Naval Build-up: Implications for Regional Order," Paper presented to the Conference on "CBMs at Sea in the Asia Pacific Region: Meeting the Challenges of the 21st Century," Kuala Lumpur: The Malaysian Institute of Maritime Affairs, 2–3 August 1994, p. 14.

5 Vice Admiral Dato' Ahmad Ramli Hj. Mohd. Nor, "The Royal Malaysian Navy's Roles: Adapting to Security Challenges?," Paper presented to the Conference on Changing Conceptions of Security in a Changing Pacific Asia, Putra World Trade Centre, Kuala Lumpur, 25–26 April 1996, p. 3.

6 "ASEAN should be 'wary of China's military expansion'," *The Sunday Times* (Singapore), 29 March 1992.

7 Siti Azizah Abod and Colonel Jamil Rais Abdullah, "Defence Reorientation in Southeast Asia – Political and Military Implications," Paper presented to ADTEX'95 Panel on Defense Re-orientation in Southeast Asia, 20–21 April 1995, New World Hotel, Manila, pp. 6–7.

8   General Dato' Che Md. Noor b. Mat Arshad, "Planning Malaysian Army for the
    Twenty-First Century," Paper Presented to the Conference on Land Forces in the
    Twenty-First Century: The Challenge for the Malaysian and Regional Armies,"
    Organized by the Malaysian International Affairs Forum, Kuala Lumpur, 20–21
    November 1995, pp. 5–6.
9   Vice Admiral Dato' Ahmad Ramli Hj. Mohd. Nor, "The Royal Malaysian Navy's
    Roles: Adapting to Security Challenges?" p. 3.
10 Ibid., p. 2.
11 Interview with *Jane's Defence Weekly*, 26 September 1992, p. 32.
12 "Malaysia: Preparing for Change," *Jane's Defence Weekly*, 29 July 1989, p. 159.
13 "Intelligence Chief Reviewed on Threat," FBIS-EAS-90-036, 22 February 1990,
    p. 41.
14 For a discussion of these factors, see Amitav Acharya, *An Arms Race in Post-Cold War
    Southeast Asia? Prospects for Control*, Pacific Strategic Papers No.8 (Singapore: Institute of
    Southeast Asian Studies, 1994).
15 On 23 July 1996, at the third ARF meeting held in Jakarta, Chinese Foreign Minister
    Qian Qichen stated that "China stands for shelving the [Spratlys] disputes while going
    in for joint development pending a solution, and has conducted consultations with . . .
    Malaysia with constructive results." "Chinese Call for Joint Development of Disputed
    Territories," *The Straits Times*, 24 July 1996, p. 12.
16 Vice Admiral Dato' Ahmad Ramli Hj. Mohd. Nor, "The Royal Malaysian Navy's
    Roles: Adapting to Security Challenges?" p. 6.
17 "Engaging China: The View from Kuala Lumpur," *Asiaweek*, 1 August 1998
    (http://ftdasia.ft.com/info-api/sh, p. 1).
18 For an authoritative study of Sino–Malysian relations during this period, see Hari
    Singh, *Malaysia and the Communist World, 1968–1981*, Doctoral Dissertation, La Trobe
    University, Melbourne, Australia, 1988, Chapter 4.
19 "China Could be Partner to ASEAN One Day: Mahathir", *The Straits Times*, 11
    December 1990, p. 15.
20 FBIS-EAS-93-141, pp. 36–7.
21 Ismail Kassim, "China's Arms Buildup No Threat to Region," *The Straits Times*, 26
    May 1993, p. 17.
22 *Jane's Defence Weekly*, 24: 20 (1995), p. 14.
23 "Trick or Treat?" *The Economist*, 10 July 1993, p21; Michael Vatikiotis, "Mixed
    Motives," *Far Eastern Economic Review*, 156: 25 (1993), p. 13.
24 "Dr Feelgood," *Far Eastern Economic Review*, 24 October 1996, p. 19.
25 "Malaysia: Premier Discusses Trade with Chinese Business Delegation," Xinhua
    News Agency, 30 April 1998 (http://ftdasia.ft.com/info-api/sh).
26 "Reviewing Overseas Investments," *Business Times (Kuala Lumpur)*, 2 May 1998
    (http://ftdasia.ft.com/info-api/sh).
27 George Hicks and J.A.C. Mackie, "A Question of Identity," *Far Eastern Economic
    Review*, 14 July 1994, p .48.
28 "China Improves Ties With ASEAN Through Manila Conference," *China Business
    Information Network*, 30 July 1998 (http://ftdasia.ft.com/info-api/sh).
29 "China Can be Misread," Editorial, *The Straits Times*, 12 August 1998, p. 36.
30 "Abdullah: China Can Help ASEAN to Rally," *New Straits Times (Kuala Lumpur)*, 29
    July 1998 (http://ftdasia.ft.com/info-api/sh).
31 "China Improves Ties With ASEAN Through Manila Conference," *China Business
    Information Network*, 30 July 1998 (http://ftdasiaft.com/info-api/sh).
32 This is evident in one of the important areas of economic dominance identified by
    David Goodman. Goodman calculated that the control of the ethnic Chinese of the
    local share capital by market capitalization was 61 per cent in the case of Malaysia,

compared to 95 per cent in Thailand, 73 per cent in Indonesia, and 60 per cent in Philippines. David S. G. Goodman, "The Ethnic Chinese in East and Southeast Asia: Local Insecurities and Regional Concerns," Paper presented to the Conference on The Economics of East Asian Security, organized by the International Institute for Strategic Studies, the Chinese Council for Advanced Policy Studies, and the Canadian National Committee of the IISS, Vancouver, 4–5 March 1997, p. 5.

33 Speech by Ambassador Dato' Abdullah Ahmad, Special Envoy of Malaysia to the United Nations at the Sixth Tun Abdul Razak Conference of Ohio University, Athens, Ohio, 18 April 1997, p. 7.

34 Jeffrey D. Young, *U.S. Military Interaction with Southeast Asian Countries*, CRS Report for Congress, 92–241 F (Washington, DC: The Library of Congress, 27 February 1992), p.12.

35 Cited in Charles Smith, "Man of the Moment," *Far Eastern Economic Review*, 157: 47 (1994), p. 18.

36 FBIS-EAS-90-036, 2 February 1990, p. 41.

37 Andrew Mack, "Naval Arms Control and Confidence-Building for Northeast Asian Waters," Paper presented to Conference on "Arms Control and Confidence-Building in the Asia-Pacific Region," organized by the Canadian Institute for International Peace and Security, Ottawa, 22–23 May 1992, p.4; Najib also offered to host the first of a series of security dialogues involving Asia Pacific nations with representatives from military and civilian organizations. "Malaysia Push for Regional Defence," *The Age*, 10 April 1992.

38 On the evolution of the ARF, see Amitav Acharya, *A New Regional Order in Southeast Asia: ASEAN in the Post-Cold War Era*, Adelphi Paper no. 279 (London: International Institute of Strategic Studies, 1993).

39 Amitav Acharya, *The ASEAN Regional Forum: Confidence-Building* (Ottawa: Department of Foreign Affairs and International Trade Canada, 1997); The ASEAN Concept Paper, Annex A and B, pp. 8–11.

40 Ah Ying, "Cooperation in Security and Security Through Cooperation," *People's Daily*, 16 July 1997, p. 6. (According to Western diplomatic sources, Ah Ying could be the pen-name of a senior official in the Chinese Foreign Ministry.)

41 "Engaging China: The View from Kuala Lumpur," *Asiaweek*, 1 August 1998 (http://ftdasia.ft.com/info-api/sh, p.1).

42 A newspaper editorial is suggestive: "China Supports EAEG: Report," *Business Times*, 6 June 1991.

43 "Malaysian PM on the Role of ASEAN, China in Promoting [*sic*]," Xinhua News Agency, 21 August 1997 (http://ftdasia.ft.com/info-api/sh).

44 "I am Still Here," Interview with Prime Minister Mahathir Mohammed, *Asiaweek*, 9 May 1997, p. 34.

45 For a conceptual elaboration of balancing and bandwagoning, see Stephen M. Walt, "Alliance Formation and the Balance of World Power," *International Security*, 9: 4 (spring 1985), pp. 3–43.

46 Third World countries such as Malaysia have been historically wary of dependence on external security guarantees, even if they have had to accept it on pragmatic grounds. In the case of Malaysia, balancing China would mean joining the stronger side (the US and its allies) against a still weaker but rising power. This would aggravate Malaysia's fear of being dominated in an unequal alliance. On the aversion of Third World countries to security dependence, see Amitav Acharya, "Regional Military–Security Cooperation in the Third World: A Conceptual Analysis of the Association of Southeast Asian Nations," *Journal of Peace Research*, 29: 1 (January 1992), pp. 7–21.

47 Derek Da Cunha's excellent analysis of Southeast Asian states' response to the China–Tawain missile crisis in 1996 supports this view. See his "Southeast Asian Perceptions

of China's Military Role in its Backyard," Paper prepared for the CAPS/Rand Joint Conference on "Chinese Security Policy and the Future of Asia," 26–28 June Waikiki, Hawaii, pp. 10–12.

48 "I am Still Here," p.34.

49 The idea of concert is derived from the nineteenth-century European Concert system, which was based on four rules: "(1) the proper way of dealing with international crises was through conference diplomacy; (2) territorial change was subject to great power approval; (3) essential members of the states system must be protected and defended; (4) great powers must not be humiliated." See Richard B. Elrod, "The Concert of Europe: A Fresh Look at an International System," *World Politics*, 28: 2 (January 1976), pp.163–6.

7

MANAGING CHINESE POWER

The view from Japan

Michael Jonathan Green

Introduction

Throughout the post-war period Japan has maintained a policy of constructive engagement toward Beijing. This strategy was established by Japan's first post-war prime minister, Yoshida Shigeru, who predicted that Japan could wean China away from Moscow by providing an alternative to dependence on the Soviet Union. In Yoshida's view, a prosperous China would inevitably become friendly with Japan and the United States. While hotly debated between the ruling Liberal Democratic Party's pro-Taipei and pro–Beijing factions in the 1960s, Yoshida's approach became the mainstream consensus view after normalization of relations with the PRC in 1972. As US–Japan relations became sour in the 1980s, this same approach became the basis for arguments that a China prosperous on Japan's terms might provide a useful counterweight to US economic hegemony. At its core, Yoshida's strategy was premised on a faith in the principles of commercial liberalism and Japan's own mercantile power.

Sometime after the end of the Cold War, however, Japan's faith in commercial liberalism began to erode. The Yoshida approach was shaken by Tienanmen, but survived more or less intact. The real changes began after Tienanmen. First, the collapse of the Japanese economic "bubble" in 1991 and Japan's poor political performance in the Gulf War undermined the confidence that had underpinned Tokyo's view of its post-war role in Asia and relationship with China. The interruption of long-term LDP rule two years later opened the foreign policy process to a more fluid and unpredictable style of political leadership. Prime Minister Hosokawa Morihiro and Foreign Minister Hata Tsutomu set the new tone with Japan's first non-LDP government in four decades by publicly pressing Beijing for greater military transparency.[1] Chinese nuclear weapons tests in 1995 then led the restored LDP–Social Democrat–Harbinger coalition to suspend $75 million in grant assistance in an unprecedented display of disapproval of Beijing's policies.[2] In 1996 the Taiwan Straits crisis, the reaffirmation of the US–Japan Alliance, and a dispute over the Senkaku (Diaoyutai) Islands reduced Sino–Japanese relations to a post-war low. These punctuated changes in official relations were accompanied by a seachange in attitude toward China demonstrated in Japanese public opinion polls and newspaper editorials over the same period.[3] In the space of only a few years, Japan's fundamental thinking on China shifted from a faith in commercial realism to a reluctant liberalism.[4]

What, then, of the traditional strategy of engagement? There is still a strong consensus in Japan that friendly relations must be maintained with the PRC. There is also a continuing search for economic, technological, and diplomatic tools to shape the growth of the Chinese economy and Chinese foreign and security policy in directions that are beneficial – or at least not harmful – to Japan. However, this traditional strategy of engagement is now tempered by a suspicion of Chinese motives, new doubts about Japanese capabilities to affect change in China, and a desire to use multilateral and bilateral security networks to balance, and even contain, errant Chinese behavior. In short, Japan has begun hedging against its earlier bets on China's future.

This chapter focuses on an assessment of the key elements in Japan's emerging approach to China and examines the potential for harnessing Japan's efforts to broader US, regional and global engagement of China. First, however, it is important to examine in more detail the structural changes in Sino–Japanese relations that have occured since the end of the Cold War.

The four pillars of Sino–Japanese relations

Japan's traditional strategy of engagement toward China rested on four distinct pillars: security; domestic politics; the legacy of history; and economics. All four pillars have shifted in the 1990s, establishing new constituencies and a new framework for Japan's approach to China.

Security

The basis of Japan's security policy in the post-war era was a close alliance with the United States, and Japan's policies toward China were formulated within the broad constraints imposed by the United States' global strategy of containment. Thus, before 1972, Tokyo followed Washington's policy of denying diplomatic recognition to the PRC and championing the Nationalist regime in Taiwan. At the same time, however, the Japanese government never saw Beijing as a military or even political threat in the same way that Washington did. The legacy of the Second World War convinced the majority of Japanese political leaders that a hostile relationship with Beijing was contrary to Japanese interests. Faith in commercial liberalism reinforced the conviction that Beijing would break from Moscow and follow a course of economic modernization modeled on Japan. Fear of becoming "entrapped" (*makikomareru*) in a US military confrontation with China over Taiwan or Southeast Asia led successive Japanese governments to deny full military cooperation with US forces, even as Japan reconstituted its own Self Defense Force (JSDF).

Japan's "conscientious objector" status in the containment of China was tolerated by Washington just as China grew increasingly comfortable with the US–Japan Alliance. The United States squeezed an official expression of support from Japan for the US defense commitment to Taiwan only once – in the 1969 Nixon–Sato Communiqué, when negotiating pressure to secure the return of Okinawa led the Japanese government to concede that the security of Taiwan is of importance to Japan. Beijing's reaction was predictably ferocious, and bureaucrats in MOFA and the Japan Defense Agency (JDA) spent the next decade retreating from any hint of a commitment to support US forces in a Taiwan contingency. Pressure on Japan to play a larger security role mounted in the 1970s despite this clever bureaucratic maneuver, however, and in 1975 the United States and Japan began negotiating Guidelines for Defense Cooperation that would establish a framework for the first deliberate military planning between the two countries. In this exercise the Japanese bureaucrats again deftly maneuvered away from explicit commitments to support US forces in a regional contingency (Article VI of the Mutual Security Treaty) and successfully locked the US side into planning for the defense of Japan from direct attack (Article V of the Treaty). As it turned out, however, the emphasis on bilateral cooperation for the defense of Japan became an important element in US global strategy as Soviet military capabilities began to expand in the Far East. In the end, Japan successfully avoided both abandonment by the United States and entrapment in US conflicts that did not directly threaten Japan.

The US–Japan Alliance increasingly served China's interests as well. Behind their fierce rhetoric against the alliance in 1951 and its revision in 1960, Chinese leaders recognized that the US–Japan Alliance contained the return of militarism in Japan. With the Sino–Soviet split in the 1960s and growing Sino–Soviet confrontation in the 1970s, the US–Japan Alliance also contributed to China's strategic objectives by containing the Soviet Union. As Washington played its "China card" in the 1970s, Japan made an even clearer tilt toward Beijing. Japan was the first nation to extend aid to China in 1972, and in 1978 the Japanese government agreed to include a transparently anti-Soviet "anti-hegemony" clause in the Peace and Friendship Treaty with Beijing.

At the end of the Cold War, this comfortable framework for sustaining mutually reinforcing security ties with Washington and commercial ties with Beijing began to unravel. First, with the demise of the Soviet threat, Tokyo's formula for contributing to US global strategy only by increasing capabilities for the defense of Japan (and not regional security) lost credibility. In the 1991 Gulf War Japan came under intense domestic and international pressure to contribute more than financial support to the multinational effort against Saddam Hussein. Unable to dispatch its shining new military forces for even rear area missions to the Gulf, the Japanese government and National Diet entered into months of intense debate which ended with new legislation that would allow some limited participation in UN-sanctioned peacekeeping missions. The legislation was successfully field tested in Cambodia in 1993, but the fundamental question of Japanese support for

US responses to regional contingencies reared its head again in 1994 with the North Korean nuclear crisis. Unable to participate in planning with the United States for maritime interdiction operations against North Korea in anticipation of economic sanctions, the Japanese government was only saved from a major political and constitutional crisis by the intervention of former President Carter in Pyongyang in April 1994. Recognizing that multilateral security and peace-keeping would be too little too late in a contingency and that steps had to be taken to provide at least rear area support for US forces responding to regional crises, the Japanese government changed its 1976 National Defense Program Outline (NDPO) in November 1995. Where the 1976 NDPO authorized preparations for defense against "limited small-scale attack," the revised 1995 NDPO cleared the way for preparing to support the "smooth and effective implementation of US–Japan security arrangements" in response to "situations that arise in the areas surrounding Japan."[5]

While carefully conditioned on Japan's legal and constitutional framework, the new regional emphasis in Japanese defense planning did not please observers in Beijing. The changes in the NDPO were followed in April 1996 by a Joint US–Japan Security Declaration that featured a revision of the 1978 Guidelines to address bilateral cooperation in regional crises. Coming on the heels of the March 1996 Taiwan Straits crisis (during which a US carrier battle group deployed from Japan), the new emphasis on regional crisis planning appeared to be aimed at Taiwan. In fact, the Joint Security Declaration was planned for the previous November and was postponed because of President Clinton's decision to skip the APEC summit to attend to the domestic US budget showdown. Moreover, the impetus for revising the Guidelines was caused by the tense situation on the Korean Peninsula rather than the situation in the Taiwan Straits. Nevertheless, the Chinese attacks on the Joint Security Declaration and the "expansion" of the US–Japan Alliance marked a change in China's policy from the perspective of Japan. Beijing's criticism of the alliance began almost immediately after the April 1996 US–Japan Joint Security Declaration and continued well into 1998 – even as the Japanese and Chinese governments were preparing for a summit that was designed to restabilize bilateral relations.[6] If China saw a reaffirmed US–Japan Alliance as inimical to its interests – a contrast to Beijing's previous tacit support for the alliance – then there was good reason to worry about long-term Chinese intentions.

This dynamic has been repeated in the debate over Theater Missile Defense (TMD). Japan embarked on a joint study of missile defense requirements with the United States in 1994 after several years of US prodding for Japanese participation in this major program. TMD, though costly and uncertain in terms of technical feasibility, had some support in Japanese industry and the JDA and MOFA as an alliance-enhancer, a technology-driver, and a potential defense against ballistic missiles – a particularly important point in the wake of North Korea's 1992 test of the Nodong missile and China's own missile demonstrations over the Taiwan Straits in March 1996. Chinese objections to

Japanese participation in TMD have been as strenuous as the objections to the revised Defense Guidelines, primarily because Beijing views Japanese-based TMD as undermining China's own deterrent. The problem with this logic from Tokyo's perspective is that Japan possesses no nuclear weapons, and therefore China's concern about its ability to strike Japan suggests that Chinese missiles not only target Japanese territory, but that China's policies of "No first use" and "No use against non-nuclear states" do not apply to Japan. Ironically, the Chinese objections to TMD have only heightened Japanese concerns about a Chinese ballistic missile threat that had been a secondary concern after North Korea in the initial discussions over TMD. At the same time, Chinese objections to TMD have reinforced its opponents in Japan just as it has emboldened missile defense activists. North Korea's August 1998 test of the Taepo-dong 1 missile over Japanese airspace solidified support for incremental movement forward on joint R&D on navy upper tier systems with the United States, but the crucial decision on whether or not to eventually develop and deploy these systems will force a further debate on strategic relations with China.

For Japan, there has also been reason to worry about long-term Chinese capabilities. Early drafts of the revised NDPO focused on the threat posed by China's growing military modernization, nuclear tests and expansionist policies in the South China Sea and the Senkaku Islands. Only after opposition from members of the Social Democratic Party of the then Prime Minister Murayama was the China-threat language removed. Prime Minister Murayama himself then used the original language in a speech to the self-defense forces in October 1995. Since then, the JDA's annual defense White Papers have highlighted the "uncertainty" caused by China's military modernization and maneuvers and these topics have been regular fare in Japanese journals, newspapers and academic symposia. For its part, the LDP's National Security Commission has repeatedly warned that Japan must "pay attention to the movement of China, especially in its modernization of Navy and Air Force, [and] its military training, which heightened the tension in the Taiwan Straits last year [in 1996]."[7]

The comfortable trilateral security dynamics of the 1970s and 1980s are over. Tightly constrained and asymmetric US–Japan military cooperation is no longer credible in Washington or Tokyo; the Chinese tolerance for the US–Japan Alliance has waned; and Japanese planners now assume that Chinese military assets could pose a potential long-term threat to Japanese interests. The new dynamics need not be confrontational, but they are no longer the same.

Domestic politics

Japanese domestic politics also contributed to the characteristic passivity of Japan's posture toward China during the Cold War. It should not be surprising, therefore, that political realignment in the 1990s is changing the patterns of Sino–Japanese relations.

Traditionally, three different levels of domestic politics locked Japan's policy of constructive engagement into place. At the interagency level, China policy was left to MOFA because the historical legacy made it too dangerous for the politicians to manage. At the interparty level, the opposition Socialists and their supporters in the mainstream media guaranteed that any criticism of the government's China policy by Beijing would cost the LDP support at election time. Finally, at the factional/intraparty level, the LDP leadership feared an ideological split between younger supporters of the Taiwan and Beijing camps who threatened to use the China issue in their bid for party leadership in the 1960s. After normalization of relations in 1972, Prime Minister Tanaka Kakuei and other senior LDP leaders established close ties with their counterparts in Beijing to ensure that domestic political debate in either country would not undermine the new course of bilateral cooperation.

In the mid-1990s the domestic political breakwaters against volatile China policy were shaken. Generational change has removed some of Beijing's closest supporters from the ranks of the LDP's active leadership. Although LDP President and Prime Minister Hashimoto Ryutaro and opposition New Frontier Party leader Ozawa Ichiro are both products of the faction of Tanaka Kakuei, neither has the same emotional or political ties to Beijing that their mentor had. Indeed, observers in Beijing tend to view both men as dangerous nationalists. Hashimoto and Ozawa are counterbalanced by more dovish leaders such as Kato Koichi (a former diplomat who served in Hong Kong), but even those advocating a "softer line" on international security lack the commitment to relations with Beijing of the previous generation.[8] Meanwhile, Beijing has lost its allies on the left in Japan. The conversion of the Socialist Party to a nominally pro-defense/pro-capitalist "Social Democratic Party" leaves only the marginalized Communist Party in Japan to defend Chinese ideology (something the party never did with any enthusiasm to begin with) and the new Democratic Party, formed in March 1998, has not established a consistent position on China. The left then surprised the Chinese in 1995 by pushing MOFA to suspend ODA in retaliation for Chinese nuclear testing. Beijing has fared poorly in the media as well. All major newspapers (except *Sankei Shimbun*) abide by a virtual censorship policy in their reporting from Beijing, but political reports from other parts of Asia and mainstream editorials are increasingly critical of Beijing. Even the *Asahi Shimbun*, which once served to amplify Chinese criticism of the LDP, is now amplifying LDP criticism of Chinese behavior in its editorials.

The atrophying ties of Sino–Japanese political elites are further exacerbated by new electoral rules and political realignment in Japan. When the pro-Taiwan and pro-Beijing factions quarreled in the LDP in the 1970s, the party leadership was able to impose the discipline necessary to prevent an open fissure. In the current context of new single-seat election districts and shifting political realignment, there is no such discipline. Thus far, political realignment has shaped China policy, even if China policy has not yet shaped political realignment. The latter possibility could increase, however, depending on larger trends in the

US–Japan–China strategic relationship. An example of what might unfold came in the summer of 1997 when LDP Secretary General Kato Koichi and Chief Cabinet Secretary Kajiyama Seiroku openly argued about whether or not Taiwan would be "included" in the newly revised US–Japan Defense Guidelines. The government clearly had no intention of undermining its one China policy or the credibility of the Guidelines by ruling one way or the other on Taiwan, but Kato used the issue to reassure the left wing of the ruling coalition, while Kajiyama responded on behalf of those who wanted to dump the socialists and form a conservative–conservative alliance.[9] LDP nationalism and anxiety regarding China was highlighted again in the summer of 1998 as MOFA attempted to negotiate a joint statement for the Jiang Zemin–Keizo Obuchi summit planned for September of that year. Beijing pressed Tokyo for a clear statement on Taiwan that would parallel President Clinton's own "three nos" enunciation in Shangai during his June summit with Jiang. Under heavy pressure from Taiwan, and resentful of Chinese pressure, the LDP rejected the possibility of any such language. Jiang cancelled his visit to Tokyo, primarily because of devastating floods at home, but there was a strong suggestion that he backed out because the Japanese side would not deliver on Taiwan.[10]

History

The third key element behind Japan's traditional engagement of China was the powerful historical legacy of the Pacific War. Overcoming the legacy of this war and rejoining the community of nations was a primary motivation behind the overall "Yoshida Doctrine" of minimal remilitarization and international commercial ambition. When Japanese commentators used the four-character phrase *dobun doshu* (same culture, same race) to describe post-war relations with China, the sentiment was profound. Even more profound, however, was the political impact of the Japanese media's (and especially *Asahi Shimbun*'s) amplification of Chinese criticism whenever nationalistic LDP politicians worshipped at the Yasukuni War Shrine or called for increased defense spending.

History no longer has the same constraining effect on Japanese policy toward China. When Japan temporarily froze grant aid to China in 1995, the Chinese Foreign Ministry spokesman responded by reminding Japan of its historical debts to China, but the ploy failed to win Beijing any support in the Japanese media as it might have done in the past. Tokyo's "economic card" and Beijing's "history card" both turned out to be jokers. Generational change accounts for the lost resonance of the war issue more than any other factor. The Japanese public has reached "apology fatigue" as Jiang Zemin learned when he finally conducted his state visit to Tokyo at the end of 1998. Jiang pressed for a formal "apology" (*owabi*) and "remorse" (*hansei*) from Japanese Prime Minister Obuchi, but Jiang refused to accept these written statements as closure on the historical problem in the way that South Korean President Kim Dae Jung had during a summit with Obuchi two months earlier. In the end, Jiang went home with only *hansei*, which left a bitter legacy from the summit for both sides. Obuchi, however, was broadly supported by the media and the major political parties for his firm stand.

Economics

Economic engagement has underpinned and stabilized Sino–Japanese relations, even in the difficult political episodes of the last few years. Trade volume increased by 25 percent in 1995 after similar gains during 1991 to 1994.[11] Japanese FDI into China mushroomed over the same period, almost doubling annually in numbers of cases and contracted investment amounts, with the increase in implemented investment not far behind.[12] In the first half of 1995, Japanese investment was larger than the same period for the previous year, despite an overall decline in FDI into China.[13] Moreover, Japan's economic cooperation with China has expanded into new sectors such as automobiles and energy.

At the same time there is a new skepticism on the economic side that parallels the concerns on the political side of Sino–Japanese relations. Pessimists are skeptical about the continued expansion of trade ties because they have seen China's economy overheat before, with disastrous effects on bilateral economic relations. Japanese companies also continue to experience intellectual property rights violations, abrupt cancellations of projects, and pressure to direct FDI to unproductive but politically important regions of the mainland.[14] Finally, Japanese worry officials increasingly about the security and environmental effects of growing Chinese demands for energy.[15] As we will see, these concerns are leading to new patterns of hedging in private sector Japanese economic engagement of China.

The emerging patterns of Japan's engagement strategy

Japan's approach to China has shifted from commercial liberalism to reluctant realism in relative rather than absolute terms. A strict realist policy based on balance of power logic would have Japan pursuing relative gains at the expense of China. Japan would cut off all aid and investment and generally adopt policies to retard China's economic growth.[16] This Japan has not done. In realist terms, therefore, Japan's response to China in recent years may be closer to the balance of threat theory.[17] Japan has hedged against growing Chinese capabilities because of a realization that China could use these capabilities against Japan and that commercial liberalism will not necessarily alter Chinese behavior. At the same time, Japan has continued to engage China and to adopt policies (with a few notable exceptions) aimed at reassuring China that Japan does not intend to become a threat.

That the shift in Japanese China policy is relative and not absolute is evident in the adjustments taken since the suspension of grant aid and the reaffirmation of the US–Japan Alliance in 1995 and 1996. Citing the twenty-fifth anniversary of Sino–Japanese normalization and the death of Deng Xiaoping, Japanese MOFA officials declared 1997 "the year of a breakthrough in China relations."[18] ODA grants were resumed and negotiations reopened on the Fourth Yen Loan package.[19] This was not the pendulum swinging back to the *modus operandi* of the 1980s, however, so much as a recalibration of Japanese policy in the wake of Clinton Administration efforts to improve Sino–US relations (this as Sino–Japanese relations deteriorated over the Senkaku Islands dispute). No matter how realist Tokyo becomes, it cannot endure a situation in which US relations with China are better than Japan's. For example, a senior Clinton administration official's comments in *Business Week* in 1996 that China is America's natural partner in Asia caused unbridled anxiety in Tokyo and prompted concerns about "Japan passing."

Even as Japan moved to the leeward side of US China policy, however, the fundamental shift in course has been clear. Traditional faith in commercial liberalism has been shattered. Japan will continue to engage China, but only while hedging its bets. Trade and investment will grow, even as MOFA and JDA view the potential of a long-term China threat and the private sector turns to other multinationals and multilateral institutions to protect its investments.

Nowhere is this new synthesis of engagement and balancing more evident than in a foreign policy strategy document prepared by the LDP in the spring of 1997. Titled "Japan's Asia-Pacific Strategy: The Challenges of Transformation," the essay was drafted primarily by China scholar turned Diet member Takemi Keizo and released by the Party's Foreign Policy Commission with official approval by the LDP executive organs. The LDP report's actual impact on policy is unclear, but it is a useful reflection of what the LDP mainstream *can* agree on in China policy (for divisions remain). The report's central statement on China says it all:

> Ultimately, China's future rests in its own hands – including how stably it will develop. Therefore, even as we seek to preserve and enhance our amicable relations with China, we must maintain a close watch on the direction China is headed and be prepared to cope with a variety of contingencies.[20]

The LDP document then spells out the specifics of what has emerged as Japan's *de facto* new strategy for engaging China. Much of the strategy is a continuation of constructive engagement, but the hedging is clear throughout. The central elements in the strategy – soft containment; multilateral engagement; multilateral economic engagement; bilateral economic engagement; aid, energy and the environment; and bilateral confidence-building – form a useful framework for assessing Japan's China strategy and are reviewed below.

Soft containment

> To make this policy work more effectively, not only must we make the
> Japan–US alliance a key dimension of our China policy, but we must
> also strengthen the cooperative countries, South Korea, and Australia –
> nations which also have reason to be concerned about China's future
> course.
>
> (Foreign Policy of the Liberal Democratic Party, p. 23)

The bulwark of Japan's hedge against the threat of future Chinese hegemony
in East Asia is the US–Japan Alliance. The reaffirmation of the alliance in April
1996 was not aimed at China – indeed, the only reference to Beijing was in the
Joint Declaration's expectation that China would be integrated as a cooperative
member of the international community.[21] With the Taiwan Straits crisis, Chinese
criticism of US presence and the US–Japan Alliance, and the confrontation over
the Senkaku (Diaouyutai) Islands, however, China quickly became the context of
the reaffirmed alliance.

Under Prime Minister Hashimoto, Japan took steps to both remind China of
the reaffirmed US commitment to forward engagement and to reassure China
that this does not represent a new strategy of containment. Speaking at Blair
House on April 25, 1997 before his meeting with President Clinton, for example,
Hashimoto reiterated that maintenance of about 100,000 US troops in the Asia
Pacific region (including close to 50,000 in Japan) was critical to regional stability,
but he indicated that this strengthened US–Japan security cooperation must be
balanced with better trilateral US–Japan–China dialogue.[22]

This triangular US–Japan–China relationship has become a major theme
for Japanese policy-makers since the 1996 Joint Security Declaration. Before
Hashimoto's trip to Washington, the editorial pages of the *Asahi Shimbun* urged the
Prime Minister to improve US–Japan bilateral coordination on China policy,
and the LDP Foreign Policy Commission urged the establishment of a trilateral
US–Japan–China summit.[23] With the Joint Security Declaration, Japan cast its
strategic vote with Washington in unmistakable terms. Now the key was to guard
against a sudden *rapprochement* between Washington and Tokyo (a repeat of the
1972 "Nixon Shock") on the one hand, or being dragged into a hostile US–China
confrontation beyond Tokyo's control on the other.[24]

Japan's confrontation with China over the Senkaku (Diaouyutai) Islands was an
early test of the strategy of harnessing US power to Japan's China policy. Tokyo's
assumption was that the US defense commitment to Japan under Article V of
the Treaty of Mutual Security and Cooperation extended to the Senkakus and
other areas under the administration of Japan. This assumption was behind
the Hashimoto administration's firm position on Japan's territorial claim to the
islands (the Japanese side even prepared to scramble JSDF helicopters if Chinese
or Taiwanese vessels attempted to land on the island).[25] When US Ambassador to
Japan Walter Mondale and State Department officials in Washington claimed

that the US–Japan Security Treaty did not apply to the Senkakus (confusing US neutrality on Japanese *territorial* claims to the islands with the long-standing US commitment to defend the islands against attack), the premise and the promise of the April 1996 Security Declaration seemed to dissipate for Tokyo.[26] Japanese diplomatic efforts went into high gear in Washington, culminating in a Department of Defense statement that the Treaty did, in fact, apply to the Senkakus.[27] Many US officials were puzzled by the Japanese Foreign Ministry's awkward insistence on an ironclad defense commitment when the possibility of Chinese hostilities was so remote. However, these officials failed to appreciate how important the Senkaku case was as a litmus test of US commitment to back Japan across the board now that the reaffirmation of the alliance had put Tokyo and China at odds for the first time.

Japanese concerns about "Japan passing" were further exacerbated by President Clinton's visit to China in June 1998, during which he declined to also visit Japan and pointedly criticized Japanese economic policy during a joint press conference with Jiang.[28] The deepening Asian financial crisis and the Clinton visit to China created a strong public impression that China was helpful and Japan was to blame for the problem. While true in part, these political atmospherics led to increased Japanese resentment of both Beijing and Washington, though Chinese criticism of Japan was harsher and contained disturbing hints of longer term competition for political leadership in Asia.[29]

Japan's strategy for locking the US in place has been paralleled by efforts to avoid abandonment by other regional actors that might seek unilateral *rapprochement* with Beijing. Thus far this soft containment is characterized not by coordinated efforts to affect Chinese behavior, so much as efforts to counteract any possible isolation of Japan by Chinese diplomacy.

The most remarkable step Japan has taken in this strategy of soft containment has been *rapprochement* with Russia. Throughout the Gorbachev era Japan warned western Europe and the United States not to trust Moscow, given the continued occupation of Japan's Northern Territories by Russian forces. In 1992 Japan separated the Northern Territories issue from overall political dialogue with Moscow (announcing a new two-track approach), but suspicion of Russia remained high. In 1996, however, Tokyo dramatically changed its policies in an effort to bring Moscow back into Asia's strategic equation as a balance to Chinese influence. Foreign Minister Ikeda Yukio visited Moscow in March 1996 and announced that he would initiate regular Russo–Japanese meetings to discuss regional security issues.[30] Japan's Foreign Ministry countered the Strategic Partnership with "second-track" US–Japan–Russia consultations and a series of new initiatives for joint confidence-building measures and peacekeeping exercises, which included a valuable "understanding" of the US–Japan Alliance announced by Russian Defense Minister Rodionov in Tokyo in May (shortly before Rodionov was sacked by Yeltsin, which left the whole endeavor in doubt).[31] A summit between Yeltsin and Hashimoto in November 1997 in Krasnoyarsk highlighted the degree to which a conservative LDP prime minister was willing to use cooperation with Russia to demonstrate the potential for Japanese leadership in Asia. On the whole, Japanese mistrust of Russia remains high and there is no solution to the Northern Territories dispute in sight. Nevertheless, Japan cannot afford to nurse old animosities in a way that allows Sino–Russian *rapprochement* at Tokyo's expense. This has been all the more so since Moscow and Beijing announced the "Strategic Partnership" in 1997.

In Southeast Asia the Hashimoto government thought it had a promising opportunity to not only counter Chinese criticism of Japan, but to coordinate engagement of Beijing. Japanese FDI in ASEAN is higher than in China, and individual ASEAN states have privately expressed support for closer political and even security cooperation with Tokyo. Hashimoto's high-profile trip to the region in January 1997 to discuss security cooperation backfired, however, because it contradicted the "ASEAN way" of avoiding open confrontation with China. Hashimoto also suffered for not allowing MOFA to coordinate the message in advance. As a result, Hashimoto was rebuffed by ASEAN leaders when he proposed regular summits and a special strategic relationship between ASEAN and Japan. Instead, diplomats from Singapore and elsewhere in Southeast Asia have responded with a counter-proposal for a summit that includes ASEAN, China, South Korea and Japan.[32] Nevertheless, Tokyo did win a statement of "understanding" of Japan's security role from Singapore and kudos from the region for extending ODA to Myanmar (a step taken to minimize Beijing's influence on Rangoon among other reasons).[33]

On the Korean Peninsula, Japanese officials worry about any expansion of Chinese influence. The worst-case scenario, according to defense and MOFA officials in Tokyo, would be a Sino–Korean continental axis against Japan and the United States. While this perspective underestimates Korea's own potential concerns about Chinese hegemony and the durability of Seoul's ties to Washington, it does reveal a deep-seated Japanese fear of political isolation from the Asian landmass. Japanese–Korean relations, already complicated by history and economic competition, have been complicated by the dispute over Takeshima (Tokdo) Island. The LDP's strategy paper captures the hope of the Japanese Foreign Ministry that these difficulties will be overcome by a more forthright accounting of history, full Japanese cooperation with Seoul in the Four Party Talks, and common desires for a successful completion of the joint Korea–Japanese 2002 World Cup Soccer event.[34] Japan and South Korea began moving towards just such a closer relationship with the Kim Dae Jung–Obuchi Summit in October 1998 and the initiation of regular trilateral diplomatic sessions with the US side thereafter.

Finally, Japan has locked in relations with Australia and New Zealand with a security-focused visit by Prime Minister Hashimoto in April. The success (and pitfalls) of the strategy were evident in an article in the *China Daily* criticizing the "military alliances that want to encircle China."[35]

Japan's strategy for soft containment has been marginally successful in the region. Tokyo has averted anti-Japanese alignments with China and sustained regional support for a more robust security partnership with the United States. However, Tokyo has failed to initiate a full security dialogue on China with any actor other than the United States and Australia. The US–Japan Alliance is diplomatically protected and Chinese diplomacy against Japan is constrained, but bilateral or trilateral coordination on China policy has proven elusive with other regional powers. And with the United States, the fear of "Japan passing" has not entirely disappeared.

Multilateral security engagement

This makes it all the more important for Japan to press China for progress in areas of arms control and disarmament and call for its active participation in multilateral talks and cooperative programs.
(Foreign Policy of the Liberal Democratic Party, p. 25)

Where active Japanese diplomatic balancing against China has failed on a bilateral basis, Japan has attempted to enmesh China in broader multilateral mechanisms. Multilateral diplomacy began attracting Japanese foreign policy strategists after the Gulf War as a hedge against US withdrawal, as an outlet for active Japanese diplomacy, and as a possible framework for cooperating with the US in broader regional security. The ASEAN Regional Forum (ARF), Asia's only effective first-track multilateral security forum, was itself in part the result of the then Foreign Minister Nakayama Taro's call for broader regional security dialogue in July 1991. Since 1995, multilateral forums such as the ARF have proved to be particularly important to Japan's strategy for engaging China.[36]

Multilateral mechanisms allow Japan to demand standards of behavior from China in ways that would simply not be as effective on a bilateral or trilateral basis. As one Japanese diplomat puts it, "Japan wants to say nice things to China bilaterally and bad things multilaterally."[37] Japan's unprecedented suspension of grant aid in 1995 failed in itself to force Beijing to sign the Comprehensive Test Ban Treaty, but implicit criticism of Beijing in the ARF meeting that same year did appear to have a major impact on Chinese thinking from Japan's perspective. China's softer approach on the Spratlys dispute also appeared to result from the solidarity displayed by other ARF members rather than from Japan's quiet prodding.

At the same time, Japan's expectations for multilateral approaches to constraining China are probably less sanguine than, for example, ASEAN's. The Chinese have long viewed regionalism and multilateralism as a cloak for Japanese interests in Asia, making Japanese initiative difficult.[38] Moreover, as the LDP's May 1997 foreign policy strategy paper warns, "China continues to favor bilateral talks over multilateral ones when issues directly affecting China's national interests are concerned."[39] Finally, Japanese-inspired institutions such as the ARF have become outlets for Beijing to criticize the US–Japan Alliance and search for fellow travelers in a new ideological campaign against "bilateral security" and for "multilateral security" in the region.[40]

While initially discouraged that Beijing's new embrace of multilateral dialogue has occurred for reasons contrary to Japanese interests, Japanese diplomats are increasingly confident in their encounters with China at these fora. The Japanese Foreign Ministry's elite new Comprehensive Foreign Policy Bureau maintains an entire "National Security Division" just for participation in first- and second-track multilateral dialogue in the region. These capable officials rebut Chinese criticism of Theater Missile Defense and the revision of US–Japan Guidelines for Defense Cooperation, arguing that these elements of the reaffirmed US–Japan Alliance are purely defensive and pose no threat to China. On the whole, Japan's Foreign Ministry is pleased with its debating record. Moreover, Japan continues to view any transparency as a win-win situation, since most suspicion of Japan in the region is viewed as misplaced to begin with. In recent years Japan has hosted the Western Pacific Naval Symposium and invited twenty-five countries to Tokyo for a transparency exercise that centered on a Japanese briefing on the Defense Guidelines.

Multilateral economic engagement

> Japan strongly supports China's bid for participation in the WTO. In view of China's position as a major power representing the region and contributing to desirable transformations throughout the world, Japan may also propose that the G-7 should accept China into its membership in addition to Russia.
>
> (Foreign Policy of the Liberal Democratic Party, p. 25)

The objective of Tokyo's bilateral and multilateral security diplomacy is to hedge against possible Chinese hegemony while integrating China into the region. While countering Chinese attempts to isolate Japan diplomatically in these multilateral institutions, Japan has not yet responded by attempting to isolate China. In fact, Tokyo continues to push for an ever higher profile for Beijing in multilateral organizations – particularly multilateral economic organizations. The WTO and the G-7 are Japan's "turf." Japan has more experience and points of leverage in these international economic organizations than it does when interacting with China bilaterally or in multilateral security fora. Multilateral economic engagement is therefore a central component of Japan's new approach to China.

Multilateral economic engagement is about more than just security, of course. Japan has a pure economic interest in using the WTO to achieve market opening for Japanese firms in China. The 1997 report on WTO compliance by the Industrial Structure Council (an advisory body of Japan's Ministry of International Trade and Industry) notes that "China's accession to the WTO, followed by implementation of its commitments for lowering tariff rates, elimination of trade restrictions, and improvements in its trade and economic systems should benefit both Japan and the global economy significantly."[41] Tokyo's specific concerns with regard to non-tariff barriers for Japanese firms include:

- Beijing's "Great Wall Mark" for quality control which blocks Japanese consumer electronic sales;
- industrial policy, local content rules and arbitrary auto standards that have complicated Japan's recent surge in FDI for auto production;
- intellectual property rights violations.

Moreover, Japan's Ministry of International Trade and Industry is concerned about the viability of the WTO to absent China. As the 1997 Industrial Structure Council report warns, the weight of China in world trade by volume has grown from 1.7 percent in 1990 to 2.8 percent in 1995, meaning that "not admitting China to the WTO may already be burdening the multilateral trading system."[42] MITI's concern is centered on US responses to China, which are increasingly turning to bilateral market access negotiations. MITI's fundamental trade strategy is aimed at moving the United States and the world trade system away from "the era of bilateralism," and "blocking unilateral actions such as the U.S. invocation of its Super 301 clause."[43] However, as long as China is out of the WTO, "there is currently no means for either WTO members or China to resolve trade disputes between them other than to try to do so bilaterally."[44] MITI questions whether the "forcible" use of Super 301 by the United States against China – even in areas of importance to Japan such as IPR protection – is "appropriate and effective." Equally disturbing for Tokyo is Washington's annual ritual debate over Most Favored Nation status for China, which "makes WTO membership of far less significance to China than it would be otherwise."[45]

Japan has attempted to use bilateral negotiations in preparation for Chinese membership in WTO in order to strike a balance between its desire to improve access to the Chinese market and to share leadership with Washington and Brussels in the WTO. Tokyo broke ranks with the United States and EU by reaching a separate agreement with Beijing over terms for membership in September 1997. MITI officials in Japan claimed that this deal paved the way for US and EU officials to complete a final agreement with China, but critics argued that Japan was merely free-riding. Ultimately, the Japanese side knows that the US position on membership terms for China will likely prevail, and that Japan's best hope for shaping the conclusion means not only applying US and EU pressure on China, but also some Chinese pressure on the West. In the end, however, as MITI's Industrial Structure Council report concedes: "we must, and beyond all else, point out that accession will mean that China's trade policies and measures must conform to WTO rules."[46]

Bilateral economic engagement

As an economic superpower, Japan is both China's best friend and strongest rival in China's pursuit of economic stature in the Asia-Pacific region.

(Foreign Policy of the Liberal Democratic Party, p. 26)

Bilateral economic relations remain the core of Japan's strategy of engagement with China. As the LDP strategy paper notes, "what is most desirable for China is to continue its present course of stable economic development until it can participate more actively in maintaining regional stability. The linchpin of Japan's efforts to bring about such a transformation in China must be economic cooperation."[47] However, this bilateral economic engagement is no longer based on the same faith in commercial liberalism that characterized Japanese trade and investment into China during the Cold War.

First, Japanese business and government officials are beginning to demonstrate concern about relative gains by China in traditional balance of power terms, even if Japanese trade and investment policy has not yet changed to reflect this. Some China watchers in Japan are warning that China will inevitably exploit its economic strength to flex greater military and political muscle in the region.[48] Japan has not yet withheld investment from China in order to stunt Chinese economic growth, but there is a growing possibility that Tokyo's traditional largesse with ODA will end. The LDP's strategy paper states the case for a long-term reassessment of economic assistance to China in this way:

> It is highly likely that China will catch up to and overtake Japan economically by around the year 2010. When this occurs, the purpose of the yen credits program, conceived 30 years earlier, will have been fulfilled. Therefore, the time has come to initiate a comprehensive reassessment of Japan's assistance to China, including discussions as to whether or not yen credits should be continued.[49]

A second departure from the pattern of bilateral economic engagement with China that was anticipated in the 1980s has been the Japanese industry's relative lack of dominance in China. In contrast to Southeast Asia, Japanese manufacturers in China are relatively new and lack well-developed supplier networks. Even in strong areas of Japanese competitiveness, such as automobiles, Japanese firms are still playing "catch-up" with the US and European competitors. Japanese FDI in China accounted for one-third of all new direct Japanese start-ups abroad in 1994 (in contrast to 1989 when only 10 percent of new start-ups were in China). However, the same survey of Japanese FDI in Asia indicated that Beijing's moves to dismantle or weaken the preferential tax treatment and other incentives for overseas investors may be slowing investment.[50] Indeed, industry surveys taken in 1998 suggested that a downturn in Japanese FDI had already begun. In general terms, Japanese FDI into China has been on a comparable scale to US investment, but Japanese firms have tended to move into China for cheaper labor costs rather than to develop new markets. This contrast to US strategy is marked in the case of automobiles, where GM has invested more than $2 billion in recent years while Toyota is still being scolded by Beijing for not investing more in China.[51] In the late 1990s, Japan's business daily, *Nikkei Shimbun*, was scolding the LDP and the government for not assisting industry investment in China as the Clinton administration did.[52]

Seventy percent of Japanese FDI in China went to manufacturing in FY '94 and much of that was, by its nature, in parallel to US and western European investment. In investments in energy and resources, however, Japanese trading companies are increasingly tying up with US firms. This also contradicts the expectations of the 1980s that Japanese industry would seek to dominate China's economic potential alone. According to Japanese trading company executives, US firms bring the financial credibility, legal expertise, and political clout necessary to deal with Chinese barriers.[53] These Chinese barriers have increasingly frustrated Japanese businesses in recent years, as the WTO report cited earlier indicates. Business surveys continue to suggest that Japanese firms expect to increase their investment in China in the future,[54] but this optimistic view is being hedged with multilateral (WTO) and trilateral (US) risk-sharing.

Aid, energy and the environment

> In the past, economic assistance to China was aimed at boosting productivity, but in the future, our financial and technological assistance should be directed toward environmental programs.
>
> (Foreign Policy of the Liberal Democratic Party, p.24)

Traditionally, any discussion of Japanese bilateral economic engagement of China would incorporate considerations of Japanese ODA. In recent years, however, Japanese financial and technological assistance to China has had as much to do with the environment and security as with economic relations. The trend began in 1991 when MOFA introduced an ODA Charter that outlined four conditions for aid recipients: fostering peace, democracy, freedom, and a market economy.[55] The temporary suspension of grant aid to China in 1995 was premised on this MOFA-established charter, though MOFA itself was forced to apply the Charter to China by the politicians. Behind the ODA Charter lies Japan's concept of "comprehensive security." Enunciated by Prime Minister Ohira Masayoshi in 1980, the comprehensive security approach broadened Japan's security debate beyond the highly contentious issue of rearmament. Through the oil shocks of 1973 and 1979, the Japanese government demonstrated that Japan faced threats – and in turn had tools to respond to those threats – that were not only military. Increasingly, these same lessons are being applied to engagement of China.

In terms of comprehensive security, the greatest concern in Japan is the Chinese environmental "threat." As Keidanren (the Federation of Economic Organizations) warns, unbridled Chinese economic growth will cause shortages in energy supply as well as increased pollution and environmental degradation.[56] From Japan's perspective, the main problems are unsafe Chinese nuclear reactors, and excessive reliance on fossil fuels to sustain Chinese development. The Japan China Energy Exchange Association estimated in 1993 that China will require 1,392 MTOE (million tons oil equivalent) by 2010. Japanese nuclear energy experts warn that if the China Nuclear Corporation's plans for increasing nuclear capacity tenfold to meet this new demand are realized, Japan would face the possibility of "multiple Chernobyl-style accidents" in which "radioactive clouds will first hit Japan and then spread around the world."[57] China's burgeoning interest in fast breeder reactors[58] has also alarmed Japanese energy authorities, which now support the concept of an Asiatom organization (modeled on Euratom) in order to strengthen the prospects for inspection and control of China's future recycling programs.[59]

In the 1980s Japan's grant aid and Overseas Economic Cooperation Fund (OECF) spending in China was almost entirely devoted to large-scale infrastructure projects. When acid rain from China began falling on Japan in the early 1990s, however, the focus of assistance was quickly rechanneled to cover environmental protection. The change in emphasis was marked with the establishment in 1991 of the $100 million Japan–China Friendship Environmental Protection Center in Beijing.[60] The portion of grant aid, OECF funds, and Export-Import Bank loans addressing environmental programs in China has steadily increased ever since. $2.25 billion of Japan's $5.52 billion Fourth Loan Package (1996–1998) are energy focused and fifteen of the forty projects under the package are environmental.[61] Through the Green Aid Plan, MITI has leveraged ODA to encourage Japanese industry associations to cooperate on large-scale environmental projects in China. The most ambitious of these, a coal liquefaction plant in China's Heilongjiang Province, was announced in April 1997 and will include eighteen major Japanese firms.[62]

These sorts of environmental projects clearly benefit Japanese corporations, but they are also strategically aimed to influence Chinese behavior in specific areas that could have a direct and detrimental impact on Japan's comprehensive security. More ambitious – and less developed – are Japanese plans for influencing China's larger energy requirements in a way that decreases Beijing's reliance on maritime sources of energy. From Japan's perspective, funding for pipelines inside China or international co-development schemes for the Spratly or Senkaku Islands increase interdependence and decrease the prospects that China will embark on a dangerous program of naval modernization to protect sea lanes of communication that are also vital to Japan.[63] The LDP echoes this theme, arguing that the establishment of an Asian Energy Community to coordinate this cooperation will be one of the most important keys to preserving the environment and building peace in the Asia-Pacific region.[64]

Bilateral confidence-building

China has gained confidence in its ability to transform itself from a large developing nation into an economic superpower. To sustain good relations with China in the future, Japan must continue to make itself attractive and indispensable.

(Foreign Policy of the Liberal Democratic Party, p. 26)

Consistent with the "balance of threat" logic behind Japan's response to China's rise, Tokyo is taking bilateral measures to reassure Beijing even while hedging against Chinese capabilities. At one level these measures involve transparency and dialogue. There is a firm conviction among China-hawks and China-doves alike in Tokyo that increased summits and defense dialogue with Beijing (and trilaterally with Washington) will improve Chinese understanding of Japan's security policies and avert a defense dilemma in relations with China. As *Nihon Keizai Shimbun* commentator Ina Hisayoshi has remarked, there is an "illusion that everything will be resolved by engagement."[65] Nevertheless, despite ferocious Chinese criticism at working-level bilateral security meetings,[66] the Japanese Foreign Ministry and LDP continue to press for higher-level talks. As the LDP strategy paper notes, "Japan must be candid with China and must not hesitate to press for more open sharing of national defense information or to request peaceful negotiations when problems do arise."[67]

Most Japanese observers of the relationship with China also argue that more forthright attention to historical issues would remove Chinese suspicion of Japan. All Japan's political parties now favor, in principle, a more honest reckoning of the legacy of Japanese wartime atrocities in China.[68] Despite a recognition of the problem, however, Tokyo has been unable to muster a consensus for a national apology or reckoning. Even under a left-wing Socialist, the government was only able to engineer more of a "triumph of carefully crafted ambiguity than a sincere apology" when announcing a Diet resolution on the fiftieth anniversary of the end of the Pacific War.[69] To make matters worse, Tokyo's lackluster apologies are usually canceled out by the rantings of one right-wing minister or another. Academic and cultural exchanges with China are on the rise, but the anecdotal information suggests that these cause as much frustration for the visiting Chinese as goodwill. Japanese China-hands express alarm at the growth of anti-Japanese literature in China, and some despair at the prospects for stemming the tide.[70]

On the whole, however, China's historical card and steady stream of anti-Japanese criticism are no longer deterring developments in Japan's China policy the way they once did. The majority of Japanese politicians and foreign and defense officials are unapologetic for the steps Tokyo has taken to strengthen the US–Japan Alliance and to engage in more active diplomacy in the region. Reluctant thought they may be, the Japanese are increasingly realists.

Conclusion: assessing Japan's approach

Because Japan's shift in strategy toward China is relative rather than absolute, and because it is about hedging rather than the pursuit of relative gains, an assessment of the success of that strategy is difficult for both Japanese observers and outsiders. Nevertheless, it is clear that a combination of commercial liberalism/engagement laced with realism/hedging has taken root and that this pattern in Sino–Japanese relations will continue for the foreseeable future. There are at least four reasons for assuming continuity along this new trajectory.

First, the shift in patterns of Japan's China policy are the result of political, cultural and institutional changes in Japan as much as they are a result of the actual dynamics of bilateral relations with China. The Japanese insecurity about the future of relative power in Asia followed from a combination of the collapse of the economic bubble *and* the steady growth in the Chinese economy (and World Bank predictions about the linear nature of Chinese growth). If China's economic bubble bursts in the near future, the Japanese side will still have angst about its own relative economic security and vulnerabilities. Moreover, the new consensus in Japan that the government must improve its crisis management system and articulation of national interest was the result of the Gulf War and domestic incidents such as the 1994 Kobe earthquake and not just Chinese demonstrations of military force in 1995 and 1996. As Japan sorts out its security role and national security institutions in the years ahead, the strategic realism in Japanese foreign policy will continue to emerge, shaped but not determined by China.

Second, Japan has not been forced to choose between its policies of hedging and engagement. The potential Chinese military threat to Japan lies in the future, and Japan has indirectly responded to any danger by improving the coordination between its own ample Cold War arsenal and the US military. Japan has not had to increase its unilateral defense spending yet in response to China (nor, of course, has the United States) and therefore economic budget priorities are not at risk. Moreover, China has not yet extracted economic punishment from the Japanese side for its more assertive political-military posture in recent years; nor has China increased its military hedging against Japan. Chinese rhetoric has been intense at times, but no commercial contracts have been canceled on security grounds and no Chinese jets have tested Japanese airspace. In short, realism has not yet had the negative effects that Japanese policy makers once thought it would.

Third, because the strategic uncertainties with China are long-term issues, Japan has by and large been able to avoid confrontation over more dangerous short-term issues. The exception would have to be in the case of the Senkakus, but on the one issue where the Chinese are clearly willing to use force – Taiwan – Japan has steered clear of danger. In the rhetorical contretemps over whether or not Taiwan would be included in the new US–Japan Defense Guidelines, the Japanese government remained appropriately vague on the geographic specifics of the Guidelines and repeated its one China policy. Tokyo has done nothing to promote Taiwan's independence or international stature (despite some pushing from pro-Taiwan elements in the Diet). Japan's more assertive position toward China has therefore not provoked Chinese responses with regard to the core security issues for Beijing.

Finally, Japan has benefited from a more than usually reliable and committed US ally in recent years. The Senkaku issue shook Tokyo's faith in how firm the reaffirmed US defense commitment was, but that was quickly sorted out by the intervention of the US Secretary of Defense, as was explained earlier. With the US side's strategy also a mix of balancing and engaging China (or integrating

China from a position of strength), Japan's own course is not too difficult to set or maintain.

Of course, each of these four elements is a variable in Japanese foreign policy that could change. Although this seems unlikely in the short term, such change could happen in the future, with profound implications for the patterns of Sino–Japanese relations. First, Japan's search for the institutions and even ideology of a normal state could conceivably create a vessel for nationalism, should economic reform and recovery fail in the years ahead and societal cleavages and disaffection result. Second, Japan could finally be forced to choose between engagement and balancing (in relative gains terms) if Chinese military power projection capabilities continue to rise and Chinese intentions become more hostile. Third, Taiwan could force a choice in Japan's dual policy by openly pushing for independence. Fourth, the United States could upset Japan's strategy by down-sizing its military presence in Asia. This is not the place for a debate about whether Japan would bandwagon with China or balance against China in the event of any of the four scenarios listed above. (For the record, I think balancing is more likely). It should suffice to say that any of the changes would render the approach described in this chapter unworkable for Japan. There is, however, no indication that Japan, Taiwan, or China will turn dangerously nationalistic or that the US will withdraw from Asia in the near future. Nor is there a possibility that China will be able to prove convincingly in the next few years that its growth does not represent a potential threat. Therefore, Japan's shift from commercial liberalism to reluctant realism will likely color bilateral relations with China for years if not decades to come.

Notes

1 Seki Tomoda, "Tai-Chu Senryaku: Sairyo no Shinario, Saiaku no Shinario," *Chuo Koron*, December 1995, pp. 54–62.
2 Christopher Johnstone, "Grant Aid Suspension Heightens Tensions in Japan–China Relations," *Japan Economic Institute Report*, No. 15, September 1996, p. 8.
3 Between 1985 and 1997 the percentage of Japanese who said they did not feel friendly relations toward China rose from 18 percent to 51 percent with the sharpest increases beginning in 1991, according to polls taken by the Prime Minister's Office in Japan. See *Asahi Shimbun*, February 27, 1997. Meanwhile, the percentage of Japanese who felt that Japan's role in Asia should focus on security doubled from 8 percent in 1994 to 14 percent in 1996 (the only other increase was in those who thought Japan should play a larger role in environmental policy, from 11 percent to 19 percent). *Asahi Shimbun*, November 9, 1996.
4 This concept and many of the arguments in the first part of this chapter are drawn from Michael J. Green and Benjamin L. Self, "Japan's Changing China Policy: From Commercial Liberalism to Reluctant Realism," *Survival*, Vol 38, No. 2, summer 1996, pp. 35–57.
5 "National Defense Program Outline in and after FY 1996" (tentative unofficial translation), Security Council and Cabinet of Japan, November 28,1995, p. 6.
6 "JCP's Fuwa Reconciles with China's Jiang: They Condemn Japan–U.S. Alliance," *Japan Digest*, July 22, 1998.

7 Research Commission on Security of the Policy Research Council, Liberal Democratic Party, "Joint Declaration and Future National Security: Implementing Review of Guidelines for Japan–US Defense Cooperation", Liberal Democratic Party, April 18, 1997, pp. 1–2.

8 Fujita Yosano, "Nicchu Kankei no Kiki o Maneku Jinteki Netowaku no Keshi" (The Destruction of Human Networks is Beckoning a Sino–Japanese Crisis) Foresight, December 1996, pp. 32–35. Fujita catalogs the decay of Sino–Japanese elite ties between the LDP-CCP, the foreign ministries, and China's Embassy in Tokyo.

9 "China Says It Won't Accept Taiwan in US–Japan Alliance," Reuters, August 22, 1997.

10 "Jiang Puts Off September Visit to Japan Because of Floods," Japan Digest, August 24, 1998; James Kynge, "Jiang's Visit to Japan Delayed by Policy Splits," Financial Times, August 24, 1998.

11 For 1995, see FBIS-EAS-96-017, pp. 10–11; and for 1994, see Hattori Kenji, "Nit-Chu Keizai Koryu no Kinmitsuka," in Kojima, ed., Ajia Jidai no Nit-Chu Kankei (Tokyo: Saimaru shuppankai, 1995), pp. 137–73.

12 Ibid., p. 50.

13 FBIS-CHI-96-013, p. 32.

14 Tanaka Akihikio, Nit-Chu Kankei, 1945–1990 (Tokyo: University of Tokyo Press, 1991), pp.107–130. Tanaka predicts (as do many of his colleagues) that the Chinese economic "bubble" will also burst. Conversely, Hattori sees repeated fluctuations in the scale of trade as a long-term problem for bilateral relations between Japan and China; see Hattori, "Nit-Chu Keizai Koryu," p. 146. In 1996 Toyota was pressured by Beijing to choose a site in the North, rather than the Shanghai site preferred by Tokyo headquarters.

15 See e.g. Kanayama Hisahiro, "The Future Impact of Energy Problems in China," Asia-Pacific Review, Vol. 2, No. 1, spring 1995.

16 The balance of power explanation is based on Kenneth Waltz, Theory of International Politics (Reading, MA: Addison Westey, 1979).

17 Stephen Walt, The Origins of Alliance (Ithica, NY: Cornell University Press, 1987). Both the balance of power and balance of threat theories are assessed in post-war US foreign policy by Michael Mastanduno in "Preserving the Unipolar Moment: Realist Theories of U.S. Grand Strategy after the Cold War," International Security, Vol. 21, No. 4, spring 1997, pp. 49–88.

18 Sankei Shimbun, February 21, 1997.

19 "LDP Okays Resumption of Aid Grants to China, Ask for Overall Policy Review," Japan Digest, February 14, 1997. Japan resumed its aid lending in December with a $1.4 billion loan for FY 96.

20 Liberal Democratic Party Research Commission on Foreign Affairs, "Foreign Policy of the Liberal Democratic Party Part I: Japan's Asia-Pacific Strategy: The Challenges of Transformation," LDP (undated: released in early May 1997), p. 23.

21 Japan–US Joint Declaration on Security: Alliance for the Twenty-first Century (Toyko, April 17, 1996).

22 Tokyo Shimbun, April 27, 1997.

23 "Anpo o Kakaru to Iu Koto" (Speaking of Dialogue on Security), Asahi Shimbun, April 24, 1997.

24 China did agree in April 1998 to a second track trialogue with the United States and Japan; see "First Japan–US–China Security Colloquy to be Held in July," Japan Digest, April 13, 1998.

25 As stated by the Air Self Defense Force Chief-of-Staff to Mainichi Shimbun, Yomiuri Shimbun, October 19, 1997.

26 Larry A. Niksch, "Senkaku (Diaouyu) Island Dispute: The U.S. Legal Relationship and Obligations," PACNET, No. 45, November 8, 1996.

27 In Hisayoshi, "Fear of U.S.–China Ties Rests on Flawed Premises," *Japan Economic Journal*, December 16, 1996.
28 "Clinton, Jiang Urge Japan to Act on Economy: Tokyo Feels Pressure, Isolation," *Japan Digest*, June 29, 1998.
29 "China Slaps Japan Hard for Failing to Lead Region Out of Crisis," *Japan Digest*, July 30, 1998.
30 *Yomiuri Shimbun*, March 21, 1996.
31 The trilateral Russian–US–Japan dialogue has included senior military officials who have met in Moscow and Tokyo. Mentioned in The Foreign Policy of the Liberal Democratic Party, p. 15.
32 Michael Richardson, "Asians Insist on Japan–China Balance," *International Herald Tribune*, September 4, 1997.
33 *Nikkei Shimbun*, January 14, 1997. On poor coordination with MOFA see "Anpo Rongi Fukamarazu" (Security Dialogue Fails to Deepen), *Asahi Shimbun*, April 14, 1997.
34 The Foreign Policy of the Liberal Democratic Party, pp. 16–20.
35 *Japan Digest*, May 27, 1997.
36 For an excellent assessment of Japan's approaches to multilateral diplomacy in the post-Cold War era, see Tsuyoshi Kawasaki (Assistant Professor of Political Science, Simon Fraser University), "Between Realism and Idealism in Japanese Security Policy: The Case of the ASEAN Regional Forum," A paper prepared for the annual meeting of the Association of Asian Studies, 16 March 1997. For a thorough Japanese treatment of multilateral diplomatic strategy see Yamamoto Yoshinobu, "Kyochoteki Anzenhosho no Kanosei", Kokusai mondai, August 1995; and Nishihara Masashi, "Ajia-Taiheiyo to Takokukann Anzenhosho Kyoryoku no Wakugumi", Kokusai mondai, October 1994.
37 Interview with Japanese official, February 1996; cited in Green and Self, "Japan's Changing China Policy," p. 52.
38 Yong Deng, "Learning to Cooperate: China and Regionalism in Asia-Pacific," A paper prepared for the annual meeting of the American Political Science Association, San Francisco, August 29–September 1, 1996, p. 4.
39 Foreign Policy of the Liberal Democratic Party, p. 25.
40 Japanese accounts of the July 13 ARF intersessional in Jakarta focused on the Sino–Japanese split; see *Tokyo Shimbun*, July 14, 1997.
41 Industrial Structure Council, *1997 Report on the WTO Consistency of Trade Policies by Major Trading Partners* (Tokyo: Ministry of International Trade and Industry, 1997), p. 300.
42 Ibid., p. 301.
43 The Japan Forum on International Relations, "The Policy Recommendations on the WTO System and Japan" (Tokyo, November 1996), p. 9.
44 *1997 Report* p. 300.
45 Ibid., p. 309.
46 Ibid., p. 300.
47 Foreign Policy of the Liberal Democratic Party, p. 23.
48 See e.g. Kanayama Hisahiro, "The Marketization of China and Japan's Response," *Asia-Pacific Review*, Vol. 1, No. 1, January 1994, pp. 123–163.
49 Foreign Policy of the Liberal Democratic Party p. 23.
50 *Toyo Keizai Geppo* (Toyo Keizai Statistical Monthly), "Seizouyou no Ajiashifuto ga Kyuukasoku) (Manufacturing Industry's Shift to Asia increases Rapidly), May 1996, pp. 19–23, cited in Christopher Johnstone, "A Level Playing Field? U.S. and Japanese Competition in the Chinese Market," (Washington, DC: Japan Economic Institute), August 30, 1996.
51 Interview with the director of Japan–China Business Council, (N: Keizai Kyokai) Tokyo, December 1, 1998; FBIS-EAS-95-231, p. 14.

52 The five-part series in *Nikkei Shimbun* runs on the front page from April 20–25, 1997 and highlights the failure of Japanese companies such as Toyota and NTT in competition with US firms for contracts in China because of poor government support from Japan.

53 Takeichi Sumi (Executive Vice President and Director of Mitsubishi International Corporation), "Global Dimensions of U.S.–Japan Relations: U.S.–Japan–China Triangle," Speech given at the CSIS-KKC Conference held at the Sheraton-Carlton Hotel, Washington, DC.

54 Johnstone, "A Level Playing Field?", p.5.

55 The ODA Charter is emphasized by the LDP in its strategy paper, p. 24.

56 Fujisawa Kazuo, *Keidanren Chugoku Iinkai Chosadan Dancho Shoken* (Report of the Delegation Head from the Keidanren China Committee Delegation), No. 1, February 15, 1994, p. 5 and No. 2 (199) p. 3.

57 Ryukichi Imai, "Japan's Nuclear Policy: Retrospect on the Immediate Past, Perspectives on the Twenty First Century," Tokyo: IIPS Paper 169E, November 1996, pp. 21–23.

58 Japanese press reports indicate a Chinese intention to construct a large-scale reprocessing plant in Lanzhou; see *Nihon Keizai Shimbun*, March 12, 1995.

59 Isaka Satoshi, "Energy Experts Promote Asian Nuclear Network," *Japan Economic Journal*, April 25, 1997.

60 Peter Evans, "Japan's Green Aid," *The China Business Review*, July to August, 1994, p. 39.

61 Peter Evans, "Official Japanese Energy and Environmental Assistance Programs to the Peoples' Republic of China," paper prepared for the US Department of Energy, November 1996.

62 *Japan Digest*, April 16, 1997.

63 Kanayama Hisahiro, "The Future Impact of Energy Problems in China," *Asia-Pacific Review*, Vol. 2, No. 1, spring 1995, p. 230.

64 Foreign Policy of the Liberal Democratic Party, p. 9.

65 Ina Hisayoshi, "Japan's Leaders Lack Depth, Objectivity in Their Thinking on the China Question," *Japan Economic Journal*, August 26, 1996.

66 Bureau-director-level security policy talks between Japan's MOFA and counterparts in Beijing have been held for several years, with increasing friction beginning in the March 1996 session; *Tokyo Shimbun*, October 24, 1996.

67 Foreign Policy of the Liberal Democratic Party, p. 22.

68 Even a study group including conservative LDP politicians endorsed the notion of historical honesty with China. See the Japan Forum on International Relations, "The Policy Recommendations on The Future of China in the Context of Asian Security", Tokyo, January 1995, p. 14. The LDP's 1997 strategy paper also endorses "honest engagement with historical issues," ibid., p. 23.

69 Nicholas Kristoff, "Japan Expresses Regret of a Sort for the War," *New York Times*, June 7, 1995, quoted in William Lee Howell, "The Inheritance of War: Japan's Domestic Politics and International Ambition," in Gerrit W. Gong, ed., *Remembering and Forgetting: The Legacy of War and Peace in East Asia* (Washington, DC: CSIS, 1996), p. 83.

70 Uemura Joji, "Chugoku de Zokuzoku Shupan Sareru 'Hanbei' 'Hannichi' no Sho" (The Continuous Publication of Anti-US and Anti-Japanese Books in China), *Foresight*, August 1996, pp. 30–37.

8

ENGAGEMENT IN US CHINA POLICY

Robert S. Ross

The United States shares with China's neighbors a dual concern for the impact of China on its immediate national interests and the growth of PRC power for regional stability and long-term US interests in a favorable East Asian balance of power. But as both a regional power and a global power with unparalleled strategic and economic influence, it has unique responsibilities in shaping the evolution of China's contribution to the regional and global order. More than any other state, how the United States balances its short-term objectives with a long-term China policy that takes into account China's expanding strategic and economic power will shape the strategic environment for the countries throughout Asia and beyond.

America's response to China's developing power will depend not only on how Washington balances short-term and long-term interests but also on the strategy it chooses to address its long-term interest in managing Chinese power and to create a favorable strategic environment in East Asia. American policy options are usually portrayed as a choice between "containment" and "engagement," with containment characterized as coercive policies designed to prevent China from developing and using its growing power to displace American influence in Asia and engagement as strategic adjustment to legitimate Chinese objectives in an effort to establish an East Asian order that is both conducive to US interests and characterized by peaceful resolution of conflicts of interest.[1]

How the United States resolves the competing pressures between short-term and long-term interests and between long-term coercive and long-term adjustment policies will be a decisive factor in determining the prospects for peace in East Asia and a stable world order in the twenty-first century. Ultimately, however, there will be no clear-cut policy choices. Rather, US policy will inevitably reflect a mix of these competing interests and this mix will evolve over time in response to ongoing evaluation and re-evaluation of Chinese behavior and objectives and to developments in US relationships with other Asian countries and, equally important, in US domestic politics.

Short-term and long-term interests in US China policy

Washington's response to the rise of Chinese power is affected by the mix of China's impact on immediate and long-term US interests. At times, these interests will be complementary, requiring a single policy response. At other times policy requirements will conflict, requiring difficult interest trade-offs. But at no time is Washington free to consider one set of interests in isolation from the other. This is the most difficult challenge in developing a contemporary China policy.

China in short-term US policy

Independent from the PRC's growing strategic weight and its destabilizing potential in the Asian balance of power, China's contemporary domestic and foreign policies impinge on a wide range of American strategic, political and economic objectives. These objectives include protection of the interests of US allies and strategic partners in Asia, protection of American domestic and international economic interests, and protection of American-led international economic and security regimes. They also include encouraging respect for funda-mental human rights in the PRC. These interests are not only at the center of contemporary US China policy but also constitute the major issues in developing a long-term China policy, thus complicating the effort to establish a regional order conducive to both US interests and stability.

Chinese interests and policy conflict with American efforts to maintain strategic partnerships with a number of key actors in Asia. The US–China conflict over Taiwan is the most difficult conflict to manage. The United States has significant strategic interests in Taiwan's autonomy. Taiwan is a potential strategic asset which Washington could utilize should US–China relations deteriorate.[2] America's commitment to Taiwan's security is a basic tenet of US Asia policy and a weakening of that commitment would call into question America's will to remain an active participant in the East Asian balance of power, possibly eliciting counterproductive reactions from American allies throughout the region.[3] Insofar as self-determination and support for democracy are fundamental American values, Americans support Taiwan's autonomy from mainland control. Thus China's insistence that Taipei acknowledge that Taiwan is part of the People's Republic of China and that global trends encourage eventual reunification elicits opposition across the American political spectrum and creates a US–China conflict of interest. This conflict has the potential to overwhelm the policy-making process and create armed conflict between the United States to determine US policy towards China on a wide range of otherwise peripheral issues.

America's relationship with Japan is nearly as difficult an issue in US–China relations as the Taiwan issue. No single country is more important to US security than Japan. The US–Japan alliance remains the foundation of US security in Asia. But in the context of apprehension over the post-Cold War viability of the alliance, potentially destabilizing bilateral conflicts of economic interests, and uncertainty over regional security trends, Washington has promoted greater Japanese military contribution to the alliance and a greater Japanese role in regional security affairs. The 1997 revisions "Guidelines of US–Japan Defense Cooperation" reflected this trend. China has expressed concern that the only conceivable target of the strengthened US–Japan alliance is China. It is also concerned for the implications of enhanced Japanese strategic initiatives for Japanese defense development. Because of the proximity of Japan to China, the recent history of Japanese expansionism, and Japan's unrealized military potential, Chinese leaders are concerned that Japan is developing the capability and the will to play an independent great power role in East Asia. Thus enhanced US–Japan cooperation elicits PRC opposition.[4]

The Taiwan issue and US–Japan strategic cooperation are only the most salient of US–China strategic conflicts in East Asia. Despite extensive US–China co-operation regarding North Korea's nuclear weapons program and in minimizing North Korean belligerence, China and the United States have different interests on the Korean Peninsula. The United States values its military presence in South Korea primarily because of the peninsula's proximity to China and its importance to Japanese security. It would welcome peaceful unification of Korea, insofar as US influence would extend throughout the peninsula. On the other hand, China benefits from the current division of the peninsula. Two small Koreas are preferable to one large Korea allied with the United States. Beijing thus aids North Korea not only to prevent regional instability but also to perpetuate the current division. Should unification occur, continued US military presence in Korea could become an issue in US–China relations.

The United Sates and China are on opposite sides of many territorial conflicts in East Asia. Regardless of the merits of the various claims to the Spratly Islands or of the strategic and/or economic importance of the islands, America's strategic interest in the South China Sea and its corresponding interest in maintaining the pro-US alignment of the maritime countries of Southeast Asia requires it to offset PRC efforts to determine the outcome of the conflict. Thus Washington has expressed a concern when the PRC has been involved in heightened tension with the Philippines over the islands.[5] A similar dynamic exists regarding the conflict between China and Japan over the Diaoyu/Senkaku Islands. Thus far the United States has remained neutral in this conflict. But insofar as Japan is both an American ally and a claimant to the islands, when conflict over the islands intensified in 1996, there was considerable pressure on the United States to support the Japanese claim and to acknowledge that the US–Japan alliance committed the United States to defend the islands against Chinese actions.[6]

American concern for the integrity of international rules governing weapons proliferation and for controlling proliferation to sensitive regions creates conflicts with China. American focus on non-proliferation regimes contributes to US–China conflict over PRC missile exports to Pakistan and Sino–Pakistan nuclear cooperation. US interest in controlling proliferation into the Middle East has led it to oppose Chinese nuclear cooperation with Algeria and Iran, despite adherence to international regimes. Chinese leaders have insisted that the missile proliferation regimes and US policy toward Iran and Libya reflect narrow US interests, rather than global norms, and that Chinese cooperation requires corresponding US cooperation regarding PRC interests, especially on arms sales to Taiwan.[7] Washington's insistence that regime violations are non-negotiable and that all violations are equally harmful to regime integrity has led it to impose technology export sanctions on China in response to PRC assistance to Pakistan.

Economic issues also compete for attention in US policy toward China. America's large and growing trade deficit with China calls attention to China's persistent use of protectionist trade measures. The resulting political pressure pushes policy makers to protect the interests of domestic constituencies by compelling China to reform its trade policy. But US demands are often detrimental to Chinese economic interests. This is the case in the market access talks between Beijing and Washington, in which the United States wants to expand exports into markets that China wants to protect to benefit nascent and troubled domestic industries. Domestic pressure also obligates US policy makers to demand immediate Chinese institutional and societal change, despite the limited capacity of the central government to enforce domestic laws on localities and individuals.

Washington's promotion of human rights in China causes it to focus on the fate of political dissidents languishing in Chinese prisons. This transforms Chinese dissidents into bargaining chips. The United States demands that China release dissidents to enable it to continue to receive most-favored-nation treatment or to hold summit meetings, and China manipulates the imprisonment and release of dissidents to maximize its ability to extract concessions from the United States. The irony is that when Chinese human rights violations are at the top of the American domestic and foreign policy agendas, China perceives little benefit from cooperating with US interests. It understands that when America is most critical of China, concessions can have minimal impact on the public debate or on policy.[8] The fate of political rights in Hong Kong after resumption of Chinese sovereignty may play a similar role in the relationship.

China in long-term US foreign policy

China has a significant impact on immediate US foreign policy objectives, but the growth of Chinese power *per se* may have an even greater impact on long-term American interests. Here the issue includes not only greater Chinese ability to affect the outcome of bilateral US–China conflicts but also the impact of greater Chinese power on the regional balance of power, with implications for US security in East Asia, and on the development of global economic and security regimes.

The mere growth of Chinese power relative to that of the United States, no matter how that power is wielded, would guarantee that China will have a greater ability to affect a wide range of US interests. Bilaterally, should greater Chinese power be reflected in enhanced PRC strategic capabilities, the territorial security of the United States will be directly dependent on the extent of US–China cooperation and resulting Chinese intentions. In addition, increased Chinese strategic confidence will enable Beijing to pose a greater challenge to the status quo in US–Taiwan relations. It will also affect the balance of leverage in bilateral negotiations over weapons proliferation and in economic negotiations, contributing to Chinese ability to resist US efforts to protect domestic constituencies and strategic industries.

The relative growth of Chinese power would affect the regional balance of power and give rise to shifting alignments on the part of smaller powers. Smaller powers will adjust to Washington's reduced ability to guarantee their security by accommodating Chinese interests. This will reduce America's regional presence and its ability to protect its interests. This process began in the mid-1970s in the context of the American withdrawal from Indo–China. Thailand accommodated itself to enhanced Chinese power in Indo–China by developing close political and military ties with China and by reducing its military cooperation with the United States. Should Chinese power experience comparable growth in maritime Southeast Asia, a similar trend would occur in the strategic orientation of Malaysia, Singapore, Indonesia, and the Philippines. The United States would thus experience reduced influence in these countries and enjoy less dependable cooperation with them on a wide range of issues, including economic relations, military cooperation, such as access to ports, territorial waters and shipping lanes from the Middle East to the western Pacific Ocean, and political cooperation, particularly in multilateral institutions and in conflict over third parties.

Finally, greater Chinese power would yield Beijing a greater voice in the global order. In the strategic realm, Chinese policy will influence whether or not military balances are characterized by unstable and dangerous arms races or by stability through arms control negotiations. Greater autonomy in great power relations would enhance its independence in the international arms trade, so that it would become a major factor affecting proliferation of nuclear, chemical and conventional weapons to Third World countries and the stability of regional balances of power and security of American allies. Such could particularly be the case in the Middle East, where tensions are always high, the balance of power is endemically unstable, the United States has enduring important interests, and China's role may grow should oil imports constitute a significant share of its energy resources and its ability to challenge US regional dominance increase.

The continued international importance of the Chinese market and the movement of Chinese exports into international advanced technology markets will increase Beijing's weight in the global economic order. Even without intent, Chinese practice will affect other countries' trade policies. Just as Japanese foreign trade success contributed to rising protectionism and economic regionalism, Chinese foreign trade success could have the same if not an even greater impact on the liberal trade order. Paralleling China's potential impact on the security realm, the PRC will play a major role in determining whether the international economic order is characterized by rule-based adjudication of economic disputes or by escalating trade crises culminating in spiraling protectionism. Even should China participate in multilateral management of the global trade, it will influence the negotiations over the content of the rules, and thus the interests of the other participants. This trend will have a unique impact on the United States, which has used its pre-eminent economic power to shape the global trade regime to maximize US interests.

Contending approaches to the rise of Chinese power

The United States has four basic policy options for contending with the rise of Chinese power. Each option, including the engagement option, reflects a different long-term strategy and each proposes a corresponding package of immediate policies. Thus, the engagement option must compete with alternative strategies. The ultimate policy outcome will reflect the combination of the preferences of administration policy makers and the impact of public opinion and congressional pressures on policy making.

The first option is to attempt to thwart China's rise to full great power status. Thus far, there is little support for this policy in the United States. This is due to widespread recognition that the rise of Chinese power will be the result of indigenous economic trends that are largely outside of US control. China's human and financial capital and its domestic market will promote long-term development. Moreover, the United States would not be able to isolate China from economic contact with other advanced industrial economies. The European countries and Japan have significant interests in developing economic relations with the PRC. Even if China could be economically isolated, this would merely slow down rather than prevent the modernization of China and the associated increase in PRC international power, while simultaneously ensuring that when China does become more powerful it will treat the United States as an adversary. Thus thwarting China's growth would require the United States to carry out preventive military measures that are simply unacceptable to both the American leadership and the public.

At the other extreme, the United States could simply accept as inevitable the rise of Chinese power and accommodate itself to a pax-Sinica premised on Chinese hegemony over East Asia. This position suggests that the inexorable rise of Chinese power will cause China's smaller neighbors to bandwagon with China, thus excluding the United States from East Asian affairs. Samuel Huntington is perhaps the most eloquent proponent of this fatalistic scenario.[9] The policy implication of this approach is that the United States should also bandwagon with Chinese power so as to avoid counterproductive conflict and to maximize the potential for cooperation in order to benefit from PRC hegemony.

The bandwagoning option has also failed to elicit even minimal support within the United States. American policy makers are loath to cede East Asia to China, and they and the American public retain considerable confidence that the United States will have the will and the material capability well into the twenty-first century to remain an East Asian power and to contend with China for the support of other countries in East Asia. Hence, while the bandwagoning approach suggests that Japan will accommodate itself to Chinese power, most Americans believe that many nations, including Japan, will choose to cooperate with Washington rather than become part of a Chinese sphere of influence.

These two strategies offer alternatives to balancing Chinese power with American power. The first proposes that the United States should preventively eliminate China's ability to contend with American power; the second proposes that the United States should bandwagon with Chinese power rather than try to contend with Chinese power. Between these two extremes is the option of balancing. While not expressed in these terms, this is the approach implicitly advocated by a broad cross-section of American foreign policy specialists. These specialists acknowledge that China will become more powerful, but also that the United States and China will compete for influence in East Asia in which neither great power will have the ability to establish region-wide hegemony.

US post-Cold War defense policy and alliance policies have had the effect of balancing China's power potential. The US defense budget, despite post-Cold War cutbacks, remains larger than the sum of the next six largest defense budgets in the world. Its acquisition of new weapons systems, including a new generation of nuclear weapons, cruise missiles, advanced fighter aircraft, submarines, aircraft carriers, anti-satellite and anti-missile capabilities, and the communications technologies supporting the "revolution in military affairs," make clear that the United States is continuing to strengthen its military power. One inevitable result of this is that for the foreseeable future the United States will maintain its advantage in the US–China military balance. American alliance policy reflects similar efforts to strengthen US power. Consolidation of the US–Japan alliance consolidates US access to Japanese naval facilities and airfields and enhances the long-term prospect that Japan will continue to use its capabilities in support of American interests. United States naval access agreements with the ASEAN states provide the United States with base equivalents throughout Southeast Asia, better enabling the United States to contend with US–China conflicts and to prepare for uncertainty over China's future role in regional security.[10]

There is a broad American consensus on America's role in Asia in the twenty-first century and in the need to balance potential Chinese power; but this consensus has not created a consensus on policy toward China. Consistent with a balance of power strategy, there remains a wide array of US policy options for developing the bilateral US–China relationship and for influencing the nature of the regional and global order. It is these choices that have led to the debate over US strategy for dealing with the rise of Chinese power between proponents of containment and proponents of engagement.

These two policy packages are both premised on the assumption that should China become more powerful, it will inevitably challenge US supremacy in Asia, but their policy preferences are premised on diametrically opposed understandings of Chinese intentions. Advocates of containment argue that once China has modernized its military it will use armed force to achieve its territorial ambitions, including reunification of Taiwan with the mainland and control over the Senkaku Islands, the Paracel Islands, and the Spratly Islands. Insofar as China will be a major importer of oil, it will seek to control the sea lanes connecting Chinese ports with the Middle East. These analysts also argue that Chinese leaders have already concluded that the United States will be the most important obstacle to realizing China's objectives and that escalated US–China conflict is inevitable. In this view, China's strategic objective is to weaken and ultimately oust American influence from East Asia to achieve its territorial objectives as well as its ultimate strategic objective – regional hegemony.[11]

Because they believe that Chinese intentions are not reactive, advocates of containment foresee little benefit in trying to reach compromise solutions to conflicts of interest. On the contrary, conciliatory US behavior simply encourages Beijing to encroach on US interests and to pursue its expansionist objectives because it suggests that the United States is neither prepared to inflict a cost on PRC "rogue" behavior nor to resist PRC hegemonic aspirations. Indeed, in this view American conciliatory behavior abets PRC efforts to subjugate smaller powers because it signals to states in the region that Washington is not prepared to challenge Chinese expansionism and that it is content that local powers, such as the Philippines, contend with China without American support.[12]

This perspective resembles US containment policies of the US–Soviet Cold War period insofar as it advocates a stiff retaliatory response to any PRC diplomatic, economic, and military initiative that challenges US interests and because it opposes PRC participation in international economic and security regimes until Beijing evidences its intent and its ability to "follow the rules." Proponents of containment criticize Washington for its inadequate response to China's military modernization program, its arms sales to the Third World, and its naval activities in disputed waters in the South China Sea. They view US–China economic ties as providing Beijing with the technological know-how and financial resources to eventually challenge US economic and strategic interests.[13]

Engagement is the other package of policy options consistent with a strategic policy of balancing PRC power. It agrees that the United States must not and will not allow China to establish a unipolar East Asia, but it also argues that within a balance of power system, policy choices can determine the levels of tension and violence that characterize conflicts of interest between the great powers. Consistent with the concept of engagement developed in Randall Schweller's chapter, American proponents of engagement argue that Chinese leaders have yet to formulate an immutable view of long-term US–China relations and that American policy can influence China's willingness to adopt cooperative policies. Washington should develop policy toward China that will balance growing Chinese power, protect US interests, and minimize the potential for global and regional instability and bilateral tension. As one advocate of engagement explained, the problem with the containment strategy is that "If you treat China as enemy, then you will have an enemy."[14] Engagement strategy, on the other hand, is premised on the possibility that if the United States treats China as a partner, then it will not become an enemy. Advocates of engagement further argue that the United States, having consolidated its alliance with Japan and its strategic presence in East Asia, Washington can use its strategic superiority to engage China from a position of strength, thus maximizing Washington's ability to encourage China to adopt cooperative policies toward regional order.[15]

Advocates of engagement generally promote three variants of the engagement strategy. The first is a bilateral approach. It stresses that how the United States addresses contemporary US–China conflicts of interest will affect the Chinese leadership's perception of US intentions and thus whether in the long term Beijing will perceive opportunities to cooperate with Washington to develop a stable regional order. On the other hand, mismanagement of PRC perceptions will lead Beijing to view the United States as an implacable adversary requiring adoption of destabilizing militant policies to realize Chinese interests and to weaken US presence in Asia. In this view, prospects for cooperation will be maximized if Washington eschews heavy-handed coercive policies. Engagement calls for negotiated solutions to conflicts of interest that avoid escalated tension and realize immediate American policy objectives. This aspect of policy is consistent with a traditional understanding of appeasement as defined in Chapter 1.[16]

The second variant of an American engagement strategy stresses a multilateral approach to promoting PRC participation and interest in a stable international order. It is this variant that separates Schweller's understanding of appeasement from engagement.[17] This strategy does not require that the necessary pre-condition to PRC membership in global institutions is immediate Chinese adherence to the rules as they now exist. In contrast to bilateral appeasement, this approach recognizes that Chinese leadership and a Chinese stake in international institutions and the global order can be a source of international stability and promote peaceful change. It stresses that Chinese entry into multilateral institutions, including the World Trade Organization and various security regimes, must be a negotiated process, so that membership does not require that China sacrifice important interests. It is premised on the understanding that for multilateral institutions to be effective, Beijing must be part of the rule-making process and benefit from the rules. Engagement advocates acknowledge that this process would necessarily be a consensual process in which the United States would not be able to maximize its interests. But they argue that US compromises reflecting Chinese interests are preferable to developing a global order without Chinese participation, one in which China would have an interest in violating its rules and undermining its effectiveness. Adherents to this policy package would agree with US Ambassador to China James Sasser, who argued that as China reveals a willingness to live in a rule-based system of institutions, it "must be allowed to help make the global rules."[18]

The third variant of American engagement stresses the importance of long-term cooperative US–China societal and institutional relationships as determinants of Chinese behavior. Engagers argue that rather than isolate China, the United States should promote Chinese societal and political interests in stable US–China relations and in a stable international order. These interests will affect PRC calculations regarding the value of revisionist foreign policies, insofar as conflictual policies would impose costs on Chinese domestic actors and political constituencies. This is the bilateral equivalent to a strategy of multilateral "binding." It is an "entanglement" strategy insofar as, by enmeshing China in a web of entangling relationships, Chinese leaders may be more inclined to tolerate a sub-optimal international order.

These three approaches toward peaceful management of a rising power – bilateral accommodation, societal entanglement, and multilateral accommodation – can be mutually complementary and reinforcing. Moreover, each has its particular policy expression in both economic and security matters. A comprehensive engagement policy would pursue all three variants in both policy arenas.

Economic engagement and US China policy

Economic engagement of China takes place in three distinct arenas. The first is bilateral negotiations over conflicts of interests. The second is US policy toward Chinese membership in multilateral economic institutions. The third is development of bilateral linkages between American and Chinese societies. A comprehensive economic engagement policy would require American application of engagement policies in all three arenas.

Economic engagement as mutual accommodation in bilateral negotiations

In bilateral economic relations, the United States has negotiated with China to resolve conflicts arising from Chinese protectionism and from Beijing's inadequate protection of intellectual property rights. In each case, Washington has used coercive tactics to elicit near one-sided Chinese compliance. But the result has nonetheless been consistent with efforts to manage conflict in ways most conducive to long-term engagement of Chinese economic power.

To contend with the large US trade deficit with China, Washington has sought an alternative to protectionist retaliation, the epitome of containment. Similar to its response to its trade deficit with Japan, it has demanded that China liberalize access to its domestic market. These "market access talks" have frequently been acrimonious. In 1992 Washington threatened to impose steep punitive tariffs if Beijing did not agree to make substantive reforms to its trading system. At the last moment Beijing agreed to make far-reaching changes. Two years later the United States Trade Representative reported that China was in substantial compliance with the 1992 agreement regarding transparency of commercial regulations and liberalization of non-tariff trade barriers, and in 1995 the United States Government Accounting Office reported that China had "taken steps to comply with most of the provisions" of the agreement.[19]

However, in the context of the rising trade deficit and mushrooming Chinese textile exports to the United States, remaining PRC trade barriers have continued to elicit US opposition. As in the past, threats of sanctions have generated PRC incentives to compromise, leading to both greater Chinese trade liberalization and promotion of US special economic interests. The February 1997 US–China trade agreement increased Chinese quotas for textile exports to the United States but also significantly liberalized China's textile market for US exports.[20]

The market access negotiations have been a successful effort to achieve both US interests and to engage China in international cooperation. Although the trade deficit has not directly harmed the US economy, so that the conflict primarily reflects US domestic politics, US use of threats has not reflected the belligerence characteristic of containment policy.[21] Because it is in China's interests to delay trade reform for as long as possible, without countervailing incentives provided by the threat of sanctions, Beijing would not change policy. Most important, this is an area in which US interests and global economic stability require identical Chinese policies. Not only is greater Chinese openness the *sine qua non* of American tolerance of its trade deficit with the PRC, but the liberal international economic trade order will not survive an economically powerful and protectionist China. Thus US efforts to open Chinese markets to American exports have had the added benefit of bringing China into compliance with the regulations of the World Trade Organization (WTO) without causing enduring tensions in US–China relations. Moreover, through their negotiations with the United States, Chinese leaders have come to understand that the PRC has an interest in ameliorating the trade deficit in order to alleviate domestic political pressure on the White House to adopt anti-China protectionist measures.[22]

The second area of economic negotiations concerns Chinese protection of intellectual property rights. In the context of the large US trade deficit with China, losses to entertainment and computer software industries from Chinese piracy of intellectual property rights have assumed considerable political importance. Thus, in a process similar to that concerning market access, Washington has used coercive tactics against Beijing, including the threat of costly economic sanctions, to gain greater protection for vulnerable US industries. This policy supported both immediate US interests and long-term Chinese engagement in the international economic order.

In 1992 the US reached agreement with China regarding PRC establishment of laws and regulations protecting intellectual property rights.[23] Although USTR was satisfied that China had fulfilled its obligations in the 1992 agreement, the agreement contained minimal guidance regarding implementation of the new regulation laws, and conflict continued. Between 1994 and 1995, the United States negotiated for better enforcement, threatening punitive sanctions if China did not close down compact disk factories pirating American products. Chinese closure of 15 plants in violation of domestic regulations resolved the immediate conflict, leading to a US–China agreement on implementation of PRC IPR legislation. Since then USTR has monitored Chinese compliance under section 306 of the 1974 Trade Act, which enables USTR to bypass special 301 provisions requiring lengthy investigations and to move directly to sanctions without prior negotiations should it conclude that Chinese enforcement is insufficient.

Washington has been generally pleased with Beijing's efforts to comply with the 1995 implementation agreement. The Clinton administration reported that China had taken "significant steps to crack down on piracy" by closing 37 illegal compact disk factories between May 1996 and March 1997.[24] Chinese government offers of rewards for information regarding IPR violators contributed to the closing of many of the factories. Equally important, in 1997 Chinese courts sentenced IPR violators to lengthy prison terms. The business climate in China had become so unfriendly for illegal corporations that many factories had left China for Singapore, Taiwan, Macau, and Hong Kong.[25]

Even if conflict over IPR continues, it should be manageable. This is because Chinese IPR violations do not significantly affect US interests. Industry estimates of losses to IPR piracy in China reflect assumptions of an inelastic demand curve for the Chinese compact disk market. If Chinese consumers had to pay US prices for computer and music CDs and entertainment videos, sales would diminish.[26] Moreover, based on industry estimates, US losses in Japan have been nearly double those in China. Piracy in the United States causes the greatest losses for US industries.[27] Finally, given ongoing widespread piracy in both developed and less-developed countries, Chinese piracy by itself does not threaten the liberal trade order.

Nonetheless, American pressure is not without benefit. First, it alleviates domestic pressure on the White House from influential interest groups to adopt punitive sanctions against China that could cause lasting harm to both the bilateral relationship and to eventual Chinese compliance with more important international economic norms. Second, it provides incentives for Beijing to improve China's IPR protection system and international support for Chinese politicians who believe an effective regulatory system to be in China's long-term economic interests. Thus US policy can take some credit for the halting progress in Chinese efforts to control IPR piracy.

Most important, given that mere dismissal of Chinese IPR violations would be politically costly and likely to lead to Americans' public support for escalatory punitive retaliation, current US policy is the least objectionable of the available options. Periodic crises and even heavy-handed threats of highly punitive sanctions have not led to permanent trade tension nor permeated the broader relationship. On the contrary, they have reduced the likelihood of greater conflict while improving China's trade practices. In this respect, US IPR policy has contributed both to resolving US–China trade disputes while minimizing the potential for future animosity and, albeit at the margins, contributing to Chinese behavior consistent with the development of an equitable international trading system.

Economic engagement as shared international leadership

Comprehensive economic engagement entails more than bilateral policy adjustments. One of the major developments of the post-World War II economic system is the development of a stable trade regime that has fostered considerable economic development throughout much of the world. Successful engagement calls for involving China in global economic leadership. It is not an exaggeration to argue that whether or not China plays a constructive role in the maintenance of the international economic order will determine the fate of that order.

China's destabilizing potential is enormous. Regardless of whether it is a formal member of the WTO, it will affect the stability of the liberal trade order. Should it fail to liberalize its economy while its exports continue to grow, other countries will adopt countervailing protectionist measures. The possibility of system-wide disruption is significant. Indeed, Japan's long-term trade surplus with the advanced industrial countries was a major factor in the development of regional trading blocs, despite Japanese membership in the General Agreement on Tariffs and Trade. Given China's potential export volume, its impact on the global economy could be far greater than that of Japan during the height of its economic growth.

Thus, international economic stability will require China to liberalize its trading system so as to promote "fair trade" and to reduce the pressures on China's major trading partners to adopt protectionist responses to inevitable trade balances. A policy of engagement would seek this objective through Chinese membership in the WTO, i.e. through multilateral engagement. For any international regime to succeed, it must reflect the interests of its most important members. The United States acknowledged this fact throughout the Cold War when it allowed significant protectionism for its NATO allies and Japan.[28] Similarly, Washington made concessions during the Uruguay Round to Japan over agricultural products and to France over agricultural and cultural products. These concessions enable France and Japan to contribute to the integrity of the overall regime.

Engagement strategists argue that a similar strategy should be used toward China. By incorporating China's voice, and thus its interests in the WTO, the international trade regime will develop in a direction that reflects a consensus of all of the major powers. This is the prerequisite to global economic stability. From this perspective, the alternative is a trade regime that isolates Beijing's voice and interests from WTO deliberations, so that the WTO will develop in a direction inimical to Chinese interests and elicit destabilizing Chinese policies.

Engagers argue that Chinese membership in the WTO will have other salutary effects. After China joins the WTO, it will be required to liberalize its policies within an agreed upon time period. By carrying out economic liberalization in compliance with an institution to which it belongs regarding commitments to which it explicitly agreed, Beijing will be less inclined to view compromises as a response to illegitimate pressure and more likely to view them as a legitimate contribution to an international order that it helps to lead. Indeed, it will be politically easier for Chinese leaders to accommodate pressure from the WTO, insofar as it would be less politicized within Beijing politics than direct pressure from the United States. Chinese membership in the WTO would also engage Chinese leaders in the international economic order by strengthening the hand of policy makers that favor a more liberal Chinese trading system. Prior to Chinese membership in the World Bank and the International Monetary Fund, many analysts argued that China's communist bureaucrats would undermine these institutions' commitments to well-established international norms. Yet just the opposite occurred. PRC membership in multilateral institutions facilitated implicit alliances between policy makers and the institution, strengthening the hand of pro-reform bureaucrats in Chinese policy making. Chinese membership in the WTO could create similar linkages, giving the WTO a voice in PRC policy making in cooperation with Chinese bureaucrats seeking implementation of Chinese commitments.[29]

Engagement policy calls for Chinese membership in the WTO. But, as Margaret Pearson shows in her chapter, whereas it is in the interest of the United States and other advanced industrial countries that China establish a liberal economic system as quickly as possible, it is in China's interest to prolong its protectionist policies. Chinese leaders believe that the long-term development of China's industrial base requires the same protectionist measures that Japan, South Korea, Taiwan, and Indonesia, for example, used to protect their nascent industrial systems prior to liberalization. Since 1989 the United States has insisted that China abide by the rules before it is admitted to the WTO. In late 1996 the US began to modify its approach and discuss a long-term liberalization schedule. Progress was then delayed in 1997 by domestic opposition to improved US–China relations. Then, at the October 1997 summit, Clinton and Jiang agreed to "intensify" their efforts to achieve PRC admission to the WTO. Progress accelerated in the weeks before Prime Minister Zhu Rongji's April 1999 visit to Washington, D.C. Although China's concessions elicited considerable private sector and bipartisan Congressional support, the administration remained concerned about domestic opposition to both an agreement and to legislation granting permanent MFN status for China, which would be required by WTO regulations. It thus sought additional PRC concessions and it remained uncommitted to Chinese admission to the WTO.[30]

Chinese absence from the WTO has been a conspicuous departure from a strategy of multilateral engagement. Moreover, bilateral trade policy alone is an inadequate response to the rise of Chinese economic power. The United States can negotiate with China to appease American domestic interests, but as long as intra-WTO negotiations continue to advance the standards of liberal trade policy, Chinese behavior will remain at variance with an international economic order that lacks legitimacy and influence in PRC policy making. In these circumstances, China's incentive to maintain protectionism will remain and the pressure on other countries to adopt countervailing polices will increase, thus undermining the global order. Until the United States uses its unique economic power and international responsibility to bring about Chinese membership in the WTO on mutually beneficial terms, containment of Chinese multilateral economic influence rather than multilateral economic engagement will continue to be an influential characteristic of US economic policy toward China.

The other important global economic institution lacking Chinese membership is the Group of Seven (G-7), the organization of the advanced industrial economies. Insofar as this is a mere "club" with no formal membership rules, it should be relatively easy to invite China to join. Indeed, when it looked as if Russian economic reforms might be successful, Russia was invited to join, making the G-7 the G-8. But despite its larger and healthier economy and its better prospects, China has not been invited to join the G-7. When in September 1998 Washington called for coordinated action on the part of the G-7 countries to respond to the Asian economic crisis, it implicitly excluded Chinese participation.[31] Yet China has been the Asian country most important to regional economic stability. Adequate current and future global economic coordination requires Chinese participation. US reluctance to expand the G-7 to include China seems to reflect administration fears of congressional charges that including China in the G-7 would certify that China is a democracy. The G-7 is an economic group, not an ideological group, and PRC membership should be an integral part of an engagement strategy that seeks to encourage PRC cooperation in global economic stability.

Economic engagement as entangling cooperation

Complementing bilateral economic relations and multilateral economic engagement is the development of US–China commercial relations and the growth of Chinese (and American) domestic interests that benefit from stable relations. The use of private sector economic engagement as a foundation of broader US cooperation is an explicit US foreign policy objective. As Under-Secretary of State Tarnoff explained, US economic ties with China "increase China's stake in cooperating" with the United States "and complying with a wide range of international norms."[32] Put differently, to the extent that the Chinese economy becomes dependent on the US market and US capital, the greater interest China has in maintaining cooperative relations with the United States, and thus accommodating bilateral and global US interests.

The administration's contribution to this process primarily entails ensuring annual granting of MFN status for China. On this basis, private commercial interests have driven the economic relationship. They have also contributed to the peaceful incorporation of Chinese power into international politics. Indeed, the development US–China trade is characterized by considerable Chinese involvement with the US economy. According to Chinese figures, in 1998 the United States was China's second largest export market, absorbing more than 20 percent of Chinese exports and earning China nearly $40 billion in hard currency.

In 1998 actual US utilized investment in China totaled over $21 billion. American statistics report even greater Chinese dependency on the US market.[33]

These economic activities play an important role in expediting Beijing's effort to modernize its economy. For this reason alone Beijing must develop a cautious US policy; but commercial ties with the United States have also created strong local interests in stable relations. The southern Chinese economy, for example, depends heavily on exports of inexpensive consumer goods to the United States. Guangdong, for example, depended on exports, a large share of which goes to the United States, for over 75 percent of its GNP in 1996.[34] Other regions, including Beijing, Shanghai, and Fujian will increasingly become enmeshed in US–China trade. Domestic economic and political stability is thus affected by the course of US–China economic relations. In a similar manner, China's new business class enjoys the wealth its derives from international economic activities and will increasingly use its informal connections with the Chinese political elite to foster stable relations.

Chinese entanglement in the American economy has already begun to influence PRC economic policy toward US–China conflicts of interests. Periodic US threats of costly economic sanctions have compelled China to make the concessions regarding IPR protection and market access discussed above. Moreover, these concessions will lead to greater US economic entanglement in the Chinese economy. As China's consumer market becomes more accessible to US businesses, American labor and financial groups with an interest in stable cooperation will extend beyond such concentrated sectors as aircraft manufacturing, power generating equipment, grain, and fertilizers and occupy a larger and more central place in the national economy. Indeed, Chinese analysts understand that Beijing's economic leverage over the United States will increase as China's economy plays an increasingly important role in US economic development.[35] Mutual engagement is the likely long-term result of US economic policy and expanded US–China economic relations.

Complementing US private sector economic engagement of China is American societal engagement of China. This process takes many forms, including educational exchanges at the university and post-doctoral levels, and cultural exchanges. These activities not only educate Chinese and Americans on each other's society, culture and political system, thus potentially contributing to reduced suspicion and to better informed elites, but also often lead to enduring ties that promote long-term cooperation. These contacts, although difficult to measure and assess, can have a significant impact on developing Chinese and American inclinations to seek negotiated solutions to conflicts stemming from China's growing power.

The United States can draw considerable satisfaction from the development of unofficial and informal non-economic US–China ties. The US government and many American philanthropic and non-profit organizations have enabled large numbers of Chinese scholars and educators to visit the United States and encouraged US and Chinese professional organizations to develop cooperative ties. This process is a non-controversial and relatively inexpensive means for the United States to contribute to long-term engagement of Chinese power.

Strategic engagement and US China policy

Paralleling economic engagement, strategic engagement can take place in three arenas: bilateral negotiations to manage conflict over conventional arms sales and proliferation of missiles and nuclear technologies; multilateral strategic engagement with China in the development of potential international security regimes; institutional linkages to develop cooperative ties among military officers and to help clarify intentions and avoid misperceptions that could make adjustment to Chinese power more difficult.

Strategic engagement as mutual accommodation in bilateral negotiations

As is the case for US–China economic conflicts of interest, the objective of American bilateral strategic engagement is negotiated solutions to contemporary conflicts of interest that realize immediate American policy objectives and avoid escalated US–China tension, thus enhancing long-term US–China cooperation. One of the most troubling bilateral strategic issues is proliferation of missiles and nuclear technologies. The issue first appeared on the agenda in 1988 when China sold CSS-2 intermediate range missiles to Saudi Arabia and silkworm missiles to Iran. Since then it has been US policy to prevent PRC proliferation that violates international regimes. The United States also wants China to refrain from transferring to the Middle East weapons that are not covered by international regimes. It has opposed Chinese sales of silkworm missiles and low-technology short-range C-802 surface-to-sea cruise missiles to Iran. It has also opposed Chinese nuclear cooperation agreements with Algeria and Iran, despite the adherence by all parties to IAEA guidelines.

American reliance on bilateral negotiations and the application of limited sanction has changed Chinese behavior.[36] In 1992 China canceled its agreement to provide M-9 missiles to Syria. In 1995 China suspended its agreement to transfer nuclear technology to Iran and in 1997 and 1998 it committed itself to not provide Iran with any nuclear technologies and privately assured US leaders that it would discontinue transferring to Iran cruise missiles. In 1996 it agreed not to aid any IAEA-unsupervised nuclear power plant, thus ending its assistance to an unsupervised plant in Pakistan.[37] Thus by late 1998 the only ongoing Chinese nuclear cooperation agreement that America opposed was China's contribution to an Algerian reactor, which dates back to a mid-1980s agreement and which, as noted above, is under the supervision of the International Atomic Energy Agency (IAEA). China has also responded to US pressure by improving its control over exports of chemical weapons precursors.[38]

The one anomaly in long-term PRC policy has been China's contribution to

Pakistan's nuclear deterrent program. In the 1980s China contributed to Pakistan's effort to develop a nuclear warhead and in the 1990s it has contributed to its effort to develop a delivery system through the transfer of M-11 missiles and technology.[39] China views a credible Pakistani deterrent as the most effective way to guarantee the security of its sole ally in Southern Asia against Indian power. India is a major power located on China's border with which the PRC has fought wars but with which it is now trying to improve relations. In this respect, China's relationship with Pakistan is similar to America's relationship with Israel. Washington and Beijing prefer that their respective smaller and vulnerable allies be able to deter attacks with nuclear threats rather than have to commit to their defense and risk complicating relations with other countries.

Washington's response to Chinese proliferation to Pakistan has been to apply relatively mild sanctions which have implicitly acknowledged China's strategic imperative in Southern Asia but which also have the effect of establishing US commitment to resist proliferation to other regions.[40] Washington has thus accommodated vital Chinese interests in Southern Asia, a region where its own interests are relatively minor, while achieving Chinese accommodation of American non-proliferation objectives in the Middle East, where the United States and not China has vital interests. This pattern is consistent with the realist understanding of strategic engagement.

While this trend suggests that US policy has achieved immediate American interests in a manner consistent with long-term cooperation, the reality is far more complex. US effort to elicit PRC cooperation is undermined by US proliferation of strategic weapons and technologies and its tolerance of proliferation on the part of its allies. Washington exports strategic missiles to England and nuclear technologies to Japan. Germany and Russia have been more important sources than China of Iranian and Iraqi military and civilian technologies, undercutting US containment of these two countries. These "double standards" question the legitimacy of US demands that China "follow the rules" of international regimes and elicit PRC criticism of US "hegemony."

Moreover, in contrast to market access cooperation and IPR cooperation, where conflict resolution allows China to benefit by maintaining mutually economic cooperation with the relatively open yet politicized US market, China's accommodation to US proliferation policies reflects Chinese compromise without any reciprocal US compromises. This is because China accommodates US interests by not proliferating into the Middle East but the United States has not accommodated Chinese interests regarding proliferation to Taiwan. The result is that Chinese leaders only grudgingly eschew arms sales to the Middle East and South Asia and resist the asymmetry in US and Chinese policies. Thus they have not formally committed China to refrain from missile proliferation, threatening to use proliferation to challenge US interests should the United States undermine PRC interests regarding Taiwan. Indeed, Beijing's expansion of its missile program with Pakistan followed Washington's decision to export F-16s to Taiwan.[41]

American policy on Taiwan not only affects US efforts to restrain PRC proliferation. More importantly, US–China differences over Taiwan have the potential to infuse the entire relationship with tension and conflict, seriously harming the prospects for maximizing contemporary US–China cooperation and for successful long-term engagement of Chinese power. As with economic issues, America's failure to finesse the Taiwan issue can be explained by domestic politics. Taiwan's development of democracy and its successful economic policies have earned it many supporters in both Congress and among the general population. In this context, Congress has made Taiwan policy that has implicitly expressed support for Taiwan independence. But unlike conflict over economic issues, domestic political pressure on US policy makers has not contributed to a resolution of the bilateral conflict that either narrows differences or benefits international stability.

The Taiwan issue is not an immutable conflict involving vital interests on both sides. Taiwan is a more important security interest for China than it is for the United States and this asymmetry allows for mutually acceptable compromises. Taiwan is off the Chinese coast, is one of China's most important economic partners, and is considered by an influential sector of the Chinese people to be Chinese sovereign territory. None of these statements apply to the US interests in Taiwan. Strategic engagement would suggest that the United States should accommodate Chinese interests while not sacrificing its own. From the early 1970s until the early 1990s it did just that. While limiting arms sales and both implicit and explicit support for Taiwan independence, Washington guaranteed Taiwan's security against Chinese power as Taiwan's economy prospered and its political system evolved into a flourishing democracy. It did this while minimizing conflict with Beijing over US–Taiwan relations.

In 1996, after its first-term failure to focus on the Taiwan problem and its acquiescence to congressional pressures, the Clinton administration began to adopt the policies of its predecessors. In the aftermath of March 1996 tension in the Taiwan straits, administration officials reassured Beijing and warned Taiwan of the so-called "three nos." US officials asserted that the United States does not support independence for Taiwan, does not support a "two-China" policy, and does not support Taiwan membership in international organizations for which sovereignty is a requirement for membership, including the United Nations. During his June 1998 visit to China President Clinton took the additional significant political step of publically supporting the "three nos."[42] Washington has also tried to assure Beijing that it will not allow Taiwan's diplomacy to damage US–China relations. In 1995, following Lee Teng-hui's visit to the United States, it told Beijing that visits by Taiwan leaders to the United States would be "personal in nature," handled on a "case-by-case" basis, and that they would be "rare."

These initiatives, in conjunction with the administration's other efforts to stabilize relations, including the October 1997 summit and the June 1998 summit, reflected the White House's effort to exercise domestic leadership over policy toward Taiwan to accommodate PRC security interests. Should US policy also include greater restraint on arms sales to Taiwan, this could alleviate PRC resentment at US "hegemony" regarding PRC arms exports and nuclear cooperation with Iran and other Middle Eastern countries.

US "Kissingerian" deals with China over South Asia and Taiwan reflect US acknowledgment of Chinese legitimate interests in exchange for China's accommodation of US interests regarding proliferation and the Middle East. These deals contribute to successful engagement by removing potential sources of PRC revisionism. The United States has carried out similar policies in Indo–China and the Korean peninsula. The US withdrawal from Indo–China in 1973 reflected American acquiescence to China's interest in a sphere of influence in Indo–China and secure borders on its southern periphery. Since then, despite the end of the Cold War and end to America's strategic imperative to cooperate with China to oppose Soviet power, Washington has not challenged Chinese influence in Indo–China. On the Korean peninsula, Washington's post-Cold War cooperation with Beijing to manage North Korean–South Korean relations is strong US recognition of China's legitimate interests on its northeast border and of its role in helping to define the strategic order on the Korean peninsula. Thus US engagement of China includes recognition that a stable regional order requires acknowledgment of China's legitimate security interests from the Korean peninsula, through Taiwan and Indo–China, and into South Asia.

Strategic engagement as shared international leadership

The United States has been instrumental in bringing about Chinese membership in both the nuclear non-proliferation treaty (NPT) and the Comprehensive Test-Ban Treaty (CTBT). Regarding the former, during the early 1980s the United States used PRC interest in establishing bilateral cooperation in nuclear energy projects to pressure Beijing to accept NPT guidelines, which China informally did in 1984.[44] China's 1992 decision to formally sign and ratify the NPT reflected American pressure as well as China's discomfort with its outlier status in the international community. Since then, China's membership in the NPT has been helpful in curtailing PRC proliferation activities and has facilitated the 1996 US–China agreement in which Beijing agreed not to assist non-IAEA supervised nuclear energy facilities.

The United States has also been instrumental in promoting China's August 1996 decision to accept the text of the CTBT. In addition to the role of image costs stressed by Johnston and Evans (Chapter 10, this volume), China's decision to join the CTBT also reflected the importance of international political pressure and great power compromise. Beijing understood that its ability to stabilize US–China relations, a priority after March 1996, in part depended on its nuclear testing policy. In addition, Japanese suspension of grant aid and delay of implementation of the fourth round of yen loans to China suggested that Chinese policy on the CTBT might affect long-term Sino–Japanese relations. Beijing also had to consider more general Chinese isolation after France agreed to a moratorium on testing and China became the lone hold-out. These international pressures and the threat of further sanctions pressured Beijing to abandon its demand that the treaty permit peaceful nuclear explosions to join the treaty, despite serious misgivings within the PLA. In this context, it is significant that the United States also compromised. It made concessions to Beijing regarding the number of votes in the CTBT Executive Council and other procedures required to trigger on-site inspection.[45]

The United States also used its negotiating leverage to encourage Beijing to join the Zangger Committee, which is the implementation arm of the export control provisions of the NPT. Prior to the October 1997 US–China summit, Washington pressed Beijing to join the Zangger Committee. Seeking to promote a successful summit and assured that the Zangger Committee would not affect PRC policy, Beijing complied. Following the summit, Washington has pressed Beijing to join the Nuclear Suppliers Group (NSG), which entails more restrictive "full scope safeguards" on exports of fissionable materials and related technologies.[46]

American efforts to bring China into the NPT, CTBT, and the Zangger Committee have made major contributions toward multilateral engagement of Chinese power. Yet they were also relatively cost-free initiatives. China was brought into pre-existing systems that supported US interests, so that PRC participation could promote but not hurt American interests. Even the basic rules of CTBT were non-negotiable, so that Washington did not have to share with Beijing responsibility for establishing the rules of the test-ban regime. A more difficult US engagement strategy involves compromise of interests to reach consensus-based rules and thus shared leadership. Washington has been reluctant to engage China in these more difficult cases.

US policy toward Chinese membership in the Missile Technology Control Regime (MTCR) has reflected American ambivalence.[47] The United States sought China's compliance with the regime's restrictions on the proliferation of ballistic missiles, but it did not include China in the drafting of the treaty and through 1997 it did not invite China to join the regime. Some US officials, in a reference to Chinese missile transfers to Pakistan, said that only when China adheres to the regime will it be invited to join. Other officials did not want the PLA to benefit from the discussions among MTCR participants regarding missile specifications and they suspected that China would use participation in the MTCR to try to extend the regime to cover exports of weapons that Washington does not want to restrict, including F-16s to, among other places, Taiwan. Thus Washington's efforts to maximize PLA weakness and its inability to negotiate with Beijing over arms sales to Taiwan undermined its ability to engage China in an important arms control treaty.[48]

But evolving US policy toward Chinese membership in the MTCR reflected the administration's growing commitment to engagement. Despite its national interest reasons for opposing PRC membership, in 1998 the United States reversed its policy and actively encouraged China to become a formal member of the regime. Following this policy adjustment Washington encountered the resistance of Chinese leaders, who linked Chinese missile exports to the Middle East, for example, with US arms sales to Taiwan.[49] At the June 1998 Beijing summit, however, China stated that it had begun to "actively study" joining the MTCR and affirmed in a US–China joint communiqué that its export policy regarding South Asia conforms to MTCR guidelines.[50] Chinese interest in joining the MTCR will continue to evolve in the context of US arms sales to Taiwan. Indeed, when the prospect of US–Taiwan cooperation on a theater missile defense system became a prominent issue in US policy debates in late 1998, Beijing became more reluctant to discuss membership in MTCR.

Despite the significant trend of engagement in US policy, Washington has not included China in all multilateral arms control arrangements. Washington has supported Chinese exclusion from the Wassenaar Arrangement on Export Controls for Conventional Arms and Dual-Use Goods and Technologies, which seeks to promote transparency of arms transfers and controls on proliferation of conventional arms and dual-use equipment in order to avoid "destabilizing accumulations" and enhanced capabilities for states whose "behavior . . . is a cause for concern." There were 33 founding members of the Wassenaar Arrangement, including Romania, Russia, and Turkey. China has been excluded, apparently because Washington and other signatories believe that they may eventually want to use the Wassenaar Arrangement to control exports to China. China is also not among the 30 countries that participate in the Australia Group, which seeks to control the proliferation of dual-use chemicals and the proliferation of biological weapons.[51]

Overall, by 1998 American policy on Chinese participation in multilateral security arrangements had adopted most of the components of engagement. Washington not only pursued cost-free but not insignificant engagement regarding Chinese membership in such institutions as the NPT, the CTBT, and the Zangger Committee; it also sought Chinese membership in the MTCR, revealing a willingness to sacrifice immediate national interests. It should not be difficult for Washington to extend engagement to the remaining institutions of international arms control. Unlike in other areas, domestic politics has not been a major determinant of US policy toward multilateral security engagement. The resulting policy flexibility may explain the progress in this area, as compared to US multilateral economic engagement of China.

Strategic engagement as bilateral institutional cooperation

Bilateral interests adjustment and multilateral engagement are the most important ways for the United States to engage China on strategic issues. Less significant but not unimportant are efforts to build cross-institutional communities of Chinese and American military officials. Such linkages can provide a number of mechanisms that could help to ease the great power adjustments associated with the rise of Chinese power. Insofar as these communities enable each side to "collect intelligence" on the other side, each side develops an interest in maintenance of these ties. This can act as an "entangling" factor in US management of conflicts of interest. Mutual intelligence collection can also enhance understanding of each side's operating procedures so that miscalculations do not occur. Finally, a security dialogue can sensitize each side to the other's security concerns while helping to alleviate misperceptions of each other's intentions, contributing to the prevention of tensions originating from misperceptions and the dynamics of the security dilemma as well as the prevention of unanticipated and unnecessary conflict.

There are a number of US foreign policies that could benefit from such linkages. Chinese suspicion of US policy toward third parties might be alleviated through bilateral discussions. A dialogue would be an important component of US efforts to explain US military initiatives in East Asia, including enhanced US–Japan security cooperation, possible deployment of ballistic missile defense systems, and possible expansion of US naval activities, including renewed access to US-built facilities at Subic Bay in the Philippines. A US–China security dialogue could also help to alleviate mutual suspicions about each country's policy toward disputed territories, including the Spratly Islands and Senkaku/Diaoyu Islands.

The United States military had a very active program of institutional cooperation with the PLA until China's June 1989 crackdown on the Beijing democracy demonstrations. This program included technology and weapons transfer projects, working-level exchanges involving experts in such areas as logistics, management, maintenance, and military medicine, and high-level exchanges involving the chairman of the joint chiefs-of-staff and various service secretaries and chiefs. There were also exchanges between the Chinese and American defense universities. These various programs enabled the two militaries to begin to develop broad-based institutional ties and a sophisticated understanding of their counterpart's strategic perspectives and its military operations.[52] The United States terminated all these programs after June 4, 1989.

During the mid-1990s, Washington took tentative steps toward restoring institutional ties between the American and Chinese militaries. The first step occurred in November 1993 when Assistant Secretary of Defense for International Security Affairs Charles Freeman visited Beijing. Freeman began discussions with Chinese leaders on four programs of cooperation with the PLA: strategic dialogue among senior officers; cooperation for conversion of PLA weapons factories to production of civilian goods; working-level visits between functional units; and cooperation in developing PLA expertise for UN peace-keeping activities. Among the Pentagon's objectives was an attempt to understand the PLA's strategic objectives, including the development of its deterrence policy, and to promote crisis prevention by learning how the PLA operates. Then, in October 1994, Secretary of State William Perry visited Beijing and finalized agreements of defense conversion and on cooperation toward improving China's military-controlled air traffic control system. He also offered Beijing technologies enabling computer simulation of nuclear tests.[53]

In the context of the US debate over Chinese human rights abuses and conflict over Taiwan, the Freeman initiative led to little immediate progress. Cooperation in peacekeeping activities was too controversial to develop, and US–China cooperation in civilian conversion of PLA weapons factories was abandoned when there were suggestions that the PLA had acquired access to sensitive advanced US technologies.[54] US domestic political controversies also obstructed development of both high-level and functional exchanges among defense officials and of a strategic dialogue.

The United States recommended US–China strategic dialogue in late 1996 when Chinese Defense Minister Chi Haotian visited Washington and the two sides agreed on an extensive agenda of defense cooperation. In 1997 the two sides exchanged visits of the Chairman of the US Joint Chiefs-of-Staff in Beijing and the Chief of the General Staff of the PLA. The two sides institutionalized the exchange of high-level officers during the October 1997 summit, creating the US–China Defense Consultative Talks, scheduled to meet annually to enhance mutual transparency through an ongoing strategic dialogue. In December 1997 General Xiong Guankai, Deputy Chief of the PLA General Staff, visited Washington to attend the inaugural session of the US–China Defense Consultative Talks. Then in January 1998 Secretary of Defense William Cohen visited Beijing.[55]

The US and Chinese militaries have also conducted dialogues among policy analysts and lower-level officials. In October 1996 the Clinton administration ended the 1989 suspension of the annual meeting program of the US and Chinese National Defense Universities. These annual NDU conferences discuss such issues as strategic doctrine and regional security perspectives. In 1997 the American NDU received Chinese NDU faculty for a short visit involving attending lectures and making presentations. There have also been cooperative programs between non-government US organizations and the PLA. The Atlantic Council in Washington, DC, has sponsored a researcher from the PLA's Academy of Military Science. In 1997 the PLA launched a program with the John F. Kennedy School of Government at Harvard University. The Kennedy School organizes two weeks of seminars and lectures for up to twenty PLA officers, including senior colonels and generals, on such subjects as US regional security perspectives and US policy-making and political processes. US military and civilian officials and elected officials have participated in these seminars.

In recent years the United States has also restored and expanded functional cooperation programs with the PLA. The programs with the most potential are the Military Maritime Safety Agreement, concluded during the 1997 summit and signed by Secretary of Defense Cohen during his 1998 visit to Beijing, and the agreement to share information concerning the use of militaries during humanitarian crises and natural disaster, seeking to foster closer coordination in relief operations. These agreements can enable the two militaries to become better informed of each other's operating procedures and will promote greater operational cooperation between the two militaries. During the June 1998 summit the two sides agreed to hold a "sand table" seminar game on joint disaster relief, a prelude to potential joint humanitarian relief military exercises. Following the summit, the US and Chinese militaries agreed to exchange observers of each other's military exercises and to cooperate to minimize environmental damage from military activities. They also agreed that a Chinese military vessel would visit the United States in 1999 and to exchange military students. There have also been regular joint exercises for humanitarian relief between US forces and Chinese forces based in Hong Kong.[56] All these activities can enhance transparency, minimize unintended tension, and consolidate cooperation more than formal high-level transparency talks.

Similar to the trend in US economic and multilateral engagement, the Clinton administration has moved to re-establish the framework of institutional strategic engagement. But progress was delayed by PRC reluctance and US domestic politics. Beijing is apprehensive that exercises with the US military and expanded transparency could be embarrassing and increase its military vulnerability. On the US side, revelations in late 1998 and into 1999 about possible Chinese espionage at US nuclear facilities politicized US–China military exchanges, reducing the Pentagon's interest in cooperation with the PLA.[57] Nonetheless, prior progress suggests that both militaries see an interest in cooperation. Over the long run, this could contribute to Chinese and American interests in stable cooperation by creating shared interests in maintaining cooperation and by enhancing understanding of each other's military procedures and strategic intentions.

Conclusion

American engagement policy toward China reflects the complexity of simultaneously seeking short-term gains and long-term interests across a wide range of policy issues in a multitude of arenas. For the most part and on a wide range of issues, the United States has been very successful at simultaneously achieving its immediate interests and many aspects of a long-term engagement policy. In economic matters, Beijing has made concessions to resolve the IPR conflict and to facilitate US access to the Chinese market. In security matters China has ended nuclear cooperation with Iran and promised not to aid non-safeguarded nuclear energy projects. It has also not transferred to Middle Eastern countries missiles covered by the MTCR and assured US leaders that it would discontinue missile sales to Iran. In response to US pressure, Beijing is also gaining better control over its exports of chemical weapons precursors. Washington has achieved these successes in a manner not inconsistent with engagement, insofar as it has relied on diplomacy and limited sanctions rather than escalatory tactics such as costly punitive sanctions.

While achieving its immediate objectives, the United States has engaged China in multilateral institutions and in US–China societal interactions. As in bilateral ties, the United States used its superior leverage to set the terms of engagement. Chinese membership in the CTBT, NPT, and the Zangger Committee all reflect American efforts to integrate China into the pre-existing international order without fundamental changes in the rules. Moreover, Washington sought Chinese membership in the MTCR after it had already secured various Chinese commitments regarding missile proliferation, particularly regarding missile exports to Iran, and it agreed to US exports of nuclear power plants to China after China established American-approved regulations governing nuclear technology exports.[58]

At times, however, in accordance with realist understanding of legitimacy, Washington has adjusted to legitimate PRC interests when accommodation has not harmed US interests. US adjustment to China's security relationship with Pakistan promotes engagement but also does not significantly affect US interests. Since the demise of the Soviet Union, US interest in South Asia has greatly declined. Similarly, US–China societal and institutional cooperation has not imposed any costs on US security or economic interests. Most importantly, the gradual evolution of the Clinton administration's Taiwan policy reflects its understanding that cooperation with China and regional stability require accommodating Beijing's one-China policy and that acquiescing to PRC interests does not require Washington to sacrifice its interest in maintaining US–Taiwan economic relations, its security commitment to Taiwan, and its support for democracy in Taiwan. To the extent that this trend continues, Washington will also ameliorate the most counter-productive aspect of treatment of US–China security conflicts – its double standards regarding the principles of non-proliferation and its "hegemonic" demands for unilateral Chinese concessions.

Through a combination of American power and concessions, the Clinton administration has pursued a strategic policy of bilateral and multilateral engagement. The limited exceptions are Chinese membership in the Australia Group and the Wassenaar Arrangement. In the economic realm, despite surprising and significant Chinese concessions to the existing international trade order, through May 1999 the White House remained unwilling to agree to Chinese membership of the WTO. In contrast to US policy toward Taiwan and South Asia, it has preferred stalemated negotiations over concessions to legitimate PRC interests, even to reciprocate PRC concessions to US interests. The long-term impact could well be very detrimental to the stability of the international economic order.

Different domestic contexts of policy making is a plausible possible explanation for the contrast in US economic and strategic policies. In economic affairs, the United States has an immediate interest in liberalizing the Chinese market, which requires opposition to China's protectionist policies; it has a long-term interest in gaining Chinese membership in the international economic order, which requires ceding Chinese shared leadership while offering short-term accommodation of Chinese protectionist interests. Its resistance to engagement through accommodation reflects the impact of US domestic interest groups. Whereas the American public is relatively uninvolved in the making of security policy, there are powerful domestic groups, including labor-intensive manufacturing industries and labor organizations, with an interest in US foreign economic policy. In addition, American human rights groups are more likely to link their policy objectives with US economic policy toward China than with security policy toward China. On the other hand, China's absence from multilateral economic organizations does not adversely affect the immediate objectives of other interest groups, so that the opposition groups can dominate the policy debate. Thus, the potential political retaliation of US interest groups against White House concessions regarding Chinese membership in the WTO and the G-7 has deterred the administration from pursuing multilateral economic engagement.

Despite the mixed picture in bilateral and multilateral engagement, Washington has actively and successfully pursued economic and strategic engagement between US and Chinese societies and institutions. With the support of countervailing interest groups, including major export industries, the White House has resisted pressure from human rights groups and protectionist industries and labor unions to attach human rights conditions to China's MFN trade status. The resulting growth in trade has promoted mutual US and Chinese interests in stable economic cooperation and served US interests in economic growth. US–China educational, societal and institutional ties have also grown, and since late 1996 the United States has encouraged engagement with the PLA. Military engagement has promoted long-term cooperation and enhanced bilateral understanding, as well as benefitted immediate US interests by improving US intelligence on the PLA and by impressing the PLA with US military superiority.

Since 1996, Washington has used its economic and strategic leverage to simultaneously achieve its immediate national interests and its long-term engagement interests in bilateral, societal, and multilateral interactions with China. When necessary, Washington has accommodated important Chinese security interests, including in South Asia, Taiwan, Indo–China and the Korean peninisula. For the most part, the United States has tried, successfully, to "engage from strength." Multilateral economic policy is the exception, reflected in US policy toward Chinese membership in the WTO and the G-7. Regarding the WTO, despite significant Chinese concessions that compromised immediate economic interests, through May 1999 domestic political interests deterred the White House from accepting full PRC membership in the international economic order, thus undermining regime development on the basis of great power consensus and the emergence of a more economically powerful yet status quo China. This may only be an exception to an otherwise successful US engagement policy, but it is an important exception which has the potential to undermine international economic cooperation.

Notes

1 For a discussion of legitimate interests in the content of mutual adjustment in the establishment of a stable strategic order, see Henry A. Kissinger, *The World Restored; Metternich, Castlereagh, and the Problems of Peace, 1812–22* (New York: Houghton Mifflin, 1973).

2 Although US officials cannot express this interest, China understands US and Chinese strategic interests in Taiwan. See Xu Yimin and Wei Wenching, "The United States Must Correct Its Stance on Taiwan," *China Daily*, January 6, 1996, in *FBIS/China*, January 11, 1996, pp. 6–7; Lu Junyuan, "Taiwan's Geostrategic Value Makes Unification Essential," *Taiwan Yanjiu*, No. 33 (March 20, 1996), in *FBIS/China*, September 4, 1996.

3 See Assistant Secretary of State Winston Lord's comments during the 1996 Taiwan Strait confrontation in Reuters, March 12, 1996.

4 See e.g. "Commentary: A Dangerous Road," Beijing China Radio International, 9 May, 1997, in *FBIS/China*, May 13, 1997; *Beijing Review*, No. 4 (January 27 to February 2, 1997), pp. 7–10, in *FBIS/China*, January 31, 1997; Ni Feng, "Enhanced U.S.–Japanese Security Alliance: Cause for Concern," June 16–22, 1997, in *FBIS/China*, June 19, 1997.

5 For a discussion of the Pentagon statement, see *Far Eastern Economic Review*, August 3, 1995. For extended discussions of US interest in East Asia and China's interests in the islands, see Douglas T. Stuart and William T. Tow, *A US Strategy for the Asia-Pacific*, *Adelphi Paper*, No. 299; Mark J. Valencia, *China and the South China Sea Disputes*, *Adelphi Paper*, No. 298. Chinese interpreted the US remarks as support for the Philippines. See the discussion in the Chinese-controlled Hong Kong newspaper *Ta Kung Pao*, June 18, 1995, in FBIS/China, June 26, 1995, p. 7.

6 See Department of State daily briefing, September 23, 1996, and October 3, 1996.

7 See e.g. the statements by the spokesmen of the Chinese Foreign Ministry on October 10, 1996, in *FBIS*, October 11, 1996; and on November 5, 1996, in Kyodo, November 5, 1996, in *FBIS/China*, November 21, 1996.

8 For a fuller discussion of this issue, see Robert S. Ross, "China," in Richard Haass, ed., *Economic Sanctions and American Diplomacy* (Washington, DC: Council on Foreign Relations, 1998).

9 Samuel P. Huntington, *The Clash of World Civilizations and the Remaking of World Order* (New York: Simon & Schuster, 1996), especially Chapter 9.

10 On the role of strengthened US–Japan security relations in US policy toward China, see the authoritative statement by former US Defense Department official Joseph S. Nye, Jr., "An Engaging China Policy," *Wall Street Journal*, March 13, 1997.

11 For a strong statement of this argument, see Richard Bernstein and Ross H. Munroe, *The Coming Conflict with China* (New York: Alfred A. Knopf, 1997); Nicholas D. Kristof, "The Rise of China," *Foreign Affairs*, Vol. 72, No. 5 (November to December, 1993).

12 Bernstein and Munro, *The Coming Conflict with China*.

13 Ibid. For a position advocating an unyielding China policy, see Robert Kagan, On Chinese admission into the WTO, see Greg Mastel, "China and the WTO: Beijing at Bay," *Foreign Policy*, No. 104 (October 1, 1996).

14 See the statement by Assistant Secretary of State Joseph Nye before the US House of Representatives, International Relations Committee, Asia and the Pacific Sub-committee, June 27, 1995.

15 See Nye, "An Engaging China Policy."

16 See Randall Schweller, Chapter 1, this volume.

17 Ibid.

18 *Christian Science Monitor*, October 8, 1998.

19 United States Government Accounting Office, "U.S.–China Trade: Implementation of Agreements on Market Access and Intellectual Property (letter report, January 25, 1995).

20 *New York Times*, February 3, 1997; Brenda A. Jacobs, "Talking Textiles," *China Business Review*, March to April, 1997.

21 On the sources and implications of the US–China trade deficit, see Barry Naughton, "The United States and China: Management of Economic Conflict," in Robert S. Ross, ed., *After The Cold War: Domestic Factors and U.S.–China Relations* (Armonk, NY: M.E. Sharpe, 1998).

22 See Under-Secretary of Commerce Stuart Eizenstat's press briefing, March 12, 1997.

23 United States Government Accounting Office, "U.S.–China Trade: Implementation of Agreements on Market Access and Intellectual Property (letter report, January 25, 1995).

24 *National Trade Estimate Report for the People's Republic of China.*

25 On the implementation of the 1995 agreement, see Office of the US Trade Representative, "Fact Sheet: Chinese Implementation of the 1995 IPR Agreement," June 17, 1996. On the prison terms, see *NYT*, April 17, 1997. On the movement of production to elsewhere in Southeast Asia, see *Wall Street Journal*, August 22, 1997, September 19, 1997. Note also that in 1997 the International Intellectual Property Alliance no longer targeted China as a priority for US foreign policy. See Jeanne Holden, "Backgrounder on 'Special 301' Trade Law Review," United States Information Agency, February 25, 1997.

26 See Marcus Noland, "The United States and U.S.–China Trade," in Robert S. Ross, ed., *After The Cold War.*

27 Berta Gomez, "Industry's Losses Estimated at $11,200 Million," United States Information Agency, May 5, 1997.

28 For a discussion of US policy, see Robert O. Keohane, *After Hegemony: Cooperation and Discord in the World Political Economy* (Princeton, NJ: Princeton University Press, 1984).

29 See Harold K. Jacobson and Michel Oksenberg, *China's Participation in the IMF, the World Bank, and GATT: Toward A Global Economic Order* (Ann Arbor: University of Michigan Press, 1990). On the benefits of engaging China within the WTO, see Nicholas R. Lardy, *China and the WTO*, Brookings Policy Briefs, No. 10 (November 1996); Robert S. Ross, "Enter the Dragon: China and the World Trade Organization," *Foreign Policy*, No. 104 (September, 1996).

30 *Xinhua* November 22, 1997, in *FBIS/China*, November 26, 1997; *AFP*, December 5, 1997; *Washington Post*, September 23, 1998; *Wall Street Journal*, September 23, 1998. On PRC concessions prior to the summit, see the report "Market Access and Protocol Commitments Process of China's WTO Accession," Office of the US Special Trade Representative, April 8, 1999. For reports on the politics of WTO, see *Wall Street Journal*, April 9, 1999, and April 12, 1999. Private sector and congressional reactions are reported in *Washington Post*, April 13, 1999, and April 14, 1999; *New York Times*, April 15, 1999. For an evaluation of Chinese compromises, see Nicholas R. Lardy, "Clinton Spurned a Great WTO Deal with China," *Wall Street Journal*, April 20, 1999.

31 *Washington Post*, September 15, 1998.

32 See Tarnoff's testimony before the Subcommittee on Asia and the Pacific, May 16, 1996, and the Subcommittee on International Economic Policy and Trade, US House of Representatives.

33 Statistics are from the United States–China Business Council.

34 Chinese State Statistical Bureau, *Zhongguo Tongji Nianjian* (Beijing: Zhongguo Tongji Chubanshe, 1997), pp. 44, 602.

35 See e.g. Chen Baosen, "Quanmian Fazhan Zhong Mei Jingmao Guanxi Gonggu

Zhong Mei Guanxi de Jingji Jichu" (Comprehensively develop China–US economic and trade relations, consolidate the economic foundation of China–US relations), *Shijie Jingji yu Zhengzhi (neibu)*, No. 3, 1992.

36 This discussion draws on Ross, "China."

37 On the Chinese cancellations, see *Far Eastern Economic Review*, May 28, 1992, interview with US State Department official. On the Iranian plant, see *New York Times*, November 10, 1995. Regarding aid to unsupervised plants, see the US Department of State special briefing, May 10, 1996. The commitment regarding transfers of nuclear technologies to Iran was reached prior to the October 1997 Washington summit. On this and the missile transfers to Iran, see the White House background press briefing by senior administration officials, October 29, 1997 "Fact Sheet: Achievements of the U.S.–China Summit," June 27, 1998; transcript of the Clinton–Jiang press conference in Tiananmen square, June 27, 1998; *Agence France Presse*, May 26, 1998, in *FBIS*, May 27, 1998; Testimony of the Honorable John D. Holum Acting Under-Secretary of State for Arms Control and International Security Affairs before the Senate Subcommittee on International Security, Proliferation, and Federal Services, June 18, 1998.

38 On China's efforts on chemical exports, see the transcript of Robert Einhorn's interview on China/non-proliferation on January 7, 1998, published in January 1998 in the United States Information Agency's electronic journal "U.S. Foreign Policy Agenda."

39 *New York Times*, August 27, 1996; *Washington Times*, November 26, 1996; *Jang* (Rawalpindi, Pakistan), January 20, 1997, in *FBIS, Daily Report: South Asia*, January 22, 1997. For a discussion of PRC motives for arms transfers, see Karl W. Eikenberry, *Explaining and Influencing Chinese Arms Transfers*, McNair Paper, No. 36 (Washington, DC: Institute for National Strategic Studies, National Defense University, 1995).

40 Ross, "China."

41 See e.g. the statements by the spokesmen of the Chinese Foreign Ministry on October 10, 1996, and on November 5, 1996, in Kyodo, November 5, 1996, in *FBIS/China*, November 21, 1996.

42 See the *Xinhua* coverage of National Security Adviser Tony Lake's meetings with the Director of the State Council Office of Foreign Affairs Liu Huaqiu in Xinhua, July 8, 1996, in *FBIS*, July 8, 1996; *Xinhua*, November 20, *FBIS*, November 22, 1996. See the White House statements issued after the October 1997 Clinton–Jiang summit in US Department of State daily press briefing, October 31, 1997 (dpb # 157); transcript of the October 29 "Background Briefing by Senior Administration Official." The President's statement occurred at the Shanghai Library on June 30, 1999.

43 See the State Department statement in "Add State Department Report," October 2, 1995; press briefing by Assistant Secretary of State Winston Lord and Director of Asian Affairs for the national Security Council Robert Suettinger, October 24, 1995. See also the report of President Clinton's remarks to Jiang Zemin during their October 1995 meeting in New York in *New York Times*, October 25, 1995. US policy on the "three-nos" dates to 1996. See e.g. US Department of State Daily Press Briefing (Dpb # 157) Friday, October 31, 1997; *Xinhua*, July 8, 1996, in *FBIS/China*, July 10, 1996; *Xinhua*, November 20, 1996, in *FBIS/China*, November 22, 1996.

44 For an analysis of the US–China negotiations in the early 1980s, see Michael Brenner, *The U.S.–China Bilateral Nuclear Accord*, Pew Case Studies in International Affairs, case No. 106 (Washington, DC: Institute for the Study of Diplomacy, Georgetown University, 1986).

45 See the Geneva press conference by John Holum, Director of the Arms Control and Disarmament Agency, August 1, 1996, and article II, section C and article IV, section D, paragraph 46 of the text of the treaty for the compromise wording. For an

analysis of Chinese decision-making, see Chapter 10 by Johnston and Evans in this volume; Alastair Iain Johnston, "Learning versus Adaptation: Explaining Change in Chinese Arms Control Policy in the 1980s and 1990s," *The China Journal*, No. 35 (January 1996).

46 On the Zangger Committee and the Nuclear Suppliers Group and on US decisions with China on PRC membership in these institutions, see the transcript of the White House background briefing on nuclear cooperation with China, October 29, 1997. See also the US Arms Control and Disarmament Agency's fact sheet on multilateral nuclear export control regimes.

47 For a comprehensive discussion of bringing China into the MTCR and other such proliferation regimes, see Charles A. Goldman and Jonathan D. Pollack, *Engaging China in the International Export Control Process* (Santa Monica, CA: RAND, 1997).

48 *Joint United States–People's Republic of China Statement on Missile Proliferation*, October 4, 1994, in *U.S. Department of State Dispatch*, Vol. 5, No. 42 (October 17, 1994), p. 702. See the report by the US Government Accounting Office, *Export Controls: Some Controls Over Missile-Related Technology Exports To China are Weak*, April 17, 1995.

49 See, e.g. the statements made by the spokesmen of the Chinese Foreign Ministry on October 10, 1996, and on November 5, 1996, in Kyodo, November 5, 1996, in *FBIS/China*, November 21, 1996. See the report of the US offer and China's response, in the briefing by US Acting Under Secretary for Arms Control and International Security Affairs John Holum, April 9, 1998.

50 See the Beijing press briefing by Mike Mccurry, National Security Adviser Sandy Berger, and National Economic Adviser Gene Sperling, June 27, 1998. On South Asia, see the US–China Joint Statement on South Asia, June 27, 1998. Chinese linkage of MTCR with the theatre missile defence issue is reported in interviews with US government officials.

51 For a discussion of the Australia Group, see Amy E. Smithson, *Separating fact from Fiction: The Australia Group and the Chemical Weapons Convention*, Occasional Paper No. 34 (Washington, DC: The Henry M. Stimson Center, 1997).

52 On these various programs, see Edward W. Ross, "U.S.–China Military Relations," in Joyce K. Kallgren, Noordin Sopiee, and Soedjati Djiwandono, eds, *ASEAN and China: An Evolving Relationship* (Berkeley: Institute for East Asian Studies, University of California, 1988), and Eden Woon, "Chinese Arms Sales and U.S.–China Military Relations," *Asian Survey*, Vol. 29, No. 6 (June 1989).

53 *Los Angeles Times*, October 21, 1994; *Financial Times*, October 18, 1994; *Washington Post*, October 18, 1994.

54 *Far Eastern Economic Review*, August 22, 1997.

55 For the 1996 planning for these initiatives, see Department of Defense press release, December 18, 1996 (Reference no. 679–696), issued press release following Minister of Defense Chi Haotian's visit to Washington. On the Defense Consultative Talks, see Department of Defense news briefing, December 11, 1997.

56 "Fact Sheet: Achievements of U.S.–China Summit," June 27, 1998; Department of Defense news briefing, July 7, 1998; US–China Joint Statement on Military Environmental Protection, September 15, 1998.

57 Interview with US military official.

58 On the linkage between China's export policies and US–China cooperation in nuclear energy, see the background briefing by a senior State Department official, October 31, 1987; China's regulations are published in *Xinhua*, September 11, 1998, in *FBIS*, September 16, 1997.

9

THE MAJOR MULTILATERAL ECONOMIC INSTITUTIONS ENGAGE CHINA

Margaret M. Pearson

Introduction

The major multilateral economic institutions that make up the global economic regime relevant to China include the World Bank, the International Monetary Fund (IMF), the General Agreement on Tariffs and Trade (GATT) and its successor, the World Trade Organization (WTO). A regional organization, the Asia Pacific Economic Forum (APEC), has a secondary and yet nonetheless significant role in bringing China into the international economic system. These organizations have tried to promote China's integration into the world economy through a logic that is quite consistent with "engagement" as defined in the Preface to this volume.[1] Moreover, judging by the evolution in attitudes of key domestic policy makers and bureaucrats within China, and changes in Chinese policies since the late 1970s, the effort of multilateral economic institutions to bring about engagement appears thus far to have been successful in encouraging China to play by the "rules of the game." At a minimum these institutions have not thwarted the goals of engagement. Although Chinese negotiators bargain hard to protect China's interests, their bargaining is within the realm of what we expect to see of any country with significant economic leverage, and does not constitute an attempt to overturn the established regime norms. In this sense, China is not a "dissatisfied rising power" (to coin the term used by Randall Schweller in Chapter 1, this volume) and engagement is an appropriate response.

Yet this generally positive assessment of the existence and results of an engagement strategy in the global economy must be tempered with two cautionary notes. First, the engagement strategy employed by the major multilateral organizations is not the *only* cause of China's expanded cooperative behavior in the global economic regime. Discipline imposed by the global market, bilateral pressure from the United States government, and especially the desires of domestic political actors, have also promoted China's cooperative behavior. Second, even when engagement is judged to be effective, its impact is not direct, but rather is channeled through domestic perceptions and domestic structures. These intervening factors can hinder or block the effectiveness of engagement as much as they can facilitate it.

To construct this argument, I draw on a number of hypotheses that have been set forth in the field of international relations to explain how transnational influence by international regimes and institutions that are attempting to engage China might work. The analysis finds positive evidence that mechanisms for engagement implicit in regime theory and transnationalism are at work, but also that domestic political structures and politics are crucial for mediating the effect of external influences on China.

The character, rationale, and mechanisms of engagement

The character of engagement

To apply the term "strategy" to the major multilateral economic organizations is somewhat misleading, as it suggests more agency than may actually exist when dealing with a particular country. Whereas in a bilateral relationship one government sets an explicit and distinct strategy toward another, this is not necessarily the case for a multilateral institution. While a multilateral institution may formulate an explicit strategy toward a country, it may alternatively act as an agent for a member country, or may treat a country according to existing rules that are broadly applied to all members. The latter strategy may be regarded as more implicit than explicit.

With regard to China's absorption into the major multilateral economic fora, we shall examine a mixture of these types of treatment. In an important sense, the dynamic behind the incorporation of China into these institutions, and particularly into the World Bank, IMF, and APEC is more one of accepting China's request to join the organization under the existing rules, and perhaps negotiating somewhat the terms of participation, than of an active (and defensive) decision to "manage" China. It may capture this dynamic better to speak of the "orientation" of these institutions toward China.[2] Yet in the case of China's negotiations to enter the GATT/WTO system, the international institution is, by and large, following the lead of the US government; the engagement strategy is closely linked to a bilateral strategy, and the institution acts more as an agent.[3]

Whether explicit or implicit, the orientation of the multilateral economic institutions reflects the liberal principles, norms, goals, and rules that have been institutionalized in the major organizations since they originated in the aftermath of World War II. The prime goal of the Bretton Woods institutions – the World Bank, IMF, and GATT – was to foster prosperity and peace, stabilize the global market, generate universal rules for free and non-discriminatory trade (primarily through the use of unconditional most-favored-nation status), and foster trade liberalization through the mutually guaranteed reduction of tariffs and non-tariff barriers.[4] The Bretton Woods system was in reality full of loopholes that permitted *de facto* discrimination. In addition, in recent years the stability of the Bretton Woods system has been brought into question by the growth of regional trade blocs, such as the European Free Trade Association and the North American Free Trade Agreement. In part to eradicate these problems, the central goal of the GATT's supersession by the WTO in 1995 was to expand the regime's scope and tighten its free trade rules. More specifically, the primary purpose of the WTO is to ensure further reduction of tariffs and non-tariff trade barriers, and to eliminate discriminatory treatment in international trade in goods and services.[5]

The essential goal of the engagement strategy can be inferred from these norms: to bring newly cooperative states into the global trading regime, and in so doing gain a commitment to the norms of the system and therefore expand the list of nations willing to play by the dominant rules of the game. Although the incorporation of non-market states into a system intended for market economies poses some problems, the core goal for these states is essentially the same as for market economies. Even though it is a regional regime, APEC's goal, too, is to enhance trade liberalization in a manner consistent with the WTO. There is even hope among some groups that APEC's formal commitment to "open regionalism" (the possibility of generalizing its regional liberalization to the world as a whole) will help push forward global liberalization, both by setting an example and because APEC's members account for nearly half the world's economy and trade.[6]

These goals of engagement are largely economic; but do political goals also exist? Specifically, do representatives of the global economic organizations, either on their own or acting as agents for member governments, wish to use engagement to achieve political ends? It is by no means logically necessary that political goals co-exist with economic ones, as markets and free trade have been shown to be compatible with a variety of political systems. Yet the possibility of a linkage between the economic and a political agenda requires further scrutiny. This is in part because advocates of free trade often argue that global markets depend upon liberal political systems to operate most effectively, and in turn can be used to encourage political liberalization. Such an assumption of the link between economic liberalization and democratization has been articulated by, for example, US Treasury official Lawrence Summers:

> Shared prosperity [through competition based on market mechanisms] advances human freedom. Think about the differences in life choices of a child born today and one born 25 years ago in Korea, or China or Chile. It cannot be an accident that most of the world's rich countries are democratic, and most of the world's poor countries are not.[7]

History also suggests the importance of examining the possibility of a political agenda, for throughout the Cold War era, "the political-security objectives of the

West, rather than systemic economic differences, [were] the driving force behind negotiations over Eastern [European and Soviet bloc] countries' bids to affiliate with the GATT."[8] The prime goal of Western countries, particularly the US, in formulating trade policies with the Soviet bloc countries was containment of Soviet power. With regard to the Soviet Union itself, the strategy of the Western countries was, first, the use of economic embargo and then, in the 1970s, trade inducements which would give the Soviet Union a stake in the global system. The strategy for eastern Europe was to divide the bloc by granting preferential treatment for some countries (such as Poland and Hungary) and not others.[9] In other words, in policy toward the Soviet bloc countries, the goal of political containment was fostered, at times, by a strategy akin to economic engagement.

Procedurally, moreover, political goals can be inserted into the economic engagement process. This is particularly true of the WTO accession. Even though non-economic conditions are supposed to be kept outside of the accession process, because the decision on admission is decided by contracting parties on a case-by-case basis (as opposed to by codified rules, as exist for admission to the World Bank and IMF), the possibility of politicization is greater.[10]

Although in the past multilateral economic institutions have been used to achieve containment, it appears in the post-Cold War era that alternative strategies to engagement are not currently present in the multilateral institutions' orientation. No coherent vision other than engagement has been articulated for these institutions by the organizations themselves or even by member governments. Two alternatives might plausibly have been articulated. The first is a "southern" strategy modeled on (or a continuation of) demands for a New International Economic Order (NIEO) that were voiced by developing countries in the 1970s and early 1980s. The NIEO was orchestrated by the developing country caucus in the UN, the Group of Seventy-seven. It criticized the exiting liberal order – seen to be embodied in the GATT, World Bank, and IMF – as systematically favoring the industrialized countries, in part by forcing open markets of developing countries. Instead, the NIEO would replace the norms of non-discrimination and reciprocity with permanent preferential treatment for developing countries' exports and support for import substitution policies.[11] In part due to some reforms in the Bank/Fund/GATT system that were designed to meet these demands, and in part because of opposition by the industrialized powers, the NIEO movement lost steam by the mid-1980s without radically altering either the norms or procedures of the multilateral institutions. Today, although development objectives are clearly at the core of World Bank goals,[12] and although the WTO charter documents make hortatory statements about the need to be sensitive to the development needs of poorer countries,[13] these institutions' development goals are to be achieved primarily through market mechanisms. Similarly, although some members of APEC – led by Malaysian Prime Minister Mahathir Mohamad – have proposed the establishment of an Asian body as an alternative to APEC that would exclude the US, Canada, Australia and New Zealand and hence protect APEC against Western domination, this proposal has not progressed very far.[14] A second alternative strategy to engagement would be containment, based on a military containment analogy for economics. The goal of such an "economic security" strategy, as noted by Schweller, would be to prevent China's further expansion. However, as will be discussed below, the idea of containment is anathema to staff members of the major economic institutions which deal with China. Thus cohesive alternative visions are not widely voiced within the organizations, and would be incompatible with the market norms that are at the heart of the multilateral economic institutions.

Within the basic strategy of engagement that lies at the core of the multilateral economic organizations, we can identify five possible and not mutually exclusive sub-goals. First, and most importantly, the central goal of engagement is to transform a country's preferences by erecting a set of positive incentives and building a domestic constituency for further integration into the global economy. Second, engagement can serve as an acknowledgment that it is legitimate for a rising world power to have a "place at the table." It is hoped that engagement will accommodate a country's "power prestige demands" without threatening the basic nature of the global market regime or economic institutions themselves.[15] Third, as a side benefit, engagement might be expected to provide information on a country's economic regime to the multilateral institutions. Fourth, engagement could facilitate access by the global economic institutions and its members to the market opportunities offered by the rising power. These first four sub-goals suggest the propriety of a "soft" negotiating posture for managing a rising power, a posture in which a multilateral institution admits the country on minimally acceptable conditions under the assumption that the institutions and its norms will influence the country once it is admitted.

A fifth sub-goal is more coercive. Engagement can be used to enmesh a country in the regime so that it is costly for the country either to breach its norms or to defect from the regime, thereby limiting its ability to disrupt the system.[16] This goal implies a "hard" negotiating posture over the terms of admission, in order to gain as much leverage or influence over the target country prior to its formal admission in the institution. A hard negotiating posture assumes that, while it is useful to have a country in the dominant regime, defection from the regime is a genuine possibility, and so the country's prior commitment to the regime should be clearly spelled out.

The rationale for why engagement can work

Although it is not often made explicit by representatives of the multilateral economic institutions, the rationale for why engagement may be effective is articulated in the IR literature on regimes and transnationalism. As noted above, the prime goal of engagement is to produce a change in a country's behavior to better fit the norms and principles of the global market regime. The underlying assumption is essentially that member countries will find it rational to comply with the international institutions.[17] Being a member of the group tends to increase adherence to group goals. For the regime's members, cooperation in the regime and the communication it engenders with other members reduces uncertainty about the international environment, in part by fostering transparency and the circulation of information. Through compliance, members can often gain material benefits – such as obtaining World Bank or IMF loans, or gaining unconditional most-favored-nation status as a member of WTO. From a more negative perspective, an "egotistic" state will comply with regime goals, even when myopic self-interest would suggest otherwise, in order to enhance its reputation as a "good player" and to avoid retaliation by other members. Social pressure from other members, and the risk that non-compliance in one regime could lead to spillover retaliation in other spheres, also encourage compliance.

Compliance of members to regime norms and rules cannot of course be guaranteed; examples of non-compliance in global economic institutions abound. Such was the case of the unilateral defection by the United States from the Bretton Woods post-war international monetary regime in 1971.[18] On the other hand, it is worth noting that the international economic institutions being considered here are undergirded by the mechanisms of the global market; the discipline on organizations' members is enforced to some degree by the marketplace, and can lead us to expect that compliance will be greater for the global trade regime than for other international regimes.

Several specific mechanisms through which international institutions promote successful engagement can be identified in the scholarly literature on international political economy.[19] In brief, international norms and rules might influence the beliefs and behavior of domestic decision makers, the positions articulated in the domestic policy debate, and, ultimately, their policies. Yet international influences must also be channeled through domestic actors and institutions, a process that may enhance or thwart external influence. In other words, the norms and rules of international institutions are made influential through their "entanglement" with the domestic political process.[20]

Four mechanisms of influence are potentially important. The first is the process by which domestic policy-makers *learn* new ideas. The concept of learning suggests that genuine (if often incremental) transformation of elite perceptions occurs as a result of exposure to international economic norms or rules. The literature on learning has focused primarily on issues of arms control – particularly the causes of Gorbachev's "new thinking" – but its utility for the issue of international economic institutions is clear.[21] To show that learning has occurred, we would need to show first that new ideas about economic integration have been trans-mitted to a country. This can happen through the business community or through agents of the multilateral institutions. This transmission of ideas through these linkages would need to lead to a shift in the dominant thinking among elites about the value of integration into the world economy, a shift that ideally leads to policy change in a direction that is consistent with the new ideas, but which can also be blocked by bureaucratic or other factors.[22] The influence of international ideas can be generational, moreover, as when ideas are adopted by a younger generation that then comes to power. It is also useful to keep in mind the conclusion that a country's leaders tend to be more open to new ideas when they face uncertainty about its current situation.[23]

Analysts of learning need to be careful not to confuse genuine learning with other possible causes of policy change, particularly strategic "adaptation." The hallmark of learning is a genuine shift in thinking in the context of a constant external environment. Adaptation occurs when change in behavior results from mere adjustment to changing external conditions – a simple re-evaluation of the costs and benefits of earlier tactics.[24] Moreover, policy change that results from bureaucratic bargaining or from turnover in domestic political institutions does not signify learning, although learning, turnover, and bureaucratic bargaining may be mutually reinforcing.

A second way that the norms and rules of the multilateral economic institutions can become entangled with domestic politics is when these ideas are used as *leverage* for domestic political actors to further their own agendas.[25] Multilateral or other external allies of domestic political actors can provide resources, including ideas, information, and arguments, to influence internal debates. For example, domestic political figures can use the ideas or rules of the international regime as the rationale for a change in domestic rules. Outside actors may also confer legitimacy on domestic actors, especially if they are seen as neutral or as possessing great resources. A more baldly instrumental use of international ideas or rules can also occur, such as when domestic actors use international rules to further interests not fully consistent with the purposes of the regime.[26]

A third path of entanglement can occur when the international institutions themselves *gain a foothold in the bureaucracy* of a country, or gain the ear of top political leaders, allowing the views and/or interests of these institutions to be articulated directly to key government actors. This can occur, for example, when a bureaucracy sets up offices to handle the relationship with the multilateral institution. It can also occur when, as a result of membership or as a condition of accession to the institution, a country's leader must engage in dialogue with international institution officials.

Still a fourth means of entanglement exists when international institutions establish explicit *positive and negative incentives* (or conditions) for compliance. The major multilateral economic organizations all establish conditions for membership. For these institutions' existing members, IMF conditionality on loans is the most well known and has been the most controversial.[27] The WTO, more so than was true of the GATT, establishes criteria for compliance with its charter and agreements, and has backed up these conditions with a dispute resolution mechanism. The World Bank also negotiates conditions for loans, but on the whole these are applied more weakly than has been the case with the IMF and GATT/WTO.

The precise way that these international ideas or rules become relevant in a country's domestic politics depends upon the domestic structure. Domestic structure refers to the degree of centralization of the political system and the pattern of state–society relations (whether policy-making is participatory or exclusionary of societal interests).[28] For a country that is centralized and exclusionary, "international rules will only affect national policy when and if authoritative officials are predisposed to the prescriptions and proscriptions embodied in international institutions."[29] The disposition of elite policy makers is obviously key; once decision-makers are on board with a program, changes based on international norms/rules may be easier to effect than in a decentralized state or one that gives voice to diverse societal interests.[30]

To the extent that a policy-making process is more decentralized to bureaucracies and localities, a different dynamic may be in effect: in a decentralized but exclusionary domestic structure, international rules will enter the debate

> when one group of policy-makers appeals to international rules [leverage] in an effort to further its own preferred strategies or to block those of other officials. However, due to the pluralist nature of the policy process, the incorporation of international rules and norms . . . does not guarantee that they will affect state policy.[31]

Bureaucratic politics models of policy making and the question of the formation of winning coalitions thus become quite relevant to arguments about domestic structure.

The engagement strategy applied to China

The general engagement strategy, its rationale, and its mechanisms as laid out above are evident in the record of China's entry into the World Bank and IMF, and its efforts to be admitted to GATT/WTO. In an important sense, China's rapidly growing presence in international markets has been viewed less as a threat to the global economic system than as an opportunity to bring China into the global economy on favorable terms. Once the Chinese leadership indicated a willingness to participate more fully in the international trade and investment system, the system responded. Market actors, seeing opportunities for new markets and sources of products, reacted immediately with trade and investment deals. Moreover, the multilateral institutions sought to bring China into the system on terms they have perceived as beneficial to both China and the system as a whole.

Although the perception of China that underlies the engagement strategy has been based more on hope than fear, worries about China's rising economic and/or political status exist. Indeed, perceptions of a threat have become more acute as the dynamism of China's economy has become clear. In particular, there is worry about the uses to which the Chinese leadership might put its economic power. Might China possess the power to flood the market with inexpensive goods, while keeping its own markets shut – thereby thumbing its nose at the principles of free trade that, ideally, underlie the global institutions? Might it convert its economic power into a military threat? The negotiations over China's admission to GATT and the WTO in recent years have felt the impact of these concerns as held by certain segments of the US government, as Robert Ross points out (Chapter 8, this volume).

Yet these worries emanate more from the status quo powers in the global economy and China's neighbors in Asia than the multilateral organizations; the IMF and World Bank, and APEC have been largely shielded from the concerns of global and regional powers. Documents produced by the World Bank, as well as interviews with staff members who work in these institutions, suggest that economically defined norms are by and large dominant. While staff members may hope that political liberalization will occur in China, such values do not appear to drive their actions. Moreover, politics of powerful countries are rarely inserted into the dealings of the World Bank and IMF, according to staff members. Interference did occur in the aftermath of the events at Tiananmen in 1989, at which time the US Executive Director of the Bank, who is under the direction of the US Treasury Department, constructed a coalition that halted lending to China for a period of several months, and restricted loans to humanitarian projects for a time thereafter. This case is said by staff members to be notable for being extreme; generally, they feel that the technocratic staff, rather than politically appointed management, dominates. Staff members express a commitment to keeping politics out of their decision making, and argue that the US government is sophisticated enough to recognize that it cannot dictate the policy of the organization.[32] Staff members in the World Bank who deal with China claim that "containment" is extremely counter-cultural to the organization, and is to their knowledge unheard of. There is a sense, moreover, that the containment debate in the US has no impact on their work. This rather benign view of China's rising economic power has greatly narrowed the expected range of responses spelled out by Schweller (Chapter 1, this volume).

China's incorporation into the IMF and World Bank

What, then, is the actual history of China's incorporation into the major multilateral economic institutions? The story of China's admission to the IMF and World Bank has been told elsewhere, and needs only to be recounted briefly here.[33] China joined first the IMF and then the World Bank in 1980. The impetus for the original contacts came from China. Chinese leaders made the decision to approach the Bank and Fund carefully, following a number of pathbreaking domestic policy changes. The most important of these were the elimination of the Cultural Revolution leadership, the decision to place economic reform at the forefront of the domestic agenda, the end of strict self-reliance, and the related legitimation of the concept of economic interdependence.

The IMF and World Bank reacted to China's overtures in mid-1979 with more delight than caution. There were, of course, negotiations over a number of key issues. In the IMF, negotiations occurred over the status of Taiwan, the size of China's quota, and the holdings of gold contributed by China, while in the World Bank, the difficult issues were China's access to various concessional tranches and, again, the status of Taiwan. Yet in hindsight these problems were resolved relatively easily. These institutions were somewhat flexible and creative in their thinking about how to involve China, but did not have to compromise their basic goals and norms. Beyond meeting its financial obligations to these organizations, the only membership requirement placed on China was for publication of data. Unlike their earlier negotiations with the Soviet Union, Bank and IMF officials assumed that China and these institutions could accommodate each other. Over the years of China's membership in the Bank and Fund, moreover, a similarly cooperative relationship has existed. Although China has been able to name executive directors and has been involved productively in the policy making of these institutions, it has not sought a major leadership role. Many of the joint projects (particularly projects involving World Bank funding) are considered to have been relatively successful. Over time, moreover, the marketization of China's domestic economy brought China more into line with the norms of these organizations.

This is not to say that some tough bargaining over terms of specific projects, and conflicts over the terms of the relationship, have not occurred. For example, IMF officials were quite displeased when, in 1980, China instituted its internal settlement rate on foreign exchange without meeting requirements to inform the organization of such an action. (The issue eventually became moot when China unilaterally discontinued use of the rate.) Moreover, China has sought to avoid IMF conditionality on its borrowings, usually by attempting to borrow through the less-conditioned tranches (thereby acting within the normal procedures of the organizations).

In its dealings with the World Bank, Chinese representatives have often bargained hard – generally harder than other countries, according to bank staff involved with China – over the terms of the covenants that lay out conditions for loans. Efforts by Chinese representatives to negotiate for favorable terms have intensified since the early 1990s, moreover. Bank staff members explain this as a function, in part, of Chinese officials' feeling more comfortable within the Bank. Staff members also point out the appearance on the scene of younger, more savvy, and generally more Westernized interlocutors who feel a need to be tough in order to prove their loyalty to Beijing. This behavior reflects a greater sensitivity to the appearance of bending to the outside world in the 1990s than was true in the 1980s. Furthermore, Chinese officials appear to be reluctant to agree to terms on which they cannot deliver.

Even though Chinese representatives bargain hard, the feeling within both the Bank and Fund is that their behavior is not out of the norm and does not attempt to challenge the institutions. Moreover, once an agreement is made, China has an excellent record of implementing it – whether in terms of repayment of loans or adherence to the terms of bank covenants. In part because China's record on project fulfillment (as well as overall economic reform) is so good, the World Bank at times agrees to somewhat less strict covenants than it would for countries with worse records. However, overall, China's treatment is not greatly different from other large countries and, in the grand scheme of things, the relationship between China and these two institutions has been constructive and non-disruptive. Jacobson and Oksenberg's definitive study of these institutions for the period up to 1989 appears to have held true in the 1990s as well: "the rules of the two institutions have not been bent for China any more than they normally are for large new entrants."[34]

The engagement strategy used by the Bank and IMF has been underlain by some, but not all, of the sub-goals outlined previously. The desire to accept China as a member seems to have been based largely on the perception that engagement would help transform China, and make China a more central player in the world economy. This move would not only benefit the status quo powers but also acknowledge China's demand for a (presumably cooperative) place at the table, as well (in the case of the Bank) as acknowledging its huge development needs. Seemingly less important but relevant nonetheless was the opportunity to gain information from China, something that would be achieved through these organizations' requirements for transparency. The more coercive goal of setting up a web of incentives and disincentives in which to entangle China is not apparent.

APEC

China joined APEC soon after it was formed as a consultative body in 1989. Though China has not taken a strong leadership role, it has been positioned to influence the norms that are becoming institutionalized in the body as it matures. APEC itself has been characterized by differences of opinion over whether to follow an "American model" that calls for setting clear and rapid timetables for compliance with binding liberalization schemes, or to follow an "Asian model" whereby liberalization is gradual, unilateral and voluntary, and operates with a looser timetable. Thus far, the latter model has been dominant. Because the forum has neither strong concrete rules to bind members nor many concrete benefits to offer them, membership does not place many burdens on China. The main incentive of membership for China is to be known as a team player and to avoid retaliation. Some Chinese analysts also hope that APEC can be a forum for finding workable compromises on the sensitive issues regarding China's entrance into WTO. Indeed, China has used APEC as a forum to demonstrate its willingness to liberalize its trade regime with an eye toward WTO membership.

All this suggests that APEC has adopted a "soft" negotiating posture toward China consistent with the strategy of engagement. At the same time, by admitting China near the founding, espousing in large part an "Asian" trade philosophy, and operating in a more consensual manner with which China is more comfortable, APEC is more open to being shaped by China than are either the Bank or the Fund.

GATT and WTO

The process of China's admission to, first, the GATT and, since 1995, the WTO has been less smooth than for the other multilateral organizations. Although as of mid-1999 membership appeared imminent, the previous thirteen years of negotiations were quite difficult. Problems with China's WTO admission reflected several factors: participation in the world trade body would require greater changes of China; the risks of admitting a non-compliant China to the WTO were higher for the status quo powers than was true with the other multilateral organizations; and Chinese officials became increasingly cognizant of the costs of participation in this regime. The complexity also reflects changes that have occurred over time in the international political context (especially US–Chinese relations), and changes in the Chinese domestic context.

China began to participate in GATT in 1982 with only "observer" status, except that it became a full member of the Multi-Fibre Arrangement (MFA). (China's participation in the MFA has been rather tense, as PRC negotiators have engaged in extremely tough bargaining to keep a generous share of textile quotas.) China applied for full membership in GATT in 1986. As with the Bank and the Fund, the impetus for application was internal. China's initial rationale was also, to a large degree, political; PRC leaders wished to be admitted to GATT ahead of Taiwan, which had indicated its own intentions to apply for membership, and did so formally in 1991. After 1989, China's leaders also calculated (erroneously) that admission into GATT would pave the way for elimination of the annual review of most-favored-nation trade status (MFN) by the US.[35]

Progress was made in the admission process during the first months after the GATT Working Party on China began to meet in 1988. During this period, negotiators representing the GATT showed quite a lot of flexibility in their treatment of China. As Jacobson and Oksenberg noted in 1990, "the outline that had emerged of the prospective protocol [for China's admission to GATT] would not force China to adopt market principles to become a contracting party of GATT."[36] But a more mixed and complicated picture of the GATT/WTO negotiations must be drawn, for even from the beginning the question of China's accession to GATT has been more problematic for both China and the institution. The GATT contracting countries, particularly the US and the major European powers, attempted from the advent of negotiations to establish rather strict terms for China's accession. They also took the stance that China's admission would be dependent upon broader economic reforms within the PRC. As a result, the early negotiating posture of the GATT contracting parties was already somewhat harder than for the IMF and World Bank. The reference point for these governments was the experience with accession of eastern European countries in the 1970s when, as noted above, a political interest in luring these countries away from Soviet dominance trumped commercial interests, and led to admission of eastern European countries on what later came to be considered overly generous terms. GATT parties judged that to use the same strategy with

China, given its potential market power, could greatly harm the commercial interests of the member countries, and would therefore be a major mistake.[37]

By the end of the decade, the attitude of the contracting parties, especially the US, toward China's accession had significantly dampened. The events at Tiananmen in 1989, which themseleves paralyzed negotiations with China for a time, also initiated the linkage in the US of China's trade status to human rights. As a result, GATT accession became caught up in the annual battle over China's most-favored-nation status. A worsening bilateral trade deficit with China, and the growing sentiment in some quarters of the desirability of containing China, added to the concern in the US that China should not be granted admission to GATT under lenient conditions. Thus, although the Working Party went on to meet periodically, and despite its declaration of support for China's accession "in principle," the cautious optimism of the earlier period dwindled.

In the context of worsening Sino–US bilateral trade relations, the process of negotiations for China's entry to GATT became increasingly important. The Working Party with whom China was to conduct negotiations was made up of representatives of the contracting countries rather than the GATT secretariat *per se*. As noted above, much more than in the cases of the Bank or Fund, the GATT is an organization of its members; when deciding to admit a new member, it can – like an exclusive club – form *sui generis* rules for admission. Moreover, the Working Party negotiations for a GATT protocol follow rather than lead the negotiations for a bilateral trade agreement with the most powerful contracting party, the US.[38] These two factors allowed domestic political agendas and narrow trade interests of contracting parties to be inserted more directly into the engagement process. All these factors remained salient for the WTO negotiations.

The negotiations for China's entry into GATT, and now WTO, therefore became even more acrimonious after the early 1990s. There has been less willing-ness of the contracting parties to rely on the hope that China will easily change its economic structure in accordance with GATT rules, much less the newer and stricter WTO rules, once a member. In other words, contracting parties are more suspicious that domestic Chinese political forces will make it difficult for the Chinese government to meet its commitments, and that the international regime will not have the desired moderating effect on Chinese behavior. Rather, an increasingly "hard" negotiating posture has been put into effect, whereby China is pressed to adhere to WTO rules – or to make clear and specific commit-ments as to how it will adhere, often on a faster timetable than allowed for other developing countries – to avoid the possibility that China will flout the rules once admitted. The sub-goal has shifted in the direction of (though not completely to) a coercive desire to entangle China with a system of negative constraints based on WTO rules. As much as there has been a change in the negotiating position and underlying sub-goal, however, the treatment of China still falls under the rubric of "engagement" insofar as it is assumed to help transform China's trade behavior by also offering positive incentives for cooperation and does not attempt to limit China's overall power. There remains no serious worry that China will make a major effort to disrupt the regime if admitted under strict conditions. And containment or exclusion of China is not offered as a viable option.

The shift to a harder negotiating strategy did not appear in isolation from changes taking place within the PRC. Chinese leaders and negotiators from the start of the accession process recognized, like their foreign counterparts, that the GATT would be more intrusive in its admission requirements than the World Bank or IMF, and that member countries are subject to substantial pressure to extensively liberalize their trade regimes and submit to greater international scrutiny. This realization led Chinese leaders to be more cautious. In its initial negotiating position, China hoped to circumscribe the breadth of negotiations, focusing primarily on the possibility of tariff reductions and arguing that China be allowed the lengthened timetables for adherence to GATT rules that are given applicants designated "developing countries."[39]

In the less favorable post-Tiananmen international political context, although China continued to press for admission to the global trade organizations, enthusiasm for WTO membership was tempered by a more realistic appraisal of the costs and benefits to China of such membership under less favorable terms than originally hoped. Some Chinese officials came to argue that China already possesses most of the advantages of WTO membership – particularly unconditional MFN from most countries (the US being the important exception) – without the obligations of formal membership. Although the US government had never promised to revoke the Jackson-Vanik amendment, moreover, Chinese officials apparently came to take the US stance more seriously, and grew more aware of the US domestic politics surrounding this issue. The MFN issue became a major irritant, and removed a major potential benefit to China.

On the cost side, moreover, the ledger grew. It became clear that Chinese negotiators would be unable to limit negotiations to tariff reductions and to gain a sweeping designation as a "developing country." Perhaps the biggest cost of which Chinese bureaucrats became cognizant was the potential competition to state enterprises that would result from the extensive dismantling of barriers to the Chinese domestic market. The threat from WTO admission was seen as particularly strong for five industries, most of which have been subjects of industrial policy: electronics, automobiles, petroleum refining, machine tools, and instruments.[40] As the fear of social unrest resulting from unemployment grew throughout China, the specter of WTO membership exacerbating this problem became worrisome.

In addition to the more realistic cost–benefit analysis, other aspects of Chinese domestic politics also affected the atmosphere in which the question of WTO admission is considered. The attitude of Chinese leaders and negotiators at times became unenthusiastic, reflecting a degree of ambivalence – and sometimes anger – toward the US. Having failed to gain admission to GATT in 1994, China's WTO negotiators accused the US of having raised the bar for membership, and of failing to trust that China would continue to make extensive reforms in its economy as it had done for the past fifteen years. Even among some Chinese officials who had previously been enthusiastic about China's admission, there was bitterness toward the US. Those negotiators who remained committed to the accession process found it more difficult to persuade key bureaucratic interests that are affected by WTO to take the process seriously. More generally, some officials complained that China should not have to accede to rules that were created by a "hegemon." The resentment of Chinese officials to what they perceive as US hostility was fed by nationalism in some quarters.

The Chinese domestic political context was made more complicated by the growing sophistication of bureaucratic actors for whom WTO admission posed a threat. In particular, certain economic ministries which projected that the state-owned enterprises under them would be subject to increased, unwanted competition from foreign enterprises mobilized. Such protectionism reflected growing influence on the part of certain core industrial bureaucracies and the localities in which they are located.[41] To some degree, officials in these ministries and local governments appear to have been behind a "who needs WTO?" fervor in 1995 and 1996. They also mobilized around the promulgation of Chinese industrial policies. Protection for these industries, largely through special funding and preferential tax policies, was considered by some Chinese officials to be vital to the development of not only a strong economy but also a strong military.

Have multilateral economic institutions successfully engaged China – or not? Assessing the results of engagement

After more than a decade and a half of experience with the strategy of engagement by multilateral economic institutions, it is possible to offer at least a partial assessment as to the efficacy of the strategy. The conclusion is mixed, although perhaps more positive than many expect. China has certainly become, or has tried to become, involved in the world's major multilateral institutions, as the above discussion illustrates. Moreover, China has neither disrupted the global system nor sought to impose its own rules. The clearest sign of this cooperation is that the global market has absorbed a huge volume of transactions and has emerged with neither a new set of "Chinese rules" nor a Chinese hegemony. There is no strong impetus within China for the establishment of an alternative Asian regime.[42] In major (if incomplete) ways, China has adopted the rules of the international game.

However, two major caveats to this relatively positive conclusion must be addressed. First, China's behavior is not totally cooperative when measured against other major powers. We see this especially with regard to negotiations over China's admission to WTO, where the engagement strategy thus far has fallen short of its goals. Second, it is not certain how much of China's greater alignment with the global economic regimes is due to the engagement strategy. While we can say that China has not thwarted the strategy of engagement, it is difficult to conclude definitively that it is engagement that has worked rather than global markets or domestic forces. It therefore remains important to examine further how these other factors have influenced China's engagement.

Evidence for the efficacy of engagement

Strong evidence that an implicit strategy of engagement has greatly increased China's integration into multilateral economic institutions lies in the fact that Chinese officials have adopted a significant number of the *policies* advocated by their World Bank, the IMF, and the GATT/WTO interlocutors. Examples of such changes in behavior, rules, and regulation abound. Chinese laws and regulations in myriad areas – from pollution abatement to banking – include content introduced by the World Bank, often through conferences with international experts. China's currency devaluations (such as in 1986), as well as the country's movement toward current account convertibility by the end of 1996, closely followed the guidelines advocated by the IMF.[43] In terms of *process*, Chinese bureaucracies now commonly use procedures for competitive bidding on projects, and offer greater regulatory transparency, both of which have been recommended by the World Bank.

The government initiated numerous additional policy changes that would bring it into line with GATT/WTO standards for international trade. For example, direct subsidies for exports have been largely phased out, and export targeting has been made more subject to market signals. Some tariff reductions were made in 1991 in the context of the bilateral "market access" agreement with the US to lower tariffs (as well as non-tariff barriers) on imports. Further tariff reductions on merchandise goods as well as in agricultural products and services were announced in 1993 and 1995.[44] The PRC government further eliminated some of the trappings of its administered foreign trade system by reducing the importance of the trade plan (particularly for exports), and by moving to a foreign trade contracting system in which, as of 1991, periodic targets were set for localities in terms of the value of exports, foreign exchange earnings, and foreign exchange remissions to the central monetary authorities.[45] Non-tariff barriers have gradually been eliminated on a large number of products since the early 1990s, culminating in Jiang's Osaka APEC announcement of the elimination or reduction of import quotas and controls on 30 percent of the items subject to import controls.[46] Throughout the second half of the 1990s talks on China's accession to the WTO appear to be moving forward, albeit slowly, on important issues such as non-discrimination (except on services), transparency, and intellectual property protection, with the Chinese government making some concessions on both terms of agreement and timetables for compliance.[47] These talks were given a huge boost by the various offers on market access and trading and distribution rights made by Premier Zhu Rongji during his visit to the US in April 1999.

The move to "open China to the outside world" that occurred in the late 1970s and early 1980s involved a genuine adoption of new ideas on the part of the

Chinese leadership; the post-Mao reformers adopted the norms of the international market, particularly the idea of comparative advantage, that undergird the major multilateral economic institutions.[48] The most obvious indications of acceptance of these norms by significant portions of the Chinese economic policy community can be found in the fact that they have been applied to the domestic economy, that China carries out enormous numbers of economic transactions on the global markets, and that China has not tried to disrupt the norms of the major economic institutions (the IMF, the World Bank, and APEC) of which it is already a member.

There are of course limits to our ability to proclaim that a paradigm shift – the adoption of the dominant international norms, ideas and rules – has been total and absolute. Even those economic policy officials who might be labeled "free traders" do not believe in an idealized vision of free trade, especially as their recognition of the costs of integration rises over time. Like most Asian market regimes undergoing trade liberalization, moreover, Chinese policy makers appear to be more comfortable with an Asian-style "concerted unilateralism" – which leaves the government greater latitude to manage how, when, and where it will liberalize – than with a fixed schedule for trade liberalizations, as required in WTO.[49] Recall, too, that Chinese negotiators have bargained hard on issues relating to membership in the major economic organizations, particularly WTO.

Yet all three of these types of evidence can be expected not only from China but also from any major status quo economic power. No country fully adheres to the goal of "free trade" stated in the regime, and regime loopholes show that these organizations fall short of this goal as well. In spite of a greater degree of comfort with the unilateral norm, moreover, China appears willing to eventually adopt stricter norms if they are required by WTO.

The extensive adoption by China of the norms and rules of the international economic regime would seem to indicate the success of an engagement strategy. But what might be the actual *causal* relationship between "engagement" and these policy changes? It will be argued below that the crucial impetus for this original "paradigm shift" was internal, not external. Nevertheless, international relations theories on the transmission of international ideas, and what has been termed "learning," also help us to unearth evidence – which is at the same time neither insignificant nor unambiguous – both that international ideas have been transmitted and genuine learning has occurred.

Significant evidence exists for one of the central mechanisms of engagement: learning from the outside economic policy community. As noted above, in order to judge that learning has occurred, we must show that new ideas which have been transmitted to China from the outside have in fact led to a shift in the thinking of policy makers (or those who will enter the bureaucracy at some point in the future). These changes in thinking must occur even when the external environment remains constant. Positive evidence of this dynamic exists. Those policy makers at the forefront of the acceptance of the global multilateral institutions, and who have been the driving force behind many of the policy changes noted above, are those directly involved with international economic policy. Dialogues between Chinese leaders and World Bank and IMF officials, as well as publications on China by these organizations, appear to have had significant influence through presenting information about China and offering policy recommendations. For example, the IMF and Chinese officials hold annual consultations on exchange rate issues. Lardy notes that, "over the past 15 or more years many of the most important Chinese decisions on exchange rate policy have been announced within a few weeks after this annual consultation."[50] Chinese officials have acknowledged directly the role played by the IMF in mid-1996 in the decision to allow foreign-invested enterprises complete access to the interbank foreign exchange market (rather than swap markets), a key intermediate step toward achieving current account convertibility.[51] Over the years, moreover, representatives of foreign businesses, foreign governments, and multilateral economic institutions have also been consulted about draft laws in areas of foreign investment, trade, intellectual property, and currency convertibility. Many of their suggestions have made their way into promulgated rules. That part of the motivation for China to subject itself to the discipline of the global economic institutions was the access to low interest funds, technical assistance, and strategic advice appears not to have lessened the commitment of the recipients to the ideas.

In addition, more and more Chinese economic policy makers have spent time abroad, often as fellows at the World Bank or IMF, and have been influenced by their exposure to those institutions' norms, even if they feel some pressure to appear loyal to their own policy status quo. New, younger officials with Western educations are also joining the Chinese government, and are slowly gaining influence. They can be presumed to bring outside ideas to their work.

A key litmus test for whether learning has occurred is whether China has been a free-rider in the global economic institutions, or whether its participation in these institutions forces it to constrain its own capabilities. It goes without saying that China has made many changes in order to benefit itself. Yet, unlike its behavior in arms control conventions, China has shown itself increasingly willing to make changes that significantly constrain its authority.[52] The major burden that joining the World Bank and IMF put on China was for transparency/information disclosure. China's willingness, in line with urging by the IMF, to move to eliminate restrictions on international payments, and to achieve current account convertibility, has already been mentioned, as has China's adoption of international competitive bidding procedures as a result of World Bank requirements. Further evidence on China's admission to the World Bank's Multilateral Investment Guarantee Agency (MIGA) shows that debates over China's entry – debates that centered on MIGA's requirement that Chinese law be subordinated to international law, international arbitration, and multilateral subrogation – were settled in favor of such subordination.[53] Some evidence of willingness to eventually make constraint-producing concessions appeared in the dramatic accession package offered in April 1999. The possible granting of trading rights to foreign firms is relevant here, as this would very clearly undermine the revenues and authority of the foreign trade corporations under the Ministry of Foreign Trade and Economic Cooperation (MOFTEC). Full national treatment of foreign firms operating in China, such as in banking and other services, would further constrain Chinese businesses.

Another mechanism for effective engagement is through generating change in the procedures or power distribution of the bureaucracy. The multilateral financial institutions have shaped China's governmental institutions in several ways. The process of joining multilateral institutions has allowed the World Bank, IMF, and GATT/WTO to gain influence in the foreign trade bureaucracies of, respectively, the People's Bank of China, the Ministry of Finance, and MOFTEC, by setting up counterpart offices. To some degree, China has tried to use these counterpart offices to mold the impact of these multilateral institutions,[54] yet the more important flow of influence has been from the outside organizations to these domestic bureaucracies. Indeed, these counterpart offices within the Chinese government often house officials who have become important allies in gaining acceptance of international norms in China.

More generally, MOFTEC as a whole has gained much greater prominence within the central bureaucracy compared to the pre-"open policy" years. It has been granted some expanded powers as well; for example, MOFTEC was put in charge of GATT negotiations, at least in part to isolate the issue from more protectionist ministries.[55] MOFTEC has helped to usher issues of the international economy into national prominence. Finally, although MOFTEC bureaucrats ultimately work at the behest of China's top leaders, as the institutional interests of MOFTEC have become increasingly aligned with the norms of the international regime, its bureaucrats have often served as able advocates within the government for China's adoption of international practices. Many of the excellent younger and highly educated officials which MOFTEC has attracted into its ranks have experience abroad, either in school, in multilateral institutions, or in foreign businesses. Those who work in the departments charged with trade relations with Western countries, and those responsible for WTO negotiations, tend to be particularly supportive of extensive integration. The careers of those in both such departments hinge on ensuring that China's trade relations run smoothly in the long term. Even MOFTEC's WTO negotiators, who are responsible for protecting China's interests, historically have been some of the most committed to China's accession.

International influences can also find their way into Chinese behavior through the mechanism of leverage, in which multilateral organizations provide ideas, information, and arguments which are used by domestic political figures as the rationale for a change in domestic rules. In policy discussions, Chinese policy makers and leaders are said to articulate the ideas put to them by international organizations, as well as the need to adopt them if China is to be admitted to WTO. This is true, for example, of officials in MOFTEC and the Ministry of Finance. (These same officials in turn argue with their WTO interlocutors that

China should be admitted quickly in part because they can use existing WTO requirements to pressure domestic actors for the changes which these officials desire.) The more instrumental use of leverage is also apparent, whereby outside views are solicited in order to provide evidence or legitimacy for ideas generated domestically.[56] Relatedly, it is also clear that the multilateral institutions are attractive to Chinese policy makers insofar as the organizations make it easier to do the things which they want to do. For example, MIGA's attractiveness to Chinese officials stemmed in part from the hope that it would provide a screen for shoddy or environmentally degrading foreign investment projects, particularly if the agency could be persuaded to use Chinese priorities as guides for what projects to guarantee.[57]

Both the direct and instrumental examples of leverage suggest that the ideas embodied in these institutions carry weight and legitimacy in Chinese policy debates. Indeed, engagement appears effective in influencing the norms and rules of international organizations in part because of the global regime's prestige in China. It is clear from numerous policy debates surrounding international economic policy, and especially the question of WTO membership, that for an important segment of the policy elite the desire to "join the club" is of high priority. It is seen as ridiculous, and even humiliating, that China – a huge trading nation with extensive ties to the market already – is not a member of *the* global trade organization. In other words, engagement fills the power prestige demands of the post-Mao regime.

It should be noted that it may be easier for Chinese officials to accept the norms and rules of multilateral institutions where they appear neutral or even favorable to China. In the case of the World Bank and IMF, acceptance appears to be eased by rules that are seen as international and evenly applied (or that favor China). China's acceptance of APEC appears to stem from the fact that it was an early member, and that its mode of operation is less rule-based than consensus-based. Conversely, Chinese attacks on GATT and WTO have focused not on the basic legitimacy of the global trade system, but rather on US dominance of the Chinese admissions process, something not as evident in the case of the other institutions.

Limits on our ability to attribute efficacy to engagement

A rather compelling argument can thus be made that a strategy of engagement, through mechanisms which transmit the norms and rules of the major multilateral economic organizations, has had at least a partially transformative effect on China as measured by changes in policy and in policy-makers' attitudes. Yet the results of engagement have not been thoroughgoing. Despite tremendous changes, there remain myriad ways in which China has not reformed its trade and investment policies to the degree desired by the US and other major trading powers. In many ways, the trade structure for imports continues to be administered and protectionist. To guard against competition from imports, the Chinese government continues to subsidize its state-owned industries and to erect significant non-tariff barriers to trade. These problem areas are by and large reflected in the issues on which, as of the late 1990s, there is a significant gap in the WTO negotiations. Problem areas include subsidies to state-owned enterprises, protected trade in agriculture and services, lack of full trading and distribution rights, and conditioning of direct investment by requirements for local content, for technology transfer, and for exports.[58] China also resisted US and European demands to retain anti-dumping and safeguard measures which protect these foreign markets. Outside of the formal WTO and bilateral negotiations another issue lurked: the question of whether the US Congress would grant China unconditional most-favored nation status (i.e. to exempt China from the Jackson–Vanik amendment).

A more important caveat about the utility of "engagement" is that it cannot be given total credit for China's evolution toward global economic norms. Although China's behavior has shifted in ways consistent with the goals of engagement held by the World Bank, IMF, and GATT/WTO, it is clear that the changes are due in part to forces that are exogenous to China but unrelated to these institutions. Much of the evolution in Chinese policy and attitudes toward international market norms is a result of China's participation in global and domestic markets *per se*, not the influence of multilateral institutions. Indeed, Chinese business transactions are, arguably, disciplined more by market forces than by international organizations.

It is also clear that change in China is due predominantly to domestic forces. The norms and rules of the international economic regime must be fed through the prism of Chinese perceptions and domestic political structures. Some attitudes and domestic structures facilitate penetration of international norms and rules. In important ways, domestic perceptions formed indigenously have worked in favor of convergence between Chinese and market economic norms. This is particularly true of the original impetus for the "open" policy; in the late 1970s and early 1980s, policy communities which favored joining the global economic regimes formed within China in isolation from international forces and made the decision to pursue participation in the multilateral economic organizations (and global markets generally).[59] The influence of outside forces came later in the process, and only after the basic decision to "open" China was made.

Consistent with this view is the perception of World Bank officials, who feel that they are influential only when a Chinese institution comes to them open to and ready for advice. One senior Bank staff member even went so far as to assert that 95 percent of the changes the Bank effects in China is due to what Chinese officials want. Moreover, the Bank is less successful in some areas than in others, working well with certain "leading" ministries (such as those responsible for power and banking) and less successfully with the "laggard" ministries (such as machine-building). According to this staff member, when the Bank can find "the right ideas at the right time, and especially can find a small group of committed guys with the ear of a Vice-Premier, the Bank can do a huge amount."[60]

As this implies, changes that align China with international regime norms require a supportive – or at least acquiescent – domestic political constituency. Conversely, external influences can be trumped by domestic concerns. As discussed above, domestic opinion has not always been favorable to further integration. There is a significant element of the Chinese policy community that, at the same time as wishing for China to gain from engaging in international trade and participating in global institutions, wants to protect China against any ill-effects of integration. Early in the era of the "open policy," this camp tended to object to further integration into the global economy on ideological grounds; Chinese leaders repeatedly expressed that they could and would adopt what was beneficial from the world economy and avoid the negative elements of integration, based on a view of the costs and benefits for the country as a whole. Concerns about loss of sovereignty were also prominent. The impetus behind recent arguments to limit engagement cite the related concern about the need to counter US hegemony in the world economy, a concern of both ideology and security. (China has found sympathy for this argument with others in Southeast Asia.[61]) In addition, however, arguments against engagement have shifted to more classic protectionist grounds, and are voiced by those in specific industries hurt by foreign competition. These protectionist voices are not, it appears, a majority, and yet – as is the classic case with trade liberalization, in which the benefits of liberalization are dispersed and the costs are concentrated – their voices tend to be loud.

Intertwined with the influence of domestic perceptions about the value of integration is the influence of domestic structure. Recall that domestic structure refers to the degree of centralization of the political system and the pattern of state–society relations (participatory or exclusive of societal interests). When the original decisions to participate in global multilateral institutions were made, and during the early negotiations over membership, the structure of decision making on the Chinese side was relatively centralized and excluded societal views. Centralization made it easier for global regime norms to have influence, once the perceptions of central elites had shifted. As "transnationalism" predicts for centralized systems, capture of the pinnacle of power by international ideas can make it much easier for outside ideas to penetrate.[62]

Over time, however, China's domestic structure has evolved; while the decision-making process still excludes societal interests, the governmental structure relevant to foreign trade has decentralized to open the way for greater influence from a multitude of bureaucracies.[63] This is quite evident in the increasingly sophisticated role that industrial ministries have come to play, particularly as they can utilize industrial policy to protect their economic interests. These ministries represent, in effect, a domestic counter-constituency that has blunted the impact of both the domestic constituency in favor of engagement, and of international forces.

Conclusion

The adoption of an engagement strategy to bring China into the major global multilateral organizations has produced mixed results. We see that many of the mechanisms for engagement that are suggested in the scholarly literature on transnationalism – especially the role of learning and leverage, and the importance of domestic structure for mediating international norms and rules – have facilitated the penetration of those market-oriented norms which the multilateral institutions intend to transmit to China. Engagement of China in the international economy, and its incorporation into major multilateral economic organizations, has enhanced China's cooperative behavior by providing ideas and incentives for change and shaping the specific nature of policy changes.

Yet the penetration of the norms of these organizations occurred only after major changes in ideology were made by the Chinese government, the impetus for which was domestic. These norms had the opportunity to exercise influence because, in the economic realm, China is not a "dissatisfied rising power," even though it opposes the US hegemony and takes expected steps to protect its domestic industry. In other words, cooperation with the global regime increased when domestic leaders were already moving in the direction of cooperation. When domestic forces have been more skeptical of change, the strategy of engagement has had more difficulty generating cooperation from China.

Notes

1 As will become clear below, however, this chapter's definition of engagement includes elements of a "binding" strategy as introduced by Randall Schweller in Chapter 1, because the most recent efforts to bring China into the WTO have become more coercive.

2 A desire to "manage" China is evident in the behavior of the Asian Regional Forum. See Alistair Iain Johnston and Paul Evans, chapter 10, this volume. At the other extreme, although markets are facilitators of engagement, they do not *choose* (in the sense of possessing agency) to engage China or not.

3 The relative youth of the WTO and the absence of a clear institutional personality contribute to the ability of member governments to greatly influence the engagement strategy for new members.

4 GATT was not intended to be more than a multilateral trade agreement, but it took on institutional status when key Western countries, notably the US, failed to ratify the International Trade Organization. The story of the origins of the Bretton Woods trade system is well told in Richard N. Gardner (1990), *Sterling-Dollar Diplomacy in Current Perspective: The Origins and the Prospects of Our International Economic Order* (New York: Columbia University Press); Jock A. Finlayson and Mark W. Zacher (1983), "The GATT and the Regulation of Trade Barriers: Regime Dynamics and Functions" in *International Regimes*, edited by Stephen D. Krasner (Ithaca, NY: Cornell University Press), pp. 273–314; John H. Jackson (1990), *Restructuring the GATT System* (New York: Council on Foreign Relations Press), pp. 9–17; and G. John Ikenberry (1993), "Creating Yesterday's New World Order: Keynesian 'New Thinking' and the Anglo–American Postwar Settlement," in *Ideas and Foreign Policy: Beliefs, Institutions, and Political Change*, edited by Judith Goldstein and Robert O. Keohane (Ithaca, NY: Cornell University Press), pp. 57–86.

5 On the origins and purposes of the WTO, see John H. Jackson (1994), "Managing the Trading System: The World Trade Organization and the Post-Uruguay Round GATT Agenda," in *Managing the World Economy: Fifty Years After Bretton Woods*, edited by Peter B. Kenen (Washington, DC: Institute for International Economics), pp. 131–171; Jeffrey J. Schott (1996), *WTO 2000: Setting the Course for World Trade* (Washington, DC: Institute for International Economics); and Asif H. Qureshi (1996), *The World Trade Organization: Implementing International Trade Norms* (New York: St Martin's Press), Chapter 1.

6 See C. Fred Bergsten (1994), "APEC and World Trade: A Force for Worldwide Liberalization," *Foreign Affairs*, Vol. 73, No. 3 (May/June), pp. 20–26; and C. Fred Bergsten (1994), "Managing the World Economy of the Future," in *Managing the World Economy: Fifty Years After Bretton Woods*, edited by Peter B. Kenen (Washington, DC: Institute for International Economics), p. 357.

7 Lawrence H. Summers (1994), "Shared Prosperity and the New International Economic Order," in Kenan (1994), p. 422. On the absence of a necessary linkage between market economies and democracy, see Charles Lindblom (1977), *Politics and Markets: Politico-Economic Systems* (New York: Basic Books).

8 Leah A. Haus (1992), *Globalizing the GATT: The Soviet Union's Successor States, Eastern Europe, and the International Trading System* (Washington, DC: Brookings), pp. 12–13. On the political uses of international trade policy, see also Michael Mastanduno (1985), "Strategies of Economic Containment: U.S. Trade Relations with the Soviet Union," *World Politics*, Vol. 37 (July), pp. 503–531. Haus does point out, however, that the founding documents of GATT did not suggest political goals.

9 Haus (1992), pp. 13–14. She further argues that the US was the most extreme in this philosophy; the French, for example, took a less negative view. Haus does not, however, distinguish clearly between the institution of the GATT and its contracting parties, and thus does not make clear whether GATT officials themselves had political goals or were merely manipulated by contracting governments.

10 Qureshi (1996), pp. 129 and 132. Politicization is also fostered by the absence of transparent admission procedures.

11 See Stephen Krasner (1985), *Structural Conflict: The Third World Against Global Liberalism* (Berkeley: University of California Press). China participated in these attacks, but was not a formal member of the Group of Seventy-seven.

12 It should be noted, however, that the World Bank has sometimes been criticized from the right for its willingness to rely on state intervention rather than pure market mechanisms, and from the left for not adequately promoting democratic and sustainable development. See Andrew M. Kamarck (1996), "The World Bank: Challenges and Opportunities," in *The Bretton Woods–GATT System: Retrospect and Prospect After Fifty Years*, edited by Orin Kirshner (Armonk, NY: M.E. Sharpe), pp. 106–127.

13 Qureshi (1996), pp. 4–5. In the 1960s, the GATT contracting parties did agree to a number of special preferences for developing countries.

14 This body would be called the East Asia Economic Caucus (EAEC). The proposal has been stonewalled by the US and Japan. See Jane Khanna (1996), "Asia–Pacific Economic Cooperation and Challenges for Political Leadership," *The Washington Quarterly*, Vol. 17, No. 1 (winter), p. 259.

15 This second sub-goal is a less accommodating version of the reasoning whereby engagement recognizes as legitimate the *interests* of a rising power, rather than just the right to be at the table. It does not suggest that it is legitimate to meet China's interests, if those interests are very different from those of the regime. For example, to the extent that China's demands to protect infant industries go beyond what is deemed appropriate to the WTO, there is no sense that the organization should accommodate these interests. That mutual accommodation is not taken seriously reflects the

hegemony of the liberal trade ideas and legitimacy of these institutions and, to a great extent, the absence of China's demand for such far-reaching accommodation. Note that Schweller categorizes this second sub-goal as part of a "binding" strategy rather than engagement.

16 Although Schweller categorizes "enmeshment" as part of a binding strategy, and thus separate from engagement, it seems more useful to consider enmeshment as a stringent form of engagement. In particular, consistent with the definition of engagement at the core of this volume, this fifth sub-goal does not attempt to limit China's overall power.

17 On the rationale for incorporation of countries into regimes, see Robert O. Keohane (1984), *After Hegemony: Cooperation and Discord in the World Political Economy* (Princeton, NJ: Princeton University Press), particularly the discussion on pp. 98–106; and Oran Young (1979), *Compliance and Public Authority: A Theory With International Application* (Baltimore, MD: Johns Hopkins University Press). Keohane observes generally that countries tend to comply with the global economic regime.

18 See Joanne Gowa (1983), *Closing the Gold Window: Domestic Politics and the End of Bretton Woods* (Ithaca, NY: Cornell University Press).

19 This section represents an attempt to be more specific about the causes/mechanisms of engagement than is often found in the policy-oriented advocacy pieces on engagement and containment. Writings on transnationalism focus on how, beyond the concrete material or financial inducements that may be offered for compliance to international rules, international norms channeled through regimes, international organizations, or transnational actors influence domestic norms in a country such as China. Of the cluster of related bodies of literature related to transnationalism that might be examined in detail – domestic structures, international "learning," ideas, and epistemic communities – it is primarily the first two that are considered here. An excellent summary of this literature is found in Matthew Evangelista (1995), "The Paradox of State Strength: Transnational Relations, Domestic Structures and Security Policy in Russia and the Soviet Union," *International Organization*, Vol. 49, pp. 1–38.

20 In this formulation, international norms/rules are the independent variables upon which arguments advocating engagement rely, while the dependent variable is change in Chinese leadership behavior and, ultimately, policy. The international forces are fed through intervening domestic variables.

21 A good summary of the literature on "learning" is found in Jack S. Levy (1994), "Learning and Foreign Policy: Sweeping a Conceptual Minefield," *International Organization*, Vol. 48 (spring), pp. 279–312. See also George W. Breslauer and Philip E. Tetlock, eds (1991), *Learning in U.S. and Soviet Foreign Policy* (Boulder, CO: Westview Press); Yuen Foon Khong (1992), *Analogies at War: Korea, Munich, Dien Bien Phu, and the Vietnam Decisions of 1965* (Princeton, NJ: Princeton University Press); and, for an application to China in the area of arms control, Alastair Iain Johnston (1996), "Learning Versus Adaptation: Explaining Change in Chinese Arms Control Policy in the 1980s and 1990s," *The China Journal*, Issue 35 (January), pp. 27–62.

22 Levy (1994, p. 312) is careful to point out that learning models alone do not provide complete explanations for foreign policy change, because they cannot explain how and under what conditions learning by individual leaders is translated into policy.

23 See Robert O. Keohane and Judith Goldstein (1993), "Ideas and Foreign Policy: An Analytical Framework," in their *Ideas and Foreign Policy*, pp. 3–30.

24 Johnston (1996), p. 31. There is disagreement within the literature on learning as to whether evidence of policy change is necessary to prove learning; for example, Levy (1994, p. 291) argues that policy change is not a necessary criterion, whereas Johnston argues that it is.

25 See Andrew P. Cortell and James W. Davis, Jr. (1996), "How Do International

Institutions Matter? The Domestic Impact of International Rules and Norms," *International Studies Quarterly*, Vol. 40, pp. 451–478. Such use of outside ideas can be consistent with genuine learning, but need not be.

26 See Evangelista (1995), p. 4, and Cortell and Davis (1996), p. 452.

27 See Cheryl Payer (1975), *The Debt Trap: The IMF and the Third World* (New York: Monthly Review Press); and Stephan Haggard (1986), "The Politics of Adjustment: Lessons from the IMF's Extended Facility," in *The Politics of International Debt*, edited by Miles Kahler (Ithaca, NY: Cornell University Press), pp. 157–186.

28 I fashion this argument about domestic structure from the following: Cortell and Davis (1996); Thomas Risse-Kappen (1995), "Bringing Transnational Relations Back In: Introduction," in *Bringing Transnational Relations Back In*, edited by Thomas Risse-Kappen (Cambridge: Cambridge University Press), pp. 3–33; and Evangelista (1995). Cortell and Davis further argue that a second intervening variable is important: domestic salience of the international norm/rule. Salience derives from the legitimacy accorded it in the domestic political context, as measured, for example, by the number of domestic declarations of support, as well as by policy actions to support, the norm/rule. This concept is not considered here.

29 Cortell and Davis (1996), p. 455.

30 This argument is made by Evangelista (1995) with reference to Gorbachev's "new thinking" on arms control in the Soviet Union. The counter-argument is that the impetus for the "new thinking" was internal and came about for economic reasons, not through the role of transnational actors.

31 Cortell and Davis (1996), p. 457. See also Evangelista (1995).

32 For example, in a 1997 report on China's economy, the World Bank "resolutely steered clear of comments on the authoritarian nature of China's Communist Government. . . . No bank official would comment on whether political reform, specifically the move toward democratic governance, was essential to further economic growth." Edward A. Gargan (1997), "World Bank Cites Weaknesses in China's Economic Boom," *New York Times* (September 19), p. A6.

33 See Harold K. Jacobson and Michel Oksenberg (1990), *China's Participation in the IMF, the World Bank and GATT* (Ann Arbor: University of Michigan Press).

34 Jacobson and Oksenberg (1990), pp. 127–128. Indonesia and Egypt are other cases where a modicum of special treatment has been given (p. 138).

35 On these reasons, see Susan L. Shirk (1994), *How China Opened Its Door: The Political Success of the PRC's Foreign Trade and Investment Reforms* (Washington, DC: Brookings Institution), pp. 71–72.

36 Jacobson and Oksenberg (1990), p. 105.

37 This argument was made in a 1986 OECD study (in which the US played a major but not exclusive role) on China's accession to GATT. Jacobson and Oksenberg (1990), pp. 88–89.

38 The negotiating positions of the EU countries, Australia, New Zealand, Canada, and Japan are said to be reasonably congruent with those of the US, though there are indications that Japanese negotiators in particular would be willing to admit China to WTO on less stringent terms than those required by the US. There are no public objections from the allies about the US position, and there is considerable agreement among analysts that the allies are quite willing to see if the US can negotiate a tough position.

39 Jacobson and Oksenberg (1990), pp. 100–101.

40 State Planning Commission Economics Research Institute Task Force (1993), "Dui huifu guanmao zongxieding diwei hou de xiaoyi fenxi he duice" ("Effective Analysis and Countermeasures after China resumes its Place in GATT"), *Guoji Maoyi* (*International Trade*), No. 2, p. 10. China's intention to write industrial policies for key

"pillar" industries was announced in June, 1994. To be considered a "pillar" industry a sector must have potential for very large output, use of advanced technology, and a large domestic (and potentially foreign) market: World Bank (1996), p. 18. On China's industrial policy, especially in automobiles, see also "China's Accession to the WTO/GATT: Investment/Industrial Policies" (Washington, DC: The US–China Business Council), 15 September, 1995.

41 In contrast, according to Shirk (1994, p. 73), the original decision to join GATT was made centrally.

42 This point is expanded upon in Margaret M. Pearson (1999), "China's Integration into the International Trade and Investment Regime," in *China Joins the World*, edited by Michel Oksenberg and Elizabeth Economy (New York and Washington, DC: Council on Foreign Relations/Brookings Institution).

43 On the role of the IMF in moving China to current account convertibility, see Nicholas R. Lardy (1999), "China and the International Financial System," in *China Joins the World*.

44 Although the 1995 reductions were announced at APEC and would not necessarily be binding on China in the WTO, they were largely seen as a signal of goodwill for the WTO negotiations.

45 On these changes, see Nicholas R. Lardy (1992), *Foreign Trade and Economic Reform in China, 1978–1990* (New York: Cambridge University Press), Chapter 3; World Bank (1994), *China: Foreign Trade Reform* (Washington, DC: The World Bank), p. xvi and Chapter 2; and He Chang (1994), "Article Views Prospects of Admission to GATT 'This Year'," *Zhongguo Tongxun She* (HK), in *FBIS*, 17 March, 1994, p. 2. The scaling back of the foreign trade plan went hand in hand with the decentralization of responsibility for the plan to local FTCs.

46 World Bank (1996), *The Chinese Economy: Fighting Inflation, Deepening Reforms* (Washington, DC: The World Bank), p. 8.

47 Of the 20 issues to be addressed in the China's WTO Protocol, 16 were said to have been agreed to. See Memo to Members of the Working Party and China from Pierre-Louis Girard, Chairman of the WTO Working Party on the Accession of China, March 6, 1997.

48 Further details of this change in economic ideology as it pertains to China's participation in the global economy are contained in Margaret M. Pearson (1991), *Joint Ventures in the People's Republic of China* (Princeton, NJ: Princeton University Press), Chapter 3.

49 On "concerted unilateralism" and its place as a central APEC norm, see Soogil Young (1996), "Political Economy of Trade Liberalization in East Asia," in *The World Trading System: Challenges Ahead*, edited by Jeffrey J. Schott (Washington, DC: Institute for International Economics), pp. 147–148.

50 Lardy (1999), fn. 11. Similar evidence for World Bank influence was provided in 1997 interviews, and in Jacobson and Oksenberg (1990), p. 33.

51 Lardy (1999), p. 11.

52 That China failed to meet this criterion in the area of arms control is argued by Johnston (1996), pp. 57–58. China's opening of the economy to international markets in and of itself constrains the country's sovereign authority, and each step that is made into the global economy creates greater constraints.

53 MIGA, part of the World Bank Group, was established in 1988 to promote foreign investment in member countries by providing political risk insurance and technical assistance. Information on MIGA is from Feng Yushu (1997), "China and the Multilateral Investment Guarantee Agency", MIGA Policy Research Working Paper 1763 (Washington, DC: MIGA).

54 David Zweig (1993), "Controlling the Opening: Enmeshment, Organizational

Capacity, and the Limits of Overseas Development Assistance in China," paper prepared for delivery at the 1993 Annual Meeting of the American Political Science Association, Washington, D.C.

55 Shirk (1994), p. 73.

56 Jacobson and Oksenberg (1990, p. 141) found this to be the case when Zhao Ziyang and his advisers solicited views of foreigners, and then used evidence gained to rebut their internal critics.

57 Feng (1997), pp. 25–26.

58 Some of these problems are discussed in World Bank (1994), pp. xvi–xvii, 39–41; and World Bank (1996), pp. 6–8.

59 This view is supported by Jacobson and Oksenberg (1990), pp. 42 and 139.

60 Interview, Washington, DC, June, 1997.

61 Similar arguments about US hegemony were voiced at the annual meeting of the World Bank and IMF in Hong Kong in the fall of 1997. Southeast Asian officials were critical of US pressure to liberalize global financial markets. See David E. Sanger (1997), "Asia's Economic Tigers Growl at World Monetary Conference," *New York Times* (September 22), pp. A1, A6.

62 See Risse-Kappen (1995) and Evangelista (1995).

63 The dynamic evident among industrial bureaucracies essentially follows what is predicted by models of "fragmented authoritarianism."

10

CHINA'S ENGAGEMENT WITH MULTILATERAL SECURITY INSTITUTIONS

Alastair Iain Johnston and Paul Evans[1]

The aim of this chapter is deceptively simple. We are interested in knowing how China's involvement in international and regional security institutions has affected its foreign policy behavior. The issue lies at the heart of the public policy debate in the United States over China policy. Advocates of engagement believe that bringing China into international institutions, sometimes more grandly termed "the international community," will moderate China's behavior and encourage more cooperative actions. But they have not articulated with much precision why they support engagement, what engagement means, and what it is supposed to do. Some, mostly in the military, see it as an opportunity to acquire more information and intelligence through closer sustained contacts with military institutions. Others see it as a way of tying China down with multiple commitments and issue linkages. Still others see it in more transformative terms as a policy aimed at changing Chinese interests or preferences. The second argument tends to be the dominant one, however. Conversely, advocates of neo-containment or some other more coercive balancing strategy believe that China's involvement in international institutions has done little to modify, restrain, or constrain China's behavior. Neither side is working from much solid empirical evidence.[2]

Policy and theory are intimately related. The arguments made by the advocates of both engagement and neo-containment run parallel to debates in international relations theory about whether "institutions matter" and how.[3] Engagement advocates have intellectual affinity with mainstream institutionalist arguments that involvement in international institutions adds new multiple costs and benefits (e.g. through side-payments, threats of sanctions, linkage to other issue areas) such that cooperation pays, even for states with opportunistic, prisoner's dilemma-like payoff preferences.[4] Other engagement advocates implicitly share constructivist arguments that institutions can socialize states, and "teach" states new interests through a complex set of ideational channels including NGOs, transnational coalitions, and domestic constituency-building.[5]

What does engagement mean in this context? Unlike the country studies in this volume, international security institutions cannot be easily treated as agents, with intentionally developed "engagement" strategies for dealing with China. Some of the institutions we discuss do exhibit elements of agency, especially the regional dialogue mechanisms including the ASEAN Regional Forum (ARF) and CSCAP (Council on Security Cooperation in the Asia Pacific) which were established with China in mind. But international arms control processes, including the Comprehensive Test Ban Treaty (CTBT), and the Chemical Weapons Convention (CWC), for instance, were not designed specifically as institutions for tying down or socializing China. In these international processes it is harder to measure the success of engagement because there is no particular actor who sets out to engage China with some measure or criteria for determining the effectiveness of the strategy. For purposes of the international security institutions, "engagement" is best understood as China's formal participation. For purposes of the regional dialogue institutions, "engagement" is a more explicit, albeit controversial strategy for involving and changing China. In both contexts we treat engagement not as an endpoint but as a process in which China, a major power, consciously chooses to participate.

Of special interest is how China's participation has been reflected back into its policy process to affect its foreign policy. This is an exceedingly complex issue. There are three levels of outcomes that an analysis of engagement needs to explore. The first is how participation at time t affects participation at time $t+n$; that is, how has the quantity of participation changed over time?

The second is whether this participation at time t has affected the quality of participation at time $t+n$. Measuring quality, of course, is fraught with method-ological difficulties, not least of which is the danger of imposing unselfconsciously held normative criteria. But one could image a range of reasons for states to adjust behavior to the anticipated preferences of others.[6] At one end, cooperation that is essentially coerced (through social or material punishments) could be considered to be relatively low-quality cooperation. At the other extreme a state's acceptance of limits on material power capabilities for normative reasons could be considered high-quality cooperation. We use this dimension plus the sophistication of participation as indicators of the quality of cooperation.

The third level of outcomes concerns more fundamental changes in Chinese calculations of interest and strategy in international institutions, and looks at spillovers into Chinese behavior outside of these institutions. Does China's engagement in international security institutions affect how it defines the relationship between multilateralism and security? Does it affect the military modernization program, military expenditures, alliance behavior, broader strategic intentions, or approaches to territorial disputes? It is tempting to conclude that there has been little connection. China's increasing involvement in international security institutions has occurred roughly coterminously with increases in military expenditures, military modernization, the development of offensive military doctrines, the sale of weapons abroad, and a demonstrated willingness to use military means to make political points as with Vietnam in 1988 and Taiwan in 1995 to 1996. Yet there is evidence that transnational "epistemic" linkages and regional security dialogues have led to some rethinking of China's interest in multilateralism as a source of security. Without access to primary documents from the decision-making process, one has to rely on counterfactual arguments to speculate as to whether behavior in most of these areas would be worse (more missile exports, more rapid military modernization, greater willingness to intimidate neighbours) if China were less involved in international security institutions.[7]

As for the causal processes that might link participation with these different levels of outcomes, there are at least five.

As the agenda of these institutions becomes more technical, China is compelled to develop expertise to handle the complexity of the issues at stake. This expertise requires organizational and bureaucratic resources. This emergent constituency of experts has a normative or organizational interest, or both, in preserving and expanding participation. Related, institutional involvement at time t explains involvement at time $t+1$, in a path-dependent process where fixed costs from involvement increase over time. This reduces the incentive to exit from an institution later on.[8]

Involvement in institutions serves other foreign policy goals. As these become more salient, the institutional behavior becomes more important. In particular, participation can be useful for developing a reputation for responsibility and co-operation, especially valuable in the context of connections to the world economy. This reputation can be banked and withdrawals can be made in other issue areas when necessary.[9]

Involvement in high-profile multilateral institutions exposes a state to social backpatting and social opprobrium. These become additional benefits and costs that enter into the calculation of cooperation strategies.

Communities of experts develop linkages with governmental and non-governmental experts in other states through which new ideas, information and interests are promoted or exchanged. These opportunities for small-group socialization lead to emergent shared identities across the community such that there are more similarities of views within this group than between the separate national communities and their respective governments.[10]

Involvement in institutions leads to constraints on action, without any obvious socialization in the norms or values being propagated by the institution. Institutions merely obstruct non-cooperative behavior, but do not change the interests motivating this behavior.

What is the evidence that any or all of these causal processes influence the three levels of outcomes we are examining?

Global institutions

Engagement and participation rates

There is no question that China's participation rates in international security institutions have increased dramatically over the 1980s and 1990s. Figure 10.1 indicates that China's accession to multilateral arms control agreements, as a percentage of all possible agreements it has been eligible to sign, increased rapidly, beginning in the early 1980s. This has not simply been a function of an increasing number of international security institutions; that is, the rate of increase in China's participation has been faster than the rate of new international security institutions. From 1982 to 1996, for example, the total number of possible treaties increased from nine to fourteen, an increase of 55 percent. China's accessions increased from two to twelve, a jump of 500 percent. By 1996, the only eligible treaties that China had not signed on to were the Partial Nuclear Test Ban (PTBT) and the Environmental Modification Treaty. In 1986, China publicly pledged to end atmospheric testing (which it had done in practice in the early 1980s), thus, in effect, unilaterally commiting itself to the major provision of the PTBT. The CTBT, in any event, makes the PTBT irrelevant.

In addition to the rather dramatic increase in the number of treaty accessions, other indicators also suggest a rapid increase in rates of participation in international security institutions. For example, the cumulative frequency of Chinese working papers presented to the UN Disarmament Commission (First Committee) in New York shows a rapid rise from zero in 1983 to three in 1988

Figure 10.1 Chinese treaty accessions as portion of eligible accessions

and to seventeen by 1994. A similar cumulative pattern shows up in China's submissions of working papers to the Conference on Disarmament in Geneva. Another indicator is the cumulative sum of arms control studies conducted by the technical arms control community based in the China Academy of Engineering Physics (CAEP), its Institute of Applied Physics and Computational Mathematics (IAPCM), and the IAPCM's Program on Science and National Security (PSNSS).[11] The cumulative sum went from zero in 1986 to ten in 1988 to over a hundred by 1994.[12] These studies have been critical in outlining the weapons community's positions on treaty bargaining, and for generating technical information essential for more active participation in international security institutions as the agendas of these institutions have evolved.

Together, these indicators suggest a strong relationship in the changing rates of participation in international security institutions over time. Indeed, the correlation matrix among these disparate arms control-related activities shows very high Pearson product moment correlations (*r*) (see Table 10.1). Put differently, relative activism in one area is accompanied by relative activism in another. If, for example, China's increased participation rates were simply busy, though shallow, responses to the changing UN agenda, with little relationship to treaty accessions or to the mobilization of talent and resources in the policy process, one would not expect these intercorrelations to be so consistently high.

The most obvious explanation for these relationships is a path-dependent one. Here the argument would be that China's initial involvement in international security institutions placed China in an environment where there were incentives to become more involved. Increasing levels of involvement lead to increasing returns from participation, returns that are distributed across new actors who emerge to handle the agenda of the institutions. These returns can involve everything from organizational gains from increased participation, access to new information and resources of use to these organizations, to social backpatting from participation in a large, highly legitimate community, among other benefits (the costs from reduced involvement are, for the most part, the opposite of these gains).[13] Path dependence, then, posits very different causal processes than institutionalist choice-constraint arguments. The latter discounts any long-term deviation from equilibria outcomes in social interaction. The former argues that small, sequentially rational decisions can lead to outcomes that deviate considerably from the best or worst equilibrium outcomes. The test of path dependence in arms control issues, then, is whether lock-in leads to outcomes that are inefficient

Table 10.1 Correlation matrix of PRC arms control activities

	DC working papers	PSNSS working papers
DC working papers		
PSNSS working papers	.96	
Arms control accession rate	.942	.947

for increasing relative power and security, but which are nonetheless too costly for other reasons to avoid.

A path-dependent explanation has two steps: Step one, why did China join certain international security institutions in the first place; Step two, how did this affect subsequent participation? China's entry into the Conference on Disarmament (CD) in 1980, after sending an observer delegation in 1979, corresponds to the beginning of the period of greatest growth in participation rate. We do not have information on the specific decision to join the CD. However, this was a period in which China began to participate more fully in a range of international institutions, many within the UN system.[14] Participation in the CD corresponded approximately with Deng Xiaoping's re-evaluation of Lenin's and Mao's inevitability of war thesis. This revision itself was related to the need to build a peaceful international environment for domestic economic development.[15]

Within this broad receptivity to fashioning a high profile in international institutions, it appears that Deng decided China should become more active in UN arms control activities. Evidently Deng personally determined that China should send a delegation to the UN Special Session on Disarmament (UNSSOD I) in 1978. There had apparently been some opposition to participation, as China had initially abstained from the vote to set up UNSSOD in the first place. The Disarmament Commission had called on all nuclear weapons states to join the CD in Geneva in the wake of UNSSOD I. Chinese leaders initially felt that they needed more time to prepare, so China did not send a delegation to the first meeting of the CD. In the second half of 1979, however, China began preparations for entry into CD in 1980.[16]

Once in the CD, there were incentives to stay there. For one thing, this was an opportunity to follow first-hand the Soviet–US competition over arms control issues. For another, it enabled China to portray itself as a responsible major power. The CD could be used to float Chinese arms control proposals. The CD was also taking up issues that at the time were considered to have potential benefits for Chinese security. For example, the CWC treaty had the potential to constrain Soviet CW capabilities.

The incentive structure appears to have been a dynamic one. Participation in the CD required a level of expertise and sophistication that in turn required training arms control experts primarily in the Ministry of Foreign Affairs (MOFA). To deal with CD issues, the MOFA set up an arms control division (the *si chu* or fourth division) in the early 1980s. Over time, the MOFA rotated over forty Ministry officials through the CD delegation, providing them with first-hand experience in multilateral negotiations.[17] In order to deal with specific scientific and technical questions on the CD agenda, however, the CD MOFA delegation had to bring in outside experts from time to time. Early on, the MOFA realized that China was handicapped without a higher bureaucratic status for its arms control community and without more efficient and regular mechanisms for drawing on scientific expertise. Thus by 1985, Chinese leaders accepted a MOFA proposal to create a separate position for an Ambassador for Disarmament (prior to 1985 the head of China's UN Office in Geneva was concurrently the Ambassador for Disarmament).[18] In 1997, due primarily to the expanded workload of the arms control specialists, the MOFA raised the bureaucratic status of the arms control division (*chu*) to that of a department (*si*). In principle, this not only means potential doubling or tripling of the number of people working on multilateral arms control, it also means, possibly, that the MOFA will have somewhat more authority in the interagency process. Prior to this elevation, the current ambassador for disarmament, Sha Zukang, was a deputy department head. This made him approximately the equivalent rank to Qian Shaojun, the official head of the arms control community in the Commission on Science Technology and Industry for National Defense (COSTIND) (now transfered to the newly created General Armaments Department), the umbrella organization under which most of China's military industrial complex is situated. Sha's elevation to departmental head may make him bureaucratically superior to Qian.[19]

Some of the institution-building has been required by new treaty obligations. For instance, under the Chemical Weapons Convention, China is required to set up a National Authority that must coordinate the regular submission of information to the international implementing organization (e.g. annual declarations of chemical production facilities). It must also develop protocols for on-site inspection and other verification-related activities. Under the CTBT China is also setting up a National Data Center as part of the treaty's global international monitoring system. These activities are highly routinized, following detailed templates, and thus require the input of scientists and technical specialists.

China's arms control diplomacy has helped to develop a community of experts beyond the MOFA. This process began in the mid-1980s. While some chemical and radiological specialists were brought to Geneva from time to time in the early 1980s, only when the nuclear winter issue captured the attention of global arms controllers in the mid-1980s did interaction between MOFA and weapons scientists became more regularized. The Chinese Ambassador for Disarmament at the time, Qian Jiadong, recommended in 1985 that China send nuclear weapons scientists to a major conference on nuclear winter taking place that year in Italy. This afforded one of the key weapons scientists at CAEP/IAPCM the opportunity to meet with other arms control scientists from the US and Soviet Union. The scientist came away feeling there was a common language with other scientists, and he was inspired to recommend that China's weapons community set up a working group to focus on arms control research that could be useful for China's arms control diplomacy.[20]

This working group served as the embryonic connection that eventually brought weapons scientists from the IAPCM and the CAEP – its parent organization – into the decision-making process with the MOFA and the PLA/GSD.[21] Indeed, this consultation process evolved into a genuine interagency one about the time of the CTBT's arrival on the CD agenda in 1993 to 1994.[22] For the CTBT negotiations, for example, the MOFA arms control division, the

COSTIND testing community (represented by CAEP and IAPCM scientists) and, to a lesser extent the GSD, held regular coordination meetings prior to and after each meeting of the CD in Geneva. The testing community was able to insert key positions (such as the insistence for much of the negotiations that the treaty allow peaceful nuclear explosions) into China's bargaining brief. Those in the technical community who work on TMD/BMD issues were also apparently responsible for the insertion of a lengthy discussion of the dangers of US TMD/BMD development into a major speech by Sha Zukang to the CD in October 1996.[23]

Other scientists associated with COSTIND's CDSTIC – an institution whose primary job is to collect, analyze and disseminate new information about weapons systems and capabilities from around the world – were involved fairly early on in arms control-related research. In 1983, the CDSTIC set up a small arms control group – later called the Arms Control and Disarmament Program – to help to prepare the CD delegation on technical issues relating to test bans and the chemical weapons convention. The group's size, budget and research scope grew at approximately the same pace as China's participation rates in global arms control. It began with three people, expanded to five in 1987 to 1988, and then to nine in 1994.[24] In addition, as the arms control agenda became heavier, this program was assigned the responsibility for organizing most of the cross-unit exchanges on arms control in Beijing – bringing together experts from NDU, IIR, CICIR, MOFA, Nuclear Materials Association, CAEP, Aerospace Ministry, etc.

With the CTBT and, most recently, the fissile material production cutoff issue moving on to the CD agenda, one of the important technical questions has been verification. In order to develop an authoritative voice on verification issues, and to study the implications of some of the more intrusive verification proposals in these negotiations, the CAEP also set up a Center for Verification Technology Studies.

Thus the requirements of participation in the CD and related activities led to the creation of a group of arms control experts in MOFA, the scientific community with an interest in this activity, and a formal process of policy coordination between these two communities and the PLA.

China's participation in global arms control processes was also responsible for institutional and research development in the uniformed military. It is much harder to discern when this occurred. But at some point in the mid-1990s, the PLA set up a small leading arms control group in the Central Military Commission (CMC)/General Staff Department (GSD). This group's task is to coordinate arms control policy research across the GSD system. It is apparently not as bureaucratically developed as the COSTIND community nor, certainly, the MOFA arms control community. While it is the third major player in the interagency process that developed over the 1990s, this group doesn't weigh in on every issue. It played a less central role in CTBT policy debates – the testing community in COSTIND being the key constituency in the military industrial complex. But on the landmine protocol question it was the key PLA actor.[25]

In order to improve the general quality and quantity of arms control research in the uniformed military, around 1996 the Academy of Military Sciences (AMS) also set up an arms control group in its Strategy Department. This group is focusing on the history of arms control, the conceptual basis of arms control, the content and scope of current arms control processes, guiding principles in the "art of struggle" in the arms control arena, and models of decision making.[26]

In reaction to the increasingly complex arms control agenda, the first major interagency linkages appeared in the mid-1980s. For example, the first major internal conference on arms control was held in 1986. Organized by the China Institute of Contemporary International Relations (CICIR) – a research arm of the Ministry of State Security – the conference drew together experts from the CICIR, The Institute of World Economics and Politics (IWEP) of the Chinese Academy of Social Sciences, the Strategic Studies Institute at the National Defense University, the General Staff Department's Intelligence Sub-department, the State Council's Center for International Studies, COSTIND's Information Center, and the Academy of Military Science's Operations Research Institute, among others. A number of participants complained about the lack of horizontal linkages and coordination within the Chinese arms control community, and some even obliquely criticized the military for not being more forthcoming with information relevent to policy discussion on arms control. As two participants from CICIR put it in their paper, those engaged in "national defense construction" could better serve the arms control and disarmament "struggle" by more quickly understanding the information needs of this struggle, and they called for establishing all-China academic conferences on arms control.[27] There was also a general recognition at the conference that China's arms control policy had been too simplistic, inflexible, and insufficiently concrete. As one of the top arms control experts at the National Defense University put it, "Merely raising principles is insufficient. We must have even more concrete topics on which to express our position."[28] In the words of an analyst from IWEP, China's leftist denunciations of arms control in the past had led to poor analysis. As a result, China's policies in the 1970s had been "limited to a few basic principles and lacked initiative and flexibility."[29] These policies only hindered China from developing responses to the widening array of arms control issues it was forced to confront as a result of its engagement in multilateral institutions like the CD.[30]

The requirements for participation in global arms control negotiation processes, such as those in the CD, were not the only impetus for the creation of arms control expert communities, however. In some cases, this constituency-building was in response to particular events or actions of other states. For example, Reagan's Strategic Defense Initiative (SDI) was a critical issue in first encouraging cross-unit research relationships that had not existed before. In reaction to Reagan's speech, CASS-IWEP organized a cross-unit meeting on SDI sometime in 1984. This brought together, for the first time in a formal meeting, participants from the AMS, GSD, COSTIND, MOFA, and Aerospace Ministry, among other groups. Prior to this meeting, inter-unit contacts were governed by strict secrecy rules and heavily compartmentalized information. The SDI research programs launched by Reagan's speech (some were based in IWEP, some in COSTIND, some in Aerospace Ministry, some in MOFA IIS, some in the Second Artillery) all required consultation among diplomatic, scientific, and strategy specialists because the issue was inherently cross-disciplinary.[31] Out of this rudimentary interagency process and consultations came reports that substantially established China's opposition to SDI, a position it took into international fora such as the CD.

In addition to all this institutional development and the creation of horizontal bureaucratic and personal linkages within the arms control community, new channels of information have been set up to disseminate arms control-related information and research. In addition to open journals on international relations and security issues, there are at least five internal publications specifically aimed at this community: *Junkong xinxi jianbao*, (Short reports on arms control information) published by the China Defense Science and Technology Information Center; *Selected Readings in Arms Control and Disarmament*, reproducing foreign-language articles and published by the CDSTIC; *Junbei kongzhi yanjiu tongxun* (Bulletin on arms control research), published by the Arms Control and Disarmament Program in the CDSTIC; an occasional papers series on nuclear and arms control issues (identified simply as "CNIC-NMC"), published by the Nuclear Science and Technology Information Research Institute (He kexue jishu qingbao yanjiu suo); and *Guowai he wuqi dongtai* (Foreign nuclear weapons trends), published by the Nuclear Science and Technology Information Research Institute, and possibly the longest running source of information on arms control-related questions for the technical community, as it was first published in 1975.

The evidence, then, suggests that activity breeds activity. The intellectual and organizational requirements of participation in international security institutions at time t is an important variable in accounting for this participation at time $t+1$. Involvement in the CD and accessions to treaties require that China act, speak and negotiate. This requires research, expertise and content. In turn this requires institutional support for this behavior. China's participation in multilateral global international security institutions has not driven the agenda or evolution of these institutions themselves. China has been relatively passive in this respect, preferring to respond to processes as these are pushed by others, but the frequency of these responses has increased over time.

Engagement and the quality of cooperation

Frequency and institutional development is one thing, but how did involvement in international security institutions affect the quality of China's participation? The codification of international rules and norms in policy institutions and their activities is one indicator of integration into international institutions.[32] But it does not really capture the kinds of arguments that are made in favor of this integration, and whether these arguments change over time as a function of initial involvement in international institutions. It is not obvious what criteria one should use to measure quality of participation. Cooperation theory is remarkably spare when it comes to describing the texture or quality of cooperative behavior. Game-theoretic metaphors rely on a unidimensional criteria – the adjustment of behavior to the anticipated preferences of others – without distinguishing much between the reasons for this adjustment. Indeed, for mainstream rational choice institutionalists, a state may cooperate in an iterated prisoners' dilemma because it is coerced by an institution's monitoring and sanctioning provisions. Interestingly, in the US debate about engagement, the criteria used to define the level of Chinese cooperation are similar. The implicit and sometimes explicit standard is whether Chinese behavior complies with US interests as American political and military leaders define them. According to this standard, China's acceptance of US arguments about the destabilizing effect of ballistic missile transfers, while putting aside arguments about the destabilizing effect of US arms transfers, would be an indicator of greater cooperation. But cooperation defined as adjusting one's behavior to the anticipated preferences of others says nothing about whether this cooperation is in some sense coerced, bought, or carried out for normative reasons. We thus need a more nuanced criteria of quality of participation which has two dimensions.[33]

The first refers simply to changes in the technical complexity of China's participation, including changes in the role it takes in the drafting of the rules and provisions of treaties, etc. China's participation has become increasingly pro-active, complex and technically sophisticated in certain areas. This has been dictated in part by changes in the international arms control agenda. Almost from the start, China's participation in CWC negotiations in the CD in the early 1980s involved offering definitions of toxity, chemical agents, etc.[34] In the early 1990s, during the end-game in the CWC negotiations, China collaborated with a number of G-21 states in submitting detailed working papers suggesting treaty language governing activities prohibited by the treaty,[35] definitions of terms, the handling of abandoned CW, on-site-inspection (OSI) provisions, among others.[36] When the CTBT moved on to the agenda in 1994, as a nuclear weapon state with a relatively primitive warhead design, China had every interest to be active in negotiations. In 1994 alone, it submitted working papers on everything from entry into force, to peaceful nuclear explosions, to verification.[37]

As a general rule, however, the working papers presented in the CD in the early and mid-1980s were primarily reiterations of China's rather vague proposals for comprehensive disarmament in conventional, nuclear, naval, and space weapons. By the 1990s, most of the working papers had to do with CWC or CTBT treaty language, or China's position on transparency in armaments (TIA).[38]

The development of a technical arms control community in COSTIND's CAEP-IAPCM and Academy of Launch Vehicle Technology over the late 1980s and 1990s has also enabled Chinese specialists to produce original studies on a range of technical subjects relating to verification of a CTBT, and the effects of theatre and ballistic missile defense (TMD/BMD) on China's deterrence, as these issues have moved on to China's arms control agenda, again in response to events outside China.[39] This technical community has also been responsible for anticipatory research. As far back as the early 1990s, well before the CTBT moved on to the negotiation stage, the COSTIND arms control community had established a research agenda focusing on extant or upcoming global issues such as nuclear testing, non-weaponization of space, a fissile material production cutoff, and deep reductions.[40] Indeed, the China Defense Science and Technology Information Center's Arms Control and Disarmament Program's task was to begin a study of the implications for China of a fissile material production cutoff at least two years prior to the opening of negotiations in the CD.[41] The program evidently also proposed as early as 1988 that China join UN-organized nuclear test ban technical verification activities.[42] The calculus was that a CTBT would eventually move on to the CD agenda for formal negotiation and China had to be prepared to deal with discussions on verification.[43] Over the last couple of years the technical community, in particular the IAPCM and arms control specialists in the PLA (and its National Defense University), have also been mandated to study the implications of a post-START III deep cuts regime for China's nuclear weapons posture, doctrine and operations, again in anticipation of the possibility of having to put Chinese weapons on a multilateral negotiation table in the twenty-first century.

In addition to the active involvement in treaty negotiations, China took the initiative beginning in 1986 in the UN Disarmament Commission to introduce resolutions on nuclear disarmament, on the prevention of an arms race in space, and jointly sponsored resolutions on naval disarmament, and a comprehensive program for disarmament.[44]

The second criterion refers to changes in the quality of cooperation. One place to start in analyzing Chinese behavior over time is to construct a typology along two dimensions. The first indicates how much China adjusted to the preferences of others, with maximal adjustment at one end, minimal at the other. In other words, how much of a shift in China's extant policy was required to bring it into compliance with the treaty commitment made as well by others? The second dimension indicates how much the state sacrifices in terms of relative capabilities to adjust its behavior. Is the commitment intrusive or non-intrusive (e.g. does it require some real constraint on relative military capabilities, programs, options or not)? One can then classify all China's treaty accessions *and* the accessions it is eligible to make into one of these four cells (Figure 10.2). If, for example, China acceded to most of the treaties in the minimal/non-intrusive cell, while avoiding most of the treaties in the maximal/intrusive cell, this would suggest a lower quality of cooperation than if China's accessions were evenly distributed across these cells. If, over time, there is a shift in the pattern of accessions from, say, minimal/non-intrusive to maximal/intrusive, this would suggest an increase in the quality of cooperation.

As a rough first cut, we classified China's accessions into one of the four cells in this matrix for each ten-year period beginning in 1950. In the 1950 to 1960

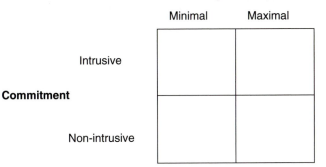

Figure 10.2 Quality of cooperation

period, China joined the only international arms control treaty that it was eligible to join, the Geneval Protocols, and this treaty required little sacrifice in terms of relative capabilities, nor did it require that China abandon its radically opposing past position on this issue. That is, for China, the treaty was situated in the minimal and non-intrusive cell.

In the 1960 to 1970 period a number of new international arms control treaties were negotiated, including at least two that, had China signed, would have required a radical change in its policy and would have entailed some constraints on relative power (e.g. the Partial Nuclear Test Ban Treaty would limit nuclear testing, and the NPT would possibly limit transfers of nuclear technology to radical Third World states).[45] In addition, there were three new treaties that China could have signed, but did not, even though these would not have required China to dramatically shift its diplomacy or restrain its relative military power. China's sole treaty accession was still the Geneval Protocols. This suggests a relatively low quality of cooperation in international arms control regimes.

From 1970 to 1980 little changed in this cooperation profile. A new treaty appeared, the Biological Weapons Convention, but China did not immediately sign on. It did sign on to the Latin American Nuclear Weapons Free Zone (NWFZ); but this was low cost, and did not involve a shift in China's position (supportive) on nuclear weapon-free zones.

The 1980 to 1990 period saw an interesting shift toward accessions to treaties that required some potential sacrifice of, or constraints on, military options (e.g. BWC and Inhumane Weapons). China also acceded to more low-cost treaties such as the Outerspace, Antarctic and South Pacific NWFZ treaties. In the 1990s, however, China has acceded to the most restrictive treaties it is eligible to sign and to the treaties or treaty proposals that it was most vociferously opposed to prior to the 1990s, namely, the NPT and the CTBT.[46] It also signed on to all the low-cost treaties (except for the Environmental Modification treaty).[47]

247

This shift over time toward acceding to most of the extant treaties and to the most restrictive ones out there (for the moment) needs an explanation. One could envisage a slightly more fine-tuned typology of outcomes that determines how willing the Chinese government has been to accede to certain agreements, namely, what are the basic incentives that underly the accessions? Here, the basic typology given above could be modified by adding one more dimension, namely, the type of cooperation: coerced (where non-accession might lead to the imposition of material sanctions or where status costs from non-accession are high); bought (where promises of material benefits are made or status image benefits accrue from accession); costless (where there are no obvious costs or benefits from accession); and normative (where accession is considered a good in and of itself, either because it may increase China's relative military power and security or because it may serve some global security interest) (Figure 10.3).

This typology establishes a continuum for the quality of cooperation. At the low quality end, cooperation would place minimal constraints on Chinese capabilities; it would not entail a dramatic shift in China's position on this issue, but it would be coerced or bought. In other words, even a relatively low-cost accession has to be coerced in some sense. At the high end, cooperation would place maximum constraints on capabilities, and would require a dramatic change in past positions, but accession would be considered a good in and of itself.[48] The interesting question, then, is how has the distribution of China's accessions across these cells changed over time? If engagement was providing maximum results, one would expect over time to see Chinese institutional behavior moving from lower level to upper right; that is, any treaties/institutions that are up there should be acceded to by China. This would be unanticipated by realist hypotheses because it would mean, in objective terms, a sacrifice of relative capabilities. We are dealing here with a small number of treaties relative to the number of cells, so distinctive patterns are less obvious. Moreover, we are hampered by the inaccessibility of the Chinese decision-making process in determining which consideration(s) made accession to which treaties attractive. Thus our coding has a large "error term".

Despite these caveats, it is clear that most of China's accessions are to treaties that are costless and have only diffuse image payoffs (Figure 10.4). This is a function of the nature of the treaties of course, not a comment on the intentions of Chinese decision-makers. The more interesting question has to do with the potentially intrusive treaties. Here, China's calculus runs the gamut. Some accessions are coerced in the sense that the image costs of opposing the treaty or agreement were weighted heavily in the decision to accede. For instance, the CTBT is a prominent pillar in the NPT regime.[49] Similarly, the image cost of opposing any limits on landmine technology was a primary consideration in the MOFA's recommendation to the State Council in early 1996 to accept protocols restricting the type of landmines for production and export.[50]

Some accessions appear to have been made for their potential non-military benefits. The primary arguments in favor of the NPT, for instance, appear to have included the positive image benefits (given the support for the NPT for most of

Type of cooperation

	Coerced		Bought		Costless	Normative	
	material	social	material	social		unilateral	common
Intrusive — Level of coop — maximal							
minimal							
Non-intrusive — Level of coop — maximal							
minimal							

Effect on capabilities

Figure 10.3 Typology of cooperation quality

Type of cooperation

Effect on capabilities	Level of coop		Coerced		Bought		Costless	Normative	
			material	social	material	social		unilateral	common
Intrusive	Level of coop	maximal		CTBT landmines	NPT?			NPT? CWC?	NPT?
		minimal						CWC? ARF?	ARF?
Non-intrusive	Level of coop	maximal							
		minimal					Geneva LA NWFZ SP NWFZ Outerspace Seabed Antartica BWC Inhumane		

Figure 10.4 The quality of China's cooperation

the G-77), the nuclear trade benefits (discuss), and the political benefits (e.g. break out of post-June 4 isolation). Some appear to have argued normatively – that the treaty was good for Chinese security to the extent that the non-proliferation regime might help to prevent nuclearization or weaponization of states around China's periphery.[51] We are not aware of any strong normative arguments made in favor of signing the CTBT, potentially the most constraining treaty which China has joined to date.[52] That is, so far as we are aware, no one has made the argument that the treaty locks in the current gap in warhead design between China and the nuclear superpowers in such a way that China is better off than without this lock-in. Indeed, arguments against the treaty, made by the testing community prior to and during the negotiation process, stressed the disadvantages of any asymmetrical lock-in. It is possible that the testing series which ended with China's signature in 1996 was successful enough to reduce the military costs of a moratorium on testing, but most specialists in the testing community, in the PLA, and even among Western specialists on Chinese nuclear weapons argue that the treaty was a "sacrifice" for China, and that there are now certain weapons designs that are closed off to the Chinese.

Among the intrusive treaty accessions, cooperation thus appears to be largely a function of either positive or negative sanctions; but, most interestingly, the positive and negative leverage appears to be related to image or reputation. Normative arguments about the "goodness" of the treaty (either its intrinsic value for relative military power or for global security) are hard to find. This concern about image, however, is a function of different kinds of normative choices and environments. Its effect depends on three factors: a particular normative view of major powers, a particular audience, and a particular sensitivity to the back-patting and opprobrium signals from that audience. Other standard accounts are not helpful in explaining the prevalence of image calculations in policy process or why one sees cooperation in first place (e.g. CTBT, landmines). The argument here requires some explanation.

At its simplest, a sensitivity to one's image is a sensitivity to social backpatting and social opprobrium. One can be sensitive to these issues for at least two reasons. The first is that image is an instrument – a good image can encourage actors to deal with you in other arenas, and can help to build trust leading to reciprocity and decentralized (uninstitutionalized) cooperation.[53] In this sense, image can also be used deceptively – one might want a positive image to convince other states to cooperate, setting them up for the sucker's payoff in some exploitative prisoners' dilemma game. There are two problems with this conceptualization, however. The first is, as Frank points out, if people know about this instrumentality, then an actor's image or reputation as a cooperator has no advantage.[54] So it is in the actor's interest to make cooperation automatic and deeply socialized, in order to make the reputation for cooperation credible. But then no advantages can be accrued, since deception is abandoned.[55] The second problem is that instrumentality assumes that the actor is seeking some concrete, calculable benefit from having a good image, an image that can be translated into leverage in some explicit, linked, immediate issue area. Yet often there are no obvious concrete benefits, or they are quite diffuse and vague. Indeed, there are sometimes concrete material costs. In this case, sensitivity to image may be related to identity.

This is the second reason for a concern about image. A particular self-image may be considered a good in and of itself. The self-image of a group, for instance, helps to maintain group cohesion, the legitimacy of political and social hierarchies within the group, and the psychological benefits from being a member of the ingroup. Thus a group will be sensitive to arguments that its behavior is consistent or inconsistent with its self-identity.[56] This sensitivity ought to depend as well on who is making these arguments. The more the audience or reference group is legitimate, that is, the more it consists of actors whose opinions matter, the greater the effect of backpatting and opprobrium.[57] The legitimacy of the audience is a function of self-identification. Actors more easily dismiss the criticisms of enemies and adversaries than they do friends and allies. Thus the strength of backpatting and opprobrium depends on two related factors: the nature of the actor's self-identification, and which other actors, by virtue of this self-identification, become important, legitimate observers of behavior. Changes in identities mean that different audiences matter differently. These are mutually constitutive processes.

The argument about China, therefore, would be as follows. Over the 1980s and 1990s China's self-identification underwent a change, a blurring. The traditional sovereign-centric, autonomous major power identity – rooted at the very least in the myths of modern Chinese nationalism – has been uneasily linked to a newer identity as a responsible major power, whose status is measured in part by participation in institutions that increasingly regulate interstate behavior.[58] This has created a tension in diplomacy between China's desire to show itself as an active, involved participant in international institutions (even those that offer no obvious costs or benefits, or that indeed require some incursion of costs), and the desire to minimize commitments and constraints that are required by this participation. But it has also meant that Chinese leaders are more sensitive to China being portrayed as an isolated, obstructionist player in international institutions, since such accusations clash with this evolving new self-identity, an identity that is supported by other actors in the system (e.g. who doesn't want China to act in a responsible, cooperative fashion, especially since it is a nuclear weapons state?).

In principle, the backpatting and opprobrium costs therefore ought to vary with the size and legitimacy of the international audience. China's participation in an institution brings it into social interaction with a particular audience. It joins the CD, for instance, and is thus involved in discussions, debates, and exchanges with at least forty other states. This means its behavior can be scrutinized or monitored by this audience, even though there are no material sanctions or rewards that might be triggered by this monitoring. The larger and more legitimate this audience, in principle, the greater the backpatting benefits and social opprobrium costs. Thus image concerns ought to play a more important role in eliciting cooperation in high-profile multilateral institutions than in lower profile bilateral relationships. This might help to explain why, for instance, image calculations have figured more prominently in decisions to sign on to multilateral treaties and processes even when these incur or may incur certain material power costs (e.g. CTBT, landmines), and why China has been more resistant to bilateral commitments to the US on proliferation issues, even in the face of substantial American criticism. American criticism can be dismissed as an expression of US power politics and hegemony. Criticisms from the G-21 in the CD, as oblique as they are at times, cannot be dismissed so easily.

The notion that backpatting and opprobrium matter for eliciting cooperation does not sit easily with influential IR theories. Neorealists, for instance, entirely dismiss the role of normative pressure.[59] At best, image is instrumental and deceptive. Yet this sensitivity cannot be dismissed so easily. For one thing, in interview after interview of arms control specialists, a common response was that China had to join such and such a treaty or process because it was part of a world historical trend, because it was part of China's role as a responsible major power, because it would help improve China's image, and, more concretely, help China to break out of the post-June 4 attempts by some Western states to isolate China diplomatically.[60] These arguments show up, as well, in internal circulation documents on multilateral diplomacy.[61]

For another, there is no sound material interest or relative power maximization explanation for the two cases that matter – where international commitments lead to a deleterious effect on military capabilities – namely, the CTBT and land-mines protocol. We know that key constituencies opposed both these processes (the PLA and the weapons community). We can guess that the concrete benefits which made it pay for China to participate in the CD in the first place (e.g. an ability to monitor the interests and actions of other states) were not particularly weighty in comparison to the possible restraints on Chinese relative power that a CTBT might impose. We know that there were no obvious side payments offered for Chinese cooperation, nor any obvious threats of economic or military punishments for non-cooperation, as a mainstream institutionalist account would suppose.

We come back, then, to one of our arguments about path dependence: from a strictly security maximizing perspective, China's accession to most of these treaties has few obvious payoffs. Most of these accessions are to costless, hence benefitless (in security terms) agreements (e.g. outer space, Latin American NWFZ). The two of interest to us – the CTBT and the landmines protocol – are potentially relative power-constraining agreements. Yet there were a multiplicity of other benefits that made avoiding, sabotaging or abandoning these processes costly. These benefits were largely functions of participation in international security institutions in the first place. China has undergone a socialization process to the extent that it is sensitive to the normative (as opposed to concrete material) image effects generated by participation in institutions, even though this socialization has not gone so far as to produce cooperation for other-regarding or cooperative security purposes. But this is progress: it could have remained outside any of these treaties – as it did in the past – without much concrete cost to its relative material power.

Engagement, socialization, and altered interests?

We have argued that participation in international security institutions has bred further participation. We have also argued that participation, in conjunction with an evolving Chinese identity as a responsible major power has generated image costs and benefits that appear to have positively influenced the quality (within limits) of Chinese participation. Has participation had any more profound effects on how Chinese decision makers conceived of Chinese interests, or the relationship between security institutions and Chinese security? Has China's involvement in international security institutions had any impact on other aspects of Chinese foreign and security policies?

The literature on Soviet new thinking in arms control, for instance, points to the critical role of Western NGOs and technical specialists in diffusing ideas about deterrence, cooperative security, etc. to Soviet arms control specialists through long-term transnational communications channels.[62] This new thinking manifested itself in everything from unilateral disarmament measures, an endorsement of minimum deterrence arguments, opposition to strategic defenses, support for new international institutions to manage East–West relations, among other breakthroughs in the Cold War. Has this phenomenon been reproduced in the Chinese case? We are interested in the kind of socialization that has gone on as a result of increased interaction with international institutions. How has all this constituency construction promoted by increased rates of participation affected foreign policy calculations, for instance? Here we move in even more speculative and anecdotal directions.

There is no doubt that many of the transnational channels that appeared in the Soviet case are now appearing in the Chinese case. In many instances the same people and organizations that established links with Soviet new thinkers are the ones that have the most extensive relationships with Chinese arms control communities. Tentative contacts between Western arms control specialists and Chinese experts began in the early 1980s, as a small number of Chinese, primarily military, analysts spend short periods doing research in strategic studies institutes in the West. In the 1990s arms control specialists from the technical and weapons communities have had the opportunity to study arms control centers, universities and NGOs in the West.

Transnational non-governmental institutional channels have also opened up in the 1990s, pushed in part by key figures in the Ninth Academy and the IAPCM. Since 1988 the US National Academy of Sciences, for instance, has held bilateral annual meetings with the Scientists' Group on Arms Control of the Chinese People's Association for Peace and Disarmament (CPAPD) to discuss *inter alia* arms control in space, non-proliferation, fissile material cut-offs, non-first use and deep reductions.[63] The Natural Resources Defense Council (NRDC) has had a number of exchanges with Chinese arms controllers in the bomb program through the 1990, 1992, and 1994 and 1996 ISODARCO seminars, a meeting with Chinese nuclear scientists on the CTB in June 1993, and another in the spring of 1996.

The Union of Concerned Scientists (UCS) has also been instrumental in influencing a younger cadre of arms control scientists in the IAPCM and COSTIND's Arms Control Program. Since 1989 the UCS has invited these specialists to attend a summer seminar on Science and World Affairs where they have had opportunities to interact with public policy scientists from the US, Europe, Russia and South Asia. Graduates of these seminars have gone on to head up arms control research offices and institutes at Fudan University, Peking University and the IAPCM. Other NGOs active in exchanges with and training of Chinese arms control specialists include the Stimson Center and the Federation of American Scientists in Washington, and the Monterey Institute of International Studies in California.

Another avenue of contact has been the biennial Beijing arms control seminar held in China and co-organized by the Rome-based International School on Disarmament and Research on Conflicts (ISODARCO), the CICIR, and the IAPCM. These seminars have brought together most of the arms control community in the military and in COSTIND with Western scientists and arms controllers associated with the UCS, Pugwash, NRDC, as well as the US weapons labs.

Individual foreigners also played a key role in introducing new ideas and agenda items into the Chinese community. Frank von Hippel, until recently the Assistant Director of the White House's Office for Science and Technology Policy, and a senior public policy scientist at Princeton University, and Richard Garwin, vice-chair of the FAS and formerly a physicist with IBM, have apparently been particularly influential. Highly respected among Chinese arms controllers in the bomb program, any new ideas or papers published by von Hippel and Garwin are apt to attract much attention, and to prompt supplementary research inside China.

Of course, the question is whether these channels have introduced new ideas about arms control into the Chinese policy process. Evidence for this remains murky, since we have a very poor understanding of this process. However, this much can be said: these channels have encouraged the development of somewhat more independently minded thinking about public policy science among a handful of younger arms control specialists. A couple of the younger arms control scientists, for instance, have came away from their training in the United States with a more sophisticated understanding of and support for minimum deterrence, putting them at odds with much of the thinking in the Chinese military on deterrence theory. There is also some evidence that Richard Garwin's arguments on the dangers of proliferation were helpful to Chinese scientists in debates in the late 1980s and early 1990s over whether China should reverse its position and accede to the NPT.[64] More recently, Theodore Postol and his colleagues in the Defense and Arms Control Program at the Massachusetts Institute of Technology have initiated discussions with Chinese nuclear weapons scientists and missile designers about the importance of the Anti-Ballistic Missile Treaty (ABM) in undergirding nuclear deterrence stability. These appear to have encouraged the Chinese scientists to take a closer look at the issue. The CAEP/IAPCM specialists on TMD pressed the MOFA to take a stronger stand in support of the ABM Treaty and against TMD/BMD. This pressure appears to have resulted in the first lengthy critique of US missile defense plans in a speech by Sha Zukang to the Disarmament Commission in New York in October 1996.[65]

Regional institutions

Multilateral security institutions in East Asia and the Asia Pacific are a comparatively recent development, emerging only as the Cold War ended in the 1990s. They were pre-dated and supported by the growth of regional economic cooperation which took concrete form in non-governmental activities including the Pacific Basin Economic Council (PBEC), and the Pacific Economic Cooperation Council (PECC) and formal governmental ones such as the Asian Development Bank and the Asia-Pacific Economic Cooperation forum. It has been these regional processes, rather than global ones such as the GATT and WTO, that up to this point have been central to engaging China in multilateral consultations on economic matters.[66]

The ending of the Cold War set the stage for an intensive period of discussion and dialogue on political and security matters, much of it promoted by nongovernmental and "track two" processes. In the late 1980s multilateral meetings on security matters were a rarity; by the early 1990s there were more than forty ongoing channels for regional discussion; and by the late 1990s there are about two meetings per week, an increasingly large percentage occurring at a formal governmental level.[67] Chinese diplomats, officers, or academics participate in all but a few. The Council for Security Cooperation in Asia Pacific (CSCAP) and the ASEAN Regional Forum (ARF), created in 1993 and 1994 respectively, are significant because they are the most ambitious and highest profile efforts to create inclusive institutions for dialogue, confidence-building and transparency. Both have established a coherent if not complete membership grouping, a regular schedule of meetings, a loose though identifiable institutional structure, and systematic work plans. CSCAP, a non-governmental or unofficial process, and the ARF, a formal governmental one, have no formal relationship to one another but are connected through objectives, work agendas, ASEAN's leadership role, and the use of ASEAN principles including consensus and non-interference in domestic affairs.[68]

China's involvement in CSCAP and ARF is instructive for several reasons. First, neither is seen by Chinese or other participants at this point as a forum for negotiation, policy coordination, or collective action, much less collective defence or collective security. Chinese officials have frequently observed that China is a participant in the ARF rather than a member of the ARF. As dialogue mechanisms, both are less threatening than many of the global institutions which make treaties or binding rules. Both operate on the ASEAN-inspired principles of consensus rather than majoritarianism, step-by-step incrementalism which proceeds at a pace acceptable to all participants, informality and the absence of elaborate bureaucratic structures. In this way, both the ARF and CSCAP are the products of an Asian, or at least ASEAN, style in an Asian setting.[69] Moreover, neither institution is seen as a tool of another great power, a rare instance in which the leadership role is played by the middle powers of a region.

Second, both institutions were created with China in mind, either as *a* principal or *the* principal reason for their existence. Both were formally launched in 1993 to 1994 against the background of uncertainty about the post-Cold War security order in Eastern Asia, and particularly the rise of China and the regional debate about the appropriate response. As both institutions were being conceived, it was frequently argued that there were already several multilateral fora for discussion among the "like-minded" members of the region. The architects of CSCAP and the ARF tended to see them as low-cost and non-provocative means for engaging China in regional processes. Yet understandings of the aims and means of engagement have varied widely. To some, engagement has meant "enmeshment" or a way of restraining or constraining China in specific conflict settings such as the South China Sea. To others, engaging China relates to a deeper and longer term process of making China more comfortable in regional institutions, bringing more Chinese into contact with multilateral processes and the habits of consultations, and increasing the chances that China will act as a responsible regional power.[70] This latter view is heavily influenced by ASEAN practices which have emphasized the socialization of its members in the direction of cooperation and away from conflict and confrontation.[71]

Third, unlike the global arena, China has had considerable influence in shaping the terms of its entry into the regional processes and the operation of these institutions. China's involvement has been "conditional" in that specific conditions were implicitly or explicitly set before China entered the institution. In the case of the ARF, which China joined at its inception, these were more implicit, and contained an understanding that issues including cross-Straits relations would not be part of the agenda of discussion. In the case of CSCAP, the conditions were more explicit. China did not join CSCAP in 1993 to 1994 because of its concern about the status of Taiwan in the organization. The issue required two years of negotiations and eventually produced an agreement very close to Beijing's terms.[72] China alone entered CSCAP on a conditional basis, underscoring both the intensity of feeling in Beijing on the Taiwan issue and the commitment of the other regional players to having China at the regional table.

The pattern of participation

The most basic point is that the Chinese have attended every meeting of the ARF since 1994 and every CSCAP meeting since China's entry in December 1996. In the ARF context, this includes about twelve meetings each year at the level of ministerial, senior official, and ARF-designated track two sessions. China co-chaired with the Philippines a meeting of the Inter-Sessional Group on CBMs, in Beijing in March 1997, the first time, the then Foreign Minister Qian Qichen stated, that China had ever hosted an official multilateral conference on security issues.[73] In the CSCAP context since entry in December 1996, representatives of CSCAP-China have been present at every meeting of the steering committee and five working groups, one of which China co-chairs with Malaysia and New Zealand. Chinese authors have presented more than a dozen papers.

The quality and tone of Chinese participation in regional security discussions has changed substantially in the past seven years and can be divided into two distinct periods. In the initial period up to 1995 it can be described as a combination of skeptical, reluctant and defensive. Officials and academics publicly expressed concerns that the region was not yet ready for multilateral processes and privately stated various worries that these fora would be dominated by other major powers, that smaller powers would use them for collective action against China, and that they would be used to "internationalize" issues including cross-Straits relations and the South China Sea that China preferred to see managed bilaterally. Chinese participants often appeared uncomfortable, stiff and wooden, frequently reading prepared texts and returning to them in responding to questions. China did not want to be excluded from regional discussions, but seemed to see little advantage in them and used them for primarily defensive purposes of reiterating existing official positions including statements of benign intentions and the Five Principles of Peaceful Coexistence.

In the second phase which began in 1995 and was especially evident at the ARF track two meeting in Paris on preventive diplomacy in November 1996, the approach has been more positive and enthusiastic. It reflects a more sophisticated grasp of the dynamics of regional discussions, a rising comfort level with them, and increased self-confidence. It has emphasized flexible interaction in formal and informal settings, detailed preparation, the use of humor, and a better understanding of the possibilities provided by officials appearing in their "personal capacities," a creative feature of track two processes.[74] Chinese participants have frequently been involved in drafting meeting summaries and reports.

Chinese officials have been fulsome in their praise of the new dialogue structures. In June 1997, for instance, Assistant Foreign Minister Chen Jian stated that "a multilateral framework seems to be the order of the day, both in the economic and security fields." In assessing the ARF, he argued that:

> we should judge the ARF by what it has achieved, not what it has done. ARF is the first ever collective endeavor in this region to carry out

institutionalized multilateral security dialogue. It represents a regional effort to form a new security order. Its progress and success is already remarkable.[75]

A month later the then Foreign Minister Qian Qichen praised the "ARF approach" and expressed support for ASEAN efforts to "to be a major driving force in the ARF."[76]

The change in approach extended beyond style into content. Chinese participants have been increasingly pro-active in advancing specific approaches and positions. In the ARF, for example, these initially covered general concerns about the pace and direction of regional discussions, including insistence on non-interference in domestic affairs, insistence on "consensus" interpreted to mean unanimity, and insistence on a gradual pace comfortable to all participants. More recently, China has advocated regional cooperation in the areas of military medicine, multilateral collaboration on defense conversion issues, the exchange of high-level visits by senior military officers, port calls by naval vessels, and joint action in search and rescue, maritime safety and marine environmental protection. A major emphasis has been the identification of the distinctive characteristics of the region which demand special approaches to confidence-building. Chinese officials have repeatedly noted the success of this regionally sensitive approach as seen in the five-power border CBM agreement it has signed with Russia, Kazakhstan, Kyrgystan, Tajikistan, and the bilateral CBMs with India.[77] All of these agreements were negotiated bilaterally without targeting third parties, and without including rigorous verification provisions.[78] Most interestingly, the five-power agreement is now touted by more commited multilateralists in Beijing as an example of "mutual security," portable with modifications to other areas of the Asia-Pacific.[79]

A dominant view in Beijing is that the ARF's main function is to build confidence and trust. Chinese officials have been hesitant about moving into two later stages outlined in the initial ARF concept paper, preventive diplomacy and "elaboration of approaches to conflict." They have been particularly anxious about what they perceive as the intrusive elements of preventive diplomacy which might include third-party mediation, use of the good offices of the ARF Chair, or a regional crisis prevention center. Mirroring positions which Chinese diplomats have adopted at the UN, they have insisted that this should only be undertaken in highly unusual circumstances when all contending parties agree, and cannot be imposed unilaterally. The pattern of Chinese thinking on post-conflict situations is less clear.

In July 1998 China published "China's National Defense,"[80] a more comprehensive statement than either the 1995 White Paper on arms control and disarmament or the annual reports presented to the ARF. Prepared by an inter-ministerial group with the lead role performed by the PLA, the document does not break new ground on the topics of defense expenditures or national defense policy. Rather, its significance lies in the motive for its creation and some new lines of thinking that emerge within it which are consonant with regional norms and practices developing in the ARF and CSCAP contexts. It uses the phrase "dialogue and cooperation" no less than fourteen times, mainly in the context of regional track one and track two processes but also extending to bilateral mechanisms which China has established with the United States, Russia, Japan, France, Canada, Australia and ASEAN. In objective and design, it parallels efforts by several other countries in the region to produce defense White Papers as an exercise in transparency. It thus serves the function of responding to complaints by China's neighbors about a lack of transparency in its defense doctrine and polices. Critics may be unimpressed by the absence of new information, but the level and kind of information provided is similar to that included in the White Papers of several other Asian countries including Indonesia, the Philippines and Thailand. Moreover, White Papers are seen as part of a process in which initial compilations provide a basis for informed discussion and interrogation on matters previously considered to be of strictly domestic concern.

Viewed from the perspective of military doctrine and security concepts, the White Paper integrates several ideas that have been mentioned by Chinese officials and academics over the past two years. Clearly influenced by the regional discussion, these ideas include "comprehensive security," "mutual security," "equal security," "cooperative security" (more precisely "security through cooperation"), and "common security."[81] In the White Paper and other recent statements, these concepts have been merged into something identified as the "New Security Concept."[82] In the White Paper it is defined to include the Five Principles of Peaceful Coexistence;[83] expanded economic cooperation; dialogue and cooperation among countries; and peaceful settlement of disputes. "Security is mutual," the document notes, "and security dialogues and cooperation should be aimed at promoting trust, not at creating confrontations, still less at directing the spearhead against a third country or infringing upon the security interests of any other nation." The concept is explicitly as a counterpoint to what is identified as a "Cold War mentality" referring to military blocs and military alliances which "run counter to the tide of the times." The border CBM agreements with China's neighbors are cited as examples of the application of the New Security Concept.

To some extent, the White Paper and its "New Security Approach" are the re-packaging of familiar ideas built around the rejection of military blocs and the Five Principles of Peaceful Coexistence. They raise, on the one hand, both immediate and tactical complaints against the US–Japan security alliance and, on the other, a philosophical foundation rooted in regional thinking that, in the long term, cooperative or comprehensive security is more appropriate to the region than traditional balance of power approaches. This can open up debating points with the United States, Japan and others on the alliance, whether it extends to Taiwan, and on issues including intrusive surveillance and notification and observation of joint maneuvers. But they also indicate a significant but subtle difference in doctrine and security philosophy. The architects of the new approach have clearly been influenced by regional norms and concepts including non-use of force and the embrace of low-key multilateral fora for dialogue and the creation of a regional consensus. Most importantly, there is a new nuance that peace must be built rather than naturally emerging from harmonious bilateral relations. Related, the emphasis on non-interference in domestic affairs and equality is counterbalanced by a new emphasis on economic interdependence.

The non-adversarial approach of these regional processes makes it difficult to assess whether Chinese participants have been much influenced by backpatting and opprobrium. On backpatting, other Asian leaders have been as effusive in their praise of Chinese participation as the Chinese have been of processes like the ARF and CSCAP. Concerning opprobrium, contrary to the expectations of some, China has rarely been isolated or cornered in ARF and CSCAP debates, with the possible exception of the preventive diplomacy agenda. Its representatives have been skillful in finding common cause with others, while, at the same time, many Southeast Asian countries have gone to considerable lengths, as seen at the ARF CBM meeting in Beijing in March 1997, to structure issues in such a way as to avoid isolating China, even as they have underscored that the principle of consensus means that all must agree. In this respect, China is in the mainstream of the discussion rather than an outlier on its margins. Yet getting to the mainstream has meant adjustments in style, vocabulary, and approach, irrefutable signs of a socialization process at work.

Institutional arrangements in China

There are several explanations of why Chinese rhetoric and style have evolved so quickly. One centers on organizational capacity and here the orchestration of Chinese participation has been impressive. Chinese officials are not alone in their uncertainty about how to bureaucratically manage regional dialogue fora. Like their counterparts in ministries around the region, they have debated two organizational issues. First, should regional dialogues on security issues be managed by geographically defined departments (e.g. the Asia Department) as compared to thematically defined departments including the International Organization Department, or the recently created Arms Control and Disarmament Department? Second, what coordinating mechanisms should be established to work with other units within the MFOA, PLA and, considering the track two nature of many of the meetings, research institutes and universities? The early dialogue mechanisms were handled by the Ministry of Foreign Affairs in an *ad hoc* way, normally having responsibility allocated to the geographical branch responsible for the hosting country. For example, governmental participants in the meetings of the Canadian-led North Pacific Cooperative Security were normally from the North American Department. This began to change with the establishment of the ARF. In an important decision in 1996, the MFOA established a special unit within the Asia Department to manage regional cooperation fora including the ARF, CSCAP, and other track two programs including the Northeast Asia Cooperation Dialogue (NEACD).

One consequence of China's participation in an increasing number of track one, track two and academic fora is the expansion of the number of Chinese attending regional meetings. Our rough guess is that fewer than 15 different individuals from China attended regional dialogues in 1992. By 1997 that number probably exceeded 100. That number would probably be at least doubled if we also included bilateral meetings. There has been a systematic effort to both train and prepare individuals who will be representing China in regional meetings. This is seen in the increasingly wide age span of Chinese participants, the increasingly broad range of organizational affiliations, and their multiple capacities in English as well as the vocabulary, style and issues of the regional discussions.

The preparation has taken several forms. One is an expansion of the number of MFOA and PLA officials visiting or doing degree programs at foreign universities and research institutes, especially in the United States. A second has been training and seminar programs linking Chinese ministries to overseas partners for training and seminar programs. The University of London conducted a summer school in June 1997 in London for the Chinese MFOA on the new global diplomacy. One example of an ongoing series is the annual "Executive Program for Senior Chinese Military Officers" at Harvard University. In another, Canada and China have held three rounds of an annual track-two seminar on "Asia Pacific Multi-lateralism and Cooperative Security," focusing on security concepts, regional issues, and multilateral structures. Chinese participants have come from the MFA, PLA, and research institutes.[84] There are also numerous other bilateral exchanges and consultations involving defence universities and official delegations.

China's entry into CSCAP has added an extra institutional layer because of the CSCAP requirement that member committees be "broad based." Interpretations of the phrase have varied widely, but it is instructive that China has created a member committee of more than thirty that is larger and more diverse than any other member committee except the American, Australian, and Canadian. It includes individuals from eight institutes in Beijing (the China Institute of Contemporary International Relations; the Institute of Strategic Studies of the National Defence University; the China Center for International Studies, the Chinese Academy of Social Sciences, the Xinhua Center for World Affairs Studies, Institute of Naval Studies, Chinese People's Institute of Foreign Affairs, and the Beijing Institute of Applied Physics and Computational Mathematics), two universities (Peking University, the National Defence University), government ministries and agencies including Defense, Foreign Affairs, Civil Affairs (the Institute of Crime Prevention), Public Security, the National Bureau of Environmental Protection, and other offices including China Daily and the China Corporation of Nuclear Industry.

CSCAP-China has held three plenary meetings. Several people who attended them commented that these were the first occasions on which such a diverse group had met within Beijing to discuss Chinese approaches to regional issues.[85] Management of the member committee and Beijing's involvement in CSCAP has been entrusted principally to former diplomats, including ambassadors Li Luye and Shi Chunlai. Chinese delegations to CSCAP working group and steering group meetings usually include a senior retired diplomat, one or two younger academics or officials, and on some occasions serving military officials. Each CSCAP working group and study group has been assigned to an institute in Beijing which is responsible for coordinating Chinese participation and preparing papers. Most active in the process have been the China Center for International Studies, soon to be integrated into the China Institute for International Studies, and the China Institute for Contemporary International Relations.

Research, training and discussion on regional security issues is also taking root in other parts of the country. An example of this is the annual summer workshop at Fudan University in Shanghai on international security problems, with a heavy emphasis on regional issues. It is significant because it includes foreign experts, mainly from the United States, and researchers and officials, mainly of the under-40 generation, from across China. Awaiting systematic studies of the scope, range and intellectual or policy influence of these new processes within China, it seems fair to say that they are unprecedented in the number of participants, the openness and vitality of discussion, and the exposure to international ideas and networks.

Changing interests and positions?

It is easy to demonstrate the seriousness and sophistication with which China has engaged these regional dialogue mechanisms. In many instances, Chinese participants are better prepared and more attuned to the pattern of the discussion than participants from other countries, including the United States. In CSCAP, the Chinese presence has raised the level of discussion. At the same time, it is also easy to demonstrate that China's positions on key regional security issues, including the Taiwan Straits, the Korean Peninsula, the South China Sea, and defense modernization, have not changed in any dramatic fashion.

This has led some Chinese and foreign analysts to assert that China is "engaged" only at the level of tactical learning about how to manipulate regional institutions and not in altering or redefining its fundamental interests. Some Chinese academics agree. In the words of one, China calculates that active involvement in the ARF and other regional institutions

> may help lessen the region's concern over China's growing strength, especially its defense modernization program. Also, as some people suspect, advocating multilateralism may serve to undermine the political and moral basis of the U.S. efforts to strengthen its bilateral security ties in the region.[86]

There are four responses to these assertions. First, regional institutions are not a very interesting testing ground because they are dialogue rather than consultative or negotiating fora where interests must be altered or compromised. Second, the change in vocabulary signifies a change in ideas that will eventually alter both doctrine and positions. The concept of mutual security and its five-power treaty exemplar, for instance, legitimates common security arguments internally, and permits proponents to operate, argue, and defend their policies in ways were illegitimate prior to China's entry into the these regional security institutions. Because these institutions are very new, there has not been sufficient time for the transformative process to develop very far. Nonetheless, there is some interview evidence that some functional specialists involved in the ARF and track-two processes have developed proto-multilateralist preferences and that they are determined to tie China into regional institutions because they judge elements of common security to be in China's interests.[87] Third, China is far from unique in using multilateral instruments, regional and global, to advance self-perceived national interests. If we ask whether China has been more or less willing than the United States to offer fresh ideas and to compromise and make high-level sacrifices, even at the rhetorical level, the answer is flattering to China. The issue is not whether Chinese leaders are sacrificing national interest in favor of promoting multilateralism. Rather, the issue is whether the promotion of multilateralism is now seen as consistent with national interests. Fourth, the most important function of dialogue fora is not the rules they create but the suspicions they allay and the norms they reinforce. In the ARF and CSCAP, perhaps the most basic norm is the non-use of force for settling disputes. At the level of rhetoric and practice, with the special exception of Taiwan, China has been as good a citizen as any other player in minding these norms of late.

The test will come if and as regional security institutions develop beyond dialogue into formal mechanisms for consultation and negotiation. It appears that the region is on the verge of moving into this new stage, with the ARF agenda trying to shift beyond confidence-building and other *ad hoc* processes such as the Four Party Talks on the Korean Peninsula struggling to move forward. Whatever else may be said, a decade ago China was both disinterested in and opposed to even entertaining serious discussion of formal regional processes. As the century turns, Chinese officials and academics are edging toward endorsement of new regional structures and might even play a leadership role in creating them, especially in Northeast Asia.

Conclusion

In this chapter we have tried to outline the institutional, ideational, and policy effects of China's involvement in international security institutions. Clearly there are multiple pressures and incentives that have, over time, led to a more sophisticated, detailed, participatory, and cooperative behavior in these institutions. In many cases there is little cost to China's cooperation. This is not so much a reflection of Chinese decision-makers' preference for "easy" cooperation as it is a reflection of the nature of the regimes themselves. They simply do not demand much from most of their participants. The interesting cases, then, are where participation is costly in terms of material power capabilities or in terms of the financial costs of compliance. Here we have seen an evolution in Chinese behavior from avoidance to participation in some instances (e.g. opposition to nuclear test bans in the 1980s to accession to the CTBT in 1996, opposition to multilateral security institutions in Asia Pacific in the early 1990s to more active and "comfortable" participation in the ASEAN Regional Forum).

The reasons for this evolution are complex. There is an element of path-dependent institutional development that has eased the process of participation. The development of arms control expertise in the nuclear weapons community, for instance, helped China to develop the research infrastructure and interagency process necessary for serious participation; but most interesting are the incentive structures to accept these instances of costly cooperation. Material incentives – promises of technology transfers, threats of economic or technological sanctions – appear to have been absent from the most interesting cases: the CTBT, the landmine protocols and the ARF. Rather, decision-makers appear to have been more sensitive to social incentives – fear of appearing to be the pariah, the saboteur of processes that were highly legitimate for a large number of states in the system; and a desire to maximize a diffuse image as a responsible major player whose identity as such required participation in major institutions regulating interstate behavior. There is less evidence that arguments reflecting the internalization of the norms of these institutions were decisive in *joining* the more costly institutions, though the NPT may be an exception here. There is some evidence, however, that after the decision to join, *participation* in some of these processes has encouraged a rethinking of Chinese interests and a normative devaluation of some of the costs of commitments. A definitive answer requires more fine-tuned analysis of the evolving thinking of policy makers in Beijing. It is precisely this kind of research that needs to precede and inform policy debates about engagement.

Notes

1 Iain Johnston thanks the United States Institute of Peace, and the Olin Institute of Strategic Studies for research support. Paul Evans also wishes to thank the United States Institute for Peace for research support. Heartfelt appreciation goes as well to all the arms control experts in the Chinese, Canadian, and American governments who provided information, assistance and insights. None is responsible for errors in fact or analysis.
2 One of the few efforts to establish an empirical baseline of knowledge about China in international institutions is a recent Council on Foreign Relations-sponsored study of the mutual impact of China's involvement in international regimes (e.g. arms control, telecommunications, environment, human rights, etc.). See Michel Oksenberg and Elizabeth Economy, eds, *China Joins the World: Progress and Prospects* (New York: Council on Foreign Relations, 1999).

3 See the debate between John Mearsheimer, Robert Keohane and Alex Wendt in the Winter (19:3) 1994/5 issue of *International Security*.

4 Lisa L. Martin, "The Rational Choice State of Multilateralism," in John Gerard Ruggie, ed., *Multilateralism Matters: The Theory and Praxis of an Institutional Form* (New York: Columbia University Press, 1993); Robert Axelrod and Robert Keohane, "Achieving Cooperation Under Anarchy: Strategies and Institutions," *World Politics* 38 (October 1985).

5 Martha Finnemore, *National Interests in International Society* (New York: Cornell University Press, 1996); Thomas Princen, Matthias Finger and Jack Manno, "Nongovernmental Organizations in World Environmental Politics," *International Environmental Affairs* 7:1 (winter 1995), pp. 42–58; Thomas Risse-Kappen, ed., *Bringing Transnational Actors Back In* (Cambridge: Cambridge University Press, 1995).

6 This is the standard institutionalist definition of cooperation. See Robert O. Keohane, *After Hegemony* (Princeton, NJ: Princeton University Press, 1984).

7 There is a fourth level that is also beyond the scope of this chapter, namely interactive international outcomes. Put differently, how does multilateral security engagement affect Sino–US relations, Sino–Japanese relations, and Sino–ASEAN relations? This requires looking at how China's involvement in international security institutions affects Chinese behavior, how this then affects American behavior, and how these two then interact to produce certain conflictual or cooperative outcomes. There is no consensus in IR theory about why inter-major power conflict occurs, and one could draw on a range of arguments, everything from power transition theory (Organski and Kugler), to ideological conflicts (Walt), to the presence of revisionist or predatory states (Schweller, Wendt), to a complex chain connecting realpolitik ideologies, enduring rivalry, arms racing, alliance polarization, and the emergence of policy hard-liners (Vasquez). Thus one would be interested in the causal processes that link China's involvement in international security institutions to the amelioration of power transition pressures (e.g. somehow engagement would have to limit the relative growth of Chinese power), to the abandonment of certain ideological sources of major power conflicts (e.g. democratization in China, or perhaps convergence of US–Chinese interests such that the US identifies China as a member of a notional ingroup in international relations), or to the transition of China from a revisionist to a status quo power.

8 Paul Pierson, "Increasing Returns, Path Dependence and the Study of Politics" (Unpublished paper, April 1997).

9 David M. Kreps, "Corporate Culture and Economic Theory," in James E. Alt and Kenneth A. Shepsle, eds, *Perspectives on Positive Political Economy* (London: Cambridge University Press, 1992), pp.90–143.

10 See e.g. Peter Haas, "Introduction: Epistemic Communities and International Policy Coordination," *International Organization* 46:1 (winter 1992); Alexander Wendt, "Collective Identity Formation and the International State," *American Political Science Review* 88 (June 1994), pp.384–396; Emanuel Adler, "The Emergence of Cooperation: National Epistemic Communities and the International Evolution of the Idea of Nuclear Arms Control," *International Organization* 46:1 (winter 1992).

11 The CAEP is principally responsible for China's nuclear weapons designs and testing.

12 These data are compiled from the Program on Science and National Security (PSNSS), *Junbei kongzhi yanjiu lunwen ji* (Collected research essays on arms control) (1994), pp.136–150.

13 For a discussion of path dependence and lock-in see Pierson, "Increasing Returns."

14 See Harold K. Jacobsen and Michel Oksenberg, *China's Participation in the IMF, the World Bank, and GATT* (Ann Arbor: University of Michigan Press, 1990).

15 In interviews with arms control specialists and practitioners in China in the spring and summer of 1996 in Beijing, this argument was repeatedly made.

16 Interview with senior arms control specialist, June 1996.

17 All told, as of 1993, seventy-four different individuals had been rotated through the CD delegation. The rate of training of new specialists is fairly constant across time.

18 Interview with former senior MOFA official, June 1996.

19 Interview with arms control specialist, January 1997. Reports from US arms control specialists engaged in bilateral discussions with China suggest that Sha has indeed become the primary interlocutor on arms control policy (conversations with US arms control specialists in the Department of Defense and the Arms Control and Disarmament Agency, June 1998).

20 Interview with senior arms control specialist, June 1996.

21 Out of this came the Program on Science and National Security Studies (PSNSS) at the IAPCM, set up in 1989. Out of this also came regular series of more informal academic seminars on technical and policy issues attended by arms control experts from the technical community, the GSD, and the MOFA. This series has been important in developing cross-unit contacts and in floating new ideas and proposals. The PSNSS has been replaced by a new Arms Control Research Office in the IAPCM, set up in 1996. In principle, this office has approved space for between thirty and forty people, many times more than the PSNSS, though the functioning number at present is fewer than that. The office focuses on CTBT OSI, fissile material production cut-off, verification, and nuclear non-proliferation (interviews with arms control specialists, January 1997, January 1998).

22 As early as the mid-1980s, there were meetings between MOFA's Fourth Department, the GSD and COSTIND specialists to discuss the drafting of documents and position papers which China took to the CD. But these meetings appear to have been less regularized and specialized than the interagency process for the CTBT negotiations. Interview with former MOFA official, May 1996.

23 Interview with arms control specialist, January 1997.

24 Interview with senior arms control specialist, May 1996.

25 Interviews with arms control official (July 1996), senior military official (July 1996), senior military arms control specialist (June 1996), and retired military officer (June 1996).

26 Interviews, Academy of Military Sciences, July 1996.

27 Huang Yanting and Song Baoxian, "Dang qian guoji caijun douzheng de tedian ji zhengce jianyi" (Characteristics of the present international disarmament struggle and several policy proposals), in *Guoji caijun douzheng yu Zhongguo* (The international disarmament struggle and China, Beijing (1987), pp. 6–8.

28 Pan Zhenqiang "Dang qian guoji caijun douzheng xingshi yu wo guo de diwei he zuoyong" (The present situation in the international disarmament struggle and our country's status and effect), in ibid., p.27.

29 Wang Shuzong "Caijun douzheng yu ji ge renshi wenti" (Disarmament struggle and a few questions of understanding), in ibid., p. 86.

30 Ibid.

31 Interview, May 1996.

32 Andrew P. Cortell and James W. Davis Jr., "How do International Institutions Matter? The Domestic Impact of International Rules and Norms," *International Studies Quarterly* 40:4 (December 1996), pp.451–478.

33 Nor does the standard definition of cooperation have much to say about whether it is good or bad for some normatively defined notion of global security. We do not comment on these criteria because we want to avoid difficult judgements about the quality of Chinese cooperation as it relates to meta-outcomes in global politics.

34 See e.g. CD/102 June 19, 1980; CD/168 March 27, 1981; CD/CW/CTC/3 March 15, 1982; CD/CW/CRP.62 August 4, 1982.

35 Language primarily designed to protect intra-developing world free trade in chemicals, the transfer of technical knowledge, etc.

36 See e.g. CD/CW/WP.415 June 26, 1992; CD/CW/WP/408 June 4, 1992; CW/CW/CP.406 June 4, 1992; CD/CW/WP.405 June 4, 1992; CD/CW/WP.415 June 26, 1992.

37 See e.g. CD/NTB/WP.123 20 June, 1994; CD/NTB/WP.167 August 23, 1994; CD/NTB/WP.78 June 2, 1994.

38 See CD/TIA/WP.23 March 10, 1994.

39 See e.g. PSNSS, *Junbei kongzhi yanjiu lunwen ji* (Collected research essays on arms control) (1994); IAPCM, PSNSS, *Arms Control: Collected Works* (Beijing 1995); and Huang Zuwei, "TMD and Global/Regional Stability," (Paper presented at Fifth ISODARCO Beijing Seminar on Arms Control, Chengdu, China, November 11–15, 1996); Li Bin, "Analysis of Fission Products – A Method for Verification of a CTBT During On-side Inspections," (Paper presented at Fifth ISODARCO Beijing Seminar on Arms Control, Chengdu, China, November 11–15, 1996), and Jin Huimin, "On Verification of the Cut-Off Treaty," (Paper presented at Fifth ISODARCO Beijing Seminar on Arms Control, Chengdu, China, November 11–15, 1996).

40 Interview with arms control scientists, ISODARCO Beijing Seminar on Arms Control, April 1994.

41 Interviews with senior arms control specialist in the technical community, May 1996, and with arms control scientist, July 1996.

42 China participated in the GSETT-2 (Group of Scientific Experts Technical Test-2) in 1991. The GSE is responsible for developing seismological, radio-nuclide, hydro-accoustic, and infrasound monitoring technologies that will undergird the CTBT's international monitoring system. See *The Monitor: Newsletter of the Nuclear Monitoring Research Office (ARPA)* 5: 2/3 (fall/winter 1995).

43 Interview with senior arms control specialists in the technical community, May 1996. The nuclear weapons community probably anticipated China's eventual involvement in a test ban negotiation as early as 1987. In that year the IAPCM's Chen Xueyin wrote a top secret report (with Hu Side of the CAEP), "Guanyu he jin shi tanpan de duice" (jimi) (On countermeasures concerning nuclear test ban negotiations) that was circulated at a COSTIND arms control seminar. See PSNSS, ed., *Junbei kongzhi yanjiu lunwen ji (Collected research essays on arms control)* (1994), p.137. However, the policy process was evidently not prepared for the speed with which the negotiations evolved after 1994. Some Chinese and Western participants believe that some of China's bargaining positions were delaying tactics to allow the interagency process time to consider new phases of the negotiations.

44 A/C.1/41/L.28 October 30, 1986; A/C.1/41/L.4 October 27, 1986; A/C.1/41/L.45 October 30, 1986; A/C.1/41/L.62 October 30, 1986.

45 It is not clear how seriously this option was considered in a general sense. With the exception of Pakistan, China's "Israel," China was generally cautious about the idea of weapons proliferation. Even in 1965, in a period of radicalizing foreign policy, foreign minister Chen Yi implied that while China supported the nuclearization of radical Third World states, it would not transfer the technology directly.

46 China has not signed the Southeast Asia NWFZ protocols as of this date; but the issue here is whether or not the treaty covers Chinese territorial waters. China cannot agree to the treaty while disputes over who controls what ocean space in the South China Sea remain unresolved. Such a commitment might prevent China from transporting nuclear weapons through its own territorial waters. We may not like its claims (though these are evolving and contracting) but the principle appears not to be to oppose the treaty because China might want to move nuclear weapons through international waters in the SEA area (which is why the US opposes it). Rather China wants to be

able to move nuclear weapons through its own waters in the SEA area. More recently, China has declined to sign the Ottawa Treaty banning anti-personnel landmines. On this score, China is joined by the US, Russia, and a number of other states. The arguments made are purely cost and security ones, and the size and nature of the anti-Ottawa treaty coalition is such that the opprobrium costs are probably bearable.

47 Our coding procedures are admittedly not very accurate, particularly when judging the impact of a treaty on Chinese relative military power. Since we do not know if China has a CW program – it says it does not, though ACDA claims it does – it is hard to judge if accession to the CWC, for instance, will require it to shut down clandestine, but potentially discoverable programs. We assume, however, that the option of developing CW becomes less credible with the CWC than without it. It is clearer, however, in relative terms, that the CWC is more constraining than, for example, the South Pacific NWFZ, since there is a more immediate military pay-off (and capability) for developing and using CW in a crisis than in developing nuclear capabilities that are deployable in the South Pacific.

48 This continuum says nothing about whether the quality of cooperation has an ameliorative effect on the broader security issue at stake. One could engage in high-quality cooperation when supporting a treaty or regime, even though the treaty's provisions might still have little effect on the problem at hand (e.g. the CTBT's effect on the likelihood of nuclear utility). We set aside the question of the value of the institution or regime for dealing with global security problems, and whether China takes the lead in strengthening the effectiveness of cooperative institutions. On this general issue, however, see Oran Young, "The Effectivenss of International Institutions: Hard Cases and Critical Variables" in James N. Rosenau and Ernst-Otto Czempiel, eds, *Governance without Government: Order and Change in World Politics* (Cambridge: Cambridge University Press, 1992), pp.160–194.

49 It is difficult to determine whether the calculus remained the same over time. The initial calculus was predominantly image-related, and cannot be explained by side-payments or threats of sanctions, or normative preferences. Key actors, such as the nuclear weapons community, opposed the treaty and thus it could not be considered a costless commitment.

50 Interview with arms control specialist, April 1996.

51 Interview with senior military arms control specialist (April 1996); interview with arms control scientist (May 1996); interview with arms control scientist in the technical community (August 1994); Yu Zhiyong, "Guanyu he bu kuosan tiaoyue ruogan wenti de zai renshi" (Additional thoughts on several questions relating to the non-proliferation treaty), in *Shijie jingji yu zhengzhi* 6 (1988), pp. 38–39; Huang Zhijian, "He kuosan – yi ge riyi yin qi shijie ren guangzhu de wenti" (Nuclear non-proliferation – a question that increasingly draws the attention of the people of the world), *Shijie jingji yu zhengzhi* 7 (1992), p. 48.

52 The degree of constraint depends, of course, on how one assesses what the Chinese military would like to do with nuclear weapons in the future and how much the treaty prevents warhead modernization that might be required by these plans. The weapons community and the PLA have consistently and explicitly argued that the treaty would freeze technical asymmetries. As late as 1994, the weapons designers argued that at that time a moratorium would prevent the development of a second generation of warheads needed for the second generation of missiles (more mobile, longer range; see "Guowai dui wo he shiyan de fanying" [Foreign reaction to our nuclear test), in *Guowai he wuqi dongtai (Foreign Nuclear Weapons Trends)* 6 (December 2, 1994), p.1. It is not clear whether the testing series that ended in July 1996 with China's signature to the treaty provided enough information for anything beyond a second-generation warhead, if that. If the testing was reasonably successful, China can proceed with

a second-generation missile capability that might go some distance in meeting the requirement for a limited deterrent. However, with the end to testing, newer generations of warhead designs (e.g. enhanced radiation, pure fusion, miniaturized, earth boring, etc.) will probably be impossible to develop.

53 Kreps, "Corporate Culture and Economic Theory."

54 Robert Frank, *Passions within Reason: The Strategic Role of the Emotions* (New York: Norton, 1988).

55 In this case, it is in the actor's interest to spend resources on convincing others that it is indeed cooperative. This might explain the instrumental use of high-profile or "principled foreign policy" rhetoric in Chinese diplomacy.

56 See Lowell Dittmer and Samuel S. Kim, "In Search of a Theory of National Identity," in Dittmer and Kim, eds, *China's Quest for National Identity* (New York: Cornell University Press, 1993), p.9.

57 Ibid., pp.14–15.

58 Ibid., p.27. This identity might be considered an amalgam of what Kim calls "UN Charter" and "Neofunctionalist" visions of world order. See Samuel S. Kim, *China in and Out of World Order* (Princeton, NJ: World Order Studies Program, 1991). It is not altogether clear what the source of new identities is. In China's case there are obvious material benefits from involvement in international institutions in general, e.g. World Bank loans, development advice, technology transfers, etc. But there were no concrete material benefits from initial involvement in security institutions such as the CD in the early 1980s. It is clear, however, that Chinese leaders do not hold visions of China any more as a radical Third World state, a leader of global have-nots, or a bastion of revolutionary Marxism.

59 Note that realist arguments fail to explain the increasing quality of Chinese arms control participation in the 1990s. If anything, in a unipolar world dominated by US military power, China ought to be more reluctant to participate in potentially relative power capabilities constraining arms control processes.

60 For example, interviews with military arms control specialists and specialists connected with military technology development, June 1996; interview with environmental scientist in the National Environmental Protection Agency, July 1996; comments by senior environmental policy-maker, May 1997; conversation with scientist in the arms control technical community, January 1998.

61 See e.g. State Council, *Wo guo guanyu quanqiu huanjing wenti de yuanze lichang* (The principled position of our country concerning global environmental problems) (Beijing: China Environmental Science Press, 1992, p.11.

62 Matthew Evangelista, "The Paradox of State Strength: Transnational Relations, Domestic Structures, and Security Policy in Russia and the Soviet Union," *International Organization* 49:1 (January 1995), pp.1–38; and Adler, "The Emergence of Cooperation".

63 This scientists' group is substantially the core of the arms control community in COSTIND and the CAEP/IAPCM system.

64 Inteview, August 1994.

65 See "Statement by H.E. Mr. Sha Zukang," First Committee Fifty-first Session of the UNGA (October 18, 1996) (PRC UN Mission Press Release), p. 8. Postol's Chinese interlocutors have been impressed by the work he and others have done showing that the development and deployment of the US Theater High Altitude Air Defense ballistic missile defense system would violate the Ant-Ballistic Missile Treaty (see Lisbeth Gronlund, George Lewis, Theodore Postol and David Wright, "Highly Capable Theater Missile Defense and the ABM Treaty," *Arms Control Today* 24:3 (April 1994), pp.3–8). Chinese scientists have since replicated the general arguments in this study. This has provided the scientific arguments for taking a higher diplomatic profile on the issue. The MFOA was initially reluctant to do so because of concerns

that the Sino–US agenda was already too complicated and conflictual. The arms control scientists evidently prevailed on this issue.

66 China entered the IMF and World Bank in 1980 and formally requested negotiations to enter the GATT in 1986. Thirteen years later these negotiations are still not concluded.

67 The pattern and impact of these dialogue activities in their formative stage has been examined in Paul Evans, "The Dialogue Process on Asia Pacific Security Issues: Inventory and Analysis," in Paul M. Evans, ed., *Studying Asia Pacific Security: The Future of Research, Training and Dialogue Activities* (Toronto: Joint Centre for Asia Pacific Studies, 1994). The multilateral dialogues up to 1994 have been chronicled since 1995 in five editions of *Dialogue Monitor*. The project, coordinated by the Joint Centre for Asia Pacific Studies in Toronto, has been expanded into a *Dialogue and Research Monitor* which will run into the year 2000.

68 The best account of the origins and evolution of the ARF is Michael Leifer's *The ASEAN Regional Forum: Extending ASEAN's Model of Regional Security* (Oxford: Oxford University Press; London: International Institute of Strategic Studies, Adelphi Paper No. 304, 1996).

69 Amitav Acharya, "Ideas, Identity and Institution-Building: From the 'ASEAN way' to the 'Asia-Pacific way'?," *The Pacific Review* 10: 3 (1997).

70 Jusuf Wanandi, "ASEAN's China Strategy: Towards Deeper Engagement," *Survival* (autumn 1996).

71 Acharya, "Ideas, Identity and Institution-Building".

72 The formula that was eventually concluded in December 1996 permitted the participation of individual experts from Taiwan in working group meetings but no formal Taiwanese membership in the Steering Committee or annual meetings. It was also agreed that relations across the Straits of Taiwan would not be part of the CSCAP agenda, though several member committees noted that any military conflict across the Straits would have major regional repercussions and thus could not be ruled out as a future issue.

73 Quoted in *Beijing Review*, August 12–18, 1996.

74 This was evident in CSCAP meetings after China's entrance in December 1996, but was already apparent in sub-regional settings two years earlier. There was a strikingly different style and level of focus in Chinese participation in the Canadian-led "North Pacific Cooperative Security Dialogue" between 1991 and March 1993, and the successor American-led "Northeast Asia Cooperation Dialogue" which began later in 1993 and is still continuing with active and sophisticated Chinese participation.

75 Chen Jian, "Challenges and Responses in East Asia." Text of speech delivered at the CSCAP Annual Meeting, Singapore, June 4, 1997.

76 Statement by Qian Qichen at the Fourth ARF Ministerial Meeting, Kuala Lumpur, 27 July, 1997.

77 With Russia and the three Central Asian Republics, "Agreement on Confidence Building in the Military Field in the Border Areas" in April 1996 and the "Agreement on Mutual Reduction of Military Forces in Border Areas"; with India, "Agreement on Confidence-Building Measures in the Military Field Along the Line of Actual Control in the China-India Border Areas," November 1996.

78 Despite the fact that the Shanghai Agreement of April 1997 had five signatories, Chinese officials have insisted that it is a bilateral agreement among multiple parties, reflecting the fact that the three central Asia republics were at one time part of the Soviet Union and that it was in fact Russia that negotiated the agreement on their behalf.

79 In Johnston's interviews in Beijing in mid-1996, for instance, it was evident that where one came down on the portability of the agreement was a litmus test of sorts about more general support for regional multilateralism. More recently, an analysis

broadcast by China Radio International in late December 1997 argued, for instance, that the five-power CBM agreement was a good example for the rest of the Asia-Pacific. It had authenticated "a new security concept completely different from the Cold War mentality and the traditional security concept. If you desire peace, you must prepare for war. This saying is a vivid description of the traditional security concept." The traditional realpolitik concepts included ideas such as maximizing military force so as to become stronger than one's opponent, a narrow focus on the security of the nation above all else and the resort to military means in the pursuit of security. See China Radio International, "The Taking Shape of a New Security Concept and its Practice in China" (December 29, 1997), *BBC-SWB* (January 7, 1998). The explicit rejection of the "parabellum" phrase, while rare in Chinese discourses on international relations, is in a sense also a repudiation of a long-standing Chinese equivalent: *ju an si wei, you bei wu huan* ("When residing in peace, think about danger. With [military] preparations there will be no calamities"). These kinds of discursive innovations in discussions of Asia-Pacific security were essentially absent prior to participation in regional security dialogues.

80 *China's National Defense* (Beijing: Information Office of the State Council of the PRC, July 1998). The English version was reprinted in its entirety in *China Daily*, July 28, 1998.

81 These are discussed in a thoughtful essay by Chu Shulong, "Concepts, Structures, Strategies and Regional Security," *Contemporary International Relations* (May 1997).

82 See Li Qinggong and Wei Wei, "The World Needs New Security Concept," *Jiefangjun Bao*, December 24, 1997, p. 5; "Conference Discussing the New Security Concept Held in Beijing," *Renmin Ribao*, December 26, 1997, p. 4; "Chi Haotian Introduces 'New Security Concept'," *FBIS Daily Report*, FBIS-CHI-98-035 February 4, 1998; and the Chinese entries (pp. 61, 62 and 74) in David Capie, Paul Evans and Akiko Fukushima, *Speaking Asia Pacific Security: A Lexicon of English Terms with Chinese and Japanese Translation and a Note on the Japanese Translation* (Toronto: Joint Centre for Asia Pacific Studies, 1998).

83 The Five Principles are mutual respect for territorial integrity and sovereignty; mutual non-aggression; non-interference in internal affairs; equality and mutual benefit; and peaceful coexistence.

84 One of its products is David Capie, Paul Evans and Akiko Fukushima, *Speaking Asia Pacific Security: A Lexicon of English Terms with Chinese and Japanese Translation and a Note on the Japanese Translation* (Toronto: Joint Centre for Asia Pacific Studies, 1998).

85 Evans's interviews in Beijing, November 1996, June and October 1997.

86 Wu Xinbo, "Integration on the Basis of Strength: China's Impact on East Asian Security," (Stanford, CA: Stanford University, Institute for International Studies Discussion Paper, February 1998), p. 8.

87 This issue is explored further in Alastair Iain Johnston, "The Myth of the ASEAN Way? Explaining the Evolution of the ASEAN Regional Forum," in Helga Haftendorn, Robert Keohane and Celeste Wallander, eds, *Imperfect Unions: Security Institutions in Time and Space* (London: Oxford University Press, 1999).

11

CONCLUSION

Alastair Iain Johnston and Robert S. Ross

How does one summarize such a rich set of empirical analyses found in this book? What comparisons can be made about the content of engagement strategies across this wide variety of states? What lessons can be drawn about how well engagement works as a strategy for dealing with emerging powers? This chapter tries to offer some tentative answers to these questions.

Descriptive comparisons

Variation in state strategies can be conceptualized along two basic dimensions (Figure 11.1). The first is an engagement–containment dimension. This dimension captures basic differences in how states react to the rising power of a (potentially) revisionist state. As Schweller notes, containment is essentially aimed at preventing the rise and perhaps actively encouraging the decline of a dissatisfied, rising power. Engagement, as the term has been used in this book, means quite the opposite – the use of non-coercive methods to ameliorate the revisionist elements of a rising power's behavior, without the intention of preventing the accretion of this state's power. The policy debates in the United States and elsewhere tend to juxtapose the two as well.[1] There can, of course, be mixes of both strategies. The dimension is an interval scale, not a dichotomous one.

A second dimension captures the degree to which states actively pursue engagement or containment; that is, the degree to which they commit economic, political, military, and human resources to these strategies. Maximal efforts imply that the state is trying to develop a comprehensive set of instruments, linked to other foreign policy interests, to pursue the strategy, and that the strategy figures prominently in the state's overall foreign policy. At the opposite end, minimal effort implies that engagement, containment, or some mix of the two is not actively pursued, or that the state relies more on the resources of other actors to implement these strategies.

In combination, these two dimensions yield typologies of behavior that typically describe the range of grand strategies toward rising powers.[2] Thus a state that pursues full-bore, maximal engagement could bandwagon with the rising power, hoping to benefit from any changes in international rules and distributions of

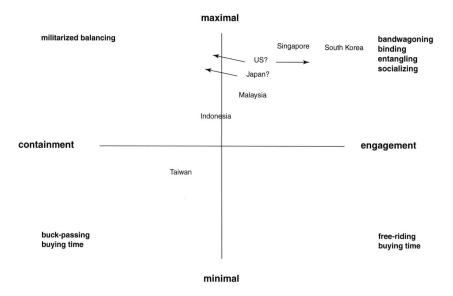

Figure 11.1 Typology of grand strategies

resources that the new power might demand. Or it could try to bind the rising power to existing international institutions, rules and norms, relying on these exogenous constraints to create new sets of interests, or new indifference curves between existing interests, that make it costly for the rising power to demand changes in the status quo. Or it could try to bind the rising state to a bilateral, Kissingerian bargain to create a condominium that would coordinate in preserving each other's legitimate interests. Or it could try to entangle the rising state in international institutional rules, responsibilities, and sanctioning procedures. Or it could try to transform the rising power's preferences and strategies through socialization in status quo institutions.

Conversely, a state that pursues full-bore containment would essentially rely on the mobilization of military power (whether through internal balancing, external balancing, or some combination of the two) to prevent the further accretion of the rising power, and indeed to reverse this trend. Foreign policy strategy would aim to shut off the state from the military and technological benefits of economic growth and to transform its political structure so that emerging elites do not endorse revisionist aims.

In contrast to maximal engagement and containment, minimalist strategies would involve, essentially, free-riding off the efforts of others to either engage or contain the rising state. It could involve, for instance, free-riding off a state pursuing full-bore containment, deriving security benefits at no or preferential cost. It could involve the opposite – free-riding off those pursuing full-bore engagement, hoping to benefit from the moderation of the revisionist state's interest, while avoiding the costs of trying to pull the state into international institutions, for instance.

The question is: Where do the actors under study in this book fall along these two dimensions? First, some caveats. The placements in Figure 11.1 are approximate ("heuristic" is the escape term!). They are generalizations drawn from the chapters and cannot capture precisely the state's strategy. There is more movement within these dimensions than the diagram suggests. Furthermore, disaggregation by actor and by time would yield a more nuanced picture of movement along these dimensions across space and time by subnational actors. Portraying the subtleties of state behavior is complicated. Still, the relative positioning of the actors can reveal interesting information about variation in engagement strategies.

Of all the actors studied here, South Korea is the actor most committed to engagement. According to Victor Cha (Chapter 2), its expectations that China's increasing power might require some form of militarized balancing are lowest. Seoul's objectives are multifaceted. Its shorter term goals are to elicit Chinese cooperation on Korean peninsula issues and to increase Seoul's prestige as a key player in, indeed a model for, China's economic transformation. Its longer term goal is to develop China's normative commitment to economic and security cooperation and to a high level of diffuse reciprocity. It is one of the few powers in this study to have such an obvious transformative concept of engagement. Seoul's policy to achieve these ends rests largely on the use of bilateral and multi-lateral economic relations. Unlike most of the other cases here, South Korea does not view military balancing as a necessary insurance policy in case engagement does not work.

Singapore has also been a strong and vocal advocate of engagement. Indeed, according to Yuen Foong Khong (Chapter 5), Lee Kuan-yew has one of the most developed conceptualizations of engagement of any of the leaderships discussed in this book. Like South Korea, Singapore views economic engagement as one of the key tools for developing status quo interests in China. Lee rejects the standard realpolitik fear that increased wealth will invariably lead to increased military power and greater interest in using military power to assert spheres of influence. Rather, China's drive for wealth can be a constraint on the exercise of its power because economic development in the late twentieth century requires involve-ment in status quo capitalist institutions. This is primarily a story of economic constraints and interest linkage, not a socialization or transformation argument. But these two arguments are not absent from Lee's concept of engagement. He argues that, as the history of many smaller Asia-Pacific states shows, one of the greatest sources of status quo preferences in China will be young Chinese returning to their homeland carrying business, economics, and technology degrees, propagating Western capitalist, globalist, and perhaps cosmopolitan notions of wealth. Despite these arguments, Singapore also hedges. Its "fall-back" position, as Khong notes, is to continue to modernize its military so that it can be prepared to balance with the United States–Japan and other ASEAN countries against Chinese power, if necessary.

Malaysia and Indonesia are more skeptical about the value of engagement, compared to Korea and Singapore. For Malaysia, this skepticism is rooted in a somewhat pessimistic view of Chinese power and intentions. China's potential military role in the South China Sea is especially worrisome for Malaysian military planners. On the other hand, for historical and legitimation reasons, Malaysian balancing with former colonial or neocolonial powers like Japan and the United States against Chinese power is politically unacceptable. Thus Malaysia's combination of relative weakness, historical memory, and political fragility requires engagement with hedging, or what Acharya insightfully calls "counter-dominance."[3] But Malaysia's theory of engagement is less well developed than Singapore's, or at least more eclectic. As Acharya notes, some Malaysians believe that economic ties will encourage Chinese interests in using diplomacy and negotiation to resolve regional territorial and resource disputes; some Malaysians hope that China and Malaysia will be able to accommodate their legitimate interests, in a Kissingerian bargain sense; some see regional economic and security institutions as mechanisms for socializing China into non-realpolitik norms of behavior, a more transformative notion of engagement. Overall, in some contrast to Korea and Singapore, Malaysia's approach to engagement is based more on faith and hope than on evidence that engagement has ameliorated China's non-status quo objectives.

Indonesia is more explicitly skeptical that engagement – a term, as Leifer points out (Chapter 4), that until recently was alien to Indonesian diplomatic vocabulary – will constrain Chinese power. In Indonesian threat assessments, China is the greatest challenge to its sovereignty. Indonesian elites believe that China's revisionist territorial interests show no signs of abating. China's rise also challenges Indonesia's self-categorization as an entitled, regional leader. Engagement is therefore a pragmatic diplomatic nod in the direction of the rest of ASEAN and the United States while Jakarta pursues different engagement strategies. It reflects on Indonesia's obligation status as an ASEAN member and as a major regional power. Jakarta also pursues engagement as an information-gathering exercise. In contrast to some proponents of engagement in the region, however, Indonesia is skeptical of multilateral engagement. It fears that Chinese involvement in the ARF, for instance, could reduce ASEAN and Indonesia's leadership role in regional security issues. Because Indonesia has very low expectations of engagement, balancing without the diplomacy of engagement is a more attractive option when dealing with China. Indonesian preferences are reflected in the rather rapid increase in Indonesian military cooperation with the United States and Australia, and its renewed interest in acquiring maritime air and blue water naval capabilities. All in all, Indonesian policy is closer to containment than that of the other ASEAN states.

Taiwan, as Goldstein points out (Chapter 3), is the actor most leery of engagement. Taiwan's leadership is worried that bilateral economic engagement, for instance, could provide Beijing with political leverage, even though economic linkages with the mainland are critical for Taiwan's plans to become a regional high technology and financial "operational center." In this context, intermittent political contacts with China seek to delay unification on PRC terms. Moreover, Taiwan has little faith that China's involvement in multilateral economic and security institutions will constrain PRC attempts to coerce Taiwan into accepting Chinese terms for unification. Nothing short of the fundamental transformation of China's political system and political culture will improve Taiwan's situation *vis-à-vis* the mainland. Rather than pursue engagement, Taiwan's policy tries desperately to encourage other states to strengthen their political and military commitments to balance against Chinese coercive diplomacy. It tries to use the United States' commitment to its security to balance against and deter China while the US *officially* eschews a policy of balancing against China.

Yet all this is complicated by Taiwan's democratization. Sentiments for continued separation, though not necessarily for independence, are strong. This encourages international political behavior that angers Beijing. Taiwan responds by trying to tie the United States more closely to its security, adding to Beijing's distrust of Taiwan's commitment to reunification. On the other hand, bottom-up economic interests in Taiwan have promoted closer economic ties between Taiwan and the mainland. Managing these ties to minimize Beijing's political leverage and protect Taiwanese business interests necessitates a more institutionalized, official relationship with Beijing. The net result, as Goldstein points out in his conclusion, is that Taiwan is at one and the same time balancing, accommodating, and hiding. Engagement, in the way this volume has defined it, however, appears to have few backers in Taipei.

The actors listed above are relatively easy to place on the two dimensions in Figure 11.1. We now come to two powers whose placement is more ambiguous or perhaps more dynamic – Japan and the United States As Michael Green discovers (Chapter 7), Japan's strategy toward a rising Chinese power has not been static. During the Cold War, he argues, Japanese leaders placed their faith in an integrationist approach to engagement: China's involvement in global capitalist institutions, combined with domestic marketization, would create vested, status quo interests. This approach undergirded a somewhat skeptical view of US anti-China containment strategies during the 1950s and 1960s. During the 1970s, the United States–Japan alliance was seen by all three players – the US, Japan and China – as an effective tool in containing Soviet power in East Asia.

The end of the Cold War, however, has seen a shift in Japanese policy toward a "reluctant realism." Green identifies a number of factors accounting for this change. First, economic integration, in the eyes of many in Japan, has not led to an amelioration of China's non-status quo military aspirations. The pace of China's military modernization, or certainly its military spending, has increased even as China has become more integrated into global capitalism and international institutions. Second, the United States has pushed Japan to adopt more intensive and extensive military commitments as part of its alliance responsibilities, commitments that have in turn increased Chinese concerns about an evolving anti-China alliance. Chinese criticisms have in turn convinced many in Japan of the need to counter Chinese power. Finally, political change in Japan is another key variable: the passing of older "friends of China" from the senior ranks of the LDP, and the alienation of the Japanese left due to China's nuclear testing, for instance, have quieted the more accommodationist voices in Japan.

Thus Japan, like some of the Southeast Asian states, has moved toward a hedging strategy. On the one hand, it continues to encourage trade and investment in China. It has been ahead of other Western economies in pushing for early Chinese entry into the WTO. On the other hand, Green notes, there is growing concern in Japan for the relative gains of economic engagement. A growing number of Japanese are arguing that rapid Chinese economic growth may not be in Japan's long-term interests if this growth feeds military modernization. Moreover, as part of hedging, Japan has begun quiet efforts to prepare the military tools to deal with conflicts that might break out with China over resources, territory, and politics in the region. It has pursued quiet diplomatic efforts to prevent China from isolating Japan in the region, including recent efforts to improve relations with Russia. Japan is also less sanguine than some of its neighbors in the ability of multilateral security dialogues to alter or constrain Chinese behavior, though participation in these fora does place Japan's regional security behavior in a more favorable light relative to China's. Whether the shift in Japan's strategy stops at hedging, or moves more concertedly toward balancing, Green suggests, is a decision which Japan's leaders do not yet have to face. But it is a direction that they have not yet ruled out.

This brings us to the United States. In a sense, the United States is the subject of the study of engagement as theory and practice in the late twentieth century (China is the object of engagement). The United States is the dominant pole in the system. The gap between its military power and economic resources and the rest is huge and growing. The global balance is as close to a unipolar system in terms of material distributions of power than it has ever been in the modern international system. As Figure 11.2 shows, using ACDA data, with the collapse of the Soviet Union, the United States share of world military expenditures jumped from about 27 percent to about 35 percent. If one uses IISS military expenditure figures the gap immediately after the collapse of the United States was even larger. In 1992 military expenditure shares, stood at 43.5 percent, 7.1 percent and 4.0 percent for the United States, Russia and China, respectively.[4] The world has entered a "unipolar moment"[5] that may be more than momentary. Despite the official Chinese line that the world is in transition to multipolarity, some nationalist conservatives and those thought to be more "pro-American" in orientation in China agree that global multipolarity is a long way off and that Beijing will have to deal with overwhelming American military and economic power.[6]

Moreover, the United States is looking to preserve its global primacy. As such, it is generally not given to empathy for or accommodation to rising powers that might challenge its primacy. This was the message of the internal draft of the Department of Defense statement in 1992.[7] As Ross notes (Chapter 8), Chinese

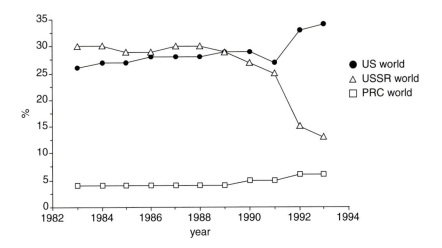

Figure 11.2 US, Russian and Chinese shares of world military expenditure
Source: ACDA 1995 World Military Expenditures

and American leaders believe that the two countries have significant conflicts of national interests.

Thus the puzzle is why has the United States adopted an engagement strategy at all? For Ross, the basic answer is that the net costs of the alternatives are considered too high. Pure balancing, or some form of neo-containment, aimed at thwarting China's emergence as a candidate great power is, despite US economic and military superiority, too expensive without allied support. Bandwagoning with Chinese power (appeasement in Schweller's lexicon) such that China is allowed to dominate political-military affairs in East Asia, is out of the question, given US strategic superiority and status quo aspirations. The default, Ross suggests, is simultaneous balancing and engagement, i.e. managed competition where, on certain issues, China is treated as a partner, but where the United States does not concede regional hegemony to Beijing. This is not the hedging strategy of smaller states, since even if China's intentions proved to be benign, this would not change the basic American interest of preventing the relative decline of US power. It is also a very difficult strategy to implement, as Schweller notes in his review of past efforts in history. It entails reassuring China that the United States sees China as a partner, while reminding Beijing of overwhelming US power and, in effect, trying to constrain Chinese behavior in a web of economic, political and security commitments. It entails reassurance signals that the United States does not intend to treat China as an enemy, but also signals that try to dispel Chinese misperceptions of US strategic weakness or lack of military stamina. It entails signaling an interest in building an inclusive, non-discriminatory security architecture in which China can fully participate, while at the same time reassuring traditional allies that China's security still rests on exclusionary bilateral ties with the United States that will be able to deter Chinese power if need be. It is not surprising, then, that there are suspicions in Beijing that engagement is merely soft containment.

Still, says Ross, US engagement policies have worked. The PRC has compromised on a range of bilateral issues (from IPR to non-proliferation). At the same time the United States has negotiated a reaffirmed security treaty with Japan (one with China scenarios increasingly in mind). It has quietly strengthened bilateral military cooperation with some Southeast Asian states. And, despite the absence of official government-to-government ties, the United States commitment to Taiwan's security is greater now than at any time since 1971. The United States has also helped to lever Chinese participation in multilateral institutions that comprise a global nonproliferation regime which is overwhelmingly advantageous to US strategic primacy. It is precisely this evidence of US leverage in the post-Cold War unipolar moment, says Ross, which suggests that the United States could be even more accommodating in order to ensure that China develops a stake even in those policies and institutions that favor US power.

US engagement policies have had the paradoxical effect of improving, relatively speaking, US leverage over the conditions and parameters within which Chinese power emerges. It is thus not obvious whether or not US engagement strategies, in the end, are designed to ameliorate the non-status quo element without hindering the accretion of Chinese power. Clearly the United States has used engagement to ensure that the accretion of Chinese power does not appreciably reduce US power.

Comparisons

How great are the differences across actors, and what explains them? On the one hand, the emergence of China has actually led to a convergence in engagement policies across most of these states. A common theme is hedging, reflecting widespread uncertainty over the trajectory in Chinese capabilities and behavior. If China succeeds in modernizing its military power, will it try to establish regional hegemony, try to establish direct control over its vast territorial claims in the region, and try to coerce deference to its interests from smaller regional powers? Or will China's growing stake in the global and regional capitalist economies and security institutions promote a profoundly status quo mentality among its leaders, who are desperate for the legitimacy that economic growth and international status can buy them?

Under conditions of uncertainty, the expected reaction is to hedge one's bets: promote engagement policies and institutions to gather information on intentions while modernizing militaries and strengthening politico–military ties with potential members of a balancing coalition. The United States, Indonesia, Malaysia, and Japan are all, to varying degrees, hedging against the rise of Chinese power, Singapore and Korea to a much lesser extent. Malaysia and Indonesia both view regional security institutions as instruments for reducing uncertainty through transparency. They also possess limited hope that such institutions will contribute to internalizing status quo rules of behavior in the Chinese policy process. Yet military planning in all of these states is increasingly taking into account the possibility of military conflict with China. Thus militaries in these states walk a fine line between engaging the Chinese military to gather intelligence and promote military transparency while simultaneously trying to send reassurance signals. Interestingly, in almost all the cases where the authors asked the question, none of these states is likely to bandwagon or appease Chinese power as a first choice, should engagement fail. The preference for most, though not all (Malaysia in particular) is a balancing coalition involving the United States, Japan, and Australian power, plus local military forces.

This raises a critical issue for policy makers. Is it possible to develop a policy which walks the fine line between signaling credible balancing that reduces the targeted state's interest in challenging the status quo and signaling unjustified coercion that encourages the non-status quo behavior which these signals are supposed to deter? On the one hand, the fact that the aggressive use of Chinese power, if our authors are right, is likely to provoke balancing needs to be communicated clearly to China, since one sometimes thinks this possibility is dismissed in Beijing.[8] On the other hand, this message could also be misread in Beijing to mean that the United States and Japan had been successful in building an anti-China front, a signal that is hardly likely to encourage a regime with shaky domestic legitimacy to accept the regional economic, political, and military status quo.

Despite the similarities across actors, there are clear differences (Figure 11.1). The governments of Singapore and Korea have placed engagement front and center of their China policies. The United States and Japan are hedging to the extent that there is concern in both countries that amelioration of Chinese non-status quo interests may require military and coercive tools. Taiwanese and Indonesian leaders are skeptical of the merits of engagement and prefer to rely primarily on balancing to cope with growing Chinese capabilities.

How are these differences explained? Is there an overarching accounting? Most behavior in world politics is over-determined, but it is worth trying to enumerate likely places to look for large effects on the dependent variable (that is, where states are placed in Figure 11.1). Typically in IR, there are a few key independent variables which different theoretical approaches tend to emphasize when trying to explain variation in degree of cooperation among powers:

Transgovernmental penetration and cross-national coalitions. Here the hypothesis might be, drawing from a neo-functionalist account of European experience, that states with more transgovernmental ties will develop cross-national coalitions that have interests in continued interaction. In China's case, however, no state has particularly intensive or extensive transgovernmental interactions with China. Singapore has been helping with experimental towns (such as the one outside Suzhou). Certain US agencies, such as the nuclear weapons labs, have established arms control links with the Chinese arms control community. Under the US–China IPR agreement, the United States is supposed to be helping to train Chinese officials in anti-piracy legal work. The US Army is running military justice exchanges with the PLA. The Canadian government and certain international agencies have helped set up an advisory council on environmental policy that involves top officials of various Chinese ministries in the state council (the China Council on International Cooperation on Environment and Development). However, despite their important effect on certain organizational ideologies and practice within the Chinese policy process, these kind of links are unlikely to explain the vast difference between, say, a Korean approach to engagement and an Indonesian one.

Degree of economic interdependence. This is the liberal trading states argument.[9] The greater the stake in peaceful economic interaction with Beijing, the more likely that engagement will be the central feature of strategy toward China. The political influence of US commercial interests on Chinese policy has been important for the evolution of the Clinton administration's engagement strategy. Economic interests have also promoted engagement in Japanese, Korean, and Singaporean policies. Yet in Taiwan's case, growing economic interaction with China on the part of private capital has reduced, or certainly not increased, incentives for the Taiwanese government to engage. If the degree of interdependence accounts for variation in the degree to which "engagement" is central to a state's China policy, there should be a strong positive correlation between the rank order of states in terms of interdependence and the rank order of states in terms of the centrality of engagement. Yet this doesn't seem to be the case.[10]

Material power differentials. This variable is often used in first cuts at explaining variation in state behavior, but it is not obvious how power differentials should effect engagement strategies. Despite vast differences in relative power *vis-à-vis* China across the states in this study, there are some behaviors that cut across most cases. We do not see unqualified bandwagoning, strategies aimed at opportunistically benefitting from Chinese interests. Even South Korea, the state with the closest strategic relationship with China, has maintained close military ties with the United States. Singapore, the smallest state among our cases, does not accept Chinese hegemony. Some local powers were publicly quiet about China's military pressure on Taiwan, but privately they welcomed Washington's challenge to China's threats to use force there. Nor do we see appeasement – opportunistic accommodation of Chinese interests to deflect pressure or buy time. Japan, South Korea, and Southeast Asian states, despite significant power differentials, have not made concessions to Chinese territorial claims. There is also a fair amount of hedging, regardless of variations in power differentials, which has involved increased military coordination with the United States, with an implicit target being Chinese power.

If variation in power differentials were to correlate either positively or negatively with variations in engagement strategies (both are possible for realist theories), one would expect that the rank order of states in terms of the centrality of engagement should roughly correlate with the rank order of states in terms of power differentials. This does not seem to be the case. The spearman rho rank order correlation between the centrality of engagement (derived from its position in Figure 11.1) and the rank order in the ratio of military expenditures *vis-à-vis* China is negative, but not significant (rho = −.071, *p.* = .86). Thus power differentials alone do not seem to be the place to turn to explain the similarities and differences in the engagement strategies of these states.

Geography. One explanation is that actors which are geographically closer will feel the most threatened by a rising power. This is primarily because the targeted state's power is more easily projected over shorter distances. Moreover, proximity contributes to territorial disputes, which leads to heightened threat perception.[11] Thus geography can affect the interpretation of power relationships. One hypothesis is that small neighbors of rising powers will appease to reduce insecurity and benefit from cooperation. Another might be just the opposite – contiguity encourages balancing with a distant power (as in the Chinese idiom "yuan jiao jin gong"). Geography plus absolute power differentials may explain the difference between South Korea and Japan. South Korea and Japan both have territorial disputes with China, but South Korea is geographically closer and strategically weaker. Consistent with the first hypothesis, this may explain its less belligerent approach toward its border dispute with China and its more sanguine attitude toward engagement, as compared to Japan. Geography plus power may also explain why both Singapore and Malaysia have resisted Chinese power. In contrast to South Korea, their distance from the mainland and the obstacle posed by the sea to Chinese power projection reduces the power differential so that, despite China's military capabilities, it lacks the ability to threaten Singapore and Malaysia. On the other hand, the Taiwan experience suggests that power and proximity alone cannot explain policy preferences. Taiwan borders mainland China, yet its policy is closer to the policies of the Southeast Asian states than to South Korea's policy.

Alliance opportunities. Despite differences in power and geography across actors, none of the powers studied in this volume have either bandwagoned or appeased. Rather, both the large and small have adopted elements of a balancing strategy. This is not surprising in the American case. Its distance from China and its power advantages give it the option of balancing Chinese power. But all of the small powers have done so to different degrees as well, despite contrasting relative power attributes. One common variable for each actor is the possibility to use US power to resist Chinese power. Some realists argue that small states balance when the opportunity to do so exists.[12] All of the smaller actors in this study have different kinds of security partnerships with the United States. The collapse of Soviet power has not appreciably weakened the range of American commitments to their security. Each of the smaller actors, therefore, has at least some option of resisting appeasing Chinese power. None has chosen to bandwagon with Chinese power.

This variable seems to provide a plausible explanation for at least some of the variation in the balancing behavior of the actors most susceptible to Chinese power. While we have not looked at these cases in this volume, a cursory examination of the contrasting examples of Thai and Burmese bandwagoning with China, for instance, suggests the presence of dependable security ties with the United States may help explain the preference of China's weaker neighbors for either balancing, appeasing or bandwagoning with China. On the other hand, both Taiwan and South Korea have reasonably tight security guarantees from the United States while both pursue very different strategies of engagement. But perhaps Taiwan's policy can be explained by the combination of geography. Although it is close to China and much weaker than China, the Taiwan strait inhibits Chinese power projection. Thus, Taiwan's policy is closer to that of Singapore than to that South Korea, which must consider China's power projection on mainland Asia.

Interests. Power disparities, mitigated by geography, and strategic alignments may explain decisions to balance or bandwagon. But they do not explain choice among options. All the countries here have balanced, but not all have engaged. The two outliers are Indonesia and Taiwan. They have neither actively sought to incorporate China into regional institutions nor enmesh China in entangling bilateral or multilateral relationships. What explains the Indonesian and Taiwan policy preferences?

Interest is perhaps the least rigorous variable in the international politics literature. The term is sufficiently malleable that it can explain almost any behavior. Interests are not structurally determined; nonetheless, certain conceptions of state interests seem to endure and have widespread support within polities. These "interests" are less arbitrary so that their explanatory power is less suspect. This is usually the case for what are known as "vital" interests. Among the actors examined in this volume, Taiwan has the most serious conflict of interests with China. It wants to expand its autonomy and retain the option of sovereignty, while the mainland wants to constrain Taiwan's autonomy and ultimately bring Taiwan under its control. Given Taiwan's relative economic and strategic weakness, it is not surprising that it views engagement in entangling relationships with China as entangling Taiwan, not China, and, given its conflict of interests, it is not surprising that it sees the risk of engagement as great. Indonesia's conflict with China is not over survival – for the foreseeable future Indonesian survival is assured by both distance and relations with the United States. But as Leifer shows, Indonesia's conception of its national interest is regional leadership. Not only does growing Chinese power challenge's Indonesia's ability to establish leadership, but engagement undermines Indonesia's authority by giving China a voice in regional multilateral institutions, the very instruments which Jakarta has used to legitimate its leadership.

Identity and historical memory. Identity is also a tricky variable to work with in the international politics literature. It seems obvious at times that the attributes which state leaders assign to themselves, their nation and other nations (responsible great power, defender of democracy, revolutionary leader, civilized, rogue, etc.) define their behavior, the interests they believe are legitimate or given, and the legitimate means for pursuing them. Yet states have multiple identities, and determining their independent effect is a difficult methodological task because the influence of identity is often semi-consciously followed. At this stage of methodological development, it is hard to determine a priori what state identity infuses leaders' world views and under what conditions. But precisely because identities vary a great deal (some states believe they hold unique ones, some believe they share basic characteristics with others in a large cross-national ingroup), identity may be a place to look for explanations for variation in engagement strategies across states that may share similar power, and geographical and economic traits in their relationships with China.

One can find key features of leadership identification of self and other that appear to influence engagement strategies toward China. Taiwan is clearly a case where historical memory (the nationalist defeat and retreat in 1949) and identity (Taiwanese-ification of political, economic, and cultural elites) combine to mediate estimations of Chinese intentions and of judgements about the success (or lack thereof) of engagement. In the American case, historical memory (fear of the cost of another cold war) and identity (American exceptionalism) both play a part in accounting for the preference for engaging China in a putative international community that respects norms of free trade and human rights. In Korea's case, while the predominant historical memory of Japanese imperialism existed both before and after the shift to an engagement strategy, and thus cannot explain this shift, it certainly impedes the option of current balancing with Japan against Chinese power. Korea's identity as a successful developmental state deserving recognition as a leader in reducing regional tensions in the 1990s has also promoted engagement with China. Indeed, as Cha notes, the South Korean leadership believes that its engagement policy has increased the international and domestic legitimacy of the regime.

Identity in ASEAN states is also a factor in the group's use of regional multilateral institutions as an element in its engagement strategy. As Acharya argues, ASEAN sees its survival as an independent entity as depending, in part, on ensuring that conflict between China, US, and Japan does not erupt or lead to a polarization of the region into balancing camps. Thus for many ASEAN states, such institutions, as long as they are not dominated by major powers, are tools for reducing the potential for conflict among these major powers. ASEAN historical memory also helps to explain engagement. As Yuen Foong Khong notes, the assumption that a wealthier, capitalist China will be more responsible, with a stake in global capitalist institutions, is based on the experience of ASEAN Tigers themselves. For Singaporeans, Indonesia is an example of this kind of socialization: economic modernization led Indonesia to abandon its revolutionary nationalism and regional hegemonist ambitions. (On the other hand, Indonesia's case underscores the difficulty of making a consistent identity argument. While it is a member of ASEAN, and presumably, shares the identity-based argument about the potentially ameliorative effects of economic modernization, its weak and skeptical approach to engagement seems to be influenced by another aspect of its identity, namely a fear of losing its self-conceived regional leadership status.)

There is also the possibility, however, that engagement itself – at least the discourse and some associated diplomatic practices – is a relatively new feature of identity, a norm of diplomacy toward China that has essentially diffused from the United States. States have bandwagoned on the strategy – borrowing its terminology, as Indonesia has – but applying it in ways mediated by prior identities and historical memories. The interesting question is: What explains this diffusion? Realist theories suggest that US power has enabled it to establish the discursive parameters of strategy toward China in other countries. Or are we seeing an unintended convergence – with some cross-national variation – in the post-Cold War period?

However, as Indonesia's case shows, like realist arguments, identity arguments are difficult to operationalize. In the end one is left with the suspicion that there is a great deal of contingency in any explanation for the differences across states in their engagement strategies; both realpolitik and non-realpolitik interpretations of the rise of Chinese power play important roles in determining engagement strategies.

Who succeeds?

What are the criteria for the success of engagement? Do actors have theories of engagement – rough causal assumptions about which engagement strategies lead to what kinds of outcomes with what kinds of probabilities and under what kinds of conditions, and that also provide explicit or implicit standards of evidence with which to measure the effectiveness of engagement? Unfortunately, actors have been vague about this because they have been uncertain about what China's intentions are and about trajectories in its power (which suggests that engagement policy requires a better research base). In addition, the criteria for success depend in part on differences across states in the range of interests involved in their relations with China.

For its part, the Clinton administration has claimed success – on such issues as nonproliferation, human rights, economic marketization, and intellectual property rights – but it is not clear why. There is no one theory of engagement that undergirds US policy. Socialization arguments are probably the least credible in Washington. They are certainly not consistent with the realpolitik part of the hybrid realist-globalization ideology of the administration. The language of norms may be part of the United States foreign policy discourse – human rights, free trade, democratic enlargement, for instance – but it is not obvious that the administration understands how these are created, promoted, and diffused. Rather, the more common causal argument is that a combination of global institutional rules and bilateral sanctioning (usually positive, but often negative) will compel the Chinese to follow their (stable, fixed) interest in promoting domestic welfare. On occasion, a Kissingerian condominium argument is made and at times Washington seems to accept that China has legitimate security interests on its periphery in South Asia, Taiwan, Indo–China, and on the Korean

Peninsula. But it is not clear whether the United States will be willing to offer China greater global or regional governance responsibilities commensurate with expanded economic and political capabilities.

As for smaller powers, since there has been less domestic challenge to engagement policies, there is less political need to look for and claim success. Nonetheless, if success means the reduction of uncertainty about Chinese intentions, then there is clearly a variation in assessments of engagement's success. As Green points out, the Japanese are disappointed with the results of engagement. Engagement has not reduced Beijing's anti-Japan invective. It has not helped to resolve territorial disputes (but perhaps it has raised the potential economic costs to Beijing of assertions of its territorial claims in the East China Sea). The realpolitik argument of Japan's "soft containers" or "reluctant realists" is that the Chinese state's interest in achieving great power status has not changed, even though it is more integrated in global institutions. What explains these realpolitik arguments? In part it is China's insensitivity to the security dilemma and to the negative effects of its own drive to build a "rich state and strong army" (*fu guo qiang bing*). The Japan case, then, illustrates the mutually reinforcing nature of perceptions of hostility.

For Taiwan, the pay-offs from engagement – as minimal as the strategy has been in Taiwanese government policy – have also been hard to see. China's coercive diplomacy between 1995 and 1996 has reinforced a growing sense of identity alienation – "China is simply not like us." The primary causal arguments underlying Taiwan's mainland policy are deterrence and democratization. Deterrence in the short term will prevent China from using force against Taiwan. Thus, for Taiwan, it is imperative to persuade the United States to deter China from use of force while Taiwan pursues efforts to expand international space. And fundamental political democratization of the mainland in the long term will lead to more stable, peaceful interactions between Taiwan and the mainland. Engagement in whatever form – binding, socialization, Kissingerian bargaining – will have little ameliorative effect on China's policies toward Taiwan.

For Indonesia and Malaysia, the success of engagement has been hard to measure. The uncertainty about Chinese political-military intentions in the region is still quite high. Malaysian decision-makers are concerned that engagement will simply signal to China that Malaysia will not oppose Chinese efforts to establish control over disputed territory in the South China Sea. The most credible evidence that engagement succeeds would be Chinese recognition of the legitimacy of some of the territorial claims of other states and reduced PLA activities in the region. These are, in a sense, tougher criteria for successful engagement than even the United States has established, for territorial concessions are much more difficult for Beijing to make than concessions on intellectual property rights, proliferation, or even human rights issues.

Singapore's theory of engagement is perhaps the most sophisticated and overt. It is essentially a liberal capitalist theory whereby the desire to maximize welfare gains brings states into institutional commitments that bind them within rules and obligations. It also entails socialization from the expected ameliorative effect of successor generations of China's societal and government elites trained in the West as economists and business people.

Korea again appears to be an outlier. According to Cha, Korean leaders had a fairly clear set of criteria for judging the success of engagement; namely Chinese recognition of South Korean interests on the peninsula and help in restraining the North. On both scores, Korea has essentially achieved what it wanted from its diplomacy toward China.

Conclusion

We have, then, a pot-pourri of hunches, guesses, hypotheses and assumptions that undergird different engagement strategies between and within different countries. Not surprisingly, assessing the effectiveness of these strategies is difficult in the absence of clear metrics for success and of any systematically arrived-at consensus about the level of Chinese "revisionism" in world politics. The default policy tends to be hedging, with outliers like Korea more fully committed to engagement, and Taiwan essentially disengaged from engagement. Hedging is prudent, and policy-makers and pundits are rarely criticized for being prudent. But prudence is not necessarily good policy if it ignores the unintended consequences of the mixed signals which hedging sends to its target. Prudence is not prudent if it is based on erroneous assessments of the target country. Specifically, hedging could be counter-productive if China is essentially a status quo power. Under this condition, it might exacerbate nascent security dilemmas. So even prudent hedging requires accurate judgements about the degree of Chinese revisionism.

Engagement is sometimes seen as a way of sending reassurance signals to China that other states pose no threat. This is one of the motivations in US and Japanese engagement policies. The hope is to avoid insecurity spirals that result from misperceived motives and capabilities. For reassurance signals to ameliorate the security dilemma, both sides must believe that they are essentially status quo powers. But hedging is based on an assumption that China may well not be a status quo power. If other states combine elements of balancing in an overall hedging strategy, Beijing may not read reassurance signals as reassuring. Indeed, it is more likely that balancing signals will provide the baseline for interpreting reassurance signals, leading Beijing to read balancing and engagement as one and the same thing – different types of containment strategies. Thus the United States' success in eliciting compromises from Beijing could, in the long term, generate resentment and revisionist goals, unless tempered by obvious and credible examples of magnanimity toward Chinese interests.

Thus the crucial prerequisite for engagement is some sort of intersubjective agreement on whether or not China is essentially a status quo state, a revisionist state, or somewhere in between, depending on issue area. There are at least three sets of issues that an informed debate on engagement needs to address. First, a score-card is needed to assess China's commitment to global norms, rules and institutions across time, across other states and across issue areas. Comparison is the *sine qua non* of sound policy analysis. It may well be that on some issues China is essentially a status quo, conservative power toward whom a policy of engagement to ameliorate the non-status quo elements of its behavior makes no sense. Rather, China could be dealt with as a "normal" power through the channels of "normal" diplomacy. Global economic issues are a case in point.

There are other issues on which China's interests require change in the status quo – territorial questions in the South and East China Seas, for instance. There are also issues on which China's behavior is converging with the extant status quo. Individual political and civil liberties or intellectual property right protection may be cases in point. There are issues in which China's behavior is no more or less different from that of many other states. China's steadfast political refusal to accept internationally negotiated constraints on its greenhouse gas emissions is premised on the rejection of the science of global warming, a rejection shared by corporate oil and coal interests in the United States and among certain OPEC states. China, like other major powers, benefits economically from selling weapons around the world, even when there is no obvious security benefit from doing so. There are also issues on which the United States and China essentially share an approach that diverges from (almost) universally accepted norms, the global ban on anti-personnel landmines, for instance. This kind of inventory-making is complex and time-consuming, but necessary.

Second, there are few agreed-upon metrics for determining what kind of engagement works and why. Policy debates often focus on action proposals for "bringing China into the international community" with no attempt to establish who constitutes this community and what are the shared global norms and rules. Is this community defined by the amount of participation in international institutions? On this score, China is over-involved for its level of development. The number of China's IGO memberships has gone from about 70 percent of the world average in 1977 to around 180 percent in 1996. By 1996 the number of its memberships approached 80 percent of the number for the United States. If one uses GNP/capita as a proxy for level of development to predict the number of IO memberships, then China has moved from being under-involved to over-involved in the 1990s (using ordinary least squares regression equations to estimate the predicted number of memberships). Figure 11.3 shows the difference between predicted and actual IO memberships since the death of Mao.

Or is this putative international community defined by its normative boundaries? How should we evaluate a state that clearly adheres to some dominant global normative discourses while rejecting others? Singapore, for instance, is one of the strongest supporters of neoclassical free trade norms, yet aligns with China in opposition to Western efforts to "universalize" individual political and civil rights. How many states have to be in this community for it to be an international one? If Beijing can muster a majority of votes to prevent the UN Human Rights Commission from condemning human rights abuses in

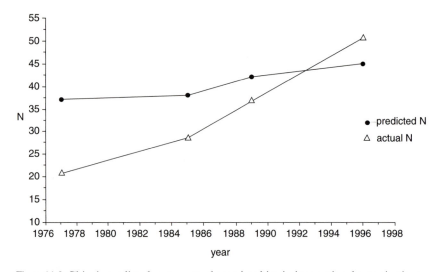

Figure 11.3 China's predicted versus actual memberships in international organizations

China, is it inside or outside the international community on human rights norms? Obviously, developing metrics that establish baselines and indicators for determining the effects of engagement is difficult, but a mere impressionistic metric based on Chinese "progress" toward accepting the "international community" serves no purpose at all.

This leads to the third set of issues. The policy debate has avoided any systematic consideration of the most important question: When China behaves in ways in which the United States (or any other state for that matter) wants it to behave, what are the possible reasons? There are at least four reasons: that Chinese leaders desired to do X; that they were coerced to do X; that they were paid to do X; or that doing X was cheap and there were no strong reasons not to do X. Equally important, which mechanisms and processes led Chinese leaders to desire to do X; what kinds of costs were most important in coercion (anticipated military, economic, political, or social); and what kinds of benefits were most important in their calculation to accept some offer to do X? Were these mechanisms bilateral or multilateral? Were they a function of the calculation of economic costs and benefits, or social rewards and punishments (status, prestige, diffuse image)?

On the one hand, US strategy has led to important status quo changes in Chinese behavior. The US market, US technology, and US capital have contributed to China's stake in sound bilateral relations. The United States–China relationship has also had a number of positive externalities for other states: US pressure in IPR carries some "free" benefits for Japanese and European companies and contributes to Chinese acceptance of WTO norms. US pressure has helped to push China to adhere formally or informally to a number of elements of the global non-proliferation regime. American-based and often government-funded NGOs have played an important role in the development of legal institutions and in village-level elections.

But the two chapters on China's involvement in international security and economic institutions strongly suggest that multilateral institutions have also constrained and transformed Chinese behavior. Initial Chinese involvement in many of these institutions reflected the regime's drive to maintain legitimacy through rapid economic growth, to use economic modernization to achieve important international strategic objectives, and to gain access to NGO economic assistance. The intellectual and bureaucratic requirements for interacting with these institutions then promoted a mix of normative and organizational interests that were more or less committed to the status quo "missions" and ideologies of these institutions. The discursive practices of these institutions themselves affected Chinese decision-makers' discussion of the missions and ideologies of these institutions. The Chinese discourse on mutual security, for instance, reflects multilateral pressure on China to contribute to the discourse in regional security institutions. Over time, an emerging commitment to these missions and ideologies may be reinforced by China's evolving identity as a responsible major power that is active in the major institutions' regulation of interstate activity. Deviant behavior may weaken the international legitimacy of the regime. At minimum, it is already clear that, once inside these institutions, China has not tried to change the rules in its favor in ways that deviate too far from the status quo.

Thus the one factor that has contributed most to the evolution of status quo interests in China has been the post-Mao drive for economic modernization, rooted in the failure of prior economic policies to maintain regime legitimacy and national security.[13] The fundamental transformation of Chinese attitudes toward modernization was not the result of other countries' engagement or containment strategies, but of domestic change. To achieve their modernization objectives, Chinese leaders developed new policies – societal, economic and political opening to the outside. It was the Dengist vision of development that generated new interests, which in turn engaged China in international institutions and engaged other states and non-state actors in China's development. This engagement, in turn, provided China with a new set of models – normative, discursive and organizational – that reinforced its new interests in the regional and global status quo.

If China has evolved from a Maoist revolutionary state to a Dengist conservative state, is it at all necessary to engage China? The answer will depend on the results of the research program outlined above. But suppose we already had much of the data. What would the data look like for the "no need to engage" case? The premise of engagement is that emerging powers are almost always dissatisfied with the status quo, hence they are a source of instability. But is China a dissatisfied power? Arguably not much of one anymore. In contrast to the Maoist era, China propagates no ideology to be spread around through the intervention in the internal affairs of others. Indeed, the predominant ideology that Chinese leaders promote today is sovereignty and autonomy, and the illegitimacy of intervention in the internal affairs of others.

China's "status quo-ization" is to some extent the result of myriad cross and transnational linkages made by individually rational, differently motivated international actors: decisions to invest, to aid village elections, to cultivate arms control communities, to train lawyers, to promote environmental education, etc. This is the result of both multilateral engagement and the perhaps unintended result of the "entangling" policies of national actors. In this respect, what is emerging is analogous to the normal diplomatic intercourse between major powers in the late twentieth century – issue-specific, institutionalized relationships, where military power is of limited relevance, where human rights, democratization, and marketization norms challenge the sovereignty and autonomy of the state. Under these conditions, state policy can emphasize promotion of multiple transnational linkages, many of which do not require central government to central government diplomacy.

Is there any remaining argument for engagement? The argument for engagement rests on evidence of Chinese dissatisfaction with the international status quo. Despite China's significant accommodation of the status quo norms and behavior in such areas as sovereignty, global capitalism, and international arms control, it remains revisionist regarding power, status, and territory. It wants to narrow the power differential between itself and the United States (though how far is unclear), it wants to resolve territorial conflicts (especially the Taiwan issue) in its favor, and it wants the status of a global power. In these issue areas, unlike in economics and, to a certain extent, unlike in global and regional security institutions, the post-Mao quest for modernity has not dramatically altered China's goals.

This brings us full circle back to the dilemma for US policy making. The policy issue for the United States is whether it and China will both be satisfied with sharing regional authority in accordance with some shared notion of legitimate interests, or whether China will seek regional hegemony while the United States mounts a strong opposition. For a US trying to preserve the regional status quo, these demands may be considered illegitimate. On one hand, the US is trying to increase China's satisfaction with the status quo through the "strategic partnership" discourse. On the other, the US is trying to prevent China from acquiring a capability to challenge the status quo in the distribution of regional and global power. If the former is persuasive, then the latter becomes less provocative in Beijing's eyes. If the former isn't persuasive, then the latter will be likely to exacerbate Sino–US rivalry. Yet it is hard to see how, under present conditions, the former can be persuasive precisely because of China's justified suspicions about the latter. For smaller states around China's periphery territorial questions, not China's status goals, still loom largest. As long as these issues remain unresolved in China's interaction with the outside world, then uncertainty remains and engagement may still be required.

How can zero-sum territorial conflicts, contentions over status, and enduring rivalries be turned into variable-sum negotiations over manageable disputes? History and theory are unclear about this. But a growing body of scholarship suggests that the amelioration of these remaining "revisionist" elements in China's behavior may require a rather more fundamental solution: namely, the liberal democratization of China. One version of the democratic peace theory holds that shared liberal democratic identity is a critical factor in reducing the causes and effects of rivalry between major power dyads. If both sides view the other as a member of a democratic in-group, instead of as an "other," they will recognize in the other a preference for resolving disputes through mediation and compromise. This recognition reduces uncertainty about intentions, thus reducing concerns in each side about any disadvantageous changes in relative material power. This puts downward pressure on security dilemma dynamics. For the most part, this version of the democratic peace argument is not that democracies no longer behave "badly." It is, rather, that the meaning of this behavior for other democracies is reinterpreted in more benign directions. The descriptive behavior of a liberal democratic China might not significantly change in many respects, but American interpretations of Chinese behavior would likely moderate, and vice versa.[14]

The evolution of French–Germany rivalry is suggestive here. Both were long-time rivals in Europe even after the emergence of a common Soviet threat. Yet over time the credibility of commitments to democratic institutions and economic, political and military integration have ameliorated a rivalry that some argue was produced by the realities of anarchy, geography and power and others argue was produced by deeply historical and internalized animosities. Democratization and the structural restraint built into the multiple, institutionalized cross-national interests that emerged from Europeanization meant that decision-makers in both countries came to believe that conflicts of interest had fewer zero-sum implications for the sovereignty and autonomy of the nation-state than in the past.

The democratic peace literature, then, would suggest that Washington would interpret an increase in a democratic China's power as far less threatening than such an increase in a non-democratic China. From the perspective of a liberal democratic China, US efforts to preserve its global military primacy would be less likely viewed as an obstacle to China's efforts to increase its status and its regional and global influence. China could become a more satisfied power precisely because other democracies would consider it a more satisfied and satisfiable power.

The problem, of course, is getting from here to there. The short-term effects of an engagement policy that aims at promoting democratization over the long-term may also be the most provocative and uncontrollable short-term policies and might also undermine long-term engagement. Direct attempts to radically influence the direction of China's political evolution would challenge the most vital interest of the Chinese leadership (its own power) and could thus dangerously exacerbate US–Chinese conflicts over particular conflicts of interest and the regional distribution of power. It could also undermine diplomatic engagement strategies by affecting Chinese evaluations of US intentions. So, we offer no policy presciptions here because the United States, or any other state for that matter, is not likely to be able to effect, or control the effects of, democratization in China in any detailed, specific, and stable way. But democratic peace arguments compel us to try to understand the complexity and enormity of the issues at stake with China's emerging power. China may not democratize. Even a democratic China may still insist on establishing a sphere of influence in East Asia in which others only enjoy limited policy flexibility, as the United States has had in Latin America. The key is, however, not how a democracy behaves, but how democratic dyads behave. Much of the theoretical and empirical evidence would suggest that a virtuous cycle of "security delights" should lead democratic dyads to interpret changes in distributions of relative power between them in more benign ways; precisely the goal of engagement. Should a stable democratic China evolve, then all security "boats" rise.

Notes

1 It is interesting that Chinese analysts tend not to see these two concepts as polar opposites. Engagement is often seen as soft containment, designed at best to prevent China from pursuing its legitimate interests, and at worst to encourage the Westernization and weakening of China. This complaint is based on an assessment of the United States' policy of engagement. Since we are interested here in engagement as a theoretical construct, the juxtaposition of these terms as ideal types still holds.

2 These generally map on to the strategies which Schweller lists in Chapter 1.

3 For a discussion of hedging as a strategy to deal with great powers, see Chapter 6.

4 This calculation uses an unofficial revision of the IISS figures for China's official budget. As a rough rule of thumb the official budget may undercount by a factor of three.

5 Christopher Layne, "The Unipolar Illusion: Why New Great Powers Will Rise," *International Security* 17:4 (spring 1993).

6 He Xin, a conservative intellectual who had access to the top leadership in the early 1990s, wrote in a letter to Deng Xiaoping in May 1992 that the trend was toward unipolarity (danji hua), not multipolarity as officialdom was declaring, and that this was definitely not in China's interest. See "Guanyu dangqian guo nei wai xingshi de yi feng xin" (a letter concerning the present domestic and foreign situation), in *He Xin zhengzhi jingji lunwen ji* (neibu yanjiu baogao) (He Xin's collected essays on politics and economics (internal circulation research reports) (Heilongjiang Education Press, 1993), p.126.

7 For reports on the classified draft, see Barton Gelman, "Keeping the United States First," *Washington Post*, March 11, 1992. For the final official statement see Dick Cheney, "Defense Strategy for the 1990s: The Regional Defense Strategy," January 1993, and Patrick E. Tyler, "Pentagon Drops Goal of Blocking New Superpower," *New York Times*, May 24, 1992.

8 Officially, at least, Beijing argued that most Asia-Pacific states were not upset with China's missile exercises against Taiwan, that they understood this was an internal affair, and that this explained their muted response. Similarly, the Chinese often seem unaware that Chinese policy, including military spending power, can make Japanese feel insecure.

9 Richard Rosecrance, *The Rise of the Trading State: Commerce and Conquest in the Modern World* (New York: Basic Books, 1986).

10 Using Figure 11.1 to show the rank order in the centrality of engagement, the list is as follows: Korea, Singapore, US, Japan, Malaysia, Indonesia, Taiwan, in that order. The rank order of export dependence (percentage of total exports that go to China, 1996) is: Korea (8.8 percent), Japan (5.3 percent), Indonesia (4.1 percent), Singapore (2.7 percent), Malaysia (2.4 percent), US (1.3 percent), Taiwan (0.5 percent). The spearman rho rank order correlation is 0.536 $z = 1.312$ $p = .1892$. The rank order of import dependence (the percentage of total imports coming from China) is: Japan (11.6 percent), US (6.7 percent), Korea (5.7 percent), Indonesia (3.7 percent), Singapore (3.3 percent), Taiwan (3.0 percent). The spearman rho rank order correlation is 0.429 z = 1.05 p = .2938.

11 On the centrality of territory in interstate conflicts see John Vasquez, *The War Puzzle* (Cambridge: Cambridge University Press, 1993), and John Vasquez, "Why Do Neighbors Fight: Proximity, Interaction, Territoriality," *Journal of Peace Research* 32:2 (August 1995), pp. 277–294.

12 On small state options regarding threat management and balancing versus appeasement, see Robert Rothstein, *Alliances and Small Powers* (New York: Columbia University Press, 1968), and Stephen M. Walt, *The Origins of Alliances* (Ithaca, NY: Cornell University Press, 1987).

13 Victor Cha's chapter on Korea wrestles with possibility. He notes that South Korea's success of engagement may have less to do with Korean diplomacy and more to do with the development of China's status quo interests in the Korean peninsula due to the need for a peaceful regional environment that is conducive to economic growth in China.

14 On the ameliorative effect of liberal and democratic ideology on interpretations of rivalry, see John M. Owen IV, *Liberal Peace, Liberal War* (Ithaca: Cornell University Press, 1997); and Bruce Russett, *Grasping the Democratic Peace*, (Princeton: Princeton University Press, 1993). See also Zeev Maos and Ben D. Mor "Learning, Preference Change, and the Evolution of Enduring Rivalries" in Paul F. Diehl (ed.), *The Dynamics of Enduring Rivalries* (Urbana: University of Illinois Press, 1998) pp. 129–164. Empirical evidence suggests that enduring rivals are more likely to view disadvantageous power shifts as threatening than are non-rival dyads; see Francis W. Wayman, "Power Shifts and the Onset of War" in Jacek Kugler and Douglas Lemke (eds), *Parity and War: Evaluations and Extensions of "The War Ledger"* (Ann Arbor: University of Michigan Press, 1996) pp. 145–62. Democratic dyads are less prone to view disadvantageous changes in relative power and status as threatening. For a thorough assessment of the claims of democratic peace literature see James Lee Ray, "A Lakatosian View of the Democratic Peach Research Programme: Does It Falsify Realism (or Neorealism)?" (Paper prepared for the International Studies Association Annual Meeting, Washington, D.C., February 1999). While many dismiss this literature, the cumulative findings are too robust to ignore out of hand.

INDEX